The Heavenly Country

*An Anthology of Primary Sources,
Poetry, and Critical Essays on Sophiology*

THE
HEAVENLY
COUNTRY

An Anthology of Primary Sources,
Poetry, and Critical Essays
on Sophiology

Edited by
Michael Martin

ANGELICO PRESS
SOPHIA PERENNIS

First published
by Angelico Press /Sophia Perennis 2016
© Michael Martin 2016

For information, address:
Angelico Press
4709 Briar Knoll Dr.
Kettering, OH 45429
www.angelicopress.com

Pbk: 978-1-62138-174-7
Cloth: 978-1-62138-175-4

Cover design: Michael Schrauzer

CONTENTS

*Dedicated to St. Edith Stein,
also known as St. Teresia Benedicta of the Cross (1891–1942),
in anticipation of the seventy-fifth anniversary
of her forced entrance into Eternity.*

Ave Crux, Spes Unica.

Acknowledgments

A PROJECT of this size and scope takes much in the way of coordination and cooperation and I am very grateful to all those, both in the temporal and eternal realms, who participated in its production.

I am thankful, first of all, to Marygrove College for the gifts of a number of research grants without which this book might never have been completed. I am particularly appreciative for my two research assistants, Shauntay Frazier-Hall and Alejandra Villegas, who worked diligently in transcribing and formatting much of the book: no mean task.

I am likewise indebted to the poets, translators, and scholars contributing new work to the collection: David Craig, Bruce Foltz, Gregory Glazov, Jennifer Newsome Martin, Daniel Polikoff, Aaron Riches, Artur Sebastian Rosman, Fr. Robert Slesinski, Lourdes Torres-Monaghan, and Arthur Versluis.

And, as always, I offer my deepest appreciation to my wife, Bonnie, and my children. I am a man rich in blessings. *mm*

Selections from the Bible are taken from the Douay-Rheims American Edition (1899).

The Book of Six Great Points by Jacob Boehme, taken from *Several Treatises of Jacob Behme*, translated by John Sparrow (London, 1661).

Selection from *The Three Principles of the Divine Essence of the Eternall, Dark, Light, and Temporary World* by Jacob Boehme, translated by John Sparrow (London, 1648).

Jacob Boehme, *Of the Becoming Man or Incarnation of Jesus Christ, the Sonne of God*, taken from *The Fifth Book of the Authour, in Three Parts the First, Of the Becoming Man or Incarnation of Jesus Christ, the Sonne of God, That Is, concerning the Virgin Mary... and How the Eternal Word Is Become Man: The Second Part Is of Christ's Suffering, Dying, Death, and Resurrection...: The Third Part Is of The Tree of Christian Faith*, translated by John Sparrow (London, 1659).

John Pordage, *Theologia Mystica, or The Mystic Divinitie of the Aeternal Invisibles, Viz. the Archetypous Globe, or the Original Globe, or World of*

All Globes, Worlds, Essences, Centers, Elements, Principles and Creations Whatsoever. A Work Never Exstant Before. By a Person of Qualitie JPMD (London, 1683).

Thomas Bromley, *The Way to the Sabbath of Rest or the Soul's Progress in the Work of the New Birth* (London, 1692).

Jane Lead, *A Fountain of Gardens Watered by the Rivers of Divine Pleasure, and Springing up in All the Variety of Spiritual Plants, Blown up by the Pure Breath into a Paradise: To Which Is Prefixed a Poem, Introductory to the Philadelphian Age, Called Solomons Porch, or The Beautiful Gate to Wisdoms Temple* (London, 1697).

Robert Fludd, *Mosaicall Philosophy Grounded upon the Essentiall Truth, or Eternal Sapience* (London, 1659).

Thomas Vaughan, *Anima Magica Abscondita* (London, 1650).

Thomas Vaughan, *Lumen de Lumine* (London, 1651).

Thomas Vaughan, *Euphrates* (London, 1655).

Johann Wolfgang von Goethe, *Autobiography: Truth and Poetry, from My Own Life*, translated by John Oxenford (1897).

Johann Wolfgang von Goethe, *Theory of Colours* (1840).

Novalis, "Christendom or Europe?," translated by Charles E. Passage (1960).

Selection from *Cosmic and Human Metamorphoses* by Rudolf Steiner. Reprinted by permission of Steiner Books.

"The Body of the Father Christian Rosencrux" by William Butler Yeats first appeared in *Ideas of Good and Evil* (1903).

Vladimir Solovyov, *Russia and the Universal Church*, translated by Herbert Rees (1948).

Selection from *The Pillar and Ground of the Truth* by Pavel Florensky, translated by Boris Jakim. Reprinted by permission of Princeton University Press, copyright © 1997.

Selection from *Sophia, the Wisdom of God: An Outline of Sophiology* by Sergei Bulgakov, translated by Patrick Thompson, O. Fielding Clarke, and Xenia Braikevitc. Reprinted by permission of Lindisfarne Press, an imprint of Steiner Books, copyright © 1993.

Nikolai Berdyaev, *Freedom and the Spirit*, translated by Oliver Fielding Clarke (1935).

Selection from *The Glory of the Lord: A Theological Aesthetics, Volume I: Seeing the Form* by Hans Urs von Balthasar, translated by Joseph Fessio and John Riches, reprinted by permission of Ignatius Press, copyright © 1982.

Louis Bouyer, *The Seat of Wisdom: An Essay on the Place of the Virgin Mary in Christian Theology*, translated by A.V. Littledale (1962).

"The Eternal Feminine" by Pierre Teilhard de Chardin, translated by René Hague (1968). Written in 1918.

Selection from *Meditations on the Tarot: A Journey into Christian Hermeticism* translated by Robert Powell. Reprinted by permission of Robert Powell.

"All in azure did my empress," "My empress has a lofty palace," and "Three Meetings" by Vladimir Solovyov, translated by Boris Jakim and Laury Magnus, from *The Religious Poetry of Vladimir Solovyov* (Angelico Press, 2014). Reprinted by permission of Boris Jakim.

Poems from *Ante Lucem* and *Verses about the Beautiful Lady* by Alexander Blok, translated by Boris Jakim, from *Poems of Sophia* by Alexander Blok (Angelico Press, 2014). Reprinted by permission of Boris Jakim.

"As when on a holiday" by Friedrich Hölderlin, translated by William S. Allen; from *Ellipsis: Of Poetry and the Experience of Language after Heidegger, Hölderlin, and Blanchot* by William S. Allen. Reprinted by permission of SUNY Press, copyright © 2007.

Selections from *Hymns to the Night* by Novalis, translated by Dick Higgins, are reprinted by permission of McPherson & Company, copyright © 1988.

"Hagia Sophia" by Thomas Merton, from *The Collected Poems of Thomas Merton*, copyright © 1963 by The Abbey of Gethsemani. Reprinted by permission of New Directions Publishing Corp.

"*Pietà*" from *New Collected Poems* by David Gascoyne. Reprinted by permission of Enitharmon Press.

"The Tutelar of the Place" by David Jones, from *Agenda* (1963). Reprinted by permission of *Agenda Poetry*.

"Rivers," translated by Renata Gorczynski and Robert Hass, and "Rivers" (prose poem), translated by Czelaw Milosz and Robert Hass, by Czeslaw Milosz, from *New and Collected Poems: 1931–2001*. Reprinted by permission of HarperCollins Publishers, copyright © 2003.

"The Heavenly Country" from *The Convections* by Robert Kelly. Reprinted by permission of Black Sparrow Books, an imprint of David R. Godine, Publisher, Inc. Copyright © by Robert Kelly.

Introduction

Sophiology: Genealogy and Phenomenon

WE LIVE in an age of untrammeled superstition: the hope that science will save us from ourselves and bless us with prosperity and, even, that it will allow us to overcome death. This is an age of the totalization of the technological and the technocratic: an age of the unreal, the artificial, the illusory, of the simulacra. Indeed, our moment anticipates the absolute technological colonization of the human person, a grotesque and horrifying apotheosis of all that is implied by the notion of "evolution." This teleological unfolding which will without question be attended by the violence implicit in such a blind (if altogether unconscious) faith in the "survival of the fittest." Thus superstition.

In this paradigm, the human person is viewed as a machine among other machines, replete with updateable hardware, a myriad number of applications, and the promise of replaceable as well as changeable parts. I, human. iHuman. As Owen Barfield has argued, "To the extent therefore that the phenomena are experienced as machine, they are believed to exist independently of man, not to be participated and therefore not to be in the nature of representations. We have seen that all these beliefs are fallacious."[1] They may be fallacious, but they are widely accepted. As Barfield implies here, accepting the human person as a machine ultimately distances the human person from *himself*, from the awareness of himself as a human person, as an integrally somatic, pneumatological, and existential being. Yet it is the machine model (though few have the courage to name it as such) that is ascendant in our own cultural moment. We see this perhaps most clearly in the burgeoning gender reassignment industry, an industry not only of technological application, but also now fully integrated into the political, corporate, and entertainment complex. Change the notion of a human person—change the notion of nature. Change the notion of nature—change cul-

---

1. Owen Barfield, *Saving the Appearances: A Study in Idolatry*, 2nd ed. (Middletown, CT: Wesleyan University Press, 1988), 51.

1

ture. But notions are plastic. Being, however elusive,—and despite what postmodern nominalism would have us believe—is not.

Rudolf Steiner, in his characteristically imaginal way, goes even further than Barfield in assessing the situation:

> Ahriman has the greatest interest in concealing from mankind that in modern intellectual, rationalistic science, in superstitious empiricism, one is dealing with a great illusion, a deception. It would be a triumph for him if the scientific superstition which infiltrates all areas of life today and which human beings even try to use as a template for the social sciences should prevail into the third millennium. He would have the greatest success if he could then arrive in western civilization in human form and find the scientific superstition as prevailing dogma.[2]

At least in a metaphorical sense, what Steiner described here in 1919 has become a twenty-first-century reality. Also cognizant of this very real crisis, Pope Francis locates its source in the "*undifferentiated and one-dimensional paradigm*" modernity has adopted in its assimilation of the technological, a paradigm which

> exalts the concept of a subject who, using logical and rational procedures, progressively approaches and gains control over an external object. This subject makes every effort to establish the scientific and experimental method, which in itself is already a technique of possession, mastery and transformation. It is as if the subject were to find itself in the presence of something formless, completely open to manipulation.[3]

This project of "possession, mastery and transformation" and the unchecked manipulation of matter it promises was during earlier times directed outwardly: toward the natural world, toward the colonization of peoples, and toward the distribution of information. It has now been turned onto the human subject himself, oftentimes with individuals allowing their own bodies to be colonized by the totalizing dictates of ideology. And we are again involved in superstition. The subject of this book offers an alternative to this superstition and provides an antidote to the ontological poison with which we have all been infected.

---

2. In Steiner's imaginary, Ahriman is a spiritual being who works to enslave human beings to technology and materialism. Rudolf Steiner, *The Incarnation of Ahriman: The Embodiment of Evil on Earth*, trans. Matthew Barton (Forest Row, UK: Rudolf Steiner Press, 2006), 22.

3. *Encyclical Letter Laudato Si' of the Holy Father Francis on Our Common Home*, §106. Emphasis in source.

What is Sophiology?

Sophiology ("the logos of Wisdom") as it is understood in this book is the theological-philosophical apprehension and perception of grace as it discloses itself (or is disclosed) in the created world, in works of art, in liturgy, and in religious experience. It is most commonly experienced as a beauty which opens the subject to transcendence, to goodness and truth. This beauty, however, does not reside in objects themselves, nor does it reside in the perceiving subject. Rather, this beauty is that which shines through phenomena, revealing what Hans Urs von Balthasar has called "splendor." By analogy, we could say that this splendor is synonymous with the light of the first day in contrast to the light of the fourth (Genesis 1:3–5; 14–19). Wisdom, furthermore, is that which God "created . . . in the Holy Ghost, and saw her, and numbered her, and measured her. And he poured her out upon all his works, and upon all flesh according to his gift, and hath given her to them that love him" (Sirach 1:9–10). Wisdom, then, according to scripture is a property of the Creation, the conduit for the Creation's participation in God and that which brings God's presence into sensory perception, a profound affirmation of an incarnational, immanental, and profoundly sacramental theology. In addition, for some, Sophia—as the passage from Sirach suggests—is a unique divine person, created, to be sure, but no less divine. Indeed, a number of sophianic mystics—the 17th-century English Protestant visionary Jane Lead, the German Romantic poet Novalis, and the 19th-century Russian philosopher Vladimir Solovyov, to name just three—experienced Sophia as just such an individuality.

Not surprisingly, then, the identification of Sophia as a divine person has proved problematic for not a few theologians. Sergei Bulgakov, a priest and arguably one of the most important Eastern Orthodox theologians of the 20th century, was officially censured for his teaching regarding Sophia, as has been typical for theologians within the Christian mainstream. And for good reason: the introduction of Sophia into the theological landscape complicates traditional understandings of the Trinity, for one, though it could also be argued that it enriches Marian theology to a significant degree. Unfortunately, the appropriation of Sophia by religious thinkers outside of the orthodox fold (whether Eastern Orthodox, Protestant, or Catholic) has often served to justify the suspicions of mainstream theologians, as the proliferation of self-styled "goddess worship," neo-paganism, and neo-gnosticism invoking the name of Sophia in recent decades has proved only so well. But such extravagances may indeed justify the serious consideration of Sophia and sophiology in the illuminating light of the Church in order for us to

3

see what truly lives in sophiology and to cleanse it of the dross of imaginative and luciferic excess.

Why this book?

The idea for a book such as this arose out of my earlier study, *The Submerged Reality: Sophiology and the Turn to a Poetic Metaphysics*, and the realization that a sophiology casebook could provide scholars, students, and others interested in the subject with a deeper, experiential introduction to sophiology by engagement with primary texts and accompanying critical discussion. Furthermore, the inclusion of a section of poetry in the book seemed to me to be imperative. As with all of the fine, performing, and practical arts, poetry is often disclosive of God's Wisdom, even though the artist in question may never have heard of Sophia—or may not even be interested in "being religious." Poetry, as Martin Heidegger has observed, is the paradigmatic site for such a disclosure and including poetry in this volume became rather an obligation, the answer to a call. One might say, then, that the sophiology of the primary texts is illustrative, the sophiology discussed in the critical studies is explanatory, but the sophiology of the poetry is (or can be) experiential. The sophiology engaged in this book, furthermore, is broadly conceived. It is not a theory superadded to an extant corpus of writings; rather, it is a property of Things disclosed phenomenologically. As a property God "poured . . . out upon all his works," Sophia is more properly understood as less a theologoumena than a law of the universe.

This book, however, is not intended to be the last word on sophiology. I have not included, for example, readings from Gnosticism, from Hinduism or Buddhism, or from the manifold appropriations of Sophia from feminist theologians or New Age innovators. Neither have I included some important early modern and Romantic German religious thinkers preoccupied with Sophia such as Gottfried Arnold, Johann Georg Gichtel, or Franz von Baader, deserving as they are.[4] My intention here, as in *The Submerged Reality*, is to trace the genealogy of sophiology from the Bible to the Protestant Reformation, to the Russian religious renaissance, to contemporary Catholic theology in order to show that sophiology is not, in fact, an innovation, but something implicit to a Christian, sacramental worldview that recognizes the cosmos, scripture,

---

4. Those interested in these thinkers and others (Louis-Claude de Saint-Martin and Leopold Ziegler among them) are referred to Arthur Versluis's superb collection *Wisdom's Book: The Sophia Anthology* (St. Paul, MN: Paragon House, 2000).

art, and liturgy as integrally united, a worldview that can heal the onto-logical, teleological, and epistemological wounds from which our age so deeply suffers.

To that end, the collection of essays which round out this volume likewise trace the genealogy of sophiology from the Bible to the post-modern moment. In "Theotokos: Sophiology and Christological Over-determination of the Secular," Aaron Riches anchors postmodern sophiology in its biblical and Russian antecedents while contributing to a vocabulary for speaking Sophia to our own times. Gregory Glazov's "On Understanding, Wisdom, and the Son of Man" excavates Old Tes-tament, Pseudopigraphic, and Apocryphal notions of Sophia inspired by the contemplative insights of the Third Order Carmelite hermit Brother Anthony Opisso. In "John Pordage and Sophianic Mysticism," Arthur Versluis investigates the sophiology of the 17th-century Anglican priest John Pordage and its greater religious implications. Brent Dean Robbins's "New Organs of Perception: Goethean Science as a Cultural Therapeutics" traces the timely significance of Goethean phenomenol-ogy, a method of investigation with sophiological overtones, while in his article Bruce V. Foltz, somewhat uncomfortable with the terminology of sophiology, nevertheless finds the Glory of the Lord implicit in the nat-ural world. In their articles, Fr. Robert Slesinski examines Russian sophiology and its applications and Jennifer Newsome Martin considers the sophiological underpinnings of the thought of Hans Urs von Bal-thasar. Finally, Artur Sebastian Rosman and I in our respective articles consider the sophiology of the poetic moment and the simultaneous immanence and transcendence of the poetic encounter.

The presence of God's Wisdom in creation—especially after Des-cartes, the Scientific Revolution, the Enlightenment, the so-called "death of metaphysics" and its accompanying "death of God," not to mention a totalizing secularism—has been almost entirely disregarded, even in religious contexts. Nevertheless, Sophia maintains a presence in the world, even if that presence, like the taking on of form in quantum mechanics, only manifests through being observed or (to speak the lan-guage of phenomenology) in response to intentionality. In this, we surely pay witness to a quality of Sophia much overlooked, even by sophiology's enthusiasts: Sophia's humility. *Ecce ancilla domini.* Sophi-ology, as this book illustrates, clearly deserves a deeper and wider con-sideration than it has heretofore been allotted.

A Note on Texts and Translation

I have chosen to not modernize early modern spellings in the chapters on Boehme, Seventeenth-Century Science, and the Philadelphians. To modify them seems to me to violate their ability to transport us into the consciousness of the age in which they were written.

I agonized quite a bit over whether or not to include original-language versions of the translated poems in Part II. Not only are poems translated from a number of languages—Latin, German, French, Italian, Polish, and Russian—but some of the selections are quite long and, considering there are also a good number of English-language poems in the collection, including poems in their original language would end up being typographically and aesthetically clumsy and obstructive. And for that decision, I apologize to both the readers and the poets.

PART I

Primary Sources

The Bible

THE WISDOM LITERATURE of the Old Testament[1] is, to risk an assertion, the canonical foundation of sophiology; for it is in this literature that Wisdom is most explicitly spoken of as a *person*. The early Church Fathers in commenting on this personification—which is obviously feminine—typically connected Wisdom to Christ, though after the Council of Ephesus proclaimed Mary the Theotokos, some theologians began to associate Mary with Sophia.[2] Nevertheless, the primary attribution of Wisdom among theologians was to the Logos, or Christ. It was only after the Protestant Reformation's emphasis on an inner understanding or illumination prompted by a personal engagement with biblical texts that a more literal interpretation of this figure found its way back into various religious ways of speaking and understanding. This was clearly the case with Jacob Boehme (though his intuitions led him more deeply into mystical speculation), with Robert Fludd, Thomas Vaughan, John Pordage, and Jane Lead, among others. What makes this all the more fascinating is the fact that a number of the Wisdom books—Tobit, Sirach, and Wisdom—were not (and are not) accepted as part of the Protestant canon. Nevertheless, the personification of Wisdom found in Sirach and Wisdom as well as in the more canonical—at least from a Protestant perspective—Proverbs informed early modern Protestant mysticism and mystical philosophy to a significant degree.

The selections that follow illustrate, among others, at least two important sophiological notions: 1) that the natural world and natural processes (*eros*) have an important role in the relationship of the believer to God; and 2) that Wisdom is a person, that Wisdom is personal, and that Wisdom is intimately involved with God, with the natural world, and in human life. The language throughout is highly metaphorical, poetic, disclosive of truth, beauty, and goodness.

1. I use the term "Old Testament" and not "Hebrew Bible" here because some of the Wisdom books are not included in the Jewish canon.
2. Celia Deane-Drummond, *Eco-Theology* (London: Darton, Longman and Todd, Ltd., 2008), 66.

9

from The Book of Proverbs

Chapter 8

¹ Doth not wisdom cry aloud, and prudence put forth her voice?

² Standing in the top of the highest places by the way, in the midst of the paths,

³ Beside the gates of the city, in the very doors she speaketh, saying:

⁴ O ye men, to you I call, and my voice is to the sons of men.

⁵ O little ones understand subtlety, and ye unwise, take notice.

⁶ Hear, for I will speak of great things: and my lips shall be opened to preach right things.

⁷ My mouth shall meditate truth, and my lips shall hate wickedness.

⁸ All my words are just, there is nothing wicked, nor perverse in them.

⁹ They are right to them that understand, and just to them that find knowledge.

¹⁰ Receive my instruction, and not money: choose knowledge rather than gold.

¹¹ For wisdom is better than all the most precious things: and whatsoever may be desired cannot be compared to it.

¹² I, wisdom, dwell in counsel, and am present in learned thoughts.

¹³ The fear of the Lord hateth evil; I hate arrogance, and pride, and every wicked way, and a mouth with a double tongue.

¹⁴ Counsel and equity is mine, prudence is mine, strength is mine.

¹⁵ By me kings reign, and lawgivers decree just things.

¹⁶ By me princes rule, and the mighty decree justice.

¹⁷ I love them that love me: and they that in the morning early watch for me, shall find me.

¹⁸ With me are riches and glory, glorious riches and justice.

¹⁹ For my fruit is better than gold and the precious stone, and my blossoms than choice silver.

²⁰ I walk in the way of justice, in the midst of the paths of judgment,

²¹ That I may enrich them that love me, and may fill their treasures.

²² The Lord possessed me in the beginning of his ways, before he made any thing from the beginning.

²³ I was set up from eternity, and of old, before the earth was made.

²⁴ The depths were not as yet, and I was already conceived, neither had the fountains of waters as yet sprung out.

²⁵ The mountains, with their huge bulk, had not as yet been established: before the hills, I was brought forth:

²⁶ He had not yet made the earth, nor the rivers, nor the poles of the world.

27 When he prepared the heavens, I was present: when with a certain law, and compass, he enclosed the depths:

28 When he established the sky above, and poised the fountains of waters:

29 When he compassed the sea with its bounds, and set a law to the waters that they should not pass their limits: when he balanced the foundations of the earth;

30 I was with him forming all things: and was delighted every day, playing before him at all times;

31 Playing in the world: and my delights were to be with the children of men.

32 Now, therefore, ye children, hear me: blessed are they that keep my ways.

33 Hear instruction, and be wise, and refuse it not.

34 Blessed is the man that heareth me, and that watcheth daily at my gates, and waiteth at the posts of my doors.

35 He that shall find me, shall find life, and shall have salvation from the Lord.

36 But he that shall sin against me shall hurt his own soul. All that hate me love death.

Chapter 9

1 Wisdom hath built herself a house, she hath hewn her out seven pillars.

2 She hath slain her victims, mingled her wine, and set forth her table.

3 She hath sent her maids to invite to the tower, and to the walls of the city:

4 Whosoever is a little one, let him come to me. And to the unwise she said:

5 Come, eat my bread, and drink the wine which I have mingled for you.

6 Forsake childishness, and live, and walk by the ways of prudence.

7 He that teacheth a scorner, doth an injury to himself; and he that rebuketh a wicked man, getteth himself a blot.

8 Rebuke not a scorner, lest he hate thee. Rebuke a wise man, and he will love thee.

9 Give an occasion to a wise man, and wisdom shall be added to him. Teach a just man, and he shall make haste to receive it.

10 The fear of the Lord is the beginning of wisdom: and the knowledge of the holy is prudence.

11 For by me shall thy days be multiplied, and years of life shall be added to thee.

¹² If thou be wise, thou shalt be so to thyself: and if a scorner, thou alone shalt bear the evil.

¹³ A foolish woman and clamorous, and full of allurements, and knowing nothing at all,

¹⁴ Sat at the door of her house, upon a seat, in a high place of the city,

¹⁵ To call them that pass by the way, and go on their journey:

¹⁶ He that is a little one, let him turn to me. And to the fool she said:

¹⁷ Stolen waters are sweeter, and hidden bread is more pleasant.

¹⁸ And he did not know that giants are there, and that her guests are in the depths of hell.

from The Canticle of Canticles (Song of Songs)

Chapter 1

¹ Let him kiss me with the kiss of his mouth: for thy breasts are better than wine,

² Smelling sweet of the best ointments. Thy name is as oil poured out: therefore young maidens have loved thee.

³ Draw me: we will run after thee to the odour of thy ointments. The king hath brought me into his storerooms: we will be glad and rejoice in thee, remembering thy breasts more than wine: the righteous love thee.

⁴ I am black but beautiful, O ye daughters of Jerusalem, as the tents of Cedar, as the curtains of Solomon.

⁵ Do not consider me that I am brown, because the sun hath altered my colour: the sons of my mother have fought against me, they have made me the keeper in the vineyards: my vineyard I have not kept.

⁶ Shew me, O thou whom my soul loveth, where thou feedest, where thou liest in the midday, lest I begin to wander after the flocks of thy companions.

⁷ If thou know not thyself, O fairest among women, go forth, and follow after the steps of the flocks, and feed thy kids beside the tents of the shepherds.

⁸ To my company of horsemen, in Pharao's chariots, have I likened thee, O my love.

⁹ Thy cheeks are beautiful as the turtledove's, thy neck as jewels.

¹⁰ We will make thee chains of gold, inlaid with silver.

¹¹ While the king was at his repose, my spikenard sent forth the odour thereof.

¹² A bundle of myrrh is my beloved to me, he shall abide between my breasts.

¹³ A cluster of cypress my love is to me, in the vineyards of Engaddi.

¹⁴ Behold thou art fair, O my love, behold thou art fair, thy eyes are as those of doves.

¹⁵ Behold thou art fair, my beloved, and comely. Our bed is flourishing.

¹⁶ The beams of our houses are of cedar, our rafters of cypress trees.

Chapter 2

¹ I am the flower of the field, and the lily of the valleys.

² As the lily among thorns, so is my love among the daughters.

³ As the apple tree among the trees of the woods, so is my beloved among the sons. I sat down under his shadow, whom I desired: and his fruit was sweet to my palate.

⁴ He brought me into the cellar of wine, he set in order charity in me.

⁵ Stay me up with flowers, compass me about with apples: because I languish with love.

⁶ His left hand is under my head, and his right hand shall embrace me.

⁷ I adjure you, O ye daughters of Jerusalem, by the roes, and the harts of the fields, that you stir not up, nor make the beloved to awake, till she please.

⁸ The voice of my beloved, behold he cometh leaping upon the mountains, skipping over the hills.

⁹ My beloved is like a roe, or a young hart. Behold he standeth behind our wall, looking through the windows, looking through the lattices.

¹⁰ Behold my beloved speaketh to me: Arise, make haste, my love, my dove, my beautiful one, and come.

¹¹ For winter is now past, the rain is over and gone.

¹² The flowers have appeared in our land, the time of pruning is come: the voice of the turtle is heard in our land:

¹³ The fig tree hath put forth her green figs: the vines in flower yield their sweet smell. Arise, my love, my beautiful one, and come:

¹⁴ My dove in the clefts of the rock, in the hollow places of the wall, shew me thy face, let thy voice sound in my ears: for thy voice is sweet, and thy face comely.

¹⁵ Catch us the little foxes that destroy the vines: for our vineyard hath flourished.

¹⁶ My beloved to me, and I to him who feedeth among the lilies,

¹⁷ Till the day break, and the shadows retire. Return: be like, my beloved, to a roe, or to a young hart upon the mountains of Bether.

from The Book of Wisdom

From Chapter 7

22 For in her is the spirit of understanding: holy, one, manifold, subtile, eloquent, active, undefiled, sure, sweet, loving that which is good, quick, which nothing hindereth, beneficent,

23 Gentle, kind, steadfast, assured, secure, having all power, overseeing all things, and containing all spirits, intelligible, pure, subtile.

24 For Wisdom is more active than all active things: and reacheth everywhere by reason of her purity.

25 For she is a vapour of the power of God, and a certain pure emanation of the glory of the almighty God: and therefore no defiled thing cometh into her.

26 For she is the brightness of eternal light, and the unspotted mirror of God's majesty, and the image of his goodness.

27 And being but one, she can do all things: and remaining in herself the same, she reneweth all things, and through nations conveyeth herself into holy souls, she maketh the friends of God and prophets.

28 For God loveth none but him that dwelleth with Wisdom.

29 For she is more beautiful than the sun, and above all the order of the stars: being compared with the light, she is found before it.

30 For after this cometh night, but no evil can overcome Wisdom.

from Sirach (Ecclesiasticus)

Chapter 24

1 Wisdom shall praise her own self, and shall be honoured in God, and shall glory in the midst of her people,

2 And shall open her mouth in the churches of the most High, and shall glorify herself in the sight of his power,

3 And in the midst of her own people she shall be exalted, and shall be admired in the holy assembly.

4 And in the multitude of the elect she shall have praise, and among the blessed she shall be blessed, saying:

5 I came out of the mouth of the most High, the firstborn before all creatures:

6 I made that in the heavens there should rise light that never faileth, and as a cloud I covered all the earth:

7 I dwelt in the highest places, and my throne is in a pillar of a cloud.

8 I alone have compassed the circuit of heaven, and have penetrated into the bottom of the deep, and have walked in the waves of the sea,

9 And have stood in all the earth: and in every people,

10 And in every nation I have had the chief rule:

11 And by my power I have trodden under my feet the hearts of all the high and low: and in all these I sought rest, and I shall abide in the inheritance of the Lord.

12 Then the creator of all things commanded, and said to me: and he that made me, rested in my tabernacle,

13 And he said to me: Let thy dwelling be in Jacob, and thy inheritance in Israel, and take root in my elect.

14 From the beginning, and before the world, was I created, and unto the world to come I shall not cease to be, and in the holy dwelling place I have ministered before him.

15 And so was I established in Sion, and in the holy city likewise I rested, and my power was in Jerusalem.

16 And I took root in an honourable people, and in the portion of my God his inheritance, and my abode is in the full assembly of saints.

17 I was exalted like a cedar in Libanus, and as a cypress tree on mount Sion.

18 I was exalted like a palm tree in Cades, and as a rose plant in Jericho:

19 As a fair olive tree in the plains, and as a plane tree by the water in the streets, was I exalted.

20 I gave a sweet smell like cinnamon, and aromatical balm: I yielded a sweet odour like the best myrrh:

21 And I perfumed my dwelling as storax, and galbanum, and onyx, and aloes, and as the frankincense not cut, and my odour is as the purest balm.

22 I have stretched out my branches as the turpentine tree, and my branches are of honour and grace.

23 As the vine I have brought forth a pleasant odour: and my flowers are the fruit of honour and riches.

24 I am the mother of fair love, and of fear, and of knowledge, and of holy hope.

25 In me is all grace of the way and of the truth, in me is all hope of life and of virtue.

26 Come over to me, all ye that desire me, and be filled with my fruits.

27 For my spirit is sweet above honey, and my inheritance above honey and the honeycomb.

28 My memory is unto everlasting generations.

29 They that eat me, shall yet hunger: and they that drink me, shall yet thirst.

30 He that hearkeneth to me, shall not be confounded: and they that work by me, shall not sin.

31 They that explain me shall have life everlasting.

32 All these things are the book of life, and the covenant of the most High, and the knowledge of truth.

33 Moses commanded a law in the precepts of justices, and an inheritance to the house of Jacob, and the promises to Israel.

34 He appointed to David his servant to raise up of him a most mighty king, and sitting on the throne of glory for ever.

35 Who filleth up wisdom as the Phison, and as the Tigris in the days of the new fruits.

36 Who maketh understanding to abound as the Euphrates, who multiplieth it as the Jordan in the time of harvest.

37 Who sendeth knowledge as the light, and riseth up as Gehon in the time of the vintage.

38 Who first hath perfect knowledge of her, and a weaker shall not search her out.

39 For her thoughts are more vast than the sea, and her counsels more deep than the great ocean.

40 I, wisdom, have poured out rivers.

41 I, like a brook out of a river of a mighty water; I, like a channel of a river, and like an aqueduct, came out of paradise.

42 I said: I will water my garden of plants, and I will water abundantly the fruits of my meadow.

43 And behold my brook became a great river, and my river came near to a sea:

44 For I make doctrine to shine forth to all as the morning light, and I will declare it afar off.

45 I will penetrate to all the lower parts of the earth, and will behold all that sleep, and will enlighten all that hope in the Lord.

46 I will yet pour out doctrine as prophecy, and will leave it to them that seek wisdom, and will not cease to instruct their offspring even to the holy age.

47 See ye that I have not laboured myself only, but for all that seek out the truth.

Jacob Boehme

JACOB BOEHME (1575–1625), a Silesian Lutheran and a cobbler by trade, experienced at least three mystical awakenings which resulted in an original and creative mysticism that reinvigorated mysticism and religious philosophy from the early 17th century onward. The first event occurred in 1610, when, "whereby according to the *Divine Drawing* and *Will*, he was in spirit rapt into the *Holy Saboath*; where he remained seven whole days by his own confession in the highest *Joy*."[1] Later that year Boehme found himself fascinated by light reflected from a pewter dish by which "he was brought to the inward ground or *Centrum* of the hidden *Nature*."[2] Finally, in 1610 Boehme's third mystical experience inspired him to commit his insights to writing, though, as the story goes, "he wrote privately and secretly for himself, by small means, and no books at all but the *Holy Scriptures*."[3] His theosophic undertakings, nevertheless, soon drew the attention of religious and secular authorities. He was denounced from the pulpit by his pastor, Gregor Richter, and even imprisoned for a time, though "as soon as his book, written in quarto, was brought from his house . . . he was released from confinement and warned to cease from such matters."[4] He did not cease. Indeed, his literary output was by any standards immense: thirty-one substantial books in fourteen years, most of them written between 1619 and 1623.

Perhaps the best way to describe Boehme's mysticism is to call it "poetic." The German Romantic poet Novalis (Friedrich von Harden-

---

1. [Durant Hotham], *The Life of one Jacob Boehmen, Who Although He Were a Very Meane man, yet wrote the most wonderfull deepe knowledge in Natural and Divine things...* (1644), A2ʳ.
2. Ibid.
3. [Durant Hotham], *The Life of one Jacob Boehmen*, A2ᵛ.
4. Ariel Hessayon, "Boehme's Life and Times" in *An Introduction to Jacob Boehme: Four Centuries of Thought and Reception*, edited by Ariel Hessayon and Sarah Apetrei (New York and London: Routledge, 2014), 13–37, at 14–15. Quoting Howard Brinton, *Mystic Will: Based upon a Study of the Philosophy of Jacob Boehme* (New York: Macmillan, 1930), 50.

berg, 1772–1801), indeed, took Boehme to be speaking an essentially poetic language, and as evidence points to the ways the mystic exalts intuition and emotion and repeatedly condemns the insufficiency of reason to truly reach into the utterance of the Divinity.[5] Friedrich Schlegel (1772–1829) went even further in describing Boehme's thought: "Its form is religious, its content philosophical and its spirit poetic."[6] To try to read Boehme as we might read a book of theology is to assure failure—which is why Boehme's prose has been described as "simply one of the most difficult reads in the history of Christian thought."[7] Boehme created his own idiom—full of idiosyncrasies and neologisms—to which it takes the reader a little time to become accustomed.

Boehme's writing on Sophia represented here is characteristic of his often polyvalent discourse—a language which needs to be read agapeically, holographically, if we wish to enter into his thought. Boehme sometimes describes Sophia as a divine principle of the universe, sometimes as a divine being resonant with the feminine Sophia of the biblical Wisdom literature. Often he associates his Sophia with the Virgin Mary and her almost alchemical role in bringing God (and therefore redemption) into the flesh and into time as Jesus Christ.

5. Kristine Hannak, "Boehme and German Romanticism" in *An Introduction to Jacob Boehme*, 163–79, at 163.

6. Friedrich Schlegel, *Die Entwicklung der Philosophie in zwölf Büchern* (Cologne, 1804–05), in Friedrich Schlegel, *Erster Teil: Philosophische Vorlesungen (1800–1807)*, ed. Jean-Jacques Anstett, vol. 12 of *Kritische Friedrich Schlegel-Ausgabe*, ed. Ernst Behler unter Mitiwirkung von Hans Eichner und Jean-Jacques Anstett (Munich: Schöningh Verlag, 1964), 259. Quoted in Hannak, "Boehme and German Romanticism," 166. Hannak's translation.

7. Cyril O'Regan, *Gnostic Apocalypse: Jacob Boehme's Haunted Narrative* (Albany, NY: State University of New York Press, 2002), 3.

Jacob Boehme

from *The Book of Six Great Points* (1620)

The First Point

The First Chapter

Of the first *Sprout and Life out of the First Principle. So to ponder and Consider it; as if it* stood alone *and were not Mixed with the other: what its Ability or potentiality* might *be.*

Not to think in such a manner, as if it were thus only in a Figure or Creature: but that Men may learn to search and fathom the Center *of Nature, and learn to* distinguish *the Divine Being or Substance from Nature.*

The First Text

1. We see and find, that Every Life is *Essential*; and find also, that it standeth in a *Will* for, the will, is the driving forth of the Essences.

2. And thus we are to conceive, as if a hidden Fire lay in the *willing*, where the will continually lifteth itself up towards the fire, and would awaken and kindle that.

3. For we understand, that every Will, without the awakening of the fiery Essences, is an *Inability*, as it were inanimate or Mute without life, wherein is no feeling, understanding or substantiality.

4. For it is only like a *Shadow* without Substance; for it hath no driver,[8] but it sinketh down and suffers it self to be driven and lead as a Dead thing or Substance; as is to be apprehended in a SHADOW, which be cometh[9] lead about *without Essence.*

5. Thus, an unessential will is an inanimate or Mute being or substance; without comprehension and Life; and yet is a *Figure*, in the Abyssal Eternal Nothing: for it cleaveth or adhereth to Corporeal Things.

6. Now as the Will without Essence is inanimate without being or Substance, so in the Essence it is a being of Substance and Image, according to the Essences, which be cometh Imaged according to the Essences: for the *willing Life* becometh generated out of the *Essences.*

7. Thus, the Life is the Sonne of the Essences and the will wherein the Lifes figure standeth, is the Father of the Essences, for no Essence *can exist* without willing: for in the willing, the Desiring becometh Originated, in which the Essences originally arise.

8. Seeing then, the *first will*, is an Abysse, to be esteemed as an Eternal Nothing: therefore we apprehend it to be *like* a Looking-Glass, in which

---

8. Of its own self.
9. As a Thought is drawn or pourtrayed in Mind.

one seeth his own Image like a Life, and yet is no Life, but a Figure of the Life, and of the Image to the Life.

9. Thus we apprehend the Eternal Abysse without and beyond Nature to be like a Looking-Glass for it is *like* an **AVGE**[10] Eye, which there seeth, & yet bringeth nothing into the Seeing, wherewith it seeth: for the *seeing* is without being or substance, whereas yet it becometh generated out of being or substance, *viz:* out of the Essential being or Substance.

10. Thus, it is apprehensible to us, that Eternal Abysse without or beyond Nature, is a Will, Like an Eye, wherein Nature lieth hidden, like *an hidden fire burneth not*, which there, is, and is not.

11. It is not a Spirit, but a form of a Spirit, like the Shimmering Glimps or Reflexion in the Looking-Glass, where *all* manner of *forms* of a Spirit is seen in the shimmering Glimps, reflexion, or Looking Glass.

12. And yet there is nothing which the Eye or Looking-Glass seeth; but its seeing is *in it self*; for there is nothing before it, which is deeper there.

13. It is like a Looking-Glass, which is a retainer of the Aspect of Nature, yet it doth not comprehend Nature, neither doth Nature comprehend the shimmering Glimps or Reflexion in the Looking-Glass: and thus the one is free from the other; and yet the Looking-Glass is really the retainer or *preserver of the Image*.

14. It compriseth the Image, and yet is impotent in respect of the shimmering Glimps or Reflexion, for it cannot retain the shimmering Glimps or Reflexion: for if the *Image departeth* away from the Looking-Glass: then is the Looking-Glass meer Glass: and the Glance *Shadow* or Reflexion is a Nothing: and yet all Forms of Nature lie hidden therein as it were Nothing and yet is truly and Entally or really, but *not* Essentially.

15. Thus we are to apprehend & understand concerning the Eternal wisdom of God, **which thus resembleth** an Eternal Eye without Being or Substance: it is the Abysse and yet seeth all; all hath stood hidden in it from Eternity, whence it hath its seeing; But it is not Essential: As the Glance shadow or Reflexion in the Looking-Glass is not Essential, and yet that receiveth, catcheth, or compriseth that which *appeareth* before it.

16. And then secondly as concerning the *Eternal willing* which is also without being or Substance, we are in like manner to understand concerning the *Spirit of God*, for No Seeing is without Spirit, also no Spirit without Seeing.

17. And understand thus, that the Seeing appeareth out of *the Spirit*, which is its Eye or Looking-Glass, wherein the will is revealed or manifest: for the Seeing maketh a *will*.

10. Boehme uses the astrological symbol for the sun in the margin: ☉

18. Thus, the Abysse of the Deep, without Number, knoweth to find no Ground nor limit, and therefore its Looking-Glass goeth into itself, and maketh a Ground in it self, that is, a *Will*.

19. Thus, the Looking-Glass of the Eternal Eye appeareth in the willing, and Generateth to it self an Eternal Ground in it self, that is, its *Center* or heart, out of which the seeing continually ariseth from Eternity: and thereby the will becometh stirring and driving forth, *viz*: of whatsoever the *Center* Generateth.

20. For, it all becometh catched or comprehended in the willing, and is a Being or *Substance*, which Eternally ariseth in the Eternal Abysse in it self: and entreth into it self, and maketh the Center in it self; receiveth catcheth or Compriseth it self in it self, but goeth with that which is comprised out of it self forth, and revealeth or Manifesteth itself in the Glance Shadow of Reflexion of the Eye, and so *appeareth* out of the being or substance, in it self, and out of it self.

21. It is its *own*, yet in respect of Nature it is as a Nothing: understand, in respect of the *Comprehensible* or palpable being or substance, as a Man may say; whereas yet it is ALL, and all originally ariseth from thence.

22. And we understand here, **the Eternal Being of Substance of Deity, with the Abyssal Wisdom**: for, the Eternal will which catcheth or compriseth the Eye; *viz*: the Looking-Glass wherein the Eternal Seeing standeth, *viz*: the Wisdom; is the *Father*.

23. And the Eternal Comprised or catched, in the Wisdom; where the Catching or Comprising, in it self compriseth a Ground or Center, out of the Abysse into a Ground, is the *Form* or Heart; for it is the Word of Life, or its *Substantiality*, wherein the Will with the Glance or Reflexion *appeareth*.

24. And the Entering into itself to the Center of the Ground; is the *Spirit*; for it is the finder, which there *findeth* continually from Eternity, where nothing is; and that goeth again from the Center of the Ground forth, & seeketh in the willing, and then the Looking-Glass of the Eye, *viz*. the Fathers and Sonnes Wisdom becometh Manifest: and thus the *Wisdom* standeth before the Spirit of God which the Abysse manifesteth in it.[11]

25. For, its vertue wherein the *Colours of the Wonders*[12] appear becometh manifest out of the Father of the Eternal willing, through the Center of his heart or ground with the out-going Spirit.

26. For it is the *outspoken*, which the Father speaketh forth out of the

11. Or "in her."
12. Of the Eternal Wisdom.

Center of the Heart with or by the Holy Spirit, and standeth in the divine *Formings* and **Images**, in the Sight of the Eye of the Holy Trinity of God; yet as a *Virgin* without generating.

27. It generateth not the Colours which appear in it, & stand manifest in the Ground and Being or Substance; But All is together an Eternal *Magia*, and dwelleth with the Center of the Heart, in it self, and with the Spirit out of the Center it goeth forth out it self, and manifesteth it self in the Eye of the Virgin-like Wisdom *in infinitum* Endlesly.

28. For, as the Being or Substance of the Deity, hath no ground, out of which it ariseth or proceedeth; so also the will-Spirit hath no ground, wherein it might *Rest*, where there might be any place or limit; but it is called *Wonderful*,[13] and its Word or Heart from which it goeth forth, is called the Eternal *Power* of the Deity; and the will which generateth the Heart or power in itself, is called Eternal *Council*.

29. Thus is the Being or Substance of the Deity, in all places and Regions, the Deep of the Abysse, *as a Wheel or Eye*,[14] where the Beginning always hath the End, and there is no place found, for it is itself the place of all Beings or Substances, and *the fulness of all things* and is apprehended or seen of Nothing.

30. For, it is an Eye in it self, as *Ezekiel* hath seen such a thing in a Figure, in the introducing his will-Spirit into God, where his Spiritual figure became introduced into the wisdom of God, with or by the Spirit of God; and there he attained the *Vision*, and otherwise that cannot be.

The Second Text

31. Thus we understand, that the Divine Being or Substance in the Trinity dwelleth in the *Abysse* in it self, yet generateth to it self a Ground in it self, *viz*: the Eternal Word or Heart, which is the *Center* or Limit of Rest in the Deity, where yet there is nothing understood concerning or as to the Substantiality, but concerning or as to a Threefold Spirit, where alwayes the one is the Cause of Birth of the other.

32. And yet that very *Threefold Spirit* is not measurable or circumscriptive, divisible or fathomable; for there is no place found for it, and it is in like manner as *the Abysse of Eternity*, which generateth itself in itself into a *Ground*.

33. And there can be no Place or Space conceivable or found, where

---

13. "For a child is born to us, a son is given to us; upon his shoulder dominion rests. They name him Wonder-Counselor, God-Hero, Father-Forever, Prince of Peace." Isaiah 9:5.

14. Ezek. 1:15–23.

the Spirit of the Trinity *is not Present*, even in all things or substances, but hidden to the Thing or Substance, dwelling in it self *as* a Substance, that equally or alike at once filleth all, and yet dwelleth not in Substance, but it self *hath a Substance* in itself; as we may find by the Bysse or Ground and Abysse, how they both are to be understood as to one another.

34. Thus we understand the *Eternity*: I. First, How it hath been, *before* the times of the Creation of this world: II. Secondly, we understand further, what the Divine Being or Substance is in it self without and *beyond* a Principle. III. Thirdly, what the Eternal *Beginning* in the Abysse is, and the Eternal *End* in its own Bysse or Ground generated in itself: *viz*: the Center to the Word, which word is the Center it self: IV. Fourthly, And yet the Eternal Geniture or Birth of the Word in the Will in the Looking-Glass of the Eternal *Wisdom, viz*: in the Virgin without generating or bringing forth; is continually effected or produced from Eternity to Eternity.

35. **In this Virgin of the Wisdom of God,** is the Eternal Principle, as a *hidden Fire*, which becometh thus apprehended as in a **Looking-Glass,** in its Colours; and hath been known from Eternity to Eternity in the *Figure*: and also thus becometh known in all Eternity in the Eternal Original in the Wisdom.

36. And in that Looking-Glass, where the Principle out of the Eternal Abysse becometh opened; is the *Substance* of the Three Principles *according* to the substance of the Holy Trinity, become *seen*, with its wonders, as in an Abyssal Deep; and that from Eternity.

37. And now it is to be understood thus; that the First Principle, in the Original is *Magicall:* for it becometh generated in the desiring in the willing, from thence then to generate its seeking or Longing and contrary *opposite* will.

38. And seeing then in the first and second Principle it is only understood as a spirit, without comprehensible or *palpable* being or substance: therefore the seeking or Longing is further, to generate the *Third* Principle: where the Spirit of the Principles might rest, and manifest it self therein in *Similitude*.

39. And although each Principle hath its Center, yet the first Principle standeth in the Magical source of quality, and its Centre is *Fire*, which cannot subsist without Substance, and therefore its hunger and desiring is after *Substance*.

40. And it is to be understood concerning or as to the first Principle, if we speak meerly of One, though it is not One alone: that the Abyssal will in the Center of the Abysse, as wherein the Eternal Word continually becometh *generated* from Eternity, is, *desirous*; for the Will desireth the Center or Heart.

41. Secondly, it desireth that the Heart might be manifest, for in the Abysse there is no manifestation or revelation: but an Eternal Nothing; a *stilness* or *vacuum* without Being or Substance or Colours and Vertues.

42. But in this *desiring*, Colours powers and vertues come to be, and yet is thus only hidden in it self; and if it should Eternally not be manifested, then there would be no Light, Lustre Bright Glance or Majesty, but a Threefold Spirit *in it self*, which would be without source or quality of any Being or Substance.

43. And thus, is the *Substance* of the Deepest Deity without beyond of besides Nature.

44. And further: the Eternal Will of the Deity, desireth to manifest it self out of its own Bysse or Ground in the Light of the Majesty.

45. Where then, the first will of the Father to the Son, and to the Light of the Majesty is apprehended to be desirous; and that in *two wayes*; the First way, to the Centre of the *Word*, the Second to the *Light* of the Manifestation or Revelation.

46. For every desiring is attractive, through in the Abysse there is Nothing which there can be drawn, yet therefore the Desiring *draweth it self*, impregnateth the *Second* willing of the Father, which *Imagineth* to the Light of the Majesty, out of the Center of his word or Heart.

47. And now is the Heart impregnated with the *Light*, and the first will impregnated with *Nature*: and yet thus there would be no manifestation, if the *Principle* were *not* generated.

48. For, the Father generateth the first Principle out of the first willing, *viz: Nature*; which in the Fire, cometh to the **highest** Perfection.

49. And then he generateth the second Principle, in and out of the second willing to the Word: in that it desireth the Manifestation or *Revelation* of the Word in the Light of the Majesty, where the Fire of the Second Principle in the Light of the Majesty is a fulfilling of the Second willing, *viz.* **Meekness**: which is set opposite to the fire of the first Principle, and *quencheth* its fierce wrath and is put into an **Essentiall Substance**, as into an Eternal Life; Where the Fire is hidden in the Light, and giveth the Light its Power, Strength, and Might, so that it is together an **Eternal Band**, and one without the other would not be.

Jacob Boehme

from *The Three Principles of the Divine Essence of the Eternall, Dark, Light, and Temporary World* (1618–1619)

Chapter 18: *Of the Promised Seede of the Woman*

33. And there the noble virgin (in the Spirit of the Prophets) did point at the seede of the Woman, at his Incarnation [or becoming Man], his suffering and dying for the poore soule of Man, that it might be delivered from the Eternall Death, and be regenerated anew, in the Sonne of the virgin: which was done after three thousand nine hundred and seventy yeares, and then the Word of the Promise, which God promised to *Adam* and *Eve* in the Paradise in the Garden of *Eden*, when they fell into sinne, (and which Imaged [or imprinted] it selfe in the Centre of the life, through which all Men that come to God are justified) became Man.

34. It continued a long time in the Covenant of Circumcision (in the life and light of the Father) with the shadows and types of the Incarnation of the Sonne: But these could not reach [or comprehend] the earnestness, of the coming againe of the body out of the grave: But the Word must become Man, if Man must rise againe out of the grave. It [the Covenant] ransomed the soule indeed, so that could stand before the Father (in the Gate of the corruptibility) in the fire of the sharpnesse, but not in the pleasant Joy, before the light of the holy Trinity; and besides it could not bring the new body forth out of the Element, for it was defiled too much with sinne.

35. Thus in that fore-mentioned yeare, the Angel *Gabriel* came, being sent of God the Father to *Nazareth*, to poore (yet chast and modest) virgin, called *Mary*, (her name signifieth plainly in the Language of Nature, *A Redemption out of the valley of misery*: and though it be plaine, that wee are not borne of the High Schooles, with many Languages, yet wee have the Language of Nature in our Schoole of Wonders [or Miracles] fixed [stedfast or perfect,] which the Master of Art, in his *Pontificalibus*, will not beleeve) and he Greeted her through God, and brought the Eternall Command of the Father, out of his will, and said to her; *Haile full of grace, the Lord is with thee thou blessed among women: And when shee looked upon him, shee was terrified at his saying, and [considered] in her thoughts what manner of salutation this was. And the Angel said to her, fear not Mary, thou hast found Grace with God, behold, thou Shalt conceive in thy womb [or body] and beare a sonne, whose name thou Shalt call Jesus, he shall be great, and be called the sonne of the most High, and God the LORD will give unto him the Throne of his Father David, and he shall be King over the house of Jacob Eternally, and of his Kingdome*

there will be no end. Then said Mary to the Angel, How shall that come to passe, since I know not a Man? And the Angel answered to her and said; the Holy Ghost will come upon thee, and the vertue [or power] of the most High will overshadow thee, therefore also that holy One, that shall be borne of thee, Shall be called the Sonne of God. Then said Mary, Behold! I am the Handmaid of the Lord, let it be done to mee as thou hast said; and the Angel departed from her.[15] Now when this Command [or Message] from God the Father came, then the nature of the Spirit of the soule in Mary was astonished, as the Text saith: for it was stirred by a gracious Guest, who went into a wonderful Lodging [or Inne].

36. But the Reader must not here understand it, as if the word, for this Incarnation, at this time did first come down, out of the highest Heaven above the Starres, hither beneath, and became Man, as the world teacheth in blindness: No, but the Word, which God spake in Paradise to *Adam* and *Eve*, concerning the Treader upon the Serpent, (which Imaged [or imprinted] it selfe in the doore of the light of life, standing in the Centre of the Gate of Heaven, and waiting perceptably in the mindes of the holy Men, even till this time) that same Word is become Man; and that same Divine Word, is againe entered into the virgin of Divine Wisdome, which was given to the soule of *Adam* neere the Word, to be a light, and a handmaid, as to the Word.

37. And the will of the Heart of God in the Father, is from the Heart entred into the will of the Wisdome, before the Father, into an Eternall contract; and the same virgin of the Wisdome of God, in the Word of God, hath in the bosom of the virgin *Mary*, given it selfe into her virgin-Matrix, and united it selfe, as a propriety, not to depart in Eternity; [you must] understand, into the Essences, and into the Tincture of the Element, which is pure and undefiled before God: in that, the Heart of God is becoming an Angelicall Man, as *Adam* was in Creation; and the going forth out of the Heart of God, with the whole fulnesse of Deity (out of which also the holy Ghost [or Spirit] of God, and out of the Spirit the virgin, goeth forth) maketh this high Angelicall Image greater than *Adam*, or ever any Angel was: for it is the blessing, and the might of all things, which are in the Father Eternally.

38. For the Word (by its being given into the Element, into the virgin-Matrix) is not severed from the Father: but it continueth eternally in the Father, and it is (in the Heaven of the Element) every where present: into which [Element] the same [word] is entred, and is become a new creature in Man: which [new creature] is called God. And you must here very highly and accurately understand, that this new creature

15. Luke 1:28–35.

in the holy Element, is not generated of the flesh and bloud of the virgin; but of God, out of the Element, in a total fullnesse, and union of the holy Trinity: which [creature] continueth with total fullnesse without ending, therein eternally; which [creature] every where, filleth all, in all the Gates of the holinesse, whose depth hath no ground, and is without number, [measure] and Name.

39. Yet you must know, that the corporeity of the Element of this creature is inferiour to the Deity: for the Deity is Spirit: and the Element is generated out of the Word from Eternity: and the Lord entered into the servant, at which all the Angels in Heaven doe wonder: and it is the greatest wonder, that is done from Eternity, for it is against Nature: and may [indeed rightly] be [called] Love.

40. And after this high Princely Angelicall Creature (in the twinkling of an eye) in the Word and Holy Ghost (in the Holy Element) was figured [fashioned, formed, or made] a selfe subsisting creature (with perfect life and light) in the Word: then also (in the same twinkling of an eye) the foure Elements (with the Dominion of the Sunne and Starres) in the Tincture of the bloud, together with the bloud and all humane Essences (which were in the body of the virgin *Mary*) in her Matrix (according to the Counsell of God) in the Element, received the creature, wholly and properly, as one [onely] Creature, and not two.

41. And the holy [pure] Element of the Heaven (which incloseth the Deity) that was the *Limbus* (or the Masculine seed) to this creature: and the Holy Ghost, with the holy Fiat, in the virgin of the Divine Wisdome, was the Master-Builder, and the first beginner; and every Regimen, built its own (in its own Center) therein.

42. The Holy Spirit of God, built the formation in the wisdome of the virgin (in the [holy] Element, in its Centre of the Heaven) even the highly worthy Princely and Angelicall formation: and the Regiment of the Starres and Elements of this world, formed the outward Man (wholly, with all Essences of our humane bodies,) with a naturall body and soule (wholly like us) in one onely Person.

43. And yet every forme hath its own height, source, [or quality] and perception: and [yet] the Divine [source] hath not so mixed, that [thereby] it is the lesse: but what it was, that it continueth to be: and that which it was not, that it is, without severing from the Divine substance: and the Word did abide in the Father: and the naturall humanity, in this world, in the bosom of the virgin *Mary*.

from *Of the Becoming Man or Incarnation of Jesus Christ, the Sonne of God* (*1620*)

The Eighth Chapter of the Virgin Mary, and of the Becoming Man or Incarnation of Jesus Christ the Sonne of God.

1. Many have attempted to write of the Virgin Mary; and *supposed* that she was *not* an Earthly Maid: them indeed hath been presented a *Glimpse* of the Eternal virginity; but the right Mark they have hitherto failed of.

2. For, many have meerly *supposed*, that she was *not* the Daughter of *Joachim* and *Anna*; because *Christ* is called the Seed of the Woman; and is so too.

3. Also he himselfe witnesseth, that *he is from above*, that *he is come from Heaven*; and therefore he must sure also be born of a Totall heavenly Virgin.

4. But that would little benefit us poor children of Eve; that are become Earthly, and carry our souls in Earthy *Vessels*; where should our poor souls become, if the word of Eternall Life, had not received it into it self.

5. If Christ had brought a soul from Heaven; *where* then should our soul become, and the Covenant with *Adam and Eve, viz: that the seed of the Woman should Crush the Serpents Head.*[16]

6. If Christ would have come and been born totally from Heaven, he should have not needed to have been born a Man, *upon Earth*, and where then would the Covenant become, in which the Name JESUS, of the *Promise*, did incorporate it selfe, in the Light of Life, that is, in the *Tincture* of the soul, instantly in Paradise when Adam fell? yea indeed *before* Adam was *Created*; as Paul faith; *We are Elected in Christ, before the foundation of the World was laid.*[17]

7. For, God, in his wisdome, knew the Fall; therefore the Name Jesus did so *instantly* incorporate it selfe into the word of Life, environed with the Virgin of Wisdom, *in* Adams Image, with the Cross.

8. For, the soul it selfe, is even a Cross-Birth: as when the soul-Fire kindleth it selfe, then it maketh in the flash, a Cross; *that is*, an Eye with a Cross, with the Three Principles, with the Character of the Holy Trinity; as in the *Third* Book or part, concerning the Threefold Life of Man,

16. Gen 3:15.
17. Eph 1:4.

is declared, and yet further in the *Fourth* Part, the forty Questions of the Soul.[18]

9. We are to understand, that Mary, in whom Christ became Man, was *truly the Daughter* of **Joachim and Anna**, according to the Outward Flesh; and was extracted out of the Seed of *Joachim* and *Anna*, according to the Outward Man.

10. But, according to the will, she was a Daughter of the Covenant of Promise, for she was the *Mark*, to which it pointed at.

11. In her, stood the *Center* in the Covenant; and therefore she was, by the Holy Ghost in the Covenant, highly *blessed among* and above all *women* [19] ever since Eve; for the Covenant opened it selfe in her.

12. You must understand it aright, according to its high precious worth: The word, together with Promise, which with the Jewes, stood in the Type or prefiguration, as in a *Looking-Glass*, wherein God, the Angry Father Imagined, and thereby quenched his Anger; that moved it selfe Now after an *Essential* **manner: which from Eternity had *not* been done before.**

13. For, when *Gabriel* the Prince, brought her the Message, that she should be impregnated or with Child; and that she consented there to; and said; *be it unto me as thou hast said*:[20] then the Center of the Holy Trinity, moved it selfe, and opened the Covenant, that is, the Eternal Virginity, which Adam *lost*, became opened in her in the word of Life.

14. For the Virgin of Gods Wisdom, *environed* the word of Life, *viz*: the *Center* of the Holy Trinity: thus the Center became Moved; and the Heavenly *Vulcan*, struck up the Fire of Love; so that the Principle in the Love-flame, became generated.

15. Understand this right; In *Maries Essences*, in the Virgin-like Essences, which perished in Adam, out of which he was to generate virgin-like Image, according to the Wisdom of God, the divine fire *became* struck up; and the Principle of Love *kindled*.

16. You are to understand that, **in the seed of Mary,** When she became impregnate, with the Soul-Spirit, that is with the *Tincture of Venus*; for, in the *Tincture of Venus*; that is, in the Source or Quality of Love; Adams first Fire, became struck up in the word of Life.

17. And in the Child JESUS, were both Tinctures perfect; just as in Adam, and the word of Life *in* the Covenant, understand, *in* the Holy

---

18. Boehme published both *The Threefold Life of Man* and *Forty Questions of the Soul* in 1620.

19. Luke 1:41.

20. Luke 1:38.

Trinity, was the *Center*; and the Principle appeared, as in or to the Fathers part.

18. Christ *became* Man in GOD, and also in MARY, in all the THREE Principles; and together therewith also in the EARTHLY *world*.

19. *He took the form of a Servant upon him,*[21] that he might be able to Master Death and the Devil.

20. For he was to be Prince, in the Place or space of this world, in the Angelical Prince-Throne, viz: *upon* the seat, and in the Authority, of the late Angel and Prince *Lucifer*, over all the Three Principles.

21. Now then, *First*: If he must be Lord over this *outward World*, then he must also dwell in the Outward World: and have its Essence and Property.

22. In like manner *Secondly*: If he must be *Gods* Sonne, then he must also be generated out of God.

23. And *Thirdly*: If he must *quench* the Fathers Anger: then he must of necessity be also in the Father.

24. And *Fourthly*: If he must be the Sonne of *Man*, then he must also of necessity be of Mans Essence and Substance: and *Fifthly*, must have a *humane Soul*, and a humane Body as we all have.

25. It is known to us, that *Mary*, his Mother, as also *Christ*, from or of his Mother, were both of the Humane Essence, with Body, Soul and, Spirit; and that Christ received a Soul of Maries Essence; *yet without* Masculine Seed.

26. Onely the great Secret *Arcanum* of God, was there opened; and the first Man, with his Secret Mystery, which fell into Death, was here generated to Life again; understand; in the *Principle* of God.

27. For, because of this, the *Deity* Moved it selfe, and struck up the Fire in the Fathers Principle, and so the deadened *Sulphur*; which dyed in *Adam*, became living again.

28. For the word had in it self heavenly Substantiality; and opened it selfe in the Heavenly Substantiality, in the virgin-like Image of the *Deity*; **this is the pure chast Virgin wherein the Word of Life became Man.**

29. And so the Outward Mary became *adorned* and *blessed* with Highly blessed heavenly Virgin, *among all Women of this World.*[22]

30. *In her*, that which was dead and shut up of the Humanity, become living again; and so the she *became* as highly graduated or Dignified, as the first Man before the Fall, and became a Mother of the Throne-Prince.

21. Phil 2:7.
22. Luke 1:41.

31. This came *not* out of *her* ability, but out of Gods ability; unless the Center of God had moved it selfe in her; she would have been *no* otherwise, then all *Eves* Daughters.

32. But, in this place, The word of Life had fixed the Mark; as also the Covenant of Promise, and *therefore* she is the *blessed* among all *Women*, and *above all* Eves Children.

33. *Not* that she is a Goddess, which Men should honour as God; for she is not the Mark; for she also said: *How shall that come to pass, since I know not of any Man?*[23]

34. But, the word of Life in the *Center* of the Father, which gave in it self, with Moving of the Deity, into the Humanity; and opened it selfe in the *Humane* Essence; that is *Mark*, that is the Goal that we must run to; in the Regeneration.

35. This is a greater wonder then in the first Adam, for the first Adam was created out of Three Principles, and his Spirit was introduced into him through the Spirit of God; and the Heart of God *needed not* to move *it selfe* in an especial manner; for Gods *Spirit* did *onely* move it self, out of Gods Heart.

36. But *now*, the center of *Heart* of God moved it selfe: **which had rested from Eternity**; and the Divine Fire was there struck up, kindled or awakened; as a Man may Express it.

The Dear or Precious Gate

37. We should *rightly* understand, the becoming Man or Incarnation of Christ the Sonne of God, *thus*: he is not become Man in the Virgin Mary *onely*, so that his Deity or divine Substantiality, did sit bolted or *fixed* therein; No, O Man; it is another Manner.

38. Let not Reason befool thee; we understand somewhat else: *as little as God* dwels alone in one onely place: but is *the Fulness of all things*,[24] *so little* also hath God moved himself in one Sparkle.

39. For God is *not divisible*, but Totall Every where: where he manifesteth himselfe, there he is Totally manifest.

40. Also, he is *not measurable*, for him, is no place found, unlesse he make a place for himselfe *in* a Creature; yet he is totally neer the Creature without or beyond the Creature.

41. When the Word moved it selfe to the opening of Life, then it opened it selfe in the divine Substantiality, in the *water* of Eternal Life, it entered in and became *Sulphur*, that is Flesh and Blood.

23. Luke 1:31.
24. Col 2:9.

42. It made heavenly Tincture, which the *Deity* did close about and fill, wherein the wisdom of God standeth Eternally, together with the *divine* Magia.

43. Understand it right: The Deity, hath longed to *become* Flesh and Bloud, and although the pure cleer Deity, continueth *Spirit*, yet is it *become* the Spirit and Life of Flesh; and worketh in the Flesh; so that we may say, *when* we with our Imagination enter into God, and wholly give our selves into him, **we Enter into Gods Flesh and Blood**, and live in God.

44. For, the Word is *become* Man, and God is the Word.

Sophiology and
Seventeenth-Century Science

Robert Fludd and Thomas Vaughan

WHEREAS the sophiology implicit to Boehme and the Philadelphians was fundamentally mystical and religious and primarily of a lay, devotional character, a sophiology much more tied to natural science also arose in England during the seventeenth century. A response to *natura pura*, Cartesian dualism, and the growing scientific materialism—foreshadowing in many ways the so-called "Enlightenment"—found voice in two natural philosophers, one a physician and the other an Anglican priest, Robert Fludd and Thomas Vaughan. For both of them, understanding *natura* is inconceivable apart from an understanding of God (not to mention scripture).

Unfortunately, posterity has not been kind to these two important thinkers, as academia has for the most part jettisoned them to the "curiosity shop" department of scholarly inquiry, no doubt a by-product of the Enlightenment assumptions that so undergirded modern and continue to undergird postmodern culture. Indeed, the prevailing interpretation of Fludd and Vaughan has not changed much since 1972 when Wayne Shumaker branded both as "abnormally eccentric Englishmen."[1] Nevertheless, the time has certainly come to reevaluate their work in the light of the call for a renewed integration of science, art, and religion.

Robert Fludd (1574–1637)

Robert Fludd is something of an outlier in the history of sophiology.[2] Seemingly unaware of Boehme's sophiology, Fludd nevertheless came to his own insights regarding Sophia through his simultaneously religious and scientific investigations of the natural world. Inspired in great part

---

1. Wayne Shumaker, *The Occult Sciences in the Renaissance: A Study in Intellectual Patterns* (Berkeley: University of California Press, 1972), 239.

2. For a full discussion of Fludd, see "*Dei Gloria Intacta:* The Wisdom of God in Robert Fludd's Mystical Philosophy" in Michael Martin, *The Submerged Reality: Sophiology and the Turn to a Poetic Metaphysics* (Kettering, OH: Angelico Press, 2014).

by the mysterious Rosicrucian manifestos,[3] in early seventeenth-century England Fludd was a highly regarded physician, scientist, and religious philosopher, and in his voluminous writings he not only argued against the encroaching scientific materialism and theological innovations of his age (he was a great opponent of the theology of *natura pura*, for example) but articulated a mystical-scientific vision of the relationship of the microcosm to the macrocosm in language that was simultaneously grounded in Christian tradition and the *avant-garde*. An important intellectual of the time, Fludd engaged in a vigorous public discourse with the scientists Johannes Kepler, Andreas Libavius, Pierre Gassendi, and Marin Mersenne among others; he was also a Fellow of the Royal College of Physicians.

Today, Fludd is little known and hardly read. His voluminous Latin works have never been translated into English (though many of Matthieu Merian's extraordinary engravings which illustrated Fludd's works have gained notice). Likewise, his few English writings have suffered from a general and universal neglect for over four hundred years. Nevertheless, Fludd's works are an amazing late-Renaissance example of an epistemology that was rapidly disappearing: one in which God's presence in the world is assumed and his participation in it is believed discernable. After Descartes, such a worldview fell into rapid decline. Furthermore, Fludd reads the natural world through the lens of the Bible, and the Bible through the lens of the natural world, detecting a synergy between the Two Books delivered by the hand of God. Indeed, Fludd's frequent citation of scripture—even of books considered apocryphal in his own Anglican religious context—justifies Urszula Szulakowska's claim that the physician and scientist wrote "primarily as a theologian," a fact that is more than obvious.[4]

In the text featured here, from the English translation of his *Mosaicall Philosophy*, Fludd explains how God's wisdom touches all things, and he presents a case for an integral, sophiological understanding of the cosmos and all aspects of human endeavor. In doing this, Fludd stands opposed to the theologians and philosophers of *natura pura*.

Thomas Vaughan (1621–1666)

The Welshman Thomas Vaughan was an Anglican priest, alchemist,

---

3. *Fama Fraternitatis* (1614) and *Confessio Fraternitatis* (1615).

4. Urszula Szulakowska, *The Sacrificial Body and the Day of Doom: Alchemy and Apocalyptic Discourse in the Protestant Reformation*, Aries Book Series: Texts and Studies in Western Esotericism (Leiden, NL: Brill, 2006), 121. William H. Huffman concurs: "Above all, the foundation of Fludd's philosophy was religious." See his *Robert Fludd and the End of the Renaissance* (London: Routledge, 1988), 101.

physician, officer in the Royalist army, mystical writer, and the identical twin brother of the Metaphysical poet Henry Vaughan (1621–1695). Between 1650 and 1655 he threw himself into a vigorous publishing campaign, issuing several volumes of mystical philosophy and engaging in a heated literary battle with Henry More (1614–1687), the Cambridge Platonist. Vaughan railed against More's intellectualism and antagonized Neo-Scholastic thinkers and their notion of *natura pura*. He likewise dismissed René Descartes's dualistic theories as *"Whymzies."*[5] Unlike the temperate rhetorical persona of his brother, Thomas Vaughan comes across a bombastic and combative soul, though his bellicosity is tempered by a wry sense of humor as well as by a holistic religious sensitivity.

Vaughan drew inspiration from the occult tradition of Renaissance magical writer Heinrich Cornelius Agrippa von Nettesheim (1486–1535), but he also bears the influence of his slightly older contemporaries Boehme and Fludd as well as that of the Rosicrucian manifestos.[6]

The three texts from Vaughan excerpted here emphasize the reciprocal relationship of God, nature, and scripture, an important theme not only for Thomas Vaughan but also for his brother Henry (who is represented in Part II). Furthermore, we can see in these texts how Vaughan's assumption of this reciprocity—which certainly has something to do with his disdain for *natura pura*—also leads his contemplation into other modes of discourse, particularly alchemy, but also eschatology and fantasy. In addition, the section from Vaughan's *Lumen de Lumine* (1651) introduces us to Vaughan's Sophia figure, Thalia, who embodies more than a few resonances with Jane Lead's visionary experiences of Sophia recounted in *A Fountain of Gardens* (see pages 70–80). Vaughan's Thalia is clearly an imaginative figure, but in her we can start to discern the misty borderlands between religious vision and poetic expression, what I have called elsewhere a "poetic metaphysics."[7] Vaughan's work clearly inhabits such a metaxological space.

5. Thomas Vaughan, *Anima Magica Abscondita* (London, 1650), 55.

6. I discuss what I call "The Rosicrucian Mysticism of Henry and Thomas Vaughan" in my chapter of that title in *Literature and the Encounter with God in Post-Reformation England* (Farnham, UK: Ashgate, 2014).

7. The notebook Vaughan kept with his wife Rebecca, *Aqua Vitæ: Non Vitis*, likewise ranges across the realms of mystical vision and scientific experiment. Donald R. Dickson, rightly in my opinion, reads Thalia as Thomas's cipher for Rebecca. According to Vaughan, Rebecca appeared to him in a dream dressed as Thalia (as in *Lumen de Lumine*, excerpted here) not long after her death in 1658. See his introduction to Thomas and Rebecca Vaughan, *Aqua Vitæ: Non Vitis* (*British Library MS, Sloane* 1741), trans. and ed. Donald R. Dickson, Medieval and Renaissance Texts and Studies 217 (Tempe, AZ: Arizona Center for Medieval and Renaissance Studies, 2001), xxix.

THE HEAVENLY COUNTRY

Robert Fludd

from *Mosaicall Philosophy Grounded upon the Essentiall Truth, or Eternal Sapience* (1659)

Wherein the originall, or beginning of the true wisdom, and consequently of the essentiall Philosophy, is opened; and then the nature and power of it, is really described.

WE PURPOSE now in the first place, to search out the originall fountain of the true wisdom, and therefore of the essentiall Philosophy. And then in the second rank, I will express the definition of it; after that, I will shew you, that it is the foundation, not onely of the true externall Philosophy, with the sciences which depend thereon, but also the discoverer of all mysteries, and hidden secrets, yea, and the onely revealer of things, as well past, as those which are to come. Concerning the originall or beginning of this sacred wisdom, I will prove by the consent and harmony of the whole Bible, that it is in God, the Father of light;[8] and therefore it must be clean contrary in nature unto the wisdom of this world, which is terrene and animal, as the Apostle hath it. *Sapientiæ dator & inventor, Deus est: The giver and inventor of wisdom is God,* as the Prophets do intimate unto us. *Sapienta & fortitudo Domini sint,* saith *Daniel; Sapience and fortitude be the Lord's.*[9] *Sapientia in antiquis est & in multo tempore prudentiæ,* saith *Job; Wisdom is of antiquity, and prudency of a long standing.*[10] Again, *Sapientiam dat Dominus, ex ore ejus prudentia & scientia,* saith *Solomon; The Lord giveth wisdom, prudency and science issue from his mouth.*[11] And again, *Sapientiam possidet Deus in principio viarum suarum, antequam quicquam faceret a principio, ab æterno ordinate eft; concepta erat cum nondum erant abyssi. God did possesse wisdom in the beginning of his waies, before he made anything, from the beginning, even from eternity was she ordained; she was conceived when there was no abysse.*[12] *Sapientia a Deo projecta est & prior omnium creata,* saith the son of *Syrach, Wisdom came from God, and was the first created of all things.*[13] And again, *Ex ore Altissimi prodivi primo-*

---

8. Baruch 1, Dan. 2:21.
9. Dan 2:20.
10. Job 12.
11. Proverbs 2:6.
12. Proverbs 8:22.
13. Sirach 1:4.

genita ante omnens creaturam, saith she in her own person; *I came or issued out from the mouth of the most High, being born before any creature.*[14] *Sapientia cælitus mittatur de sanctis cælis, ut mecum sit, & mecum laboret,* saith *Solomon* in another place: *Let wisdom be sent from thy holy heavens to assist me, and to labour with me.*[15]

And againe he expresseth the time of her election, the manner of her election and way to seperate her truth from falsehood in these few words which are golden ones, *Sapientiam dei ab initio nativitatis investigabo & ponam in lucem, nec præteribo veritatem, I will find out the wisdome of God even from the beginning of her nativity, and I will put her into light, neither will I passe over, or omit the truth.*[16] By all these places and many more which I could produce, it is made manifest that this excellent spirit of which we intend to treat in this place is the true wisdome, and withall it must needs follow that the philosophy which dependeth on it, is the essentiall, perfect and only reall one, forasmuch as it is from the father of lights, according unto the Tenent of the forementioned Apostle and divine philosopher. Now we proceed to shew you briefly what this wisdome is, and how is was produced, and that according unto the mind of the wise Solomon, *Sapientia* (saith he) *est vapor virtutis Dei & emanatio quælam claritatis omnipotentis dei sincera, et candor lucis æterna, et speculum sine macula Dei maiestatis, et imago bonitatis illius. Wisdome is the vapor of the vertue of God, and a certaine sincere emanation of the brightness of the omnipotent God, and the beauty of the eternall light, and the immaculated or unspotted mirror of the majesty of God, and the image of his goodness.* And the Apostle, *Christ is the brightness of the glory and the ingraved forme of his person which beareth up all things by his mighty word.*[17] Whereby it is an easie thing for wisemen to discern, what a main difference there is between the false Ethnick and mundane wisdom which is terrene, and that true and essentiall one which is from above, and hath his originall from the Father of light, forasmuch as the fountain thereof is the Word, or voice of the Lord. *Sapientiæ fons* (saith the Text) *verbum Dei in excelsis, & ingressus illius mandata æterna: The fountain or beginning of wisdom is the word of God from above, and her entrance the eternall Commandments.*[18] Having then expressed unto you, what this onely true wisdom is, I will endeavour to

14. Ibid., 24:5.
15. Wisdom 9:10.
16. Ibid., 6:24.
17. Heb 1:3.
18. Sirach 1:5.

open and discover also her catholick vertues, in the which she acteth and operateth, as well in general, as in particular, over all the world: Nay verily, what can she not do and effect, when she *is all in all, and operateth all in everything,* as the Apostle teacheth us.[19] For this reason also is Christ, the true wisdom, said, in the forementioned Text, *to sustain and bear up all things by the word of his vertue.*[20] This omnipotent power of hers, in the over all things in this world, is most excellently explained and set down thus, by the Divine Philosopher *Paul: Christus est imago Dei invisibilis, primogenitus omnis creaturæ, quoniam in ipso condita sunt universa in cælis & terra, visibilia & invisibilia, sive throni, sive dominationes, sive principatus, sive potestates, omnia per ipsum & in ipso creata sunt, & ipse ante omnes, & omnia in ipso constant. Christ is the image of the invisible God, the first begotten of every creature, because that in him, all things visible and invisible, in the heavens and in the earth, were made, whether they be thrones, or dominions, or principalities, or potestates, all were created by him and in him; and he is before all creatures, and all things consist in him.*[21] This may seem very strange doctrine unto such Academick persons, as are too confident in the Ethnick Philosophy, forasmuch as it doth acknowledge no such wisdom from above, no such a Christ, or sacred Word, which was the Creator of heaven and earth, and who made the Angelicall Intelligences, and in whom, and by whom, all things were, and do yet exist. But it telleth us of subalternat efficient natures, namely, of Intelligences, of Stars, or Elements, and such like things, which operate or effect, of themselves, all things above and beneath, and will have the world to be eternall, and without all beginning; when contrariwise this true Philosophy telleth us, that God *created all things in and by his word* and wisdom; that *he operateth all in all,* and, *that he is all, and in all.* For the plain words of the precedent Text is, *Omnia in ipso constant, All consist in him.* But to the purpose. The foresaid Text seemeth to confirm this of the wise *Solomon: Sapienitam possidebat in principio viæ suæ: ante opera sua, ante ullum tempus, ante seculum, cum nulla essent abyssi, edita erat ipsa, cum nulli essent fontes abundantes aquis, ante montes fundati essent, cum nondum fecerat terram, cum aptaret cælos ibi erat, cum statueret ambitum in superficie abyssi, cum forticaret superiores nubes superne, quando roborabat fontes abyssi, quando ponebat mari statutum suum, cum statueret fundamenta terræ, erat sapientia apud ipsum cuncta componens. Jehovah*

---

19. 1 Cor 12:6.
20. Heb 1:3.
21. Col 1:15.

did possesse wisdom in the beginning of his waies, before any of his works, and before there was any time, before the world was made; she was brought forth before there was any abysse, and before there was any fountains that did abound with water, before the mountains had their foundations, when as yet he had made no earth. When he did adapt and make fit the heavens, she was there; when he did ordain a compasse, or appoint margins for the surface of the abysse. When he did fortifie the highest clouds above, when he did corroborate the fountains of the deep, when he did set bounds unto the sea, when he did establish the foundations of the earth, then was wisdom with him, composing or making all things. Whereby he argueth, first, the antiquity of the eternall wisdom; and then he proveth, that she was the composer and maker of Heaven and Earth, and consequently of every thing, as well invisible, as visible therein. And this agreeth in all things with that of our sacred and essentiall Philosopher *Moses*, where he acknowledgeth first an abysse without form; then that the informed matter of the abysse was by the presence of Gods emanating Spirit, universally informed and called waters.[22] Then how by the acting of the divine or essential voice or word, *Fiat*, which was uttered by the mouth of the Omnipotent, the light or created form was produced in the waters and afterwards by the will of the Creator, the word was pronounced the second time, and the waters above were divided from the waters beneath by the firmament, and so the heavens were made by the second fiat; as by the third, the division of the lower waters into elements, was effected by the assistance of this one and self-same word, or the Spagerick operation of this divine and catholick Spirit, *Elohim*, but in a various property. Doth not David in few words affirm so much, saying, *Verbo Domini firmati sunt cæli & Spiritu ab ore eju omnis virtus eorum: By the word of the Lord the heavens were made, and by the Spirit of his mouth each vertue thereof.*[23] Again, *In Sapientia omnia fecisti; Thou hast created all things in wisdom.*[24] And St. *Peter, Cæli erant prius & terra de aquæ, & per aquam existentes verbo Dei: The heavens were first, and the earth of water, and by water, consisting by the word of God.*[25] And doth not St. *John say, By it all things were made, and without it nothing is made. The world was fashioned by this word or essentiall spirit, which was pure light, but the world did not know it.*[26] And Solomon, *Sapientia Deus*

22. Gen 1.
23. Psalm 32:6.
24. Ibid., 103:24.
25. 2 Peter 3:5.
26. John 1.

fundavit cælos, stabilivit terram in prudentia: By wisdom God made the heavens, and by his prudency he laid the foundations of the earth.[27] In conclusion, the whole harmony of holy Writ, which is too long for me punctually in this place to rehearse, doth testifie thus much, that all things, of what nature or condition forever, were made, disposed, and effected, in, by, and through this divine vertue or emanation, which is God himself, forasmuch as it is the divine act, whose root is the word. *Ex ipso* (saith St. *Paul*) *per ipsum, & ipso sunt omnia: Of him, by him, and in him, are all things.* But because some of the learned of this world may reply, that through it is true, that God by his divine Spirit or Word, did create all things; yet it followeth not, that he doth act immediately, and exist essentially in every thing. But after that this eternall Spirit of wisdom, had bestowed on each creature a peculiar vertue in its creation, then the creature can act of it self by a free-will, which is absolutely; and distinguished, and divided from the immediate act of God. I answer, that by our founded rules in Divinity, the true essence of the Deitie is individuall, and therefore God doth impart no essentiall act or vertue unto any creature which can be discontinued or seperated from Himself. And for this reason, Christ who is the eternall spirit of wisdom is said to fill all. I marry (will our learned say) that is vertually, but not substantially or essentially. I would fain know (laying all such school distinctions apart, of which St. *Paul* biddeth *Timothy* to beware)[28] if the vertue of God be not his essence, or whether the one can be divided from the other? If they reply and say, that this vertue of God is no essence but an accident: Verily they must needs erre in saying so, being that it is most certainly known unto the very Jewes and Gentiles themselves that God hath not any accidents in him, seeing that he is absolutely essentiall, and reall of himself, for where his divine act is, there is also vertue, and, where his vertue is, there is he truly said to be essentiall: for else the word or divine act which doth vivifie and quicken every creature, should seem to be but an Accident, and that divided from the divine essence: which, how absurd it is, the immortality and root of it doth argue: For *David* in his forsaid text sayeth, *spiritu ab ore ejus omnis virtus eorum; from the spirit of his mouth doth issue every vertue of the heavens.*[29] I imagine that there is no man of an upright sense that will esteem this vertue to be an Accident; which being so, then must it needs be essentiall, and consequently in God, and of God, and therefore not

27. Proverbs 3:19.
28. 1 Tim 6:4.
29. Psalm 32:6.

divisible from his spirit: But what needs more words when Scriptures do confirme this every where? St. *Paul* sayeth, in the text before mentioned, *Quoniam in ipso condita sunt universa in cælis et in terra tam visibilia quam invisibilia, omnia in ipso et per ipsum creata sunt; et omnia in ipso constant. Because all things in heaven and earth are made in him, as well visible as invisible, all things are created in him and by him all consist in him;*[30] *Ergo,* nothing without him. Again, St. *John* saith, *In verbo erat vita; Life was in the Word.*[31] And therefore the creature is annexed unto him by a continuated tye of one and the self-same spirit of life which is in the creature, without the which it cannot exist one minute. And for this cause the Psalmist saith, *O Lord, how manifold are thy works, in wisdom thou hast made them all. The earth is full of thy riches; so is the wide sea, and the innumerable creeping things therein both great and small. Thou givest unto them, and they gather it, thou openest thine hand and they are filled with good things; but if thou hide thy face, they are troubled, if thou takest away their breath they die, and return unto dust. Again, if thou sendest out the Spirit, they are re-created and revive, and thou renewest the face of the earth.*[32] Whereby we see, that it is the immediate act of the Spirit of wisdom, that worketh these things, by which God is said to vivifie all things, and that by him we breathe, and live, and have our being. And not onely we, but also all other flesh whatsoever, as it appeareth by the foresaid Text; as also by this testimony of *Job, Si Deus apponens ad hominem animum suum, spiritum seu flatum ejus ad se reciperet, desiceret & exspiraret omnis caro simul, & homo in cinerem reverteretur: If God setting his heart or mind upon man, should receive or draw unto himself his Spirit or breath of life, all flesh would die together, and man would return unto dust.*[33] And the Prophet, *Deus dat flatum populo qui est super terram & spiritum calcantibus eam. God giveth breath unto the people which is on the earth, and a spirit unto the creatures which tread on it.*[34] Now I beseech you, How is it possible, that this spirit of life should be present with, and in, all things, and therefore essentially in every thing, and yet it should cease to act immediately, that is, in *persona sua,* when it is the most swift and mobil in his active nature and agility, of all things, as the wise man telleth us. That he is present in all things, it is apparent, because all things do act and live in him, and by

---

30. Col 1:16.
31. John 1:4.
32. Psalm 104: 24, 29–31.
33. Job 34:14.
34. Isaiah 42:5.

him; for *St. Paul's* Text before mentioned saith, *Omnia in ipso constant,*
All consist in him. And again, *Ipse operatur omnia in omnibus, He wor-*
keth all in all. And St. *Peter, The heavens and the earth which were of*
water, exist by the word.[35] And *Solomon, Incorruptibilis Dei spiritus inest*
omni rei, The incorruptible Spirit of God is in all things.[36] And again,
Spiritus disciplinæ sanctus implet orbem terrarum, The spirit of wisdom
filleth the earth.[37] And the Prophet *David, whither shall I go from thy*
Spirit, or whither shall I flee from thy presence? If I ascend into heaven,
thou art there; if I lie down in hell, thou art there. Let me take the wings of
the morning, and dwell in the uttermost parts of the sea, yet thither shall
thine hand lead me, and thy right hand hold me. If I say, yet the darkness
shall hide me, even the night shall be light about me, yea the darknesse
hideth not from thee; but the night shineth as the day, the darknesse and
night are both alike.[38] Therefore it is his reall Spirit that filleth all things,
and not any accidentall vertue, as is falsly imagined by some. And the
Prophet *Isaias, Cælum est sedes mea, & terra scabellum pedum meorum,*
saith the Lord, *The heavens are my seat, and the earth my foot stool.*[39]
And *Jeremy, Cælum & terram nunquid impleo, Do not I fill the heaven*
and the earth?[40] Now that you may know more particularly how this is
done, hearken unto *David, In sapientia* (saith he) *omnia fecisti, replete*
est terra possessione tua; Thou madest all things in wisdom, and the earth
is full of thy possession or riches;[41] he meaneth with his Spirit, which
replenisheth, inacteth, and informeth all things. And therefore saith the
son of *Syrach, Sapientiam effudit Deus super omnia opera sua, & super*
omnem carnem secundum datum suum: God powred out his wisdom
upon all his creatures, and upon all flesh, according unto the measure that
he bestoweth it:[42] That is to say, The Spirit of wisdom is more or lesse in
all things, according as it pleased God to impart it unto this or that creature. And for this reason, *Solomon* in another place, *Sapientia operatur*
omnia, Wisdom worketh or acteth all things.[43] Which agreeth with this
Text of the Apostle, *Deus operatur omnia in omnibus.*[44] Why should we

35. 2 Peter 3:5.
36. Wisdom 12:1.
37. Ibid., 1:7.
38. Psalm 139:7–12.
39. Isaiah 66:1.
40. Jer 23:24.
41. Psalm 104:24.
42. Sirach 1:10.
43. Wisdom 8:5.
44. 1 Cor 12:6.

not infer then, that this spirit is essentiaily, and presentially in every thing? To conclude therefore this general discourse of the true Philosophy, *Moses* teacheth us, that after the foundation of the Heavens and Elements, every creature that was framed or composed of them, and lived and moved in them, did exist and was preserved by the self-same spirit; namely, the Sun, Moon, and other Starrs in heaven, the seeds, trees, herbs, and such like vegetables, and the creeping and four-footed beasts of the earth, and fishes of the seas. And lastly, Man was created, by one and the self-same spirit; but God imparted unto him a greater proportion of his Spirit, that thereby he might excell in perfection all other creatures. It were too infinite to expresse and set down the main scope of this businesse in writing, as Scriptures do at large recite it; for look into the works of *Moses,* the books of *Joshua* and *Judges,* the history of *Kings* or *Chronicles,* the reports of *Job,* the *Psalms* of *David,* the *Proverbs, Ecclesiastes, Cantiques,* and *Wisdom of Solomon,* the monuments of the *Prophets,* the subject of *Ecclesiasticus* and *Maccabees*; and lastly, the relations or stories of *Christ* and his *Apostles,* and we shall find, that this sacred wisdom, with her essential vertues and acts, in the vast cavity of this world, both above and beneath, is the ground and firm foundations of their doctrine and science, as well concerning naturall, as supernaturall businesses; or rather touching the acts of God in his naturall Tabernacles, or watry and humid mantles, which he assumeth or putteth off at his pleasure, as Scriptures do testifie. And yet I would have no man so far to mistake me, as not to think, that as God is not excluded from the creatures, so he is not included by any of them. I will now descend unto particularities, and shew you how this eternall wisdom is the fountain or corner-stone, first, of the higher Arts, namely, of *Theology, Physick,* or the art of Curing, *Astronomy, Musick, Arithmetick, Geometry, Rhetorick*; and after that, how the *Meteoro-logicall* Science onely dependeth on his act; then how true *Morall* learning, and *Politick* government is derived from the instructions and directions on this onely wise Spirit. And lastly, how all *mysticall* and *miraculous Arts* and discoveries, are effected and brought to light by it, confirming that place in Scripture, where it is said, *Cætera sunt ancilla hujus, All sciences are but the handmaids unto this wisdom.* Of each of these therefore, in order.

THE HEAVENLY COUNTRY

Thomas Vaughan

from *Anima Magica Abscondita* (1650)

BUT LAYING aside such *Proofs*, though the *Scripture* abounds in *Them*, let us consider the *Exercise* and *practise* of *Nature* here below, and we shall finde her *Game such* she can not *play it* without this *Tutor*. In the first place then I would faine know *who taught* the *spider* his *Mathematicks*? How comes he to *lodge* in the *Center* of his *Web*, that he may sally upon all *Occasions* to any part of the *Circumference*? How comes he to *præmeditate*, and *forecast*? for if he did not first know and imagine that there are *Flies*, whereupon he must *feede*, he would not watch for them, nor spin out his *Netts* in that *exquisite form*, and *Texture*. Verily we must needs confesse, that *he* who *ordain'd Flyes* for his *sustenance*, gave him also some *small light* to know, and *execute* his *Ordinance*. Tell me if you can, who taught the *Hare* to *Countermarch*, when she *doubles* her *Trace* in the *pursuit* to *confound* the *sent*, and *puzzle* her *persecutors*? who *counsels* her to *stride* from the *Double* to her *Form*, that her *steps* may be at a *greater distance*, and by consequence the more *difficult to finde* out? Certainly this is a *well order'd policy*, enough to prove that *God* is not *absent* from his *Creatures*, but that *Wisdom reacheth mightily from one end to another*,[45] and that *his Incorruptible spirit filleth all things.*[46] But to speak something more immediately apposite to our purpose. Let us consider the several products that are in *nature*, with their admirable features, and *symmetrie*. We know very well there is but one Matter out of which there are form'd so many different shapes, and Constitutions. Now if the Agent which determinates, and figures the matter, were not a *discerning* Spirit, it were impossible for him to produce anything at all. For let me suppose *Hyliard*[47] with his *Pencill*, and *Table* ready to *pourtray* a *Rose*: if he doth not *inwardly apprehend* the very shape, and proportion of that which he intends to limne he may as well do it without his eyes, as without his *Intellectualls*. Let us now apply this to the Spirit which worketh in Nature. This moves in the *Center* of all things, hath the matter before him, as the Potter hath his *clay*, or the *Limner* his *colours*. And first of all he exerciseth his *chymistry* in severall *Transmutations*, producing *Sinews, Veines, bloud, flesh*, and *bones*: which work also

---

45. Wisdom 8:1.
46. Ibid., 12:1.
47. Elizabethan miniature painter and craftsman, 1537–1619.

includes his *Arithmetick*, for he makes the Joynts and all Integrall parts, nay, as *Christ* tells us, the very Hairs of our Heads, in a certain determinate Number; which may conduce to the beauty and motion of the *Frame*. Again in the outward *Lineaments*, or *symmetrie* of the *compound*, he proves himself a most regular *Mathematician*, proportioning Parts to Parts, all which Operations can proceed from nothing but a *Divine, Intellectual spirit*. For if he had not severall *Ideas* or *Conceptions* correspondent to his several *Intentions*, he could not distinguish the one from the other: And if he were not sensible, if he did not foresee the work he doth intend, then the End could be no Impulsive cause, as the *Peripateticks* would have it.

The Consideration of these severall offices which this spirit performs in Generation, made *Aristotle* himself grant, That in the Seeds of all Things there were *virtutes similes Artificiis*.[48] We should therefore examine who weaves the flowers of Vegetables? who colours them without a pencil? who bolts the branches upwards, and threads (as it were) their Roots downwards? for all these actions include a certain Artifice which cannot be done without Judgement, and Discretion. Now our Saviour tells us, *My Father worketh hitherto*;[49] and in another place, it is *God cloathes the Lilie of the Field*,[50] and again *not one Sparrow fals without your Father*.[51] Verily this is the *Trueth*, and the *Testimony* of Trueth, notwithstanding *Aristotle* and his *Problems*. Neither should you think the *Divine Spirit disparag'd* in being president to every generation, because some Products seem poor, and contemptible: For verily as long as they conduce to the Glory of their Author, they are noble inough, and if you reflect upon *Egypt*, you will finde the basest of his Creatures to extort a *Catholick Confession* from the *Wizards*: *Digitus Dei est hic*, The *Finger of God is here*.[52] That I may come then to the point, These invisible, *Centrall Artists* are Lights seeded by the First Light, in that *primitive Emanation*, or *sit Lux*, which some falsely render *Fiat Lux*. For *Nature* is the Φωνή του Θεοῦ,[53] not a meer sound or Command, but a substantiall active Breath, proceeding from the Creatour, and penetrating all things. God Himself is Λόγος σπερματικός,[54] and this is the only sense wherein a Form may be defined as Λόγος τῆς ὀυσίας.[55] I know this will seem

48. "Potencies like unto artifices."
49. John 5:17.
50. Matt 6:28–29 and Luke 12:27–28.
51. Matt 10:29.
52. Exodus 8:19.
53. *Phonê tou Theou* = "voice of God."
54. *Logos spermatikos* = "spermatic form."
55. *Logos tes ousias* = "form of essence."

harsh to some Men, whose *ignorant zeal*, hath made them *Adversaries* to *God*, for they *rob him* of his Glory, and give it to his Creature, nay sometimes to fancies, and Inventions of their own. I wish *such Philosophers* to consider, whether in the beginning there was any life, or wisdom beyond the Creator, and if so, to tell us where. Verily (to use their own Term) they can never finde this *Ubi*. For they are gracious concessions, or Talents which God of his free will hath lent us, and if he should resume them, we should presently return to our first Nothing. Let them take heed therefore whiles they attribute Generation to Qualities: lest the true Author of it, should come against them with that charge, which he brought sometime against the *Assyrian*. *Shall the ax boast it self against Him that heweth therewith? or shall the saw magnifie it self against him that shaketh it? as if the Rod should shake it self against them that lift it up, or as if the staffe should lift up it self, as if it were no wood.*[56] Let them rather cashier their *Aristotle*, and the Errors wherewith he hath infatuated so many Generations. Let them approach with confidence to the Almighty God, who made the world, for none can give a better account of the work then the *Architect*. Let them not despair to attain his Familiarity, for he is a God *that desires to be known*, and will *reveal himself*, both for the *manifestation of his own glory*, and the *Benefit* of his *Creature*. There is no reason then why we should decline this great, and glorious *School-Master*, whose very Invitation speaks more then an Ordinary Incouragement. *Thus saith the Lord, the Holy One of Israel, and our Maker: Ask me of things to come concerning my Sons, and concerning the Work of my Hands Command you Me. I have made the Earth, and created man upon it; I, even my hand, have stretched out the Heavens, and all their Hostes have I commanded.*[57] But it will be question'd perhaps, how shall we approach to the Lord, and by what means may we finde him out? Truely not with words, but with workes, not in studying ignorant, *Heathenish Authors*, but in perusing, and trying his Creatures: For in them Lies his secret path, which though it be shut up with thornes and Briars, with outward worldly Corruptions, yet if we would take the pains to remove this luggage, we might *Enter the Terrestrial Paradise*, that *Hortus Conclusus* of *Solomon*, where God descends to walk, and drink of the sealed Fountain. But verily there is such a generall prejudice, such a customary opposition of all Principles which crosse *Aristotle*, That trueth can no sooner step abroad, but some *Sophister* or other flings Dirt in her Face. It is strange that none of these Schoolmen consider, how the severall distinctions, and divisions translated from *Logick*

56. Isaiah 10:15.
57. Isaiah 45:11–12.

to *Divinity*, have set all Christendom on fire: How they have violated the Peace of many flourishing Kingdoms, and occasion'd more sects in Religion, then there are opinions in Philosophie. Most seasonable then and Christian is that Petition of Saint *Augustine*: *A logica libera nos Domine!*[58] And here I must desire the Reader not to mistake me; I do not condemn the Use, but the Abuse of Reason, the many subtleties, and Fetches of it, which Man hath so applied, That truth and Errour are equally disputable. I am One that stands up for a *true Naturall knowledge*, grounded as *Nature is*, on Christ Jesus, who is the true *Foundation* of all things visible and Invisible. I shall therefore in this Discourse, touch neerly upon those mysteries, which some Few have delivered over to posterity, in difficult, obscure termes; That if possible, the Majesty of trueth, and the Benefit they shall receive from it, may settle Men in a new way, and bring them at last from vain, empty Fansies, to a Reall, sensible Fruition of Nature.

You may remember how in my former discourse of the Nature of Man, I mention'd a certain triplicity of Elements according to their severall Complexions in the severall Regions of the world. I shall now speak of another triplicity much more obscure and mysticall, without which you can never attain to the former, for these three principles are the *Clavis* of all *Magick*, without whose perfect knowledge you can never truly understand the least *Idioms* in *Nature*. The first Principle is *One in One*, and *One from One*. It is a pure, white *Virgin*, and next to that which is most pure, and simple. This is the first created unity. By this all things were made, not actually, but Mediately, and without This Nothing can be made either *Artificiall* or *Naturall*. This is *Uxor Dei*, & *stellarum*.[59] By mediation of this, there is a descent from One into *Four*, and an ascent from *three* by *four* to the *invisible, supernaturall Monas*. Who knows not *This*, can never attain to the *Art*, for He knows not what he is to look for. The second Principle differs not from the *first* in substance and dignity, but in *Complexion* and Order. This *second* was the *first*, and is so still Essentially, but by *adhæsion* to the *Matter* it contracted an impurity, and so fell from its *first unity*, wherefore the Magicians stile it *Binarius*. Separate therefore the *Circumference* from the *Center per Lineam Diametralem*,[60] and there will appear unto thee the Philosophers *Ternarius*, which is the third *Principle*. This third is properly no principle, but a product of *Art*. It is a *various* Nature, Compounded in one sence, and Decompounded in another, consisting of

---

58. "Deliver us, O Lord, from logic."
59. "The wife of God and the stars."
60. "The center by a diagonal line."

Inferior and superior *powers*. This is the Magicians *Fire*, This is *Mercurius Philosophorum, celeberrimus ille Microcosmus, & Adam.*[61] This is the *Labyrinth* and *Wild* of *Magick* where a *world* of *students* have *lost themselves*: a *thing* so *confusedly* and *obscurely* handled by such as knew it, that it is altogether impossible to find it in their *Records*. There is no late writer understands the *full Latitude*, and *universality* of this *Principle*, nor the genuine *Metaphysicall* use thereof. It moves here below in shades and *Tiffanies*, above in *white aethereall Vestures*; neither is there any thing in Nature expos'd to such a *publique prostitution* as *this* is, for it *passeth* thorough all hands, and there is not *any Creature* but hath the *use* Thereof. This *Ternarius*, being reduc'd *per Quaternarium* ascends to the *Magicall Decad*, which is *Monas Unitissima*, in which state *Quæcunque vult, potest*; for it is united then *per Aspectum* to the *first, eternall, spirituall unity*.

from *Lumen de Lumine* (1651)

I could see between me and the *Light*, a most exquisit, divine *Beauty*. Her *frame* neither *long*, nor *short*, but a meane decent *Stature*. Attir'd she was in *thin loose silks*, but so *green*, that I never saw the *like*, for the *Colour* was not *Earthly*. In some places it was *fansied* with *white* and *Silver Ribbands*, which look'd like *Lilies* in a *field* of *Grasse*. Her *head was overcast* with a thin floating *Tiffanie*, which she *held up* with one of her hands, and look'd as it were from *under* it. Her *Eys* were *quick, fresh*, and *Celestiall*, but had something of a *start*, as if she had been *puzzl'd* with a suddaine *Occurrence*. From her *black Veile* did her *Locks* breake out, like *Sun-beams* from a *Mist*; they ran *dishevell'd* to her *Brests*, and then return'd to her *Cheeks* in *Curls* and *Rings* of *Gold*. Her *Haire* behind her was *rowl'd* to a curious *Globe*, with a small short *spire* flowr'd with *purple*, and *skie-colour'd Knots*. Her *Rings* were pure, intire *Emeralds*, for she valued no *metall*, and her *Pendants* of burning *Carbuncles*. To be short, her whole *Habit* was *youthfull* and *flowrie*, it *smelt* like the *East*, and was thorowly *ayr'd* with rich *Arabian Diapasms*. This and no other, was her *appearance* at that *Time*: but whiles I admir'd her *perfections*, and prepar'd to make my *Addresses*, shee prevents me with a voluntarie *Approach*. Here indeed I expected some *Discourse* from her, but she looking very seriously and silently in my face, takes me by the hand, and softly whispers, *I should follow her*. This I confesse sounded strange, but I thought it not amisse to obey so *sweet* a *Command*, and especially one that *promised* very much, but was able in my Opinion to *performe* more. The *Light* which I had formerly *admir'd*, proved now at last to be her

---

61. "Mercury of the Philosophers, that most celebrated Macrocosm and Adam."

Attendant, for it moved like an *Usher* before her. This *Service* added much to her *Glorie*, and it was my only care to *observe* her, who though she *wandr'd* not, yet verily she *followed* no *known path*. Her *walk* was *green*, being *furr'd* with a fine small *Grasse*, which felt like *plush*, for it was very *soft*; and purl'd all the way with *Daysies* and *Primrose*. When we came out of our *Arboret* and *Court* of *Bayes*, I could perceive a strange *Clearnesse* in the *Ayr*, not like that of *Day*, neither can I affirme it was *night*. The *stars* indeed *perched* over us, and stood *glimmering*, as it were on the *Tops* of high *Hills*, for we were in a most deep *Bottome*, and the *Earth* overlook'd us, so that I conceived we were *neer* the *Center*. We had not walk'd very far, when I discovered cerraine thick, white *Clouds*, for such they seemed to me, which fill'd all that part of the *Valley*, that was before us. This indeed was an *Error* of mine, but it continued not long, for comming neerer, I found them to be firm solid *Rocks*, but *shining* and *sparkling* like *Diamonds*. This rare and goodly *sight* did not a little *incourage* me, and great desire I had to heare my *Mistris* speake (for so I judged her now) that if possible, I might receive some *Information*. How to bring this about, I did not well know, for she seem'd *averse* from *Discourse*; but having resolv'd with my self to *disturb* her, I ask'd her if she would favour me with her *Name*. To this she replied very familiarly, as if she had known me long before. *Eugenius* (said she) *I have many Names, but my best and dearest is* Thalia: *for I am alwaies green, and I shall never wither. Thou doest here behold the* Mountains *of the* Moone, *and I will shew thee the* Originall *of* Nilus, *for she springs from these Invisible Rocks. Looke up and peruse the very* Tops *of these* pillars *and* Clifts *of Salt, for they are the true, Philosophicall,* Lunar Mountains. *Didst thou ever see such a Miraculous, incredible thing?* This speech made me quickly look up to those glittering *Turrets* of *Salt*, where I could see a stupendous *Cataract*, or *Waterfall*. The *streame* was more *large* than any *River* in her full *Chanell*, but notwithstanding the *Height*, and *Violence* of its *Fall*, it descended without any *Noyse*. The *Waters* were *dash'd*, and their *Current* distracted by those *Saltish Rocks*, but for all this they came down with a dead *silence*, like the still, soft *Ayr*. Some of this *Liquor* (for it ran by me) I took up, to see what strange *wollen substance* it was, that did thus *steale* down like *Snow*. When I had it in my hands it was no *Common water*, but a *certaine* kind of *Oile* of a *Waterie Complexion*. A *viscous, fat, mineral nature* it was, *bright* like *Pearls*, and *transparent* like *Chrystall*. When I had viewd and search'd it well, it appear'd somewhat *spermatic*, and in very Truth it was *obscene* to the *sight*, but much more to the *Touch*. Hereupon *Thalia* told me, it was the *first Matter*, and the very Naturall, true *Sperm* of the *great World*. It is (said she) *invisible*, and therefore *few* are they that *find* it; but many believe it is *not* to be *found*. They believe indeed that the *world* is a dead *Figure*, like a *Body* which hath been sometimes *made*, and *fashion'd* by that *spirit*, which *dwelt* in it, but *retaines* that very *shape* and *fashion*, for some short *time*, after that the *Spirit* hath *forsaken* it. They should rather *consider*, that every *Frame* when the *Soule* hath *left* it, doth *discompose*, and can no longer *retaine* its former *figure*, for the *Agent* that *held* and *kept* the parts *together* is *gone*. Most excellent then is that speech, which I heard sometimes from one of my own Pupils. *Mundus hic ex tam diversis contrariisque partibus in unam formam minimè convenisset, nisi unus esset, qui tam Diversa conjungeret; Conjuncta vero Naturarum ipsa Diversitas invicem discors, dissociaret, atque divelleret, nisi unus esset, qui quod nexuit, contineret, Non tam vero certus naturae ordo procederet, nec tam dispositos motus Locis, temporibus, efficientiâ, Qualitatibus explicaret, nisi unus esset, qui has Mutationum varietates manens ipse disponeret. Hoc quicquid est, quo Condita manent, atque gubernantur, usitato cunctis Vocabulo Deum nomino.* This world (saith he) of such *divers* and *contrarie parts* had never been made *one thing*, Had not there been *one*, who did *joyn together* such *contrary things*. But being *joyn'd together*, the very *Diversitie* of the *Natures* joyned, fighting one with another, had *Discompos'd* and *separated* them, unlesse there had been *one* to *hold* and *keep* those *parts together*, which he at *first* did *joyn*. Verily the *order* of *Nature* could not *proceed* with such *certaintie*, neither could she move so *regularly* in severall *places, times, effects* and *qualities*, unlesse there were *some one*, who *dispos'd*, and *order'd* these *Varieties* of *Motions*. This, whatsoever it is, by which the world is preserved and govern'd, I call by that usuall name, *God*. Thou most therefore *Eugenius* (said she) understand, that all *Compositions* are made by an *active, intelligent life*; for what was done in the *Composure* of the great world in *generall*, the same is perform'd in the *Generation* of every *creature*, and its *sperm* in *particular*. I suppose thou doest know, that *water* cannot be *contained* but in some *Vessell*. The *naturall Vessell* which God hath appointed for it, is *Earth*. In *Earth* water may be *thickned*; and brought to a *figure*, but of it *self*, and *without Earth*, it hath an *indefinit flux*, and is subject to no *certaine figure* whatsoever. *Ayre* also is a *fleeting indeterminat substance*, but water is his *Vessell*: for *water* being *figured* by means of *Earth*, the *Ayr* also is *thickned*, and *figur'd* in the *Water*. To ascend higher, the *Ayr* coagulats the *liquid fire*, and *fire incorporated* involves and confines the thin *Light*. These are the *Means* by which God *unites*, and *compounds* the *Elements* into a *Sperm*, for the *Earth* alters the *Complexion* of the water, and makes it *viscous* and *slimie*. Such a *water* must they look, who would produce any *Magicall extraordinary Effects*; for this *Spermatic water* coagulats with the *least heat*, so that *nature* concocts, and hardens it into *metals*. Thou seest the *whites* of *Egs* will *thicken* as soon as they *feel* the *fire*, for their *moysture* is temper'd with a *pure subtill Earth*, and this subtill, animated *Earth*, is that which *binds* their *water*. Take *water* then my *Eugenius*, from the *Mountains* of the *Moon*, which is *water*, and *no water*: Boyl it in the *fire* of *Nature*, to a two fold Earth, *white* and *red*, then feed those *Earths* with *Ayr* of *Fire*, and *Fire* of *Ayr*, and thou hast the two Magicall *Luminaries*. But because thou hast been a servant of mine for a long time and that thy patience hath manifested the Truth of thy Love, I will bring thee to my *Schoole*, and there will I shew thee what the world is not capable of.

from *Euphrates* (1655)

Let any man read those Majestick and Philosophicall *Expostulations* between God and *Job*; or in a word, let him read over both Testaments and he shall find, if he reads *attentively*, that *Scripture*, all the way, makes *use* of *Nature*, and hath indeed discovered such *natural Mysteries* as are not to be found in any of the *Philosophers*. And this shall appear in the following Discourse. For my own part, I fear, not to say, that *Nature* is so much the business of *Scripture*, that to me, the *Spirit of God*, in those sacred Oracles, seems not onely to mind the *Restitution of Man* in *particular*, but even the *Redemption of Nature* in *generall*. We must not therefore *confine* this *Restitution* to our own *Species*, unless we can confine corruption to it withall, which doubtless we can not do: for it is evident that Corruption hath not onely *Seiz'd* upon *Man*, but on the *World* also for man's sake. If it be true then that *Man* hath a Saviour, it is also as true, that the whole Creation hath the same; God having reconciled all things to himself in Christ Jesus. And if it be true, that we look for the *Redemption* of our *Bodies*, and a *New man*: It is equally true, that we look for a *New Heaven*, and a *New Earth*, wherein dwelleth Righteousness: for it is not Man alone, that is to be *Renued* at the general *Restauration*, but even the *world*, as well as *Man*, as it is written: *Behold! I make all things New.*[62] I speak not this to disparage man, or to match any other Creature with him: for I know he is *principall* in the *Restauration*, as he was in the *Fall*, the *Corruption* that succeeded in the *Elements*, being but a Chain, that this prisoner drags after him: but I speak this to shew, that God minds the *Restitution* of *Nature* in general, and not of *Man alone*, who though he be the noblest part, yet certainly is but a small part of Nature. Is scripture then misapplied, much less vilified, when it is applied to the object of *Salvation*, namely to *Nature*, for that is it, which God would save, and redeeme from the present *Depravations*,

---

62. Rev 21:5.

to which it is subject? verily, when I read *Scripture*, I can find nothing in it, but what concernes *Nature*, and *Naturall things*: for where it mentions *Regeneration, Illumination,* and *Grace,* or any other *spirituall gift*, it doth it not precisely, but in order to Nature, for what signifies all this, but a *New influence* of *Spirit*, descending from God to assist Nature, and to free us from those Corruptions, wherewith of a long time we have been opprest? I suppose it will not be denied, that God is more *Metaphysicall*, than any *Scripture* can be, and yet in the work of Salvation, it were great impietie to separate *God* and *Nature*, for then God would have nothing to save, nor indeed to work upon. How much more absur'd is it in the Ministry of Salvation to separate Scripture and Nature: for to whom I beseech you doth Scripture speak? Nay, to whom is salvation minister'd, if *Nature* be taken away? I doubt not but man stands in *Nature*, not above it, and let the *School-men* resolve him into what parts they please, all those parts will be found natural, since God alone is truely *Metaphysicall*. I would gladly learn of our Adversaries, how they came first to know, that *Nature* is *Corrupted*; for if Scripture taught them this physicall truth, why may it not teach them more? but that Scripture taught them, is altogether undeniable: Let us fansie a Physician of such Abilities, as to state the true temperament of his patient, and wherein his Disease hath disorder'd it. Doth he not this to good purpose? Questionless, he doth: and to no less purpose is it in my opinion, for the spirit of God, Whose patient nature is, to give us in Scripture a Character of nature, which certainly He hath done in all points, whether we look to the past, present, or future Complexion of the World. For my own part, I have this Assurance of *Philosophy*, that all the *Mysteries* of *Nature* consist in the *knowledge* of that *Corruption*, which is mention'd in *Scripture*, and which succeeded the *Fall*: namely to know what it is, and where it resides principally: as also to know what Substance that is, which resists it most, and retards it, as being most free from it, for in these two consist the Advantages of *life* and *death*. To be short: *Experience*, and *Reason* grounded *thereupon*, have taught me, that *Philosophie* and *Divinity* are but one, and the same science: but *Man* hath dealt with *knowledge*, as he doth with *Rivers*, and *Wells*, which being drawn into severall pipes are made to run severall wayes, and by this Accident come at last to have severall names. We see that *God* in his work, hath united *spirit* and *matter, visibles* and *invisibles*, and out of the *union* of *spirituall,* and *naturall substances* riseth a perfect *Compound*, whose very *Nature*, and *Being* consists in that *union*. How then is it possible to demonstrate the *Nature* of that *Compound* by a divided *Theory* of *Spirit* by it self, and *matter* by it self? For if the nature of a *Compound* consists in the Composition of *Spirit* and *matter*, then must not we seek that *Nature* in their *separation*, but in their *mixture* and *Temperature*, and in their mutuall *mixt Actions*, and *Passions*. Besides, who hath ever seen a spirit without matter, or matter without spirit, that he should be able to give us a *true Theory* of *both principles* in their *simplicitie*? Certainly, no man living. It is just so in *Divinity*, for if by evasion we confine *Divinity* to God in the abstract, who (say I) hath ever known him so? Or, who hath received such a *Theologie* from him, and hath not all this while delivered it unto us? Verily, if we consider God in the abstract, and as he is in himself, we can say nothing of him *positively*, but we may something *Negatively*, as *Dionysius* hath done,[63] that is to say, we may affirme, what he is not, but we cannot affirme, what he is. But if by Divinity, we understand the Doctrine of Salvation, as it is laid down in Scripture, then verily it is a *Mixt doctrine*, involving both *God* and *Nature*. And here I doubt not to affirme, That the *Mysterie* of *Salvation* can never be fully understood without *Philosophie*, not in its just latitude, as it is an *Application* of *God* to *Nature*, and a *Conversion* of *Nature* to *God*, in which *two Motions* and their *Meanes*, all spirituall and naturall knowledge is comprehended.

To speak then of God *without Nature*, is more than we can do, for we have not known him so: and to speak of Nature *without God*, is more than we may do, for we should rob God of his glorie, and attribute those Effects to Nature, which belong properly to God, and to the spirit of God, which works in nature. We shall therefore use a mean form of speech, between these extremes, and this form the Scriptures have taught us, for the Prophets and Apostles, have used no other. Let not any man therefore be offended, if in this Discourse we shall use *Scripture* to prove *Philosophie*, and *Philosophie* to prove *Divinity*, for of a truth our *knowledge* is such, that our *Divinity* is not without *Nature*, nor our *Philosophie* without *God*. Notwithstanding, I dare not think but most men will repine at this course, though I cannot think, wherefore they should, for when I joyne *Scripture* and *Philosophie*, I do but joyne *God* and *Nature*, an union certainly approved of by God, though it be condemned of men. But this *perverse ignorance*, how bold soever it be, I shall not quarrel with, for besides Scripture, I have other grounds, that have brought me very fairely, and soberly to this *Discourse*.

---

63. (Pseudo-)Dionysius, *The Mystical Theology.*

The Philadelphian Society

THE PHILADELPHIAN SOCIETY for the Advancement of Piety and Divine Philosophy (more commonly known as the Philadelphian Society) was formally organized in England in 1694, but the group had been in existence (though perhaps not by that name) from at least the middle of the century. The members were deeply influenced by Boehme (they were known as "Behmenists") and they flourished for a time, putting a decidedly English stamp onto the burgeoning Protestant mysticism that had begun to manifest itself during the Civil War and into the Restoration.

John Pordage (1607–1681)

John Pordage was a physician and Anglican priest with a propensity for radical religion whose encounter with the works of Jacob Boehme profoundly altered his own religious sensibilities.[1] Installed as rector of Bradfield, probably in November of 1646,[2] he gathered around him a number of like-minded believers.[3] The group was noted for its female visionaries: Ann Bathurst, Joanna Oxenbridge, and, especially, Pordage's first wife, Mary Pordage—all later to be superseded by Jane Lead.[4] Some of their contemporaries disparaged the Pordage circle with charges of "enthusiasm" and accused Pordage himself of erratic behavior: he was reputed to have fallen into a trance while preaching one Sunday, finally "running out of the Church, and bellowing like a Bull, saying that he was called and must be gon."[5] But this description, however invariably it is quoted in Pordage criticism, should not be accepted

1. Nigel Smith believes Pordage became interested in Boehme by no later than 1651, though some of Pordage's followers show evidence of Boehme's influence before that date. See his *Perfection Proclaimed: Language and Literature in English Radical Religion, 1640–1660* (Oxford: The Clarendon Press, 1989), 189.

2. Ariel Hessayon, "Pordage, John (*bap.* 1607, *d.* 1681)," *Oxford Dictionary of National Biography* (Oxford: Oxford University Press, 2004).

3. B.J. Gibbons, *Gender in Mystical and Occult Thought: Behmenism and Its Development in England* (Cambridge: Cambridge University Press, 1996), 106–7.

4. Gibbons, *Gender in Mystical and Occult Thought*, 107–8.

5. *A most Faithful Relation of Two Wonderful Passages* (1650), 2. Quoted in Ariel Hessayon, "Pordage, John (*bap.* 1607, *d.* 1681)."

uncritically, seeing that it derives from a pamphlet smearing Pordage, the anonymously published *A most faithful Relation of Two Wonderful Passages Which happened very lately in the Parish of Bradfield in Berkshire*.[6] Pordage, due to the scandal, was eventually ejected from his living at Bradfield in December of 1654, though he had defended himself in print in his publication *Innocencie Appearing Through the Dark Mists of Pretended Guilt* (1655).

Pordage's writing, however, though highly mystical, hardly shows evidence of being written by a crackpot. Indeed, he was learned in theology and in Christian doctrine, though he wrote for those interested in encountering God, not for the learned. He published only one full-length book in English, *Theologia Mystica* (excerpted here), though he wrote several books that were immediately translated into German for a Pietist readership (among them his masterwork, *Sophia: das ist Die Holdseelige ewige Jungfrau der Gottlichen Weisheit*, in 1699), the English originals of which are, as far as anyone knows, lost to us.[7]

Thomas Bromley (1629–1691)

While a student at Oxford, Thomas Bromley first heard John Pordage preach there in 1654 and soon thereafter left his fellowship to join the latter's community at Bradfield. He was on familiar terms with Anne, Viscountess Conway as well as the Cambridge Platonist Henry More. All accounts of him tell of a man who lived simply and was very charitable to the poor. He published his only work, *The Way to the Sabbath of Rest*, in 1655. It was soon translated into German, Dutch, and Swedish.

Jane Lead (1621–1704)

Jane Lead was born Jane Ward and christened on 9 March 1624 at the parish church of St. Andrew, Letheringsett, Norfolk. Lead had probably met Pordage by 1668[8] and, after the premature death of her husband, became a member of his household in about 1674. Lead, deeply religious and inclined to mystical experiences from a young age, found in Pordage and his circle a supportive environment for her own religious sensibilities.

---

6. *A most faithful Relation*, 2–3.

7. A number of Pordage's works were promised in an advertisement included in Lead's *A Fountain of Gardens* (1697): *Philosophia Mystica, The Angelical World, The Dark Fire World, The Incarnation of Jesus Christ, The Spirit of Eternity, Sophia*, and *Experimental Discoveries*. They never appeared.

8. Julie Hirst, *Jane Leade: Biography of a Seventeenth-Century Mystic* (Aldershot, UK: Ashgate, 2005), 23.

When the Philadelphian Society was announced publicly in 1697, Lead was already seventy-three-years old, obese and rapidly losing her eyesight (probably due to untreated diabetes). She guided the Society until her death in 1704, and her followers, the Anglican clergymen Richard Roach and Francis Lee among them, were devoted to her and believed deeply in her visionary abilities.

Her name first appeared in print with the publication of her book *The Heavenly Cloud Now Breaking* in 1681. In 1683 she provided an introduction for the posthumous publication of Pordage's *Theologia Mystica*, and in the same year, the first edition of her book *The Revelation of Revelations* saw print. Soon thereafter, the German nobleman Baron Freiherr von Knyphausen discovered her work in the Behmenist Loth Fischer's German translation (unknown to Lead at the time) of the *Heavenly Cloud*. Knyphausen offered to pay for the publication of anything Lead would write—in both English and German editions—and with his support Lead's publishing career accelerated at an astonishing rate, and she issued new editions of her works from the 1680s as well as at least nineteen additional works, including three volumes of her massive spiritual diary, *A Fountain of Gardens* (1697–1701). It was a remarkable output for an elderly woman hampered by blindness, health problems, and poverty.[9]

In the selections that follow, the Behmenist mysticism of the three Philadelphians illustrates three essential qualities: Pordage's intellectual, esoteric approach; Bromley's gentle spirituality; and Lead's visionary speculation: three diverse aspects of a fascinating moment in English religion.

9. For more on Lead, see chapter five, "The Pauline Mission of Jane Lead," in my *Literature and the Encounter with God in Post-Reformation England* (Farnham, UK: Ashgate, 2014).

John Pordage

from *Theologia Mystica, or The Mystic Divinitie of the Aeternal Invisibles*

The *Third Wonder* which was presented to my intellectual sight was *God's Wisdom*, concerning whom I shall speak under these three heads.

First I shall speak of the Birth and Nativity of the Wisdom of God.
Secondly of its Nature.
Thirdly and lastly of its office.

1. First then, as to the Birth and Nativity of Wisdome, we are to know that spring's[10] and flows from God's Eternal Eye, as from its Eternal root and original, and here it is fixed as in its proper seat and center; for it is by this Wisdom, that all the desire and motions of the Deity are most wisely Ordered, conducted and governed, for it proceeds from and is seated in the same Eye with his desiring mind, and willing will, these three are in one another and penetrate through one another, and make up but one inseparable, indivisible power. I say they *all three exist in the Eye as one power, yet distinguishable, and without the least disorder of confusion*; the first is the wisdom, then the mind, and next the will; for as the wisdom proceeds from the Eye, so the mind proceeds from the wisdom, and the will from the mind. And thus much for the birth and Nativity of Wisdome.

2. I come now in the next place to speak of the second head, *viz.* what the *Nature of the Wisdom is*: I say then, that the Divine Wisdom is a flowing, moving power, a moving motion immediately proceeding from God's Eternal Eye. God's Wisdom is a bright ray, or glance issuing from the Eye of Eternity: therefore she is termed the brightness or Clarity of the God-head, and a pure breath or efflux from the Majesty of the Almighty. We can say nothing of her but that *She is the brightness and glance of the Eye of Eternity*; who as she proceeds from the Eye, so she is moved by, and only the same; for she is a meer passive bright shining virtue, that swiftly passeth through and pierceth all things, by reason of her high purity and subtilty, which can be compared to nothing better, than to a lustrous shining glance, being perfectly passive and moving only according to the motion of the Eye of the Father, which makes her more swift and piercing than any thing whatsoever.

---

10. *Sic*—Pordage (or his typesetter) add apostrophes for odd reasons upon occasion.

But for further illustration of Nature of God's Wisdom, I shall a little enlarge my self upon these following Particulars, which are so many Essentiall properties of the said Wisdom.

I. In the first place this *Wisdome is Co-essential with the Holy Trinity*: Because as hath been said it proceeds from the Trinity, as an outgoing ray, glance or brightness; now nothing doth immediately proceed from God, but *what is of the same nature and Essence with him*, and consequently what can this *bright shining glance* from the Eye of the Majesty be else, but pure Deity, as proceeding from, and fixed in the Eye of Eternity.

II. The second Essential property of this *Divine Wisdom*, is this, that she is *Co-eternal* with the ever-blessed Trinity. *God was never without his wisdom, nor the Eye of Eternity without this glance and bright ray which proceedeth from it*; for else God could not have been an All-wise and All-knowing God. Therefore *according to order of time the Divine wisdom, is Co-eternal with the Holy Trinity*, though in order of Nature and dignity, the Holy Trinity are before *Wisdom*, which is *nothing else but a passive efflux from the ever-blessed Trinity*. Wherefore you are *not* to imagine that the wisdom of God, as she is Co-essential and Co-eternal, *is also Co-equal* with the holy Trinity, *because* as was said before, *she is perfectly passive*, and moves not herself, but as the Eye is moved, whereas the Blessed Trinity is all Act, all acting power; *she is indeed said to be a Co-operator with the Trinity*, but *yet so as that she moves not, except she be moved*, nor acts except she be acted: *thus far indeed* she may be said in some sense to be *Co-equal* with the Trinity, *forasmuch as she fills with her glance and brightness the whole still Eternity*; but this cannot amount to a proper co-equality, because she is wholly passive, and depending of the Trinity. Besides *she is clearly distinguishable from the Eye*, and *the Spirit of the Eye*, as being only a brightness, Glance or ray proceeding from it, and is consequently inferior, and subordinate to the Blessed Trinity.

III. The third and last Essential property of the *Divine Wisdom*, is her *Virgin Purity*, which *consists in this, that she is free from all desire, will and motion of her own*. She desire's and wills nothing, but as the Eternal mind, and will, desires and wills in her; she moves not, but as she is moved, and acts not, but as *she is acted* by the *Spirit of Eternity*; for she is nothing but a bright passive glance from the Eye of Eternity. She is *an Eternal stillness in her self*. She is not the Majesty it self, nor the Eye, but *she is only the beauty, glory, brightness, lustre, and glance of the Majesty in the Eye, and that such a transparent clarity and brightness as is without all spot or blemish*. And in a word, She is nothing but perfect, absolute purity, she is a thousand times brighter, and purer than the Sun, and fairer then the Moon, and indeed nothing can be compared to the Excellence of that her Virgin-purity.

But *her pure virginity doth* not only *consist* in this, that she is free from all manner of spot, blemish or mixture, but *especially in this*, that *her bright glance is from all Eternity fixed upon the flaming heart of God's love, which is the Center of the Holy Trinity.* This *flaming heart of Love is the sole Object* to which her regard is fastned continually: she receives nothing into her self but this divine Love, from the heart of God. She espouseth her self to nothing, inclineth her self to nothing, but only to this Essential Love, the Word of God, fixed in the Heart of the Deity. Thus *the Holy Trinity have their delight with wisdom, and again the whole joy and delight of wisdom is the flaming Love of the blessed Trinity.* She is exalted above all things, because of her beauty and immaculate purity; she is the highest purity; *she is purity and virginity in the abstract. She cannot be touched by sin, evil or self,* because she cannot mix with, nor incline to anything, but only the essential Love of God. *She is free from all essences whatsoever, being nothing else but the unspotted mirrour of the glory and excellency of God*: and thus we have declared to you what that pure Virginity is, which is one of the essential properties of God's wisdom.

3. I now proceed to the third and last head, *viz. What the office of Wisdom is in the Still Eternity.* I find that Wisdom dischargeth these two offices, *viz.*

1. She is a revealer of the Mysteries, and hidden wonders of the Deity.

2. She is an enlightner of the still Eternity.

First, As for the first of these, Scripture and Revelation assure us, That *Wisdom is the revealer and manifester of the unsearchable Secrets of God*: she is the golden Key of the Eternal Eye, by which all the wonders of the Trinity are unlocked. As *the office of the Holy Ghost is to effect and create all things*, so the office of *Wisdom* is to manifest and reveal all things. *She never brings forth anything, and upon that account also, is called a pure Virgin,* but only discovers and manifests whatsoever the Holy Trinity, by their effecting-creating-power, are pleas'd to bring forth. This *Wisdom is the companion of the Eye of Eternity,* by her outgoing glance, revealing the wonders contained in it. She is as an *Handmaid* waiting upon the Holy Trinity, to declare, publish and make known their counsels, secrets and wonders.

Secondly, The other office of Wisdom is to give Light to the deep Abyss of the still Eternity. *It is Wisdom's bright glance which is the day and light of this most holy mansion,* not a created Light, but *a pure divine*

Light, in that sense as God is called a Light in whom is no darkness at all, and no otherwise.

But you will object, That *the Holy Scriptures and Divine Philosophers seem to give a different account concerning Wisdom than I have here given?*

To which I answer, That I easily grant that the Scriptures of Truth, and holy enlightened Men, have spoken concerning Wisdom after another manner, than here I have done; and the reason of it is plain, for *they speak of Wisdom after the production of Eternal Nature, as Wisdom is introduced into the seven forms of Eternal Nature;* whereas *I speak of Wisdom's existence with the Holy Trinity, in the Still Eternity, before ever Eternal Nature was brought forth.*

XIX. *In the mixture of these Eternal Elements observe with me these following Particulars*

First, *Wisdom's Art* appears *in the manner of their mixture,* they are mixed one with another, and one through another; Fire with Water, Light with Darkness, and penetrate through and through one another, neither can their contrariety hinder or oppose the Art and Power of Wisdom.

Secondly, *The Art of Wisdom* appears not only in mixing them, but *in reducing them to a harmony* and equal temperament, she doth proportion them to an equality in Number, Weight and Measure.

Thirdly, *Wisdom's Art* appears in that being thus proportionally tempered together, *they qualifie act and move in and through* one another, and that *in the greatest* harmony and friendship, as the members of one body: the fierceness of the fire is mitigated and allayed by the Water, the harsh astringency of the Darkness, is dissolv'd in the meekness of the Light, and so of the rest.

Fourthly, *Wisdom's Art* appears, in this, that in the harmonizing of these four Eternal Elements, *she hath made all their contrary properties to be useful one to another*: The Harsh Darkness is serviceable to the Meek Light, for Darkness is the subject through which Light displays it self, were there no Darkness, there would be no Light: the fierceness of the Fire, gives strength to the Meek Water-Essence, and meekness of the Water allays the fierceness of the Fire: so Air is very useful to the Fire to keep it from being suffocated; and the Earth is useful to them all, because it gives them a Body to act and move in: We may yet *further consider the usefulness* of the Elements to one another, *as they stand harmonized and tempered together by the Hand of Wisdom.* The Fire gives Life, Mobility and Strength to the Meek Water, and the Water gives Food and Nourishment to the Fire, and thereby allays the fierce hunger of the Fire: so that Darkness subsists in the Light, and the Light in the Darkness, and satisfieth the harsh bitter hunger of the Darkness, being as food unto it: and in *this their serviceableness to one another consists their Natural Goodness*: for how can any evil be in them, since they serve the Will of their Creator, and are useful to one another; the Darkness is as useful as the Light, and the Fire as the Water, and consequently *they are all good, their contrarieties* being harmonized, and reconciled *by the skillful hand of omnipotent Wisdom.*

Fifthly, *Wisdom's Art* appears in that, in this temperature of the *Eternal Elements, she makes them qualifie* and serve one another *in triumphing joyfulness*, and to rejoyce in each other's qualifying; for though these *Eternal Elements are not understanding Spirits*, yet they have an innate hunger in themselves (which is their intrinsecal form) which makes them desire each other: thus the Fire-Essence hunger's[11] after the Meekness of the Water, as its dayly food, wherewith its ravenous fierceness may be satisfied and allayed: and again the Water hunger's after the Fire, as its Life, Strength and Motion. The astringent Darkness hunger's after the Meek Light, and the Light after the Darkness, that it may shine through it, and subsist in it. And from *this inbred Hunger it is that they rejoyce to qualifie one with another*; it is as *their sport and past time* to penetrate one through another, and to be sometimes above and sometimes under another in *this wrestling wheel of Nature. For you must know that all these qualifying powers of Nature have sensibility and mobility in themselves*, whereby they can feel and taste one another's properties, and are sensible of the pleasure and satisfaction they receive one from another, which continually awakens the hunger in every property, to qualifie one with another. So the Fire is sensible that the Meek Water doth allay its fierceness, and therefore it doth hunger after it; the anguishing Darkness is sensible, that the amiable pleasantness of the Light is a refreshment to it; and thus each property feels and tastes the other's goodness, and this makes them still to hunger after one another, and to penetrate one another with all triumphing Joyfulness. 'Oh let us for ever admire this unsearchable Art of the Divine Wisdom! who alone can perform this Masterpiece.'

Sixthly, *Wisdom's Art* appears *in nothing more than in the orderly placing of these Elements*; for *Wisdom* makes the Fire, with all its Harsh, Bitter, Dark, Anguishing and Brimstony properties to descend, and makes its elevating pride to buckle, bow and become a Servant to the Water-Essence; and causeth the Water with its Meekness, Gentleness

11. *Sic.*

and Ponderosity to ascend and command the Fire; the Light to rule over Darkness; the Meekness over Fierceness; and the joyfulness of the Light over the Anguish. For *Divine Wisdom well understood the force of self elevating Fire*, and therefore she caused it to sink down, and become a Servant to the Meek Light: she foresaw that the Fire-life with its fierce properties would be but *an ill Governor, therefore she made the elder, viz.* the Fire-Spirit, *to serve the younger, viz.* the Water and Light-Essence, which could be done by no other Hand but that of Omnipotent Wisdom. *If we proceed to consider of this order how incomprehensible will the Skill of Wisdom appear!* For the Darkness was hid in the Light, and though it was there with all its properties, yet nothing of it was to be seen or felt; for it was swallowed up of the Light, as the night is swallowed up of the Day; so the fierceness, bitterness and Anguish of the fire were perfectly dissolv'd in and swallow'd up of the meekness, mildness, softness, and pleasantness of the Water, and nothing remained but the pleasant glances of the Fire arising from the mixture of Fire and Water. This *was the Beauty and excellence of Eternal Nature, that all her divided, contrary properties were united into one undivided property in the Eternal Earth, where all their contrarieties were reduced to the most perfect union, agreement and harmony.*

Thomas Bromley

from *The Way to the Sabbath of Rest or the Soul's Progress in the Work of the New Birth*

Chapter VII

The Soul having now attained to the Death of that which so long hindered its growth in the pure Life (and to the Enjoyments of those spiritual Objects, which exceedingly refresh and quicken the Heart, in the midst of all Discouragements) proceeds cheerfully in the strait way of Resignation;[12] offering up its Sin Offering daily as a Sacrifice to the Father's Justice. For now the daily Oblation is restored in the Holy Place, which must continue till the Death of Sin, and the rending away the Vail of Flesh[13] from before the most Holy. Now therefore the Circumcising Knife of God's Power constantly cuts off the fleshly Part, which is offered up in the Fire of Justice, and consumed before the Lord. Now the Soul sees it must resist to Blood, that is, to the Death of the Body of Sin,[14] which is wholly to be separated from the Spirit, with all its Members. For this is that false Covering it hath wrapped itself in through the Fall, instead of that naked Innocency in which there was no uncomeliness, and therefore no Shame:[15] Except therefore this fore-skin of the Flesh be cut off, the Angelical Robe cannot be put on: And as that falls off, this is assumed; increasing as that decays: For, they cannot both rise and fall together; for while the outward Man Decays, the inward Man is renewed Day by Day.

Here it clearly appears, we must forsake all; otherwise we cannot be Christ's Disciples.[16] All Objects of our Carnal Affections, all Complacency in fleshy Things; all Self-Propriety in the Will of Nature, which came in through the Fall, and the Soul's departing from the universal Charity, (the true Ground of heavenly Community) into the particular Objects of Self-Affections, which as it hath been awakened by the Soul's going out of God's Will, into its own: so it must be crucified by returning from itself into the pure eternal Will of God, which we can never attain, till we are dead to the Affections of the sensitive Part.[17]

12. Rev 1:6.
13. Heb 10:20.
14. Ibid., 7:4.
15. Gen 2:25.
16. Luke 14:33.
17. Gal 5:24.

For Carnal Love, Joy, Hope, Fear, Desire, Displeasure, are all the selfish Motions of the Natural Man, the corrupt Members of the Body of Sin, together with earthly Pride, Covetousness, Envy, Jealousy, Emulation, Wrath, Strife, all which are the Legs of the Earthly Adam, and therefore to be cast away and destroyed;[18] and in their Fall, the Will comes to be crucified to all their Objects, and to all selfish Propriety. Here we come to lose our own Lives, to hate our selfish Motions, to be slain to all fleshy Things, the Will hath espoused, instead of God in Christ. Here we begin to be truly Poor, renouncing all for Christ, in a resigned Will and mortified Affections, as also a Moderate, Charitable and Sanctified use of all temporal Things.[19] And as to the Case of Propriety in Earthly Estates, it is good to know and declare Impartially, the full and perfect thing design'd to be brought forth in the Church, that Christians of this Day may at least wish and pray for it; tho' it seems indeed to be almost impracticable in the present degenerated State of the Christian Church: Nor to be set upon without an Aid and Concurrent Power of the Holy Ghost, like that in Pentecost, where no Man call'd any thing that he had his own, but they had all things in Common. It is certain that Covetousness in the desire of the natural Man, hath been the cause of all those Engrossings of Land and Money, which most are Involved in, and Christ with his Disciples, and his Disciples afterwards with their followers, gave a Pattern, and made a Beginning of the Renewal of the Law of Love; which regards our Neighbour or Brother as our self. And the least we can do in this Point at this Day, must be for those that have Estates, to be as tho' they had them not, and to use them as Stewards for God and Christ, and also with regard to his Body or Members, being Communicative according to the Will of God, in the more enlarg'd and generous Proportions of Wisdom, Goodness and Love. We are also in this to see our present Shortness, and bemoan the loss of the Spirit and Power of Primitive Christianity; and stand ourselves so loose and indifferent to all things, that if, or whenever God may please to restore the Primitive Spirit, Power and Life of Christianity again, we may be in a Posture prepar'd and ready to give up all, and Concur in the more perfect Manner of such a blessed Day. *viz.* In a Heavenly Community here on Earth which may Imitate the Holy Angels and the Glorified Saints above, who inherit their Eternal Substance, as their Eternal Joys, without any Self-appropriation, in blessed Unity and Community.

18. Col 3:5.
19. Matt 19:27.

Here we likewise die to, and forsake earthly Relations,[20] as part of that we call Ours: And though we are not to destroy natural Affection, nor to neglect the performing of any due Obligation laid upon us by the Law of Nature, as it accords with the Will and Justice of God; yet we are to die to all such Propriety of Affection, as flows from corrupt Nature, and hinders the impartial Communication of our Love to every one, according to the perfect Example of our Heavenly Father, who takes in no fleshy Respects, in the giving forth of his Love to his Creatures, which is our Pattern to imitate; for we are to be perfect as our heavenly Father is perfect.

Here those that have Wives, are as though they had none, in Sanctification of the Marriage Bed, and subordination of inferior Desires, by a superior regard to Christ the Spouse of the Church, whereof they are here appointed a Holy Figure. Thus forbearing to Idolize the Woman of the World, and returning to the true Mother and Spouse of the Soul in Christ Jesus, viz. The Virgin *Sophia*, or the Heavenly Wisdom, who is the unspotted Mirror of the Eternal World, the first and Chief Spouse of Christ, see *Rev.* xii. 2. And they who can receive it, follow the Example of Christ, who lived and died in Virginity, as he was born of a Virgin: And this they do for the Kingdom of Heaven's sake, according to that precept, *Mat.* xix. 12. *He that is able to receive it, let him receive it;* where Christ speaks concerning the abstaining from Marriage, and of those that had made themselves Eunuchs for the Kingdom of Heaven. Whence it is clear, that a greater degree of dying to, and crucifying the Root, whence the enjoyment in that State comes, is to such, a real mean to the greater growth and encrease of God's Kingdom in the Soul, which is to be presented as a Chaste Virgin to Christ (2 Cor 11:2) and St *Paul*, (1 Cor 7: 21, 32, 33, 34, 35) prefers the Virgin State far before the Married; and therefore Verse the 7th saith, *I would that all Men were as I am*: Which certainly he spake according to true Light, sound Judgment and great Experience in the Work and Progress of Regeneration.

But in a Word, in this State before described, we come to see, that we our selves are not our own, but the Lord's, and that we are to consecrate our Bodies, Souls and Spirits to him, and to resign up all we call ours to him, whose is the Kingdom, and the Power and the Glory, for ever. And truly our gradual Incorporation into the Body of Christ, with the Enjoyment of new Relations and Treasures, which are Spiritual and Eternal, make it the more easy to die to, and forsake all earthly Things;

20. Rev 8:16. Though I hint at the mystical sense of the Beast in Rev 13, yet I deny not the Historical as it hath been truly applied to a Succession of Persons in the signally lapsed or Antichristian Church. [Bromley's note].

which being of a lower Nature, shew their Rise by their Fall; for being of the Earth, they are Earthly, and return to Earth, as utterly incapable to enter with us into the Kingdom of Love.[21] As we leave the Spirit of the World, they leave us; and so we arrive to a good degree of Conquest and Victory over that Beast,[22] which rules the whole World, which gives the Soul occasion thus to express itself in praise.

> *Blest be that Power, by which the Beast*
> *Is made to serve, and we releast*
> *From that base servile Drudgery,*
> *Which some mistake for Liberty.*
> *Sad Liberty! That chains poor Souls to Dust,*
> *And soils immortal Things with mortal Rust.*

Chapter XIII

By this time the Soul experienceth the happy State of being freed from the principle of Selfishness, in returning to God from the Spirit of the World, and sees the real Progress it hath made from the Outward thro' the Inward dark World, into the inward Paradise; where Adam lived before his Fall; and where Christ conversed, between the time of his Resurrection and Ascension. In this spiritual Region the Curse is not manifest, there being a perpetual Spring. Here are the Ideas of all visible Bodies, in much Beauty and appearing Lustre. Here are those bright Clouds which overshadowed Christ on the Mount, and when he was received up into Heaven; in which he will descend when he comes again to judge the Earth.[23]

Now the Soul having attained to the state of this Angelical Garden, knows what it is to turn and become as a Child, and to attain a secret and quiet Life of Innocency and pure Love, free from those Passions and evil Affections it had formerly groaned under.[24] And here it experienceth what it is to be born of Water and the Spirit,[25] as a necessary qualification to do the Will of God: And sees its Conception in the Womb of Wisdom (which is our new Mother) who here distills the Milk of the eternal Word, (from the eternal World) to feed and nourish the Soul: Whither it now Travels as fixing its Sight upon that pure River of Water of Life, clear as Christal,[26] proceeding out of the Throne of God, and of

21. 1 Cor 15:50.
22. Rev 13:16–17.
23. Ibid., 1:7.
24. 1 Pet 2:2.
25. John 3:5.
26. Rev 22:1.

the Lamb. But now likewise the Soul lives the Life of Spiritual Vegetation and grows like a Willow by the Water Courses, [27] or a Lilly in the Garden of the Lord, being continually refreshed with the Dews of the eternal Heavens, and quickened by the Beams of the Sun of Righteousness, and cherished with the enlivening Gales of the holy Spirit. All that are in this State, are like the harmless Flowers in a fruitful Garden, springing from the same Ground, yet differing in Colour, Virtue, Smell, and Growth, according to their several Natures, and Times of Planting; yet all serving to express the Power, Love and Wisdom of their Creator, without any Strife or Contention for Eminency, Place, or Esteem, being all satisfied with what God affords them, and their different Capacities fit them for.

O what a sweet Harmony is here! What a beautiful Consent in expressing the Goodness of the great Creator of all Things! How far are Spirits here from envying the different Beauties and Ornaments one of another! How sweetly do they incline to mutual Love and agreement! As being the Branches of one pure Root, as enjoying the same kind of Nourishment, and receiving Life from the same quickening Spirit![28] How is all Wrath and Contention here forgot! How amiable do Spirits now begin to grow in the Eye of Christ, by their innocent Childishness! And truly in this Dispensation, we come to be cloathed with Humility, wrap'd up in Meekness; expressing nothing but the blessed Effects of Heaven upon Earth; here we are full of Love-meltings towards Christ, who baptiseth us in the soft Water of spiritual Meekness; which over-spreads the Soul, not suffering any fire of Passion to spring up. In this State, the Soul is very watchful over every Motion, in the outward and inward Man, fearing to step down again into Nature, where before it had so much Trouble and Bitterness;[29] whereas now it is in a sweet pleasant Rest, lying upon the Bed of Innocency, solacing itself in the sweet Embraces of its Saviour,[30] who now begins to shew itself very clearly, and to afford almost continual Refreshments: In a Word, this is a life of Stilness, Silence, and spiritual Simplicity; in which the Soul turning its Eyes from Nature, looks directly forward to Eternity;[31] and strongly breathing after its arrival there.

And here we come to know the Work of the fifth Day in our new Creation, answering the fifth of those seven Spirits, which are the Eyes of the Lamb of God (Rev 5:6).

27. Hos 14:5.
28. 1 Cor 12:13.
29. Heb 12:15.
30. Cant 2:6.
31. Heb 12:2.

If Harmony doth in this Fifth arise,
What will it be, when thou dost Sabbatise,
In that last Day, where all variety
Concenters in a perfect Unity!
Then stand thou fast, poor Soul, and keep thy Ground,
Till with eternal Love thou shalt be Crown'd.
Take heed of Lust which unlock'd Adam's Eyes,
And cast him to the Earth from Paradise.

Jane Lead

from *A Fountain of Gardens*

The First Vision that appeared to me
was in the Month of April, 1670. *Which was on this wise;*

BEING MY LOT at that time to visit a Friend in a Solitary Country-
place, where I had great advantage of Retirement, often frequenting
lonely Walks in a Grove or Wood; contemplating the happy State of the
Angelical World; and how desirous I was to have my Conversation there,
my thoughts were much exercised upon *Solomon's* Choice, which was to
find the Nobel Stone of Divine Wisdom; for by acquainting my self with
her, all desirable good in Spiritual things would meet upon me. The
Report and Fame that *Solomon* gave of Wisdom, did much excite me to
seek her Favour and Friendship; demurring in my self from whence she
was descended, still questioning whether she was a distinct Being from
the Deity or no? Which while in this debate within my Mind, there
came upon me an overshadowing bright Cloud, and in the midst of it
the Figure of a Woman, most richly adorned with transparent Gold, her
Hair hanging down, and her Face as the terrible Crystal for brightness,
but her Countenance was sweet and mild. At which sight I was somewhat amazed, but immediately this Voice came, saying, Behold I am
God's Eternal Virgin-Wisdom, whom thou hast been enquiring after; I
am to unseal the Treasures of God's deep Wisdom unto thee, and will be
as *Rebecca* was unto *Jacob*, a true Natural Mother; for out of my Womb
thou shalt be brought forth after the manner of a Spirit, Conceived and
Born again: this thou shalt know by a New Motion of Life, stirring and
giving a restlessness, till Wisdom be born within the inward parts of thy
soul. Now consider of my Saying till I return to thee again.

This Vision took great Impression on me, yet I kept it for the
present hid, but it Operated so much upon me, as indeed I was incapable to converse with any Mortals; which was taken notice of, that some
extraordinary thing had happened; for the which I begged my Friends
excuse, and desired that she would give me liberty to be much alone,
and to walk in the silent Woods; where I might contemplate what had so
lately happened. Now after three days, sitting under a Tree, the same
Figure in greater Glory did appear, with a Crown upon her Head, full of
Majesty; saying, Behold me as thy Mother, and know thou art to enter
into Covenant, to obey the New Creation-Laws, that shall be revealed
unto thee. Then did she hold out a Golden Book with three Seals upon
it, saying, Herein lieth hidden the deep Wonders of *Jehovahs* Wisdom,

which hath been sealed up, that none could, or ever shall break up, but such as of her Virgin-Offspring shall appear to be; who will her laws receive, and keep, as they shall spring daily in the New Heart and Mind. This Appearance, and Words, was wonderfully sweet and refreshing in my Soul; at which I bowed, prostrated at her Feet; promising to be obedient to all her Laws. So the Vision shut up for that time.

Pondering this in my Heart, with great comfort, that this Day-star had visited me from on high; I returned to *London* to my own Habitation, retiring my self from all my Acquaintance, saving one Person that was highly Illuminated, who encouraged me still to wait upon this Vision; for he was acquainted with somewhat of this kind. So after six days the Vision appear'd again, with a Train of Virgin-Spirits, and with an Angelical Host; and called to me to come and see the Virgin Queen, with her first-born Children; asking me, Whether I was willing to be joyned amongst this Virgin Company? At which I reply'd, All willing to offer up my self most free: Then immediately I was encompass'd about with this Heavenly Host, and made a Spirit of Light. Then these Words from the Virgin proceeded saying, I shall now cease to appear in a Visible Figure unto thee, but I will not fail to transfigure my self in thy mind; and there open the Spring of Wisdom and Understanding, that so thou mayst come to know the only True God, in and by the formation of Christ, the anointed Prophet in thee; that shall reveal great and wonderful things unto thee, that are to be made known, and publick, in its time and day: Therefore be watchful, and to thy Mother Wisdom's Counsel give good heed, and thou shalt greatly prosper and succeed the Prophets and Apostles to perfect what was left behind, for compleating as to Christ the Fulness of God's great Mystery: So go, and nothing fear, or doubt; for I thy Glass for Divine Seeing shall evermore stand before thee. Then my Spirit replyed, According to thy Word let all this be fulfilled. And so this Glory withdrew; but an inward Glory did my Heart fill, for a burning Love to all of those Heavenly Beings did kindle within my Heart vehemently.

In the Month of *August*

The Mind of Wisdom thus opened it self in me, as I waited in my Spirit upon her, she did shew me what Key would open the *Great Mystery,* which lay deeply hid in my self. It was wrought and carved out of such pure Gold, as had passed through many Fires; many Keys I had tryed, but could not turn in this secret enclosed Lock, but still it shut upon me, though I thought I had that Key which was compounded of such Metals, as would have made its entrance, as Love, Faith, Patience, Humility, which with strong Supplication and Prayer, I presented, as the Key of work. All which was too short to reach it. Whereupon I was put to a loss altogether to seek how this Gate should be opened, having compassed the Holy City, and waited and tried every way, where I might find passage, Circling from one Path to another, from Prayer to Prayer, and from Faith to Faith; so that in good earnest I began to consider I had not found the wonderful Key, for want of which I might run out in wast all my days, and grope as in the dark, yet never find the Door which opens into my true Shepherd's Fold. Whereupon being cast into a deep astonishing silence and stillness, the Word of *Wisdom* thus opened it self unto me; Oh thou deep searching Spirit, marvel not thou hast been so long frustrated, for as to thy present state and dispensation, thou couldst never reach me to all Eternity, for my Birth in thee lies deeper then thy present Gift of Faith and Prayer can open; thou hast with many others been in great mistake. But in as much as thou ownest and bewailest thy unskilfulness, I will make known to thee what Key will turn this great Wheel of my Wisdom, so as it may move, and manifest it self in thee, through all thy Properties, if thou canst bid up to the Price of it. For understand that it is compounded of all pure Gold, subsisting in Burning Furnace of many Fires: And although this wonderful Key is of Wisdom's carving out, and her free gift, yet, Oh thou seeking Spirit, she will cost thee very dear, if ever thou obtainest her. Yet she goeth about seeking such as are worthy of her, and will shew her self within the Walls of the Mind, and meet them in every thought that waits for her Laws and Counsel, and brings a Kingdom which will be well worth thy selling all for. But the great thing, saith Wisdom, now is to discipline and make thy Spirit a cunning Artist, to give it Knowledge of what Matter in Number, Weight and Measure this pure Key is made of, which is all pure Deity in the Number THREE; which is weighty indeed, being one exceeding weight Glory, sitting in the Circle of the Heavens within Man's Heart, measuring with the Line of His Power, the Temple and inward Court, with the Worshipers therein. This is Wisdom's Key, which will make our Hands drop with sweet smelling Myrrh upon the Handle of her Lock. Which while I was opening her Privy-Door, with this Key, my Soul failed within me, and I retained no strength, my Sun of Reason, and the Moon of my outward Sense were folded up, and withdrew. I knew nothing by my self, as to those working Properties from Nature, and Creature, and the Wheel of the Motion standing still, another moved from Central Fire; so that I felt my self Transmuted into one pure Flame. Then came that Word to me, This is no other then the Gate of my Eternal Deep, canst thou subsist in this Fiery Region, which is *Wisdom's* Mansion, where she meets with holy abstracted Spirits, and gives forth a fiery Law, which if there unto thou canst give heed, so as to come up to her Requirings, then no Secret shall be withheld from thee. Thus far am

I admitted to, come into the entrance of her House, where I must stop till I hear further from her.

Now as I was attending to obtain a fresh Visit, being entred into this first Mansion of her House, to hear and learn further, she said on this wise, That I was greatly beloved, and she would be my Mother, and so should I own her and call her, who would now be to me as *Rebecca* was to *Jacob*, to contrive and put me in a way how I should obtain the Birth-right-Blessing. For if I would apply my self to her Doctrine, and draw my Life's Food from no other Breast, I should then know the recovery of a lost Kingdom; At which Salutation I was dissolved and melted, the fervent heat of this Love strongly impulsing me to a resolve, for to obey her in all things.

Which pure Oil from *Wisdom's* Vessel stopping, it opened again not till *October* the 20th in the Morning-Watch; then heard I her Voice thus; Sequester and draw out of thy Animal Sensitive Life, that is too gross: I cannot appear till that disappear. There must be Spirit with Spirit, Light with Light. No sooner had I this caution, but I felt Power which suspended the active busie mind, which for a time was expired into silence: Know then (said the same Voice) thou shalt supplant thy Brother *Esau*, who according to the Figure, is a cunning Hunter in the out-birth and field of Nature. While he with his subtilty seeking it abroad, in the wild Properties of External Region; I will now help thee to it near at Hand, even in thy own enclosed Ground. There the true Scape-Goat feeds, of which I will make savoury Meat, such as God thy Father loves. Hearing this Salutation from my late known Mother, I was deadly ravished in the Spirit, in the Light of the Lord, and feared to returned to the dark House of my outward Senses again; which opened a Spring of Intercession in me, that as one of the Friends of the Bridegroom, I might hear his Voice still, which indeed was so pleasant and sweet, as I could well have admitted of a dissolution of my Elementary Being, rather than this Conference should not still be maintained with this renowned Pearl of Wisdom. But I have learned to observe her Time and Seasons, I witness her opening as in the twinkling of an Eye, a pure, bright, subtil, swift Spirit, a working Motion, a Circling Fire, a penetrating Oil.

November the 10th. 1673.

In the Morning, about the fifth Hour, my Spirit was called forth to attend Wisdom's Oracle again, to know further into that mysterious thing, she discovered with me, in order to the obtaining the Birth-right-Blessing. Oh thou Fiery Soul, know thy self now out of thy own Creaturely Being. Whereupon I was environed with sweet burning Flames, which devoured and consumed all the Bryars, Thorns, and accursed

Emanations that did offer to put forth. So that Scripture was witnessed, feeling God's being a Wall of Fire, which separates the Earthly part from the Heavenly. Then uttered Wisdom her Voice: Oh sollicitous Spirit, I am now come to shew thee what is required of thee, as in the beginning of my parling I shunned not to declare, what it would cost thee to purchase the Key, that unlocks the Gate which gives thee entrance into that pure and transparent City, where thou art to be an Inhabitant in the Lambs's Nature for ever. I tell thee, God requires an Offering from thee, as he did of *Abraham*, there is no sparing any part; an whole Burnt-offering through the Eternal Spirit must be given up. Understand me thus, thou hast an Earthly Principle that hath dilated and overspread thee, and got into dominion, and covered thee safe from my Heavens within thee; but these Thrones and Powers must be cast down, their Place must be found no more. Thou hast made great Complaints, for want of constant near Alliance and Freedom with God thy Creator: but marvel not the Cause lies here in dying, yet thou art not totally dead. This is the first Baptism thou art to know, and how many have herein fallen short in not giving their earthly Self a Through-wounding and killing Blow? Therefore to thee, O beloved of thy Mother *Rebecca*, I commend to thee my Flaming Sword. Be thou now valiant, and let it do full Execution in the Camp of Nature; slay utterly Old and Young whatever in thee bears not my Mark and Name, which is my Image. Few in this latter Age have come thus far. Therefore I have had so little pleasure to inhabit with, and to reveal my self to the Children of this Generation; in that a pure Crystalline Mind is so rarely to be found, and in no other will thy God appear. Therefore hear and learn of me, who well knows what will qualifie thee for the reception of thy Fountain-Light and Joy, which may be an abiding Friend and Comforter to thee, which was the Heritage of Jacob, thy forerunner in the Line and Blessing. Now having made known what thy Offering is to be, which is one remove that makes way for the returns of thy Bridegroom; the second thing required is the Venison that must be presented to thy Father; that he may eat thereof, that so the Love from his Heart may flow into thee, wherein the Blessing will be known; but of this thou shalt have my Counsel, as thou art faithful in answering to this preparative Work.

As these Sayings of my Mother I well pondered all, tending to resining me out of my Earthly Life, feeing I must offer it up, and that time of my departure out of the first Principle, is drawing nigh upon me, as Wisdom has plainly shewed me; that thought I had come with many Offerings, yet till all was consumed by that one whole Burnt-Offering, I could not be made perfect in the Virgin-State, where Christ's Second Birth in pure Spiritual Humanity should appear in me. Which Wisdom told me, was the true right Venison, that God my Father would receive from my Hand, who could favour no other Meat Offering but what should be made up and dressed by the Hand of Virgin-Wisdom, who further shewed me that place, where she would make ready the savoury Meat, which was in the fiery Essence of my Spirit. Which in very deed I did feel going to work in her own kindled Furnace, where she shewed me her Golden Pot. No Vessel was to be used but of that pure Metal, wherein was ordered all the several Ingredients, which I implored her Friendship to let me see; which was granted unto me, and hitherto I had observed her Charge, and her Secrets should be with me, and that I should know such things from a deep Ground, as had not been broken up of late Ages: if I could bear that hot fiery Furnace, which should boil away the Scum of all that which of the earthly part had yet its remainder with me. Which Counsel begot this Exploration with my Mother, as fearing I should not come up to these her pure and high Accomplishments.

Disponding therefore, I said, Oh my Mother-Wisdom, the terms of thy Requirings are hard, considering I constrained am to reside in the Out-Birth of Mortal Shadow, where Millions of Spirits do me tempt to keep me from this high and noble Ascent. What an overturning must here be made, that so a Renewing may be on the face of my old Earth? Which Renovation well answers to that Scripture, *We shall not all dye, but suffer a change, or Translation.*[32] Oh how little did I understand, till Wisdom unsealed and opened her Testimony, lighting my Lamp from her Seven Pillars of Fire, which now go before me, that my Way may no more be dark: Who hath made good her Promise, for I felt her strong Impulse, and her Furnace prepared, burning as an Oven. By which I well know what that Word of Record means, *The Day comes that shall burn as an Oven.*[33] She told me, She was now come to make ready the Venison, that I might have access to God my Father with it. While I was pondering, seeing only the Vessel and the Fire, with *Isaac* I was ready to say, Where is the Lamb? Then uttered she this Word, Thou thy self must be this Paschal Lamb, which must be slain: Then was I taught to say or pray, strike upon that Life-Vein, which may abundantly return again; thus yielding my self up to Love's Flaming Sword, I felt a separation was made. Oh how sweet is it to feel the Life's Blood run into the Fountain of that Godhead, from whence it came? Let none henceforth fear in the Lord to dye, for Life shall spring again as to one that awaketh out of a Sleep, into another Principle, or begotten into a New World in which with other Inhabitants, with whom I now my Conversation have, in the

32. 1 Cor 15:51.
33. Malachi 4:1.

light of the Deity I do dwell. O dear *Sophia*, what am I, that hitherto thou hast me brought, that I should know of thy Magick-Art, and from thy holy Flames be inspired, which foreruns the Day of Pentecost, which shall known again be to those who follow hard the prize to take. This feeling, Divine Power had me touched as the Key that unlocked the Gate of the Eternal Deep; I further emboldned was to ask my Mother Wisdom, how and when she would compound that savoury Meat, on which the Blessing entailed is, for I as one impatient am till the Birth-right confirmed be to me. Upon which there was presented as in a Charger, Kid lying in a Composition Liquor of Milk, Oil, and Blood, with several spices, as Spikenard, Myrrh and Cinnamon, giving forth strong Odours. Then *Wisdom* called to me. O go and see what I have compounded and prepared a Banquet-Feast, whereto thy Father will come down with his dear Son thy Elder Brother, and I thy Mother, and will hereof take and feed, so that the Fountain of *Jacob* may be thy Blessing, which the Eternal Father accordingly pronounced, saying, From the Upper and Supercelestial Planets let thy Eternal Nativity again renew, as from its own Originality; by which the lower Constellations and Elements shall to these subjected be and bow; as a Globe upon which thy Feet shall stand; and both the upper and neather Springs command. The Dews of Heaven, and the Fat Things of the Earth shall together upon thee meet: This is the Fulness of all Blessings, where with the Triune Unity do thee greet. Henceforward now observe, and obedient be, to what shall be further Communicated to thee.

After this my Spirit still attended, eagerly longing to lay my Mouth to *Wisdom's* Breast, from which the Word of Life so sweetly did flow. Then she with Flaming Heart did present herself to me. Out of which Heart sprouted forth a Tree, with Twelve Branches, having upon the Root of it engraven, GOD is the Pith, Life and Virtue, that maketh the Heart thus Fruitful, in various opening and quickning Powers, giving forth according to each Branch, a different and peculiar Fruit. Then said she to me, Here doth lie the Mystery: do thou it come and see, how out of the Flames these Branches put forth green palpable Fruits, that are not yet grown, yet thou with Patience must still wait till to perfection of ripeness they be grown in thee, then of the first Fruits of this Tree thou shalt bring to thy God as an Offering, that will draw down the Life's Blessing; read and see what engraven is for thee, and let thy Mind be staid a while, till thou to this ripe Age shall arrive and comforted be, that this shady Heart as a fruitful Vine shall overspread within the Walls of thy Mind, a River of Oyl shall here outspring, which will make thy Flames burn still, till so hot the Furnace may come to be which as the Sun for vehemency shall transmute this Fruit to a Golden Colour. Then thou with savoury

Meat to thy God shall come, who will himself feed upon their pleasant Fruit, which nourished has been from the Life's Blood; Come now and into Love's deep descend with me, that thou mayst know the various operation of this Tree, and every Branch thereof, namely as the living sense shall spring in thee according to which thy lot will be, as relating to the Blessing promised, the which will require perseverance still in the Faith, till to perfection in Colour the Fruit be brought. No other charge I shall leave with thee, but to abide within this Shady Rock, where Love's Flames shall be thy Food continually. Oh how pleasant is it here to be, all encircled with Love's flaming Breast?

January the 22nd. 1674.

Wisdom's Word opened yet again to me, saying Arise, swiftly follow me: I will shew thee Greater Things then what hath yet been known to thee. Whereupon I felt a mighty attractive Power drawing up my Spirit for Ascension; but surprized I was with a potent Enemy, which did me encounter highly, charging me with a breach to Nature's Laws and how I stood obligatory to her, in as much as I had an outward Body, which I ought to take in the Sense of its Elementary requirings, and accordingly make Provision, as the rest of my fellow Creatures in the World, which were under the Government of that great Monarch *Reason,* to whose Scepter all must bow that live in the Sensitive Animal Life. These and such Arguments I was assaulted with, and pursued as *Jacob* was by *Leban,* when he took his Flight to return to his Father's House, so greatly distressed was my Spirit, seeing it self so oppressed that it could not tell where to make its escape, or how to discharge my self from being a Subject to his Starry Kingdom: as I stood in the Line of Nature. I was under the dominion of the Starry Region, in the strife of the four Elements, which brought in the Curse, where Care and Fear, and the toil and labour of the Body did consist. Saith the Prince of earthly Life, How wilt thou acquit thyself from my Laws, and break the Brother *Esau's* Yoke from off thy neck?

Thus in obedience having drawn up my Charge, and having good proof and witness hereof, I presented it to the view of my Mother, who said, Are these things so indeed? I shall advise with the Deity how to destroy them of thy inward Coasts, seeing thou dost not join or take any part with them; but hast brought in Evidence against them as Traytors to the Crown, Dignity, and Dominion of the Lamb, whose Power they would depose him of, in his chosen and elect Seed: and though these evil seducing Spirits think their Mountain so strong, that is never to be moved, yet know their Day of Judgment is hastening on apace, and they will be given up to be tryed by the Fiery Law, which issueth forth from the

Ancient of Days, who hath appointed a Day, in which he will average his Elect, that cry mightily to him, as oppressed by these invading Spirits. Be of good Comfort, the Judge is nominated, the Jury is chosen, by whom the Verdict will be given; therefore be true to the Interest of my Son, who is appointed to judge the World in thee, and to cast out Hell, Sin and Death, the Beast and his retinue into the Lake, where there shall be no return out thence, to assault thee more with their Dregs and Poysonous Floods. This is to be done by joining Issue and Power with me, whom am come to help thee against the great *Leviathan*, who makes war most, where he sees his Time of Reigning is almost worn out, and that he must have no more place; who thinks it very great Injustice to be cast out of Man's Nature, before the laying down of the Mortal Body. But oh, to thee let me commend this present state, that in my Virgin-Purity thou mayst still be found; for I delight thee all fair to see: then with my presence frequently I would visit most satisfiedly, wherein you tell me all your Joy doth lie: Then droop not, but most pleasant be; as those whose Name and Place is ever with me. Call in also those who of doubtful Heart are apt to be: Unanimously go forward, remembering what the true *Nazarite* is to be, of Holy Courage and Divine Magnanimity: no more must such hang down the Head, or to feebleness of Mind give way, but the Power display, which in the Seven Locks concealed are; it is but needful that you all Force do draw out; for while these Earthly Spirits do border upon your Land, they will be scouting out: therefore without my proved Armour dare not with them to parley; this is the Charge I shall leave with thee.

September the 29th. 1676.

This Night approaching to Morning, great Spiritual Travail came upon me; and I was in Soul-heaviness, through the sharp Pangs which I was overtaken with. For I felt the Birth strong to make way for its deliverance: mighty throws of Spirit did work, and I therewith co-working was, that if by any means I might embrace the first-born of Might, to whom the Throne-Power and Government was to be established. While I thought on these things, my Spirit thus burst out, Ah my Lord, I have often been in these strong travelling Cries, but yet too feeble am, to bring forth that which is to be the Ruler of Nations, even he, who is to be cloathed with Royal Glory, Strength, and Majesty, to attend the Throne of the Deity; who will admit only such dignified Spirits there to resort and dwell, who are born again of equal quality within; so is it may be no Robbery to derive from thee, O God, this Fire-Birth, which makes the pure *Nazarite*: Whose Proceeding, as also Working forth must be from that everlasting Womb of Eternity; which does miraculously introduce it self into a poor despicable Corporeity, which is not perceived, till it cometh to a full grown Body, impregnated with Life in every part, and so growing till it comes to its full Birth-hour: which I did believe was after the manner of a Spirit to be effected. For this Word was expresly spoken to me, Fear not, thou shalt have this same also, which shall be caught up and nourished for a certain time, and then shall come again to thee; For while he is a Babe, and in Minority, Dangers and Perils will beset him, from this envious World. Therefore his Birth must be hidden and concealed, and there needs to be no Proclamation of it, because none but Spiritual Powers and Invisible Hosts were called forth to be privy to this secret Birth.

Then I beheld, till I saw the Virgin, who travelled to ascend, after the Child, therein wrapped up out of fight, freed from all Malice and Despight, being kept, and for while reserved within the Eternal Circle of Light. Then the Voice in me cryed, and said, Behold that which thou hast seen to ascend out of the Forms of Nature, shall again descend in a full grown God-Manhood, to accomplish, all, that hath been predicted and declared by the Spirit, who hath searched out the Depths of the Birth of Wisdom. Then upon this was revealed and presented to me, the Figure of a Lamb all white, having Seven Heads, upon which were Seven Crowns like Garlands, with fresh Roses and Lilies. And one riding in the similitude of a Woman, cloathed with a Flaming Garment, like the Sun for Glory and Brightness, with a Cup of Pearl-Royal in her Hand, filled full of flaming Liquor of Gold. Then the Spirit said, This is the Lamb and the Bride, which shall the Dragon and the Beast, with all his horned Power ride down, with all his Mark and Name, which the whole World hath worshipped and admired. He hath had long his Time, to impose strange Laws, and Injunctions: and hath been in Universally obeyed. Whose Sorceries, Witchcrafts, and Deceits have worn out many Generations, who was ignorant of the Depths of this subtle Serpent, and who hereby have died short of their Kingly Crown; The seducing Prophet perswading them, that they were under a necessity, of owning this false usurped Power and Authority, which so well agreed and answered to the Apostatized Life of Sensuality. But oh, to you, whom I have seen Revolters from this strange King, and his Government, I the Spirit of Jesus am sent, to declare to you the Father's Love and Intent. Whose Heart is set to redeem you, from all Sins oppressing Tyranny, from the World's Spirit, and all that is Rudimental. I have sought out for such, as for what my purpose might be, who are resolved to deny, and throw off all weights, and thronging Spirits, that would traffick within my Holy Place. For assuredly, I do of such take special notice, who do forsake all this low Orb for me, to follow my new revealed Tracks. Then cryed my Spirit, since, O my Lord, I have thus far found Grace in thy sight, give me to understand the meaning of this last Representation, to wit, of the Seven Crowned Lamb, with the Effigies of a Woman riding on him.

So this was opened unto me by the divine Intelligencing Spirit, which informed me, that the Lamb which I saw with Seven Crowns, signified Jesus, who yet never assumed his Reigning Power on the Earth for any duration. For while he was Personally in the World, he was under Suffering and Reproach: and ever since he hath been vailed and obscured in his Spirit; the Earthly part hath yet been too hard in the Lamb's Warriours. But now to any such, in whom the Virgin Bride is come down, to travel in the greatness of Strength, to bring forth this mighty Birth of the God-like Nature, they may expect and look for great things to be produced, as the effects of this wonderful Birth. Which is caught up to the Throne of God, and will not return back, till he comes with all full command, to give the Seventh Number Crown, and fix it on them, to whom he is first to appear; conveying most freely and clearly his Soveraignty to them. But that which is the most deep thing in the Vision, is the great Mystery of the Woman, which sate upon the Lamb, with a cup in her Hand, Whose Representation is to shew, that this is the Virgin of *Sion*, the Mother of the *New Jerusalem*, who is come to divest, and lay open the Harlotry Spirit, that hath brought in the Abomination of all Idolatry, and hath made drunk the several Sects with the Wine of Luciferian Spirit, enchanting all Nations through her Magnificency and Power, having the Riches and Honours of this World, to give as a Reward to her Worshippers: Therefore to countervail, and the more highly to excell all that, this Princely Virgin, the Eternal Wisdom and Power of God, hath appeared with the Lamb in the Spirit's Soveraignty, to let thee know, she is the only Mother and Bride to whom is given the Cup of Blessing. From whence are substantial, durable Riches, Power, Dignity, and Soveraignty, that shall know no limit or end of Glory and Kingly Dominion: and thereof also will be to all Eternity an encrease. Therefore let it not repent you, who have been Lover and Admirers of the illustrious *Stone of Wisdom*: trust to her, expect all from her, looking only to her united Power with the Lamb; who will assuredly come in you to Reign. For the Anointing Oyl is in his Horn, and the melted Liquor of Gold in the Cup, to which you are called to take a full sup: then you will know another manner of Reward then all the Enchanting Principle of the Beast, and Sin trimmed Whore can afford; who will be all dispoiled, as the Lamb and Wisdom in you shall yet more evidently appear, to imprint the Mark and Name of the Great *Salem*. Upon whom faith the Spirit of the Bride-Love, wait, and fix, and stir not therefrom; for so she will be your Springing Garland.

Sophiology
and Romanticism

THE ENLIGHTENMENT PERIOD was not one conducive to sophio-logical thought. Nevertheless, in Romanticism's rebellion against the tyranny of reason promulgated by the Enlightenment's totalizing demands for obeisance, sophiology started to creep back into the Western cultural imaginary. As poet and engraver William Blake told his friend Crabb Robinson, "Bacon, Locke, and Newton are the three great teachers of Atheism or of Satan's doctrine. Every thing is Atheism which assumes the reality of the natural and unspiritual world."[1] Following the rise of Cartesian dualism, science's ascendance began, and was answered reciprocally in the master culture by theology's decline. As Kate Rigby has described it, "the disenchanted world of modern science was one from which the divine had largely been expelled."[2] Long after this period, poet William Butler Yeats gave voice to a sentiment common to his Romantic forebears:

> I cannot get it out of my mind that this age of criticism is about to pass, and an age of imagination, of emotion, of moods, of revelation, about to come in its place; for certainly belief in a supersensual world is at hand again.[3]

Indeed, his words could be repeated today without compromising their combined hope and anxiety.

The writers and thinkers represented in this section are hardly an exhaustive cross-section of sophiological ideas appearing between the late-eighteenth and early-twentieth centuries. They do, however, clearly articulate the Romantic and Idealist commitment to an alternative view

---

1. Henry Crabb Robinson, *Diary, Reminiscences and Correspondence*, 2 vols., ed. Thomas Sadler (Boston: Houghton, Mifflin and Company, 1898), 2:27.

2. Kate Rigby, *Topographies of the Sacred: The Poetics of Place in European Romanticism* (Charlottesville, VA: University of Virginia Press, 2004), 21.

3. See the complete essay, 107–8.

to that of the encroaching scientism and materialism that was so much a part of the master culture's epistemology in their own times—an epistemology which persists into ours.

The section begins with two excerpts from the writing of Johann Wolfgang von Goethe (1749–1832), unquestionably the most multifaceted genius of his age. The first passage comes from his *Autobiography* and tells of his childhood intuition to raise an altar to the "God who stands in immediate connection with nature, and owns and loves it as his own work ... who might be brought into closer relationship with man, as with everything else, and who would take care of him, as of the motion of the stars, the days and seasons, the animals and plants." This notion is central to what Goethe identified as *Ehrfurcht*, "reverence," which he considered a much-needed component of inquiry that had been summarily dismissed and discounted by Enlightenment science (and much of the science that came after). This is followed by an excerpt from his *Theory of Colours* describing his phenomenological method, an implicitly sophianic mode of scientific inquiry. (An excerpt from the second part of Goethe's *Faust* appears in Section II of this volume.)

Next comes Novalis's *Christendom or Europe?*, a unique and imaginative document which stirred much controversy throughout its publishing history—even among some of Novalis's closest friends. Novalis (pseudonym of Georg Philipp Friedrich Freiherr von Hardenberg, 1772–1801) wrote *Christendom or Europe?* not long before his premature death at the age of twenty-nine, and in it he looks longingly at the idea of a Europe united by both faith and a holistic understanding of human culture and human flourishing. Novalis's Catholic sympathies are patent throughout the piece (clearly the source of the work's controversy), and the sophiological character of his worldview is clearly evident throughout it as well. Complementing *Christendom or Europe*, we have included excerpts from Novalis's masterpiece *Hymnen an die Nacht (Hymns to the Night)* in Part II.

After Novalis, we come to a nineteenth- and twentieth-century Austrian philosopher, educator, esotericist, and virtuoso who had been deeply influenced by both Goethe and Novalis, but whose genius took him into startlingly unexpected directions: Rudolf Steiner (1861–1925). Studied in the phenomenology of Franz Brentano, like Martin Heidegger (whose mentor Edmund Husserl was also a student of Brentano), Steiner developed a healthy suspicion of the scientific revolution's fascination with technology and the impact such a fascination might have upon being human. Steiner gave over six thousand public and private lectures on a bewildering number of topics. His ideas, influenced by Blavatskian Theosophy (though this influence waned more and more over time) and early Rosicrucianism, may strike many readers as bizarre. Nevertheless, Steiner's contributions to education (the Waldorf movement), medicine (Anthroposophically-extended medicine), agriculture (the Biodynamic method), and work with the handicapped (the Camphill movement), to name just a few, are not so easily dismissed. The lecture excerpted here was given in 1920 and is from a cycle entitled *Cosmic and Human Metamorphoses*. In it, Steiner contemplates the cosmological significance of Christianity and the relationship of the human person to the person of Christ, notions inherently sophiological—if highly idiosyncratic in their presentation.

Finally, poet William Butler Yeats (1865–1939) closes the chapter on Romanticism with his brief 1895 essay "The Body of the Father Christian Rosencrux," a lament and a prayer resonant in many ways with Novalis's contemplation of his own times in *Christendom or Europe?*

Johann Wolfgang von Goethe

from *Autobiography:*
Truth and Poetry, from My Own Life

HE CAME to the thought that he might immediately approach the great God of Nature, the Creator and Preserver of Heaven and Earth, whose earlier manifestations of wrath had long been forgotten in the beauty of the world, and the manifold blessings in which we participate while upon it. The way he took to accomplish this was very curious.

The Boy had chiefly kept to the first article of Belief. The God who stands in immediate connection with nature, and owns and loves it as his own work, seemed to him the proper God, who might be brought into closer relationship with man, as with everything else, and who would take care of him, as of the motion of the stars, the days and seasons, the animals and plants. There were texts of the Gospels which explicitly stated this. The Boy could ascribe no form to this Being: he therefore sought Him in His works, and would, in the good Old Testament fashion, build Him an altar. Natural productions were set forth as images of the world, over which a flame was to burn, signifying the aspirations of man's heart towards his Maker.

He brought out of the collection of natural objects which he possessed, and which had been increased as chance directed, the best ores and other specimens. But the next difficulty was, as to how they should be arranged and raised into a pile. His father possessed a beautiful red-lackered music-stand, ornamented with gilt flowers, in the form of a four-sided pyramid, with different elevations, which had been found convenient for quartets, but lately was not much in use. The Boy laid hands on this, and built up his representatives of Nature one above the other in steps, so that it all looked quite pretty and at the same time sufficiently significant. On an early sunrise his first worship of God was to be celebrated, but the young priest had not yet settled how to produce a flame which should at the same time emit an agreeable odour. At last it occurred to him to combine the two, as he possessed a few fumigating pastils, which diffused a pleasant fragrance with a glimmer, if not with a flame. Nay, this soft burning and exhalation seemed a better representation of what passes in the heart, than an open flame. The sun had already risen for a long time, but the neighbouring houses concealed the East. At last it glittered above the roofs, a burning-glass was at once taken up and applied to the pastils, which were fixed on the summit in a fine porcelain saucer. Everything succeeded according to the wish, and the devotion was perfect. The altar remained as a peculiar ornament of the room which had been assigned him in the new house. Every one regarded it only as a well-arranged collection of natural curiosities. The Boy knew better, but concealed his knowledge. He longed for a repetition of the solemnity. But unfortunately, just as the most opportune sun arose, the porcelain cup was not at hand; he placed the pastils immediately on the upper surface of the stand; they were kindled, and so great was the devotion of the priest, that he did not observe, until it was too late, the mischief his sacrifice was doing. The pastils had burned mercilessly into the red lacquer and beautiful gold flowers, and as if some evil spirit had disappeared, had left their black, ineffaceable footprints. By this the young priest was thrown into the most extreme perplexity. The mischief could be covered up, it was true, with the larger pieces of his show-materials, but the spirit for new offerings was gone, and the accident might almost be considered a hint and warning of the danger there always is in wishing to approach the Deity in such a way.

from *Theory of Colours* (Preface to 1810 edition)

It may naturally be asked whether, in proposing to treat of colours, light itself should not first engage our attention: to this we briefly and frankly answer that since so much has already been said on the subject of light, it can hardly be desirable to multiply repetitions by again going over the same ground.

Indeed, strictly speaking, it is useless to attempt to express the nature of a thing abstractedly. Effects we can perceive, and a complete history of those effects would, in fact, sufficiently define the nature of the thing itself. We should try in vain to describe a man's character, but let his acts be collected and an idea of the character will be presented to us.

The colours are acts of light; its active and passive modifications: thus considered we may expect from them some explanation respecting light itself. Colours and light, it is true, stand in the most intimate relation to each other, but we should think of both as belonging to nature as a whole, for it is nature as a whole which manifests itself by their means in an especial manner to the sense of sight.

The completeness of nature displays itself to another sense in a similar way. Let the eye be closed, let the sense of hearing be excited, and from the lightest breath to the wildest din, from the simplest sound to the highest harmony, from the most vehement and impassioned cry to the gentlest word of reason, still it is Nature that speaks and manifests her presence, her pervading life and the vastness of her relations.

And thus as we descend the scale of being. Nature speaks to other senses—to known, misunderstood, and unknown senses: so speaks she with herself and to us in a thousand modes. To the attentive observer she is nowhere dead nor silent; she has even a secret agent in inflexible matter, in a metal, the smallest portions of which tell us what is passing in the entire mass. However manifold, complicated, and unintelligible this language may often seem to us, yet its elements remain ever the same. With light poise and counterpoise, Nature oscillates within her prescribed limits, yet thus arise all the varieties and conditions of the phenomena which are presented to us in space and time.

Novalis

(Georg Philipp Friedrich Freiherr von Hardenberg, 1772–1801)

Christendom or Europe?

Once there were fine, resplendent times when Europe was a Christian land, when one Christendom occupied this humanly constituted continent. One great common interest united the remotest provinces of this broad spiritual realm. Without great worldly possessions, one Head guided and unified the great political forces. A numerous guild to which everyone had access stood directly beneath him and carried out his behests and strove with zeal to confirm his beneficent power. Every member of this organization was universally honored, and if the common people sought comfort or help, protection or counsel from this member, and in return were happy to provide generously for his manifold needs, he also found protection, respect, and a hearing among the more powerful, and everyone cared for these chosen men, equipped with miraculous powers, as for children of Heaven whose presence and favor spread manifold blessing abroad. Childlike faith bound men to their pronouncements. How cheerfully every man could fulfill his earthly labors when, through the agency of these holy persons, a secure future was prepared for him and every misstep forgiven, when every discolored spot in life was obliterated by them and made clean. They were the experienced helmsmen upon the great unknown sea, in whose keeping one might disdain all storms and count on a sure attainment of the coast and a landing at the world of the true home.

Before their words the wildest and most voracious propensities were obliged to yield respect and obedience. Peace proceeded from them. They preached solely love for the holy and wondrously beautiful Lady of Christendom, who, endowed with divine powers, was prepared to rescue any believer from the most dread perils. They told of celestial persons long since dead who, by virtue of adherence and loyalty to that Blessed Mother and to her divine and benevolent Child, withstood the temptation of the earthly world and achieved honors and had now become protective and beneficent powers to their living brethren, willing helpers in tribulation, intercessors for human infirmities, and efficacious friends of mankind before the heavenly throne. With what serenity people used to depart from the beautiful assemblies in the mysterious churches, which were adorned with cheering pictures, filled with sweet fragrances, and animated by holy and exalting music. Therein the consecrated remains of former God-fearing men were gratefully preserved in precious reliquaries. And through them was manifest the divine goodness and omnipotence, the powerful beneficence of these happy saints, in splendid wonders and signs. In this way loving souls preserve locks of hair or bits of writing of their departed loved ones and feed the sweet flame thereby until reuniting death. With heartfelt care people used to gather from everywhere whatever had belonged to these beloved souls, and each man considered himself fortunate who was able to procure, or so much as touch, such a consoling relic. Now and again the heavenly grace seemed to have descended especially upon some strange picture or upon a grave. Thither streamed people then from all regions with lovely gifts and carried away heavenly gifts in return: peace of soul and health of body.

Assiduously this powerful peace-creating organization sought to make all men sharers in this beautiful faith and sent their colleagues into all parts of the world to proclaim everywhere the Gospel of Life and to make the Kingdom of Heaven the only kingdom on this earth. With good cause the wise Head of the Church countered insolent excrescences of human talents at the expense of the sacred sense, as well as untimely, dangerous discoveries in the area of knowledge. Thus he prevented bold thinkers from asserting publicly that the earth was an insignificant planet, for he realized that humans, together with respect for their dwelling place and their earthly homeland, would also lose respect for their heavenly home and for their race, would prefer circumscribed knowledge to infinite faith, and would become accustomed to scorning everything great and worthy of wonder and look upon these as dead legalisms. At his court assembled all the clever and reverend men in Europe. All treasures flowed thither, Jerusalem destroyed had avenged itself, and Rome itself was Jerusalem, the holy residence of divine government on earth. Princes laid their disputes before the father of Christendom, willingly laid their crowns and their splendor at his feet. Indeed, they deemed it a glory to conclude the evening of their lives as members of that high guild in godly contemplation within solitary cloister walls. How beneficial this regimen, this arrangement was, how appropriate to the inner nature of man, was shown by the mighty upsurge of all the other human powers, the harmonious development of all capacities, the tremendous height to which individual men attained in all departments of knowledge of life and of the arts, and by the universally flourishing traffic in spiritual and earthly wares within the boundaries of Europe and outward to the most distant Indies.

Such were the fine essential characteristics of the truly Catholic or truly Christian times. For this splendid kingdom mankind was not ripe, not developed enough. It was a first love, which died away amid the press of business life, whose memory was crowded out by selfish cares, and whose bond—afterwards cried down as imposture and illusion and judged in the light of subsequent experiences—was sundered forever by a large proportion of Europeans. This great inner cleavage, which was attended by destructive wars, was a noteworthy sign of the harmfulness of culture to the sense for the Invisible, or at least of the temporary harmfulness of the culture of a certain stage. Annihilated that immortal sense cannot be, but it can be troubled, lamed, crowded out by other senses. Protracted intercourse of human beings decreases their affections, their belief in their race, and accustoms them to devoting their entire aim and endeavor solely to the means of wellbeing. Their needs and the devices for the satisfaction of their needs become more complex; and the greedy man requires so much time to get to know them and to acquire skills in them, that no time is left for the quiet composure of the spirit, for attentive observation of the inner world. In cases of conflict, present concerns seem to touch him more nearly, and thus faith and love, the fair blossoms of his youth, fall and yield place to the tarter fruits, knowledge and possessions. In late autumn one recalls the springtime as a childish dream, and with childish simplicity one hopes that the full granary will hold out forever. A certain solitariness seems to be necessary for the thriving of the higher senses, and hence a too extensive association of persons one with another will inevitably choke out many a sacred stalk and frighten away the gods who flee the unquiet tumult of distracted societies and the transactions of petty occasions.

We have, moreover, to do with times and periods, and for such, is not an oscillation, an alternation of opposing movements, essential? And is limited duration not characteristic of them? Is growth and decline not their nature? But also, is not resurrection and rejuvenation in new and vigorous form to be expected with certainty of them? Progressive, ever augmenting evolutions are the stuff of history. What now does not attain fulfillment, will attain it upon a future trial or upon a reiterated one. Nothing is perishable which history has taken up. Out of untold transmutations it emerges again in ever riper forms. Christianity had once appeared in full force and splendor; down to a new world-inspiration its ruin and its Letter endured amid ever increasing feebleness and derision. Infinite inertia lay heavy upon the now safe guild of the clergy. In the feeling of its esteem and its comfort it had stopped moving, while the laity had wrested experience and erudition from its hands and had taken mighty strides ahead of it on the way to culture. In the forgetfulness of its true office, which was to be the first among men in intellect, insight, and culture, base desires had grown rank, and the vulgarity and baseness of their mode of thinking became still more repugnant because of their garb and their vocation. Thus respect and confidence, the props of this and every kingdom, fell gradually away, and therewith that guild was undone. The actual mastery of Rome had, long before the violent insurrection, silently ceased to be. Merely clever, and therefore also merely transient, measures still held the corpse of the organization together and protected it from too rapid dissolution, into which category fell, for example, primarily the abolition of marriage for the clergy—a measure which, applied analogously, could bestow a redoubtable solidity upon the parallel military caste and confer upon it long extension of life. What was more natural than that finally a mind quick to take flame should preach open rebellion against the despotic Letter of the former organization, and with all the greater success because he himself was a member of the guild.

The insurgents rightly termed themselves Protestants, for they protested solemnly against the usurpation of the conscience by an inconvenient and seemingly illegal force. For the time being they reappropriated, as though it were free, their silently surrendered right to the examination, determination, and choice of religion. They also set up a number of right principles, introduced a number of praiseworthy things, and abolished a number of pernicious laws. But they forgot the inevitable result of their procedure, they separated the inseparable, divided the indivisible Church, and sacrilegiously wrenched themselves loose from the universal Christian community, through which and in which alone was possible the true, the enduring rebirth. The condition of religious anarchy must not be more than transitory, because there remains constantly operative and valid the reason for dedicating a number of people exclusively to this high vocation and for making this number of people independent of temporal force with regard to these affairs. The establishment of consistories and the retention of a kind of clergy was of no help toward this requirement and was no adequate substitute for it. Unfortunately the princes had intruded themselves into this schism and many of them used these contentions for the re-enforcement and extension of their sovereign power and incomes. They were happy to be exempt from that former high influence and now took the new consistories under their paternalistic protection and guidance. They were most zealously concerned with preventing the total unification of the Protestant churches, and thus religion was irreligiously contained within the boundaries of states, whereby was laid the foundation for the gradual undermining of cosmopolitan religious interest. Thus religion lost its great political influence for the creation of peace and its proper role as unifying, individualizing principle, the role of Christendom. Religious peace was settled according to thoroughly erroneous principles antithetical to religion, and by the continuation of so-called Protestantism something entirely contradictory—a revolutionary regime—was declared perpetual.

Meanwhile, at the foundation of Protestantism there lies by no means merely that pure concept. Rather, Luther treated Christianity quite arbitrarily, misjudged its spirit, introduced another Letter and another religion, namely the holy universal validity of the Bible, and therewith unfortunately was injected into religious affairs a different, highly alien, worldly science—philosophy—whose corrosive influence becomes henceforth unmistakable. Out of a dim perception of this error he was himself elevated by a large proportion of Protestants to the rank of evangelist and his translation canonized.

This choice was highly injurious to the religious sense, for nothing so crushes its sensitivity as the Letter. In the previous situation this latter could never have become so harmful, considering the large compass, the flexibility, and the copious matter of the Catholic faith, as well as the esotericizing of the Bible and the sacred power of the councils and of the spiritual Head. But now these counterforces were abrogated, the absolute accessibility of the Bible to the people was asserted, and now the inadequate contents, the rough, abstract sketch of religion in these books, became all the more obvious and for the spirit of holiness infinitely weighed down free animation, penetration, and revelation.

Hence the history of Protestantism shows us no great and splendid manifestations of the supernatural any more. Only its inception gleams through a transitory blaze of heaven, and soon thereafter the desiccation of the spirit of holiness is already evident. The worldly has gained the upper hand. The sense for art suffers kindred-wise. Only rarely does a genuine, eternal spark of life leap forth here and there and a small congregation form. It expires and the congregation dissolves again and drifts with the current. Such were Zinzendorf, Jakob Böhme, and others. The moderates get the upper hand, and the era feeds on a total atony of the higher organs, on the period of practical disbelief. With the Reformation, Christendom came to an end. From then on there was no such thing anymore. Catholics and Protestants or Reformed stood further apart from one another in sectarian division than from Mohammedans and heathens. The remaining Catholic states went on vegetating, not without imperceptibly feeling the harmful influence of the neighboring Protestant states. Modern politics first developed at this point in time, and individual powerful states sought to take over the vacant universal Chair, which had been transformed into a throne.

To most princes it seemed a humiliation to be inconvenienced for a powerless cleric. For the first time they felt the weight of their physical power on earth, beheld the heavenly powers idle before offense to their representatives, and now sought gradually and without fuss to cast off the burdensome Roman yoke from subjects of theirs who still inclined zealously to the Pope, and to make themselves independent on earth. Their uneasy consciences were set at rest by clever soul-keepers who had nothing to lose if their spiritual children arrogated to themselves the control of church property.

To the good fortune of the old organization there now advanced a newly arisen order on which the dying spirit of the hierarchy seemed to have poured out its uttermost gifts, which equipped the old with new strength, and which applied itself with marvelous insight and perseverance, more astutely than had ever happened before, to the Papal kingdom and its mightier regeneration. No such society had ever been met with before in world history. Not even the ancient Roman senate had devised plans for world conquest with greater certainty of success. No one had with greater sagacity yet contemplated the execution of a greater idea. This society will ever be a model of all societies that feel organic desire for infinite expansion and everlasting duration—but also a proof forever that unguarded time alone undoes the cleverest enterprises and that the natural growth of the entire species incessantly suppresses the artificial growth of any subsection. All that is specialized unto itself has its own measure of ability; only the capacity of the race is infinite. All projects must fail which are not projects fully consonant with all the natural inclinations of the race. This society becomes still more noteworthy as mother of the so-called secret societies, a growth still unripe but surely of genuine historical importance. The new Lutheranism—not Protestantism—surely could not have a more dangerous rival. All the magic of the Catholic faith became still more potent beneath its hand. The treasures of the sciences flowed back into its cells. What had been lost in Europe they sought to regain multifold in other continents, in the furthest Occident and Orient, and to acquire and vindicate the apostolic dignity and vocation. Nor did they lag in their efforts for popularity, and they well realized how much Luther had owed to his demagogic arts, his study of the common folk. Everywhere they instituted schools, penetrated confessionals, assumed professorial chairs, and engaged the presses, became poets and sages, ministers and martyrs, and in their tremendous expansion from America across Europe to China remained in the most extraordinary agreement as to deed and doctrine. From their schools they recruited with wise selection for their order. Against the Lutherans they preached with devastating zeal and sought to make the cruelest extermination of these heretics, as actual confederates of the devil, the most urgent obligation of Catholic

Christendom. To them alone the Catholic states, and in particular the Papal See, owed their long survival of the Reformation, and who knows how old the world would still look if weak leaders, jealousy of princes and other clerical orders, court intrigues, and other odd circumstances had not checked their bold course and with them had not all but wiped out this last bulwark of the Catholic organization. It is sleeping now, this dread order, in wretched form on the outskirts of Europe. Perhaps from thence, like the nation that is sheltering it, it will someday spread abroad with new force over its old homeland, perhaps under a different name.

The Reformation was a sign of its time. It was significant for all Europe, even if it had openly broken forth only in truly free Germany. The good minds of all nations had secretly come of age and in the illusory feeling of their vocation revolted the more sharply against obsolete constraint. The erudite is by instinct the enemy of the clergy according to the old order. The erudite and the clerical classes, once they are separated, must war to the death, for they strive for one and the same position. This separation advanced ever further, and the erudite gained the more ground the more the history of European humanity approached the age of triumphant erudition, whereas knowledge and faith entered into more decisive opposition. It was to faith that people looked to find the cause of the general impasse, and this they hoped to obviate by keen knowledge. Everywhere the sense for the holy suffered from the manifold persecutions of its previous form, its former personality. The end product of the modern manner of thinking was termed "philosophy," and under that head was reckoned everything that was opposed to the old, hence primarily every objection against religion. The initial personal hatred of the Catholic faith passed gradually over into hatred of the Bible, of the Christian faith, and finally of religion in general. Still further, the hatred of religion extended itself quite naturally and consistently to all objects of enthusiasm. It made imagination and emotion heretical, as well as morality and the love of art, the future and the past. With some difficulty it placed man first in the order of created things, and reduced the infinite creative music of the universe to the monotonous clatter of a monstrous mill, which, driven by the stream of chance and floating thereon, was supposed to be a mill in the abstract, without Builder or Miller, in fact an actual *perpetuum mobile*, a mill that milled of itself.

One enthusiasm was generously left to poor mankind and, as a touchstone of supreme culture, was made indispensable to every shareholder in it—enthusiasm for this grand and splendid "philosophy" and more particularly for its priests and initiates. France was fortunate enough to become the womb and the seat of this new faith, which was pasted together out of pure knowledge. Yet, decried as poetry was in this new church, there were nevertheless some poets in its midst who, for the sake of effect, still made use of the old adornments and of the old light, though in so doing they ran the risk of setting the new world system on fire with the old flame. Shrewder members, however, knew how to pour cold water at once upon such listeners as had waxed warm. The members were tirelessly busy cleaning the poetry of Nature, the earth, the human soul, and the branches of learning—obliterating every trace of the holy, discrediting by sarcasm the memory of all ennobling events and persons, and stripping the world of all colorful ornament. The Light, by virtue of its mathematical submissiveness and its insolence, had become their favorite. They rejoiced that it yielded to refraction sooner than to play with colors, and thus they took from it the name of their great undertaking: Enlightenment. In Germany this undertaking was prosecuted even more thoroughly. The educational system was reformed. An attempt was made to impart to the old religion a more modern, more rational, more general meaning by carefully washing it clean of all that was marvelous or mysterious. The whole of scholarship was enlisted to cut off refuge in history, while people strove to elevate history itself to a domestic and civic portrait of manners and families. God was made into the disengaged spectator of this great, touching drama which the scholars were mounting, at the conclusion of which He was expected to entertain and solemnly admire the poets and players. By downright preference the common people were enlightened and educated to that cultivated enthusiasm, and in this way there arose a new European guild: the Lovers of Mankind and Enlighteners. What a pity that Nature remained so wondrous and incomprehensible, so poetic and infinite, in defiance of all the efforts to modernize her. If somewhere an old superstition about a higher world and the like turned up, a hue and cry was straightway raised on all sides and wherever possible the dangerous spark was quenched into ashes by "philosophy" and wit. And yet Tolerance was the watchword of the cultured, and particularly in France was reckoned synonymous with "philosophy."

This history of modern disbelief is highly significant and the key to all the tremendous phenomena of recent times. It has its first beginning in this century, especially in the latter half, and in a brief span has grown to incalculable size and diversity. A second Reformation, more comprehensive and more specifically characteristic, was inevitable, and it had to strike first in that country which was most modernized and which, from lack of freedom, had lain longest in an asthenic state. The supernatural fire would long since have burst forth and set at naught the clever plans for enlightenment, had not secular pressure and influence come to the latter's support. But at that moment, when dissension arose between the erudite and the new regimes, between the enemies of religion and their whole fellowship, it necessarily emerged as a third, tone-setting, conciliating member, and this emergence must now be acknowledged by every friend thereof and proclaimed aloud, even if it should not be especially evident. That the time of resurrection has come, and that precisely those circumstances which seemed to be directed against its animation and which threatened to complete its destruction, have become the most favorable signs for its regeneration, this cannot remain in doubt to a person with a sense of history. Genuine anarchy is the creative element of religion. Out of the annihilation of all that is positive it raises its glorious head as a new creator of worlds. As though of himself, man rises toward heaven when nothing else holds him bound; the higher organs rise for the first time of their own will out of the general uniform mass and out of the total dissolution of all human abilities and powers, as the primeval seed of earthly formation. The spirit of God hovers over the waters and a heavenly island is discernible above the retreating waves as the dwelling place of the new man, as the river-bed of eternal life.

Let the true beholder contemplate calmly and dispassionately the new state-toppling era. Will not the state-toppler seem to him like Sisyphus? Now he has attained the summit of equilibrium, and already the mighty weight is rolling down the other side again. It will never remain on high unless an attraction toward heaven holds it poised on the crest. All your props are too weak if your state retains its tendency toward the earth. But link it by a higher yearning to the heights of heaven, give it a relevancy to the universe, and you will have in it a never-wearying spring, and you will see your efforts richly rewarded. I refer you to history. Search amid its instructive coherency for parallel points of time and learn to use the magic wand of analogy.

Is the Revolution to remain the French one, as the Reformation was the Lutheran one? Is Protestantism once again, contrary to nature, to be fixed as a revolutionary regime? Shall the Letter make way for the Letter? Are you seeking the seed-germ of deterioration in the old order too, in the old spirit? And do you imagine yourselves on a better tack toward the understanding of a better spirit? O would that the spirit of spirits filled you and you would desist from this foolish effort to mold history and mankind and to give it your direction! Is it not independent, not self-empowered, as well as infinitely lovable and prophetic? To study it, to follow after it, to learn from it, to keep step with it, to follow in faith its promises and hints—of these things no one thinks.

In France a great deal has been done for religion by withdrawing its right of citizenship and leaving it solely the right of tenancy in the household, and this not in One Person but in all its countless individual forms. As a strange, unprepossessing waif it must first win hearts again and be universally loved before it can be publicly worshiped again and be drawn into secular matters for friendly advice and the harmonizing of spirits. Historically noteworthy remains the attempt of that great iron mask which, under the name of Robespierre, sought in religion the mid-point and the strength of the Republic. Likewise the insensibility with which theophilanthropy, that mystique of modern Enlightenment, was taken up. Likewise the new conquests of the Jesuits. Likewise the approach to the Orient through recent political circumstances.

Of the other European countries besides Germany it may be prophesied only that, with *peace*, a new and higher religious life will begin to pulse within them and that this will soon consume all other secular interests. In Germany, on the other hand, the traces of a new world can already be demonstrated with total certainty. Germany is proceeding, at slow but sure pace, ahead of the other European countries. While the latter are occupied with war, speculation, and partisan spirit, the German is developing himself with all industry into a partaker in a higher epoch of culture, and this advance cannot fail to give him a great advantage over the others in the course of time. In learning and in the arts one detects a mighty ferment. Infinitely vast intelligence is being developed. Requisition is being made from new and fresh lodes of ore. Never was learning in better hands, never did it arouse greater expectations. The most varied aspects of objects are being explored. Nothing is being left unstirred, unjudged, unexamined. Everything is being worked. Writers are becoming more individualized and more powerful. Every old monument of history, every art, every branch of knowledge is finding friends, is being embraced with new love and made fruitful. A versatility without parallel, a wonderful profundity, a splendid polish, comprehensive knowledge, and a rich and mighty imagination are to be found on this side and on that side, often daringly combined. A tremendous intimation of the creative will, of the boundlessness, of the infinite multiplicity, of the sacred particularity and universal capability of the inner man seems everywhere to be astir. Awakened from the morning dream of helpless childhood, a section of the race is exerting its first powers against serpents that entwine its cradle and seek to filch from it the use of its limbs. All these things are still only intimations, incoherent and raw, but to the historical eye they give evidence of a universal individuality, a new history, a new mankind, the sweetest embrace of a young and surprised Church and a loving God, and the fervent reception of a new Messiah within its thousand members. Who does not, with sweet shame, feel himself pregnant? The newborn child will be the image of his father, a new Golden Age, with dark and infinite eyes, an Age prophetic, wonder-working, miraculously healing, comforting, and kindling eternal life—a great Age of reconciliation, a Savior who, like a good spirit, is at home among men, believed in though not seen, visible under countless forms to believers, consumed as bread and wine, embraced as a bride, breathed as air, heard as word and song, and with heavenly delight accepted as death into the core of the subsiding body amid the supreme pangs of love.

We now stand high enough to smile amicably at those previous ages mentioned above and also to recognize remarkable crystallizations of historical matter even amid those odd follies. Gratefully we wish to press the hands of those scholars and "philosophers." For that illusion had to be exhausted for the benefit of posterity and the scientific aspect of things had to be validated. Lovelier and more colorful stands poetry, like an India adorned, opposed to the cold, lifeless peak of that closed-room intelligence. In order that India may be so warm and resplendent in the middle of the globe, it was necessary that a cold and rigid sea, dead cliffs, fog instead of starry sky, and a long night should make both extremes inhospitable. The profound significance of mechanics lay heavy upon those anchorites in the deserts of Reason. The charm of first insight overwhelmed them; the old took its revenge upon them. To the first awareness of self they sacrificed the holiest and most beautiful things in the world in astounding denial, and they were the first to acknowledge anew through deeds and to proclaim the sacredness of Nature, the infinitude of Art, the ineluctability of knowledge, respect for the secular, and the omnipresence of the genuinely historical; and they were the first to put an end to a higher, more universal, and more terrible dominion of ghosts than they themselves had thought.

Only through more exact knowledge of religion will the dread begotten of religious sleep, those dreams and deliria of the sacred organ, be better judged, and only then will the importance of that gift be properly appreciated. Where no gods are, ghosts prevail, and the actual development time of European ghosts—and this fairly completely accounts for their forms—was the period of transition from Greek doctrines of gods into Christianity. Come, therefore, you Lovers of Mankind and encyclopedists, into the pacific lodge and receive the fraternal kiss, cast off the grey net, and with youthful love behold the wondrous splendor of Nature, of History, and of Mankind. I shall lead you to a brother, and he shall speak with you so that your hearts shall leap up, and so that you shall clothe your dead, beloved intuition with a new body, and so that you shall embrace again and recognize what hovered before you and what the sluggish earthly intelligence could not grasp for you.

97

This brother is the heartbeat of the new era. Whoever has felt it no longer doubts of the era's coming, and with sweet pride in his contemporaneity steps forth even from among the multitude to the new band of disciples. He has made a new veil for the Holy One, which, clinging, betrays the heavenly mold of her limbs and yet conceals her more decorously than any other. The veil is to the virgin what the mind is to the body, its indispensable organ, whose folds are the letters of her sweet annunciation. The infinite play of the folds is a cipher-music, for speech is too wooden and too insolent for the virgin: her lips open only for song. To me it is nothing less than the solemn call to a new primeval assembly, the mighty wing-stroke of a passing angelic herald. These are the first pangs: let everyone prepare for delivery in birth!

The highest development in natural philosophy is now at hand and we can the more easily now survey the learned guild. The indigence of the external sciences had become the more evident in recent times the more familiar we became with them. Nature began to look ever more indigent, and, accustomed to the brilliance of our discoveries, we saw more plainly that it was only a borrowed light and that with known instruments and by known methods we would not find and construe the essential thing we sought. Each investigator had to confess that one branch of knowledge was nothing without the others, and thus there arose attempts at mystification in the branches of knowledge; the wayward soul of philosophy, demonstrated as a mere scientific element, fell into place in a symmetrical basic figure of the sciences. Others brought the concrete sciences into new circumstances, promoted a lively interchange among them, and tried to set clear their natural historical classification. And so it continues, and it is easy to estimate how favorable must be this association with both the external and internal worlds, with the higher cultivation of the intellect, with the knowledge of the former and the stimulation and culture of the latter, and how under these circumstances the weather must clear and the old heaven must again come into view, and with it the yearning for it, the living astronomy.

Now let us turn to the political spectacle of our time. The old world and the new world are engaged in battle. The defectiveness and shortcomings of the organization of states up to now have become apparent in dreadful phenomena. What if here, too, as in the branches of knowledge, closer and more multiple connections and contacts of European states were the primary historical goal of war? What if a new stirring of hitherto slumbering Europe were to come into play? What if Europe were to reawaken and a state of states, a political theory of knowledge, were to confront us! Might perhaps hierarchy, that symmetrical basic figure of states, be the principle of unification of states, as the intellectual concept of the political ego? It is impossible for secular forces to put themselves into equilibrium; only a third element, which is at once secular and superworldly, can solve that problem. Between the conflicting powers themselves no peace can be established. All peace is mere illusion, mere truce. From the standpoint of cabinets or the common consciousness, no unification is conceivable. Both parties have great and urgent claims and must make them, driven as they are by the spirit of the world and of mankind. Both are indestructible powers in the heart of man: on the one side reverence for antiquity, dependence upon historical system, love for the monuments of ancestors and of the ancient and glorious family of the state, and joy in obedience; on the other side delightsome sensation of freedom, unlimited expectation of tremendous provinces of activity, pleasure in things new and young, effortless contact with all members of the state, pride in the universal validity of man, joy in one's personal rights and in the property of the whole, and the powerful feeling of citizenship. Let neither of these two hope to destroy the other. All conquests are meaningless here, for the inner capital of every kingdom lies not behind earthwalls and is not to be taken by siege.

Who knows whether there has been enough of war? But it will never come to an end unless someone grasps the palm branch, which a spiritual power alone can proffer. Blood will wash over Europe until the nations perceive the fearful madness which is driving them about in a circle; until, arrested by holy music and soothed, they approach former alters in multi-hued fusion and undertake works of peace; until a great feast of love is celebrated as a festival of peace amid hot tears upon smoking battlefields. Only religion can waken Europe again, and reassure the peoples, and install Christendom with new splendor visibly on earth in its old peace-establishing office.

Do nations have about them everything of the human being—except his heart?—except his holy organ? Will they not become friends, as men do, beside the coffins of their loves? Will they not forget all that is hostile when heavenly compassion speaks to them?—and one misfortune, one sorrow, one emotion has filled their eyes with tears? Will sacrifice and surrender not seize them with irresistible force? And will they not yearn to be friends and allies?

Where is that old, dear faith, which alone can render blessed, in God's government on earth? Where is that heavenly trust of humans in one another, that sweet piety amid the outpouring of a God-inspired heart, that all-embracing spirit of Christendom?

Christianity is of a threefold form. One is the creative element of religion, the joy in all religion. One is intercession in and of itself, faith in the universal capacity of all earthly things to be the bread and wine of eternal life. One is faith in Christ, His Mother, and the Saints. Choose which one you will. Choose all three, it makes no difference. You will thereby become Christians and members of a single, eternal, ineffable community.

Applied, vitalized Christianity was the old Catholic faith, the last of these forms. Its omnipresence in life, its love of art, its profound humanity, the inviolability of its marriages, its communicativeness benevolent to man, its joy in poverty, obedience, and loyalty, render it unmistakable as genuine religion and comprise the basic features of its system.

It had been purified in the river of eras. In intimate and indissoluble combination with the other two forms of Christianity it will ever make fortunate this earth. Its accidental form is as good as annihilated.

The old Papacy lies in its grave and Rome for the second time has become a ruin. Shall Protestantism not cease at last and make way for a new, enduring Church? The other continents await Europe's reconciliation and resurrection in order to join with it and become fellow-citizens of the heavenly kingdom. Should there not be presently once again in Europe a host of truly holy spirits? Should not all those truly related in religion become full of yearning to behold heaven on earth? And should they not gladly join together and begin songs of holy choirs?

Christendom must come alive again and be effective, and, without regard to national boundaries, again form a visible Church which will take into its bosom all souls athirst for the supernatural, and willingly become the mediatrix between the old world and the new.

It must once again pour out the cornucopia of blessing over peoples. From the holy womb of a venerable European Council shall Christendom arise, and the task of awakening will be prosecuted according to a comprehensive divine plan. Then no one will protest any longer against Christian and secular compulsion, for the essence of the Church will be true freedom, and all necessary reforms will be carried out under its guidance as a peaceful and formal state process.

When and when sooner? The question is not to be asked. Patience only! It will, it must come, that sacred time of endless peace when the new Jerusalem will be the capital of the world. Until then be cheerful and courageous amid the dangers of the time. Partakers of my faith, proclaim with word and deed the divine Gospel, and to the veritable and everlasting Faith remain true unto death.

Rudolf Steiner

from *Cosmic and Human Metamorphoses*

Now, what was above all demanded of these priests It was necessary in a certain sense that they should know that if they made themselves acquainted with what streamed down from the universe for the fructification of earth life, and especially if they used it in their social knowledge, they must be capable, having thereby become much cleverer, of establishing the principal laws and other rules for government during the coming year.

It would at one time have been impossible to establish laws or social ordinances, without first seeking guidance from those who were able to receive the secrets of the Macrocosm. Later ages have retained dim and dubious echoes of this greatness in their superstitious fancies. When on New Year's Eve people pour melted lead into water to learn the future of the coming year, that is but the superstitious remains of that great matter of which I have described. Therein the endeavor was made so to fructify the spirit of man that he might carry over into the earth what could only spring from the universe; for it was desired that man should so live on the earth that his life should not merely consist of what can be experienced here, but also of what can be drawn from the universe. In the same way, it was known that during the summer time of the earth we are in a quite different relation to the universe, and that during that season the earth cannot receive any intimate communications from thence. The summer mysteries were based upon this knowledge, and were intended for a quite different purpose, which I need not go into today.

Now, as I have said, even less has come down to us in tradition concerning the secrets of the course of the year, than of those things relating to the rhythm between day and night, and between sleeping and waking. But in those olden times, when man still had a high degree of atavistic clairvoyance, through which he was able to experience in the course of the year the intimate relations between the universe and the earth, he was still conscious that what he thus experienced came from that meeting with the Spiritual world, which he cannot now have every time he sleeps. It came from the meeting with the Spiritual world in which dwell those Spiritual beings we reckon as belonging to the world of the Archangels—where man will some day dwell with his innermost being, after he has developed his Life Spirit, during the Venus period. That is the world in which we must think of Christ, the Son, as the directing and guiding principle. (Man had this meeting in all ages, of course, but it was formerly perceived by means of atavistic clairvoyance.) We have, therefore, called this meeting, which in the course of the year man has in any part of the earth where he makes Christmas in his winter: the meeting with the Son. Thus in the course of a year, a man really goes through a rhythm which imitates that of the seasons of the year, in which he has a meeting and a union with the world of the Son.

Now we know that through the Mystery of Golgotha, that Being whom we designate as the Christ has united Himself with the course of the Earth. At the very time this union took place, the direct vision into the Spiritual world had become blurred, as I have just explained.

We see the objective fact: that the Event of Golgotha is directly connected with the alteration in the evolution of mankind on the earth itself. Yet we may say that there were times in the earth's development when, in the sense of the old atavistic clairvoyance, man entered into relation with Christ, through becoming aware of the intimate duologue held between the earth and the Macrocosm. Upon this rests the belief held by certain modern learned men, students of religion, with some justification:—the belief that an original primal revelation had once been given to the earth. It came about in the manner described. It was an old primeval revelation. All the different religions on the face of the earth are fragments of that original revelation, fragments fallen into decadence. In what position then are those who accepted the Mystery of Golgotha? They are able to express an intense inner recognition of the Spiritual content of the universe, by saying: That which in olden times could only be perceived through the duologue of the earth with the cosmos, has now descended; it dwelt within a human being, it appeared in the Man, Jesus of Nazareth, in the course of the Mystery of Golgotha. Recognition of the Christ who dwelt in Jesus of Nazareth, recognition of that Being who was formerly perceptible to the atavistic clairvoyance of man at certain seasons of the year, must be increasingly emphasized as necessary for the Spiritual development of humanity. For the two elements of Christianity will be then united as they really should and must be, if on the one hand Christianity, and on the other humanity, are each to develop further in the right way. The fact that in the old Christian traditions the Legend of Christ Jesus was part of the yearly celebration of the Christmas, Easter, and Whitsuntide Festivals, is connected with this; and, as I stated in a former lecture, the fact that the Festival of Christmas is kept at a fixed date, while Easter is regulated according to the heavenly constellations, is also connected with this. Christmas is celebrated in accordance with the earth conditions, it is kept in what is always the very depth of winter and this hangs together with the meeting with Christ, with the Son, which meeting really takes place at that season. Christ, however, is a being belonging to the Macrocosm. He descended from thence, yet is One with it; and this is expressed in the fixing of Easter by the heavens in spring, according to the constellations of sun and moon—for the Easter Festival is intended to show that Christ belongs to the whole universe, just as Christmas should point to the descent of Christ to the earth. So it was right that what belongs to the seasons of the year through their rhythm in human life, should be inserted into the course of the year as has been done. For this is so profound a thing, as regards the inner being of man, that it is really right that these Festivals relating to the Mystery of Golgotha, should continue to be held in harmony with the rhythm of the great universe, and not be subject to the alteration which in modern cities has taken place in the hours of sleeping and waking.

Now, among the things that are perhaps the most found fault with in spiritual science by certain religious sects, is, that according to spiritual science the Christ impulse must once again be bound up with the whole universe. I have often emphatically stated that spiritual science takes nothing away from the traditions of religion with respect to the mystery of Christ Jesus; but rather adds to them the connection that surrounds that mystery extending, as it does, from the earth to the whole universe. Spiritual science does not seek Christ on the earth alone, but in the whole universe. Here we have something in which man should not as yet exercise his freewill, something in which each year the consciousness should come to him, that, though he can no longer come into touch with the great universe through atavistic clairvoyance, there is still something living within him which belongs to the universe and expresses itself in the course of the year.

It is indeed not easy to understand why certain religious confessions so strongly condemn this connecting of the Christ impulse with cosmic events. This attitude would be comprehensible if spiritual science wished to do away with the traditions of Christianity; but it only adds to them, which should be no reason for censure, but so it is; and the reason is that people do not wish anything to be added to certain traditions.

There is, however, something very serious behind all this, something of very great importance to our age. I have often drawn your attention to the fact, which is also mentioned in the first of my Mystery Plays,[4]

4. Steiner wrote four so-called "Mystery Dramas" between 1910 and 1913. They are highly esoteric affairs concerned with themes of reincarnation and karma and are still tinged with ideas common to Blavatskian Theosophy, though transformed through Steiner's unique genius. Rarely performed, even by Anthroposophists, the plays are certainly an acquired taste. An English translation is available under the title *Four Mystery Dramas*, trans. Ruth Pusch and Hans Pusch (1972; reprt., Great Barrington, MA: Steiner Books, 2007).

that we are approaching a time in which we can speak of a Spiritual return of Christ. I need not go more fully into this today, it is well known to all our friends. This Christ Event will, however, not merely be an event satisfying the transcendental curiosity of man, but it will above all bring to their minds a demand for a new understanding of the Christ impulse. Certain basic words of the Christian faith, which ought to surge through the whole world as holy impulses—at any rate through the world of those who wish to take up the Christ impulse—are not understood deeply enough. I will now only call to your remembrance the significant and incisive words: "My kingdom is not of this world." These words will take on a new meaning when Christ appears in a world that is truly not of this world, not of the world of sense. It must be a profound attribute of the Christian concept of the world to cultivate an understanding of other human views and concepts, with the sole exception of rough and crude materialism. Once we know that all the religions on the earth are the remnants of ancient vision, it will then only be a question of taking seriously enough what was thus perceived; for later on, because mankind was no longer organized for vision, the results of the former vision only filtered through in fragmentary form into the different religious creeds. This can once again be recognized through Christianity. Through Christianity a profound understanding can be gained, not only of the great religions, but of every form of religious creed on the earth. It is certainly easy to say this; though at the same time very difficult to make men really adopt these views. Yet they must become part of their convictions, all the wide world over. For Christianity, in so far as it has spread over the earth up to the present time, is but one religion among many, one creed among a number of others. That is not the purpose for which it was founded; it was founded that it might spread understanding over the whole earth. Christ did not suffer death for a limited number of people, nor was He born for a few; but for all. In a certain sense there is a contradiction between the requirement that Christianity should be for all men and the fact that it has become one of many creeds. It is not intended to be a separate creed, and it can only be that, because it is not understood in its full and deep meaning. To grasp this deep meaning a cosmic understanding is necessary.

One is compelled today to wrestle for words wherewith to express certain truths, which are now so far removed from man that we lack the words to express them. One is often obliged to express the great truths by means of comparisons. You will recollect that I have often said that Christ may be called the Sun Spirit. From what I have said today about the yearly course of the sun, you will see that there is some justification for calling Him the Sun Spirit. But we can form no idea of this, we cannot picture it, unless we keep the cosmic relation of Christ in view, unless we consider the Mystery of Golgotha as a real Christ Mystery, as something that certainly took place on this earth, and yet is of significance for the whole universe and took place for the whole universe.

Now, men are in conflict with one another about many things on the earth, and they are at variance on many questions; they are at variance in their religious beliefs, and believe themselves to be at variance as regards their nationality and many other things. This lack of unity brings about times such as those in which we are living now. Men are not of one mind even with regard to the Mystery of Golgotha. For no Chinese person or Indian will straightway accept what a European missionary says about the Mystery of Golgotha. To those who look at things as they are, this fact is not without significance. There is, however, one thing concerning which men are still of one mind. It seems hardly credible, but it is a commonplace truth and one we cannot help admitting, that when we reflect how people live together on the earth, we cannot help wondering that there should be anything left upon which they are not at variance; yet there still are things about which people are of one mind, and one such example is the view people hold about the sun. The Japanese, Chinese, and even the English and Americans, do not believe that one sun rises and sets for them and another for the Germans. They still believe in the sun being the common property of all; indeed they still believe that what is extraterrestrial is the common property of all. They do not even dispute that, they do not go to war about these things. And that can be taken as a sort of comparison. As has been said, these things can only be expressed by comparisons. When once people realize the connection of Christ with these things that men do not dispute, they will not dispute about Him, but will learn to see Him in the Kingdom which is not of this world, but which belongs to Him. But until men recognize the cosmic significance of Christ, they will not be of one mind with respect to the things concerning which unity should prevail. For we shall then be able to speak of Christ to the Jews, to the Chinese, to the Japanese, and to the Indians—just as we speak to Christian Europeans. This will open up an immensely significant perspective for the further development of Christianity on the earth, as well as for the development of mankind on the earth. For ways must be found of arousing in the souls of men, sentiments that all people shall be able to understand equally.

That will be one thing demanded of us in the time that shall bring the return, the Spiritual return, of the Christ. Especially with respect to the words: "My Kingdom is not of this world," a deeper understanding will come about in that time; a deeper understanding of the fact that there is in the human being not only what pertains to the earth, but something supra-earthly, which lives in the annual course of the sun. We must grow to feel that as in the individual human life the soul rules the body, so in everything that goes on outside, in the rising and setting stars, in the bright sunlight, and fading twilight, there dwells something Spiritual; and just as we belong to the air with our lungs, so do we belong to the Spiritual part of the universe with our souls. We do not belong to the abstract Spiritual life of an outgrown Pantheism, but to that concrete Spirituality which lives in each individual being. Thus we shall find that there is something Spiritual which belongs to the human soul, which indeed is the human soul; and that this is in inner connection with what lives in the course of the year as does the breath in a man; and that the course of the year with its secrets belongs to the Christ Being, who went through the Mystery of Golgotha. We must soar high enough to be able to connect what took place historically on the earth in the Mystery of Golgotha, with the great secrets of the world—with the Macrocosmic secrets. From such an understanding will precede something extremely important: knowledge of the social needs of man. A great deal of social science is practiced in our day, and all sorts of social ideals mooted. Certainly nothing can be said against that, but all these things will have to be fructified by that which will spring up in man, through realizing the course of the year as a Spiritual impulse. For only by vividly experiencing each year the image of the Mystery of Golgotha, parallel with the course of the year, can we become inspired with real social knowledge and feeling.

What I am now saying must certainly seem absolutely strange to people of the present day, yet it is true. When the year's course is again generally felt by humanity as in inner connection with the Mystery of Golgotha, then, by attuning the feelings of the soul with both the course of the year and the secret of the Mystery of Golgotha, a true social ruling will be the true solution, or at any rate the true continuation of what is today so foolishly called (in reference to what is really in view) the social question. Precisely through spiritual science people will have to acquire knowledge of the connections of man with the universe. This will certainly lead them to see more in this universe than does the materialism of today.

William Butler Yeats

The Body of the Father Christian Rosencrux

The followers of the Father Christian Rosencrux, says the old tradition, wrapped his imperishable body in noble raiment and laid it under the house of their order, in a tomb containing the symbols of all things in heaven and earth, and in the waters under the earth, and set about him inextinguishable magical lamps, which burnt on generation after generation, until other students of the order came upon the tomb by chance. It seems to me that the imagination has had no very different history during the last two hundred years, but has been laid in a great tomb of criticism, and had set over it inextinguishable magical lamps of wisdom and romance, and has been altogether so nobly housed and apparelled that we have forgotten that its wizard lips are closed, or but opened for the complaining of some melancholy and ghostly voice. The ancients and the Elizabethans abandoned themselves to imagination as a woman abandons herself to love, and created great beings who made the people of this world seem but shadows, and great passions which made our loves and hatreds appear but ephemeral and trivial phantasies; but now it is not the great persons, or the great passions we imagine, which absorb us, for the persons and passions in our poems are mainly reflections our mirror has caught from older poems or from the life about us, but the wise comments we make upon them, the criticism of life we wring from their fortunes. Arthur and his Court are nothing, but the many-coloured lights that play about them are as beautiful as the lights from cathedral windows; Pompilia and Guido are but little, while the ever-recurring meditations and expositions which climax in the mouth of the Pope are among the wisest of the Christian age. I cannot get it out of my mind that this age of criticism is about to pass, and an age of imagination, of emotion, of moods, of revelation, about to come in its place; for certainly belief in a supersensual world is at hand again; and when the notion that we are "phantoms of the earth and water" has gone down the wind, we will trust our own being and all it desires to invent; and when the external world is no more the standard of reality, we will learn again that the great Passions are angels of God, and that to embody them "uncurbed in their eternal glory," even in their labour for the ending of man's peace and prosperity, is more than to comment, however wisely, upon the tendencies of our time, or to express the socialistic, or humanitarian, or other forces of our time, or even "to sum up" our time, as the phrase is; for Art is a revelation, and not a criticism, and the life of the artist is in the old saying, "The wind bloweth where it listeth, and thou hearest the sound thereof, but canst not tell whence it cometh and whither it goeth; so is every one that is born of the spirit."[5]

5. John 3:8.

Russian Sophiology

AFTER OVER two hundred years at the theological margins, sophiology entered the consciousness of the religious mainstream in the late nineteenth century through the writing of the man who has been called Russia's greatest philosopher: the thinker, mystic, and poet Vladimir Solovyov. Solovyov brought Sophia and the problems of sophiology into the Church and compelled theologians in Russia and Orthodoxy to take seriously the problematics of the Wisdom of God, eventually influencing even a number of Catholic theologians. He established a genuine sophiology in the Orthodox Church and paved the way for a number of thinkers, theologians, and poets who found his work a source of inspiration and sustenance. Though the thoughts of the Russian sophiologists are often called into question, they cannot be ignored.

Vladimir Solovyov (1853–1900)
Born in Moscow, Solovyov's entrance into sophiological history is inextricable from a series of religious experiences he had, the first of which occurred on the Feast of the Ascension, May 1862, when he was nine years old.[1] Later, as a young scholar, Solovyov undertook a trip to London to make use of manuscripts concerning Gnosticism and kabbalah in the British Museum and experienced a second vision of one whom he called his "Eternal Friend" and who instructed him to meet her in Egypt. Solovyov boarded a ship for Cairo and met her once more in the desert. He recorded these experiences with her in his autobiographical poem, "Three Meetings" (included in Part II of this volume), though he never describes her by name: "eternal beloved, I will not name you, / But my tremulous song will reach your ears." However, Solovyov, a formidable thinker, is not easily discounted as a garden-variety mystical

---

1. The story of Solovyov's visions of his Eternal Friend is oft repeated. See the account of his nephew, Fr. Sergey M. Solovyov, *Vladimir Solovyov: His Life and Creative Evolution,* trans. Aleksey Gibson (Fairfax, VA: Eastern Christian Publications, 2000), 35–36 and 129–36; Paul M. Allen, *Vladimir Soloviev: Russian Mystic* (Blauvelt, NY: Steiner, 1978), 23–28 and 109–19.

drunkard. Indeed, it is not without reason that some have read him as a sort of split personality, "critical analyst by day, visionary poet by night."[2] He was a one-man Russian theological revolution.

Because his thought sweeps across realms of logic and intuition, his conceptual framework—particularly when speaking of Sophia—can be notoriously fluid. In *Russia and the Universal Church* (excerpted here), Solovyov calls Sophia "the guardian angel of the world" and the agent of "pan-unity," another of Solovyov's key philosophical/theological insights.[3] Furthermore, he connects Sophia to Christ, the Virgin Mary, and to the Church. His language is startling, as if words alone cannot contain the concept.

Pavel Florensky (1882–1937)

Pavel Florensky is one of the most impressive figures in Russia's intellectual history.[4] A priest and theologian of the Russian Orthodox Church, Florensky was also a gifted mathematician, scientist, and electrical engineer, and he also made an impact in the disciplines of art history and linguistics. For good reason, he has been called "the Russian Da Vinci." So valuable were Florensky's formidable talents to the Bolsheviks that, though a priest who always wore a cassock, he was not forced to leave Russia in 1922 following the banishment of so many like-minded intelligentsia, but was invited (read: ordered) to stay in order to help design and implement Russia's electrical grid.[5] Eventually his priestly vocation became a hindrance to his work for the government and he was sent to a Siberian gulag in 1933. He was eventually martyred on 8 December 1937.[6]

---

2. George M. Young, *The Russian Cosmists: The Esoteric Futurism of Nikolai Federov and His Followers* (Oxford and New York: Oxford University Press, 2012), 96.

3. Vladimir Solovyev, *Russia and the Universal Church*, trans. Herbert Rees (London: Geoffrey Bles, 1948), 167. Florensky, for one, even though he follows Solovyov in many regards, criticized this concept of Solovyov's as a badly veiled pantheism. On this point, he writes, "Our entire work, in its antinomian spirit opposes Solovyov's conciliatory philosophy." See *Pillar and Ground of the Truth: An Essay in Orthodox Theodicy in Twelve Letters*, trans. Boris Jakim (Princeton: Princeton University Press, 1997), 433. It may be that, like Bulgakov following his own ordination, Florensky was anxious to prove his doctrinal orthodoxy by distancing himself from Solovyov in a rather Oedipal gesture.

4. The best biography of Florensky available in English to date is that of Fr. Robert Slesinksi, *Pavel Florensky: A Metaphysics of Love* (Crestwood, NY: St. Vladimir's Seminary Press, 1984). Also available, interesting but suffering from some serious critical bias, is Avril Pyman's *Pavel Florensky: A Quiet Genius: The Tragic and Extraordinary Life of Russia's Unknown Da Vinci* (New York: Continuum, 2010).

5. Robert Slesinksi, *Pavel Florensky*, 34.

6. Loren Graham and Jean-Michel Kantor, *Naming Infinity: A True Story of Religious Mysticism and Mathematical Creativity* (Cambridge: Harvard University Press, 2009), 143–5.

In 1914, Florensky published *The Pillar and Ground of Truth*, a revised and greatly expanded version of his Master's thesis. It is an extraordinary work and has rightly been called "one of the most unusual books" of the 20th century.[7] It is one of the most curious works extant in the literature of Orthodoxy. Written as a series of letters addressed to "My meek, my radiant friend!," the book is by turns mystical treatise, theological meditation, and emblem book. The effect of Florensky's fluid rhetorical and epistemological commitments is pleasantly destabilizing. He deconstructs the reader's reliance on conventional forms of religious discourse, preferring instead to have his text inhabit a metaxological space between theology, poetry, Church history, and aesthetics, between the exoteric and the esoteric, between objectivity and subjectivity.

The section from *The Pillar and Ground of the Truth* excerpted here comes from Florensky's "Letter Ten: Sophia" and in it he explains Sophia's ontology as well as her relationship to the Trinity.

Sergius Bulgakov (1871–1944)

The Orthodox priest, philosopher, and theologian Sergius Bulgakov created what is to date the most fully realized sophiology of the modern era. He was the first to present a systematics of Sophia and has rightly been called "one of the . . . truly great theologians of the twentieth century."[8] Bulgakov's sophiology in many respects intersects with those of Solovyov and Florensky, and like them he reads sophianicity in the integral wholeness of creation, identifies Sophia as the *ousia* of the Trinity and a kind of fourth hypostasis, and interprets the Virgin as the exemplar of both Sophia and sophianicity. Bulgakov emphasizes the two aspects of Sophia, as simultaneously created and divine, and he also entertains the notion of Sophia as "world soul." Furthermore, for Bulgakov, because the world's relationship to God is structured sophiologically, the Church itself "is the Divine Sophia and the creaturely Sophia united."[9]

The selection from Bulgakov included here comes from his important text known in English as *Sophia, the Wisdom of God: An Outline of*

---

7. Boris Jakim, Translator's Preface and Acknowledgements to Pavel Florensky, *The Pillar and Ground of Truth: An Essay in Orthodox Theodicy in Twelve Letters* (Princeton: Princeton University Press, 1997), vii.

8. John Milbank, *The Suspended Middle: Henri de Lubac and the Debate concerning the Supernatural* (Grand Rapids, MI and Cambridge, UK: William B. Eerdmans Publishing Company, 2005), 104.

9. Sergius Bulgakov, *The Bride of the Lamb*, trans. Boris Jakim (Grand Rapids, MI: William B. Eerdmans Publishing Company, 2001), 271.

Sophiology, his apologia. In it he explains the relationship between the created and uncreated, the earthly and the heavenly aspects of Sophia.

Nikolai Berdyaev (1874–1948)

Nikolai Berdyaev was one of the most original and creative religious philosophers of the twentieth century. A close friend of Bulgakov, like his priestly friend he also traveled the pathways through atheism, Marxism, and finally to an impassioned and highly original religious faith that ultimately led, as it did Bulgakov, to exile in Paris. Deeply influenced by Solovyov—and even more so by Boehme—Berdyaev made significant contributions to what became known as *religious existentialism* in the mid-twentieth century. His thought is visionary in both its audaciousness and its eschatological scope. The Church, for Berdyaev, is nothing if not a cosmological reality.

In the selection from his *Slavery and Freedom* (1936) included here, Berdyaev's debt to Boehme is very clear—but so is his engagement with the Fathers and with ecclesiastical history. Berdyaev here gives evidence of a thoroughly mystical philosophy as well as a complementary philosophical mysticism. His project, like that of his mentor Solovyov, is nothing less than the regeneration of Christian culture.

Vladimir Solovyov

from *Russia and the Universal Church*

The Threefold Incarnation of the Divine Wisdom

Et formavit Futurus Deorum hominem—pulvis (sic) *ex humo—vajitser Jahveh Elohim eth haadam haphar min haadamah*: If the earth in general signifies the soul of the lower world, the dust of the earth indicates the state of abasement or helplessness of this soul when it ceases to assert and exalt itself in the blind desire of an anarchic existence, when repelling all lower suggestions and abandoning in perfect humility all resistance or antagonism to the heavenly Word, it becomes capable of understanding its truth, of uniting itself to its activity and of establishing in itself the Kingdom of God. This state of humiliation, this absolute receptivity of earthly Nature, is objectively marked by the creation of Man (*humus—humilis—homo*); the sensitive and imaginative soul of the physical world becomes the rational soul of humanity. Having attained an interior union with the heavens, contemplating the intelligible light, it can include by consciousness and reason all that exists in an ideal unity. Ideally a universal being in his rational potentiality as the image of God, Man must become effectively like God by the active realization of his unity in the fullness of Creation. Child of the Earth by the lower life which it gives him, he must give it back transformed into light and lifegiving spirit. If through him, through his reason, Earth is raised to Heaven, through him also, through his activity, the heavens must descend and fill the Earth; through him all the world outside the Godhead must become a single living body, the complete incarnation of the divine Wisdom.

In man alone the creature is perfectly, that is, freely and reciprocally, united to God, because, thanks to his two-fold nature, man alone can preserve his freedom and remain continually the moral complement of God, while achieving an ever completer union with Him by a continuous series of conscious efforts and deliberate actions. There is a marvellous dialectic in the law of life of the two worlds. The very supernatural perfection of the freedom enjoyed by a pure spirit, the absence of all external limitation, means that this freedom, manifesting itself completely, is exhausted in a single act; and the spiritual being loses its freedom by reason of the very excess of freedom. On the other hand, the hindrances and obstacles presented by the external medium of the natural world to the realization of our interior acts, the limited and conditional character of human freedom, make man freer than the angels in that he is allowed to retain his freewill and exercise it continually, and to remain, even after the Fall, an active co-operator in the divine work. It is for this reason that eternal Wisdom does not find her delight in the angels, but in the sons of Man.

Man exists primarily for the interior and ideal union of earthly potentiality and divine act, of the Soul and the Word, and secondarily for the free realization of this union in the totality of the world outside the Godhead. There is, therefore, in this composite being a center and a circumference, the human personality and the human world, the individual man and the social or collective man. The human individual, being in himself or subjectively the union of the divine Word and earthly nature, must begin to realize this union objectively or for himself by an external reduplication of himself. In order really to know himself in his unity, man must distinguish himself as knowing or active subject (man in the proper sense) from himself as known or passive object (woman). Thus the contrast and union of the divine Word and earthly nature is reproduced for man himself in the distinction and union between the sexes.

The essence or nature of man is completely represented by individual man (in the two sexes); his social existence can add nothing to it; but it is absolutely necessary for the extension and development of human existence, and for the actual realization of all that is potentially contained in the human individual. It is only through society that man can attain his final end, the universal integration of all existence outside the Godhead. But natural humanity (Man, Woman, and Society), as it emerges from the cosmic process, contains within itself only the possibility of such integration. The reason and consciousness of man, the affections and instinct of woman, and finally the law of solidarity or altruism which forms the basis of all society, these are but a foreshadowing of the true divine-human unity, a seed which has yet to sprout, blossom and bear its fruit. The gradual growth of this seed is accomplished in the process of universal history; and the threefold fruit which it bears is: perfect Woman, or nature made divine, perfect Man or the God-Man, and the perfect Society of God with men—the final incarnation of the eternal Wisdom.

The essential unity of the human being in Man, Woman and Society, determines the indivisible unity of the divine incarnation in humanity. Man properly so-called (the masculine individual) contains already in himself *in potentia* the whole essence of man; it is only in order to realize that essence in actuality that he must, first, reduplicate himself or render his material side objective in the personality of Woman, and secondly, multiply himself or render objective the universality of his rational being in a plurality of individual existences, organically bound together and forming a corporate whole—human Society. Woman being only the complement of Man, and Society only his extension or total manifestation, there is fundamentally only one human being. And its reunion with God, though necessarily threefold, nevertheless constitutes only a single divine-human being, the incarnate Σοφία, whose central and completely personal manifestation is Jesus Christ, whose feminine complement is the Blessed Virgin, and whose universal extension is the Church. The Blessed Virgin is united to God by a purely receptive and passive union; she brought forth the second Adam, as the Earth brought forth the first, by abasing herself in perfect humility; there is therefore here, properly speaking, no reciprocity or co-operation. And as for the Church, she is not united to God directly, but through the incarnation of Christ of which she is the continuation. It is then Christ alone Who is truly the God-Man, the Man Who is directly and reciprocally (that is, actively) united to God.

It was in the contemplation in His eternal thought of the Blessed Virgin, of Christ and of the Church that God gave His absolute approval to the whole Creation when He pronounced it to be *tob meod, valde bona*. There was the proper subject for the great joy which the divine Wisdom experienced at the thought of the sons of Man; she saw there the one pure and immaculate daughter of Adam, she saw there the Son of Man *par excellence*, the Righteous One, and lastly she saw there the multitude of mankind made one under the form of a unique Society founded upon love and truth. She contemplated under this form her future incarnation and, in the children of Adam, her own children; and she rejoiced in seeing that they justified the scheme of Creation which she offered to God: *et justificata est Sapientia a filiis suis* (Matt. xi. 19).

Mankind reunited to God in the Blessed Virgin, in Christ and in the Church is the realization of the essential Wisdom or absolute substance of God, its created form or incarnation. In truth, it is one and the same substantial form (designated by the Bible as *semen mulieris, scilicet Sophiae*) which realizes itself in three successive and permanent manifestations, distinct in existence but indivisible in essence, assuming the name of Mary in its feminine personality, of Jesus in its masculine personality, and reserving its proper name for its complete and universal appearance in the perfect Church of the future, the Spouse and Bride of the divine Word.

This threefold realization in mankind of the essential Wisdom is a religious truth which Orthodox Christendom professes in its doctrine and displays in its worship. If, by the substantial Wisdom of God, we were to understand only the Person of Jesus Christ, how could all the texts of the Wisdom Books which speak of this Wisdom be applied to the Blessed Virgin? Moreover, this application, which has been made from the earliest times in the Offices of the Latin Church as well as of the Greek Church, has in our own days received doctrinal sanction in the Bull of Pius IX on the Immaculate Conception of the Most Holy Virgin. On the other hand, there are texts of Scripture which Orthodox and Catholic doctors apply sometimes to the Blessed Virgin, sometimes to the Church; for instance, the passage in the Apocalypse concerning the Woman clothed with the sun, crowned with the stars, and with the moon beneath her feet. Finally, there can be no doubt as to the close link and complete analogy between the individual humanity of Christ and His social humanity, between His natural Body and His mystical Body. In the sacrament of Communion the personal Body of the Lord becomes in a mystical but real manner the unifying principle of His collective Body, the community of the faithful. Thus the Church, human Society made divine, possesses fundamentally the same substance as the incarnate Person of Christ or His individual Humanity; and since this latter has no other origin or substance than the human nature of the Blessed Virgin, the Mother of God, it follows that the organism of the divine-human incarnation, having in Jesus Christ a single active and personal center, possesses also in its threefold manifestation one single substantial basis, namely, the corporal nature of the divine Wisdom, as both latent and revealed in the lower world; it is the soul of the world completely converted, purified and identified with Wisdom itself, as matter identifies itself with form in a single concrete and living being. And the perfect realization of this divine-material substance, this *semen mulieris*, is glorified and resurrected Humanity, the Temple, Body and Spouse of God.

The truth of Christianity, under this positive aspect—the complete and concrete incarnation of Godhead—has particularly attracted the religious soul of the Russian people from the earliest times of their conversion to Christianity. In dedicating their most ancient churches to St. Sophia, the substantial Wisdom of God, they have given to this idea a new expression unknown to the Greeks (who identified Σοφία with the Λογός). While closely linking the Holy Wisdom with the Mother of God and with Jesus Christ, the religious art of our ancestors distinguished it clearly from both and represented it under the form of a distinct divine being. It was for them the heavenly essence clad in the appearance of the lower world, the luminous spirit of regenerate humanity, the Guardian Angel of the Earth, the final appearance of the Godhead for which they waited.

Thus, side by side with the individual human form of the Divine— the Virgin-Mother and the Son of God—the Russian people have known and loved, under the name of St. Sophia, the social incarnation of the Godhead in the Universal Church. It is this idea, revealed to the religious consciousness of our ancestors, this truly national and yet absolutely universal notion, that we must now expound in reasoned terms. It is for us to formulate the living Word which old Russia conceived and which new Russia must declare to the world.

Pavel Florensky

from *The Pillar and Ground of the Truth: An Essay in Orthodox Theodicy in Twelve Letters*

from "Letter Ten: Sophia"

Sophia is the Great Root of the whole creation (cf. *pasa hē ktisis* [Rom. 8:22]). That is, Sophia is all-integral creation and not merely *all* creation. Sophia is the Great Root by which creation goes into the intra-Trinitarian life and through which it receives Life Eternal from the One Source of Life. Sophia is the original nature of creation, God's creative love, which is "shed abroad in our hearts by the Holy Spirit which is given unto us" (Rom 5:5). For this reason, the true I of a deified person, his "heart," is precisely God's Love, just as the Essence of Divinity is intra-Trinitarian Love. For everything exists truly insofar as it communes with the God of Love, the Source of being and truth. If creation is torn away from its root, an inevitable death awaits it. Wisdom itself says: "For whoso findeth me findeth life, and shall obtain favour of the Lord. But he that sinneth against me wrongeth his own soul: all they that hate me love death" (Prov. 8:35–36).

With regard to creation, Sophia is the Guardian Angel of creation, the Ideal person of the world. The shaping reason with regard to creation, Sophia is the shaped content of God-Reason, His "psychic content," eternally created by the Father through the Son and completed in the Holy Spirit: God thinks *by things*.

Therefore, to exist is to be thought, to be remembered, or, finally, to be known by God. They whom God "knows" possess reality. They whom God does "not know" do not exist in the spiritual world, in the world of true reality, and their being is illusory. They are empty, and in the Triradiant Light it becomes clear that they do not exist at all, that they only appeared to exist. In order to exist one must "be known by God" (cf. John 10:14 and Matt. 7:23). One who exists in Eternity "knows" in Eternity, but that which he "knows" in Eternity appears in time at a single, definite moment. God, the Supratemporal, for Whom Time is given in all its moments as a single "now," does not create the world in Time. But, for the world, for creation, which lives in time, the creation of the world is necessarily linked with definite times and seasons.

The question may be asked, Why is it linked precisely with these times and seasons, and not with others? In my opinion, this question is based on a misunderstanding, namely, on the confusion of cosmic Time with time in the abstract. Cosmic Time is a succession and, as a succession, it imparts the character of successiveness to all that has succession. In other words, cosmic Time is an internal organizedness each term of which is necessarily situated where it is situated. The succession of everything else, which occurs through (mathematically speaking) its "correspondence" with this fundamental, succession-generating, "taxogenic" series, must also be organized. The correspondence between moments of Time and phenomena occurs owing to the inner kinship of each given moment of Time and each given phenomenon. The essence of a given moment also contains the fact that this moment is connected by correspondence with such-and-such and such-and-such phenomena. And once such a correspondence has been established, to ask why a phenomenon arose at some particular time and not at some other time is as meaningless as to ask why 1912 comes after 1911 and not after 1915.

But one must speak wholly differently about time in the abstractness of rationality. For rationality rips away the external form of Time from its inner anatomical structure. Rationality takes the form of succession but removes from this form the content of succession. What results is an empty, indifferent schema of succession. To be sure, in this schema one can transpose any two successive moments, yet, owing to the impersonality of these moments, what is obtained does not differ in any way from what it has been obtained from. When this essentially meaningless concept is passed off as Time, the following absurd question must certainly arise: Why did God create the world so many thousands of years ago, and not at some other time? This is the error committed by the famous Origen, among many others. God created the world for us when it was appropriate for it to be created. That is the answer to such questions. Without citing various patristic texts in support of the conception of Time expounded here (this would lead us too far afield), I will mention only the testimony of St. Gregory of Nazianzus.

Prior to the creation of the world, outside the essence of the Holy Trinity, "the World-generating Reason also considered, in His mind's great representations, the images of the world formed by Him, this world which was generated later, but, which, for God was present even then. Everything is before God's eyes: what will be, what was, and what is now. For me such a division is set by time: that one thing is ahead, another thing behind. But for God all merges into one, and all is held in the arms of the Great Deity."[10]

"Of the worlds," says the same holy father, in another place, "one was created first. This is another heaven, the habitation of the God-bearers, contemplated by reason alone, the radiant habitation. Into this habita-

---

10. Gregory of Nazianzus, *Oration 4, On the World.*

tion, the man of God will subsequently enter, when, having purified his reason and his flesh, he becomes a god. But the other world, the corruptible one, was created for mortal men, when both the splendor of the celestial lights that preach God by beauty and grandeur and the royal palace for the Image of God had to be established. But these two worlds were created by the Word of the great God."

"We," says Clement of Alexandria as well, "already existed before this world, because our creation was decided by God long before our actual creation. Before our creation we therefore existed in the thought of God, we who later turned out to be intelligent creatures of the Divine Word. Thanks to Him, we are very ancient in our origin, because 'in the beginning was the Word.'"[11]

But let us return to the question of Sophia.

She is the Eternal Bride of the Word of God. Outside of Him and independently of Him, she does not have being and falls apart into fragments of ideas about creation. But in Him she receives creative power. One in God, she is multiple in creation and is perceived in creation in her concrete appearances as *the ideal person of man*, as *his Guardian Angel*, i.e., as the spark of the eternal dignity of the person and as the image of God in man. To speak of this Divine "spark" is impossible here, for this would require us to make a survey of virtually all mystical teachings. I will limit myself to mentioning the name given to this Divine light in the Apostolic Epistles. This, for an individual man, is his "building of God, an house not made with hands, eternal in the heavens" (2 Cor. 5:1), the "house which is from heaven" (2 Cor. 5:2) in which man will be clothed when his "earthly house" is destroyed. The "earthly house" will necessarily be destroyed, not because it is on earth but because it is of earth (*epigeios*), i.e., because it is corruptible in its essence. And although that house is now "in the heavens (*en tois ouranois*)," not this is essential for it, but the fact that it is a house "from heaven (*to oiktērion hēmōn to ex ouranou*)," i.e., what is important is its nature, not its location. The earthly and heavenly houses are opposite according to their nature, not according to their location. In hell there is pure fleshiness, although hell does not have to exist on earth (indeed, the Lord's Earth will not tolerate hell on itself). In heaven, there is pure spirituality, though a saint can approach it even in life. The ideal aspect will be revealed in illuminated creation, in transfigured man. The earthly "hovel (*skēnoma*)," i.e., the corruptible empirical character, is also mentioned in the Apostle Peter (2 Pet. 1:13–14), while the opposite character, the ideal one, is called "an inheritance incorruptible, and

11. Clement of Alexandria, *Exhortation to the Greeks*.

undefiled, and that fadeth not away, reserved in heaven. . . ." (1 Pet. 1:4). These are the "everlasting habitations (*aioniai skēnai*)" (Luke 16:9) or *types of spiritual growth* about which the Lord Jesus speaks in the parable of the unjust steward.

The combination of these "many mansions," these ideal images of that which exists, makes up the true house of God (Heb. 3:6), in which man is a steward (1 Cor. 4: 1–2), and often a dishonest steward, turning the House of the Lord into a "house of merchandise" (John 2:16). "In my Father's house are many mansions" (John 14:2), says Jesus Christ. Individual mansions, like the cells of a honeycomb, make up the House of God, the Holy Temple of the Lord, or, in an expanded version of the same image, the Great City, Holy and Heavenly Jerusalem (Rev. 21:2, 10; Heb. 12:22, etc.). The Holy Spirit lives in this City and shines on it (Rev. 22:5), and the keys to the City are possessed by the bearers of the spirit, which know the mysteries of God (Matt. 16:17–19; Rev. 3:7–9; Matt. 18:18, etc.). On the ontological plane, the fall of creation consisted in the expulsion from the heavenly house, in the lack of conformity between the empirical disclosure of the likeness of God and the heavenly image of God: "the angels which kept not their first estate . . . left their own habitation" (Jude 1:6). The abandoned conformity is achieved anew only in the Holy Spirit. For this reason this City of God, or Kingdom of God, has itself only in the Original Kingdom of God, in the Holy Spirit, just as this Wisdom has itself only in the Original Wisdom of God, in the Son, and this Motherhood has itself only in the Original Parenthood, in the Father. Permeated with Trinitarian Love, Sophia *religiously*, not rationally, almost merges with the Word and the Spirit and the father, as with the Wisdom and the Kingdom of the Parenthood of God. But, *rationally*, Sophia is wholly other than each of these hypostases.

Sergei Bulgakov

from *Sophia, the Wisdom of God: An Outline of Sophiology*

The Divine Sophia and the Creaturely Sophia

In what is revealed about creation it is emphasized that is has a "begin-ning." "In the beginning God created the heaven and the earth" (Gen. 1:1), "The Lord possessed me in the beginning of his way" (Prov. 8:22). To this it is natural to add John 1:1: "In the beginning was the Word." It is usual to interpret this "beginning" as a matter of temporal succession and to see no more in it than an indication of the order or sequence of events. This is especially strange in relation to John 1:1. If what has been argued above holds good, this "beginning" imports rather a divine prin-ciple of life, the essential Wisdom of God. If we adopt this interpreta-tion, then all these texts become evidence for a principle in God which gives rise to the world: God created the world by his divinity, by that Wisdom whereby he eternally reveals himself unto himself. It is for this reason that the same revelation (John 1:1) includes the Word and the Holy Spirit.

In general, our position here is to maintain that God in his three per-sons created the world on the *foundation* of the Wisdom common to whole Trinity. This is the meaning which underlies the narrative of the creation of the world in six days (Gen. 1:3–31). We have then the follow-ing general scheme of creation: God creates by his Word, calling things into existence by his creative *fiat*, "God said. . . ." We can distinguish here the person of the Creator—God the Father, "The Father Almighty, maker of heaven and earth and of all things visible and invisible"; his creative Word; and its accomplishment. Certainly, the Word, which con-tains in itself every word of God concerning creation, and the Spirit, who brings all to fulfillment, are equally persons in the Holy Trinity. It is quite obvious, however, from the text, that it is precisely the Father in person who initiates this act of God, while the Son and the Holy Spirit participate in creation only in virtue of their self-determination in Sophia, the words of the Word and the fulfillment of the Spirit. It is not the Word itself which speaks the creative word, but "God"—the Father—who affirms it by his command "Let there be. . . ." Although the tri-personal God creates the world with each person participating in accordance with its personal character, nevertheless, the very manner of this participation is differently determined for the different persons of the Holy Trinity. In creation the Father alone acts "hypostatically" in the name of God, while the Son and Spirit abandon themselves to the will of the Father as his word and action. It is the Father who speaks and not the Son, through the words are those of the Word, as it is the Father who creates and not the Spirit, though the Spirit's is the quickening power. Son and Spirit participate in creation not hypostatically so much as sophianically, revealing themselves in Wisdom. So it is said of the Son, "All things were made by him; and without him was not anything made that was made" (John 1:3), and of the Holy Spirit that by the breath of the Father's mouth the strength of the heavens is established (Ps. 33:6; and 104:30 in the Slavonic version).

We can, therefore, say that God the Father creates the world by Sophia, which is the revelation of the Son and the Holy Spirit. At the same time we should bear in mind that Sophia does not exist in God independently of the divine hypostases, but is eternally hypostatized in them. Yet it is quite possible to draw a distinction within the self-revelation of the Godhead to the effect that this self-revelation may be predominantly determined by reference either to the hypostases, or to Sophia. In the one case we have a revelation predominantly hypostatic, in the other sophianic. So the creation of the world displays the following relationship: the hypostatic Creator is the Father, who, being the principle of procession in the Holy Trinity, creates the world by an act of the whole Trinity in its unique wisdom. In this act the Second and Third Hypostases participate not as separate persons, but somehow "kenotically," concealing themselves in the hypostasis of the Father, from whom initiates the will to create.

The divine Sophia, as the revelation of the Logos, is the *all-embracing unity,* which contains within itself all the fullness of the world of ideas. But to the creature also, God the Creator entrusts this *all,* withholding nothing in himself and not limiting the creature in any way: "All things were made by him [the Word]" (John 1:3). In Sophia the fullness of the ideal forms contained in the Word is reflected in creation. This means that the species of created beings do not represent some new type of forms, devised by God, so to speak, *ad hoc,* but that they are based upon eternal, divine prototypes. For this reason therefore the world of creatures also bears a "certain imprint" of the world of God, insofar as it shares the fullness of the divine forms or ideas. This is clear from the fact that on accomplishing the work of creation God "rested from all his work" (Gen. 2:1–3). This similitude implies the exhaustive fullness of creation, whose two-fold aspect as the creation of both "heaven and earth," the world of angels and the world of humans, does not affect the general postulate that the primary foundation of the world is rooted in divine Sophia.

God bestowed on the world at its creation not only the fullness of its ideal form as present to his own mind, but also the capacity to maintain its own distinct existence. This is the life which it derives from the Holy Spirit. "When thou lettest thy breath go forth, they shall be made. When thou takest away their breath, they die" (Ps. 104:29–30). The action of the Holy Spirit consists in the direct or indirect application of the creative *fiat* to the different aspects creation: "Let the waters, let the earth, bring forth. . . ." (Gen. 1:20, 24). The quickening activity of the Holy Spirit bestows on creatures in general the capacity to exist, prior to the emergence of their specific forms: "The Spirit of God moved upon the face of the waters" (Gen. 1:2), that is to say, over prime matter, communicating the capacity for existence to the *tohu-bohu* of the "void." The Holy Spirit, who thus imparts to ideal forms their reality, represents the power of *Beauty* or the divine Glory. The Father confers glory on creation after the likeness of divine Glory. The divine approval of creation is repeated as a sort of ratification of the work of each "day"—starting with the third: "and God saw that it was good" (Gen. 1:10, 12, 18, 21, 25). This culminates in the general appropriation of everything created. "And God saw everything that he had made and, behold it was very good" (5:31). "His work is worthy to be praised and had in honor" (Ps. 111:3). This the Slavonic renders, "His work is glory and beauty."

Thus God created the world by the Word and by the Holy Spirit, as they are manifested in Wisdom. In this sense he created the world by Wisdom and after the image of Wisdom. That Wisdom, which is an eternal reality in God, also provides the foundation for the existence of the world of creatures. Once again here we may repeat the dogmatic assertion that the world is created out of "non-being" or "nothing." Yet its capacity to exist, and its abiding reality, is not without some ground. This it finds precisely in the Wisdom of God. To admit this is to affirm, in a sense, the fundamentally divine character of the world, based upon this identity of the principle of divine Wisdom in God and in the creature. Wisdom in creation is ontologically identical with its prototype, the same Wisdom that exists in God. The world exists in God: "For of him, and through him, and to him, are all things" (Rom. 2:36). It exists by the power of his Godhead, even though it exists outside God. It is here that we find the boundary which separates Christianity from any kind of pantheism. In the latter the world is identical with God, and, therefore, strictly speaking neither the world nor God exists, but only a world which is a god in process of becoming. In the Christian conception on the other hand, the world belongs to God, for it is in God that it finds the foundation of its reality. Nothing can exist outside God, as alien or exterior to him. Nevertheless, the world, having been created from "nothing," in this "nothing" finds its "place." God confers on a principle which originates in himself an existence distinct from his own. This is not pantheism, but panentheism.

The created world, then, is none other than the creaturely Sophia, a principle of relative being, in process of becoming, and in composition with the non-being, of "nothing": this is what it means when we say that *the world is created by God from nothing*. Nevertheless, through the positive principal on which the world is based belongs to the being of God, the world as such maintains its existence and its identity distinct from that of God. Although its whole being depends upon the divine power of the creaturely Sophia within it, nevertheless the world is not God, but only God's creature. There is no such ontological necessity for the world that could constrain God Himself to create it for the sake of his own development or fulfillment; such an idea would indeed be pure pantheism. On the contrary, God creates the world in the freedom of his superabundant love. The self-sufficiency of God's being is completely realized in the tri-hypostatic life of the consubstantial Deity; nothing else can add to it or give it further fulfillment. In this sense, that is, for his own sake, God does not need the world.

Nevertheless the divine freedom which has manifested itself in the creation of the world is not something haphazard, nor some casual whim of such a kind that the world might equally well have been created or not. The reason for its creation is to be found in a quite different, free "necessity"—the force of God's love overflowing beyond the limits of its own being to found being other than his own. In any other view God's absoluteness would set a limit to the Absolute itself. In the creation of the world any such limitation is transcended by God's omnipotence. Through the act of creation the Absolute descends into the relative. That which does not exist is brought into being by the omnipotence of the Absolute, who is in fact the God who is Love. The Absolute then abides not only within its own absoluteness, but also outside itself, so that the world finds a God in it. This diffusion of God's love into creation is accomplished not in virtue of any *natural* necessity (as Plotinus, for example, thought). It is a *personal* creative act of God, his voluntary self-abandonment in love *ad extra*. But in creating the world by his omnipotence from "nothing" God communicates to it something of the vigor of his own being, and, in the divine Sophia, unites the world with his own divine life. Insofar as the creature is able to bear it, God communicates Sophia, the creaturely Sophia, to creation.

Already as far back as the time of Philo, and later during the Arian controversies, the question had arisen of the need for some meditating principle between God and the world. This problem remained unsolved during the period of christological controversy. The necessity of some such meditation cannot be denied, wherever the distinction of the world from God is held together with its participation in his being. Nevertheless the hypostasis of the Logos cannot provide such a unifying principle between God and the world. This assumption inevitably led to the subordinationism evident in the Christology of Tertullian and Origen, and, more particularly, of Arius. The principal we require is not to be sought in the person of God at all, but in his Nature, considered first as his intimate self-revelation, and second as his revelation in the world. And here we have at once Sophia in both its aspects, divine and creaturely. Sophia unites God with the world as the one common principal, the divine ground of creaturely existence. Remaining one, Sophia exists in two modes, eternal and temporal, divine and creaturely. It is of the first importance for us to grasp both the unity and the "otherness" in this unique relation of the creature to its Creator.

The act of the creation itself remains a mystery to the creature. It is a mystery which goes deeper than the being of the creature, to the production of existence from non-existence through the omnipotence of God. Nevertheless we can dimly discern the limitations of created being, since we come upon them in our inward and outward experience inasmuch as we ourselves belong to this world of creatures. The fundamental mark of the created world is becoming, emergence, development, fulfillment. As a process this involves succession, variety, limitations of space, restriction—all these are aspects of being in the state of becoming. But although this becoming constitutes development, it does not represent evolution from nothing, in the way that this is usually interpreted in theories of evolution, for *ex nihilo nihil fit*. On the contrary, this development represents the germination of the divine seeds of being in the soil of non-being, the actualization of divine prototypes, of the divine Sophia in the creaturely. Nevertheless the seed remains only a seed and not the plant itself. The world of becoming must travel by the long road of the history of the universe if it is ultimately to succeed and reflect in itself the face of the divine Sophia, and be "transfigured" into it. The creaturely Sophia, which is the foundation of the being of the world, its entelechy, *entelecheia* (in Aristotelian language), is at present in a state of potentiality, *dynamis*, while at the same time it is the principle of its actualization in finality. The world is created in all its fullness, and God "rested from his works" after creation. This fullness, however, only applies to the contents of the world as God intended it to be when he created it; it is not true of the present state of the world. The world created from nothing both is, and at the same time is not, the creaturely likeness of divine Sophia; it only approximates to this likeness in the course of the world process.

It is possible to ask: Is not the creation of the world, as it were, a sort of duplication of the divine Sophia? But the whole conception of correspondence is inapplicable to the relation between the eternal and becoming. Indeed, it is nearer the truth to speak of unity, even identity, as between the divine and the creaturely Sophia, for nothing is doubled in God. At the same time, however, and without equivocation, we can speak of the two different forms of Sophia in God and in creature. They are distinguished, on the one hand, as the simple and simultaneous perfection of eternity, as against temporal becoming, and, on the other, as divine, as against participated being. The identity and distinction, the unity and duality of Sophia in God and in creation, rest on the same foundation.

This *coincidentia oppositorum* finds its expression on this account in a relation of type and antitype, an identity in distinction, and distinction in identity. This is the primary and ultimate antinomy of sophiology. And this sophiological antinomy only serves to express the still deeper antinomy from which all theological thought springs and to which it inevitably returns: that of the identity and distinction of God and the Absolute. Absolute being, self-existent and self-sufficing, while maintaining all its absolute character, yet establishes as it were alongside or outside of itself a state of relative being, to which it stands as God. The Absolute is God, but God is not the Absolute insofar as the world relates to him. We find this theological antinomy reflected in a whole series of paradoxical relationship: God and the world, the divine and the creaturely Sophia, the type and the anti-type.

Nikolai Berdyaev

from *Freedom and the Spirit*

The interior life of God is realized by man and the world. The interior life of man and the world is realized by God. Man, who is at the center of being and called to play the most important role in the life of the universe, can have no positive life-content without God and without the world, that is to say, without that which is above and below him. He cannot remain solitary for he has no source of life in himself alone upon which to draw. When man stands alone before the void of non-being he is attracted towards it, and feels it is a part of himself. If nothing exists but man in his solitariness then there is neither man nor anything else at all. An exclusive psychologism involves the affirmation of non-being and the destruction of man's very core. Human beings cannot build up their lives on themselves. The creation of life always presupposes for man the existence of another. If this Other Being Who is divine does not exist for him, he determines his life in reference to another which is of a lower nature. In separating himself from God and the higher world man submits himself to the lower world and becomes enslaved by it.

The submission of man to the elements of the natural world means the destruction of the ordered hierarchy of the universe. The relative position of the higher and lower elements in it is reversed, and everything is thrown out of place. Man, the king of the universe, becomes the slave of nature and necessity. Man is separated from God and the world from man, so that the world becomes something external to man which forces him to submit to its own laws. Man loses his spiritual independence. He begins to be determined from without and not from within. The sun ceases to shine upon him and to be the light of the world as before. It now becomes part of the nature which is external to man, the life of which depends entirely on illumination from without. The whole universe being separated from God ceases to have an inner radiance; it needs a source of light exterior to itself. The principal result of the Fall is just this loss of inner illumination and the subordination of everything to an external source. When man dwells in God, then the cosmos is in man; he has the sun within himself. When God and man are separated, the cosmos and man are separated too. Necessity reigns in the cosmos and it is no longer subject to man's command.

St. Simeon the New Theologian said,

When Adam was driven out of Paradise, the whole creation refused to submit to him any longer. Neither the moon nor any of the stars would appear; the springs refused to send forth their waters and rivers stopped in their courses; the air was minded to keep so still that sinful Adam might not even be able to breathe. When the beasts and all the terrestrial animals saw that he had lost the garment of his first glory they began to despise him; the heavens were ready to fall upon him and the earth desired to support him no longer. But what did God do, He Who is Creator of man and all things? By His creative power He retrained them and in His mercy and goodness He did not suffer the elements forthwith to loose themselves upon man. He ordained that creation should continue subject to Adam and that having become ready to perish it should serve man who was in a like case and for whom it had been created. Nevertheless, when man is born again and becomes spiritual, incorruptible, and immortal, creation, which has been subjected to man by God, will be freed from this task and will likewise be born again becoming incorruptible, and in a measure, spiritual.[12]

Thus does a great mystic describe the day in which man lost his central position in the cosmos, and the bond which now fetters him to it.

Once separated from God and the spiritual world, man loses his independence and his spiritual individuality; he is subject to the laws of the animal world, becomes an instrument of the racial principle, and is condemned to live dominated by tradition in families and states in which this principle is a preponderating factor. Man is born and perpetuates the race of fallen Adam, which is subject to an indefinite process of birth and death, to that bad infinity of endless generations born only to die. The hopes of personality for eternal life are destroyed by this racial principle or element. Instead of eternal life and that fullness which personality demands there is nothing but the endless dissolution of generations which rise and then disappear. The link which binds birth and death cannot be broken by the racial element. Birth carries within it the seed of death, the breaking-up of individuality, and the loss of its hopes. He who begets is himself condemned to die and condemns to death those who in their turn come to birth. In the racial element on which the sinful life of natural humanity is based there is no victory over death and no achievement of the life incorruptible.

Sex, with its generative function which subjects man to natural law

---

12. From Homily 45.3, available in English in Saint Symeon the New Theologian, *The Sin of Adam and Our Redemption: Seven Homilies* (Saint Herman of Alaska Brotherhood, 1979), 68–69.

and links him with the natural world, is the result of sin and separation from God. Through birth man bears the consequences of sin, but, even if he redeems it, he is unable to overcome corruptible nature and to attain eternal and immortal life. The new spiritual race of Christ is not a race born on earth according to the laws of the animal world and so prone at all times to the temptations of a lower element. Separation from God meant for man precisely the loss of his integrity, chastity, and virginity; in other words, of the "male-female" image of the Divine Being.

According to the ingenious doctrine of Boehme, man lost the eternal Virgin (Sophia) who departed from him and took refuge in heaven. This separation of the feminine element from "male-female" humanity meant that femininity became something apart from man, and the object of a tormenting attraction from which there was no escape. But while in his integrity and chastity man dwelt in God, he had been able to comprehend femininity in Him. And it is here that we rediscover all that concerned man and the cosmos, for sin is above all the loss of integrity and chastity, which involves division and dissension. A virtuous integrality is precisely a synthesis of chastity or virginity, that is to say, the union in man of the masculine and the feminine. Sensuality and depravity are the result of this loss of integrality, an inevitable consequence of the division which has taken place within man. Everything has become, as it were, externalized and mutually exclusive. It is the same with regard to masculinity and femininity. The feminine element is an external, attractive, and seductive element without which the masculine cannot exist. Man cannot remain in a state of division, a mere incomplete half of his true self. This is why the human race suffers, for it has a desperate longing for this reunion and reintegration, and the full realization of its complete "male-female" being. But in the racial element, which bears the marks of this division, integrality is never acquired, the "male-female" image is never restored, man's ardent longing for eternity and for his virgin remain unfulfilled. Each individual man or woman is in different degrees bi-sexual and it is just this fact which makes the whole of life so complex.

The teaching of Boehme about Sophia is precisely that of the Virgin and the "male-female" image of man. "Through lust Adam was parted from the Virgin, and through lust he gained his wife; but the Virgin is always waiting for him and if he only desires to be born again she will receive him and crown him with glory."[13] "The Divine Wisdom is the eternal Virgin and not woman, she is unsullied purity and chastity and

---

13. From Boehme's *Three Principles*, 12.60.

she appears as the image of God and the image of the Trinity."[14] "The Virgin is from all eternity, she is uncreated and unbegotten; she is the Divine Wisdom and the image of Divinity."[15] "The image of God is the masculine virgin and not woman or man."[16] "Christ on the cross delivered our virginal image of masculinity and femininity and in His divine love He dyed it crimson with His heavenly Blood."[17] "Christ was born of the Virgin in order to hallow afresh the *Tincture* of femininity and to unite it to the masculine principle so that man and woman might become alike 'male-female' as was Christ."[18]

Wisdom is eternal virginity and not eternal femininity, for the wisdom-cult is that of the Virgin and not that of the feminine principle which is the result of division and the Fall. That is why the cult of Wisdom is almost identical with that of the Virgin Mary, the Mother of God. In her, nature became virginal and she conceived by the Spirit. Thus there arose a new humanity, the seed of Christ, which is immortal and triumphs over the bad infinity of birth and death. The integrality of man's image is restored through the Virgin Mary and her conception of Him Who is both Son of God and Son of Man. It is the way of chastity, purity, virginity, the way of mystical love.

The doctrine and cult of virginity have always had a more profound significance for Christianity than the doctrine of marriage and the sanctification of procreation, which alike have received insufficient emphasis. The revelation of the mystical and positive meaning of love between man and woman (*eros* not *agape*) is part of Christian problematics. The mystical significance of love has not received dogmatic elucidation, and what the Fathers of the Church have to say on this subject is poor and inadequate. The Christianity of the Fathers teaches us to acquire virginity by means of asceticism, but reveals nothing of the mystical significance of love as the way to virginity, the reestablishment of man's image in its integrity, and eternal life. Christianity has been right in justifying and sanctifying marriage and the family for sinful humanity, for in this way it preserves and spiritualizes fallen sex-life, but it says nothing about transfiguration or the coming of a new sex. This form of transfiguration has, like many other things, failed to receive its proper emphasis in Christianity. The sanctity of motherhood possesses cosmic significance, though to say that does not solve the question. The gulf which

14. From *The Three-fold Life of Man*, 5.44.
15. Ibid., 11.12.
16. From *Mysterium Magnum*, 23.44.
17. Ibid., 19.7.
18. Ibid., 58.46.

separates racial love (the love that begets) and the mystical love whose goal is eternity creates an antinomy for Christian thinking. The Church teaches that sex which is fallen and divided against itself is transformed in the Virgin Mary into an illumined virginity and motherhood, and receives into itself the Logos of the world Who is born of the Spirit. But it seems that no deduction has been drawn from this with regard to the positive methods by which the old racial element, that is the sexual element, can be illumined and transfigured. The positive religious significance of love, the link which unites it to the very idea of man as an integral being, is not revealed. This is due to the insufficient attention paid to anthropology within Christianity. Love, like so many other things in the creative life of man, remains unexplained and unsanctified, outside the pale, as it were, condemned to a tragic destiny in the world. The Christian doctrine of marriage and of the family, like that of government and of the state, has a profound meaning for the natural and sinful world, and for the racial element in which man undergoes the consequences of sin. But the problem of the meaning of that love which is the result neither of physical attraction nor of childbearing, nor yet of the social organization of the human race, is not even broached. Love by its nature occupies the same place as mysticism. It, too, is aristocratic and spiritual, and incapable of being assimilated to the democratic "psychical" and corporeal organization of human life. Love is bound up with the initial idea of man. We have no vision of the religious meaning of love except in the symbolism of the relations between Christ and His Church.

Catholic Sophiology

SOPHIOLOGY in Catholicism since at least the medieval period has been, as I have argued elsewhere, a "submerged reality." It has always been implicit in some forms of theological thinking and particularly in mysticism, but did not really start to emerge until the twentieth century, as Russian sophiology, particularly as found in Solovyov and Bulgakov, began to influence some Catholic theologians, especially those connected with the *Ressourcement* movement, also known as *Nouvelle Théologie*. An important element of the *Ressourcement* was the thought of Henri de Lubac (1896–1991), who challenged Neo-Scholasticism's idea of *natura pura* and opened the way for a vigorous and explicitly Catholic appropriation of sophiological ideas.[1] Unarguably, from his inspiration and that of others a new era of Latin Catholic theology had begun. Often debated, often ridiculed, *Ressourcement* nevertheless reset the terms of debate in twentieth- and twenty-first-century Catholic theology.

Hans Urs von Balthasar

Hans Urs von Balthasar (1905–1988) was and remains one of the twentieth century's most influential theologians—Catholic, Orthodox, or Protestant. Balthasar's religious imagination was exceedingly rich, and he often found previously undiscovered riches for the Catholic tradition in a variety of orthodox Catholic (Aquinas, the Fathers) and apparently heterodox (Barth, Solovyov, Origen) sources. Sophiological intuitions inhabit much of his dogmatic theology in several different ways, particularly in his notion of "splendor" which he articulates in the outline of the "theological aesthetics" found in his *Herrlichkeit* (1961–1969), known in English as *The Glory of the Lord*.

In the selection from *Herrlichkeit* excerpted here, Balthasar explains his notion of *theological aesthetics*, an "immanental self-transfiguration on the part of the world," an important concept in the light of sophiology.

---

1. See in particular John Milbank's *The Suspended Middle: Henri de Lubac and the Debate concerning the Supernatural* (Grand Rapids, MI/Cambridge, UK: William B. Eerdmans Publishing Company (2005).

Louis Bouyer

A convert from Protestantism and a former Lutheran pastor, Louis Bouyer (1913–2004) entered the Catholic Church in 1939 and was active in the theological and liturgical maelstrom that resulted from Vatican II—the latter of which he strongly repudiated afterwards.[2] Early in his religious life, while still a Protestant Bouyer met a number of Russian Orthodox thinkers and prelates then living in exile in Paris, including the formidable Fr. Sergius Bulgakov, whose sophiology clearly had an impact on the young scholar and theologian. Bouyer's *Le Trône de la Sagesse* (*The Seat of Wisdom*) can be read as the first systematic attempt to provide an outline for a Catholic sophiology.

In "Wisdom and the Assumption" (taken from *The Seat of Wisdom* and excerpted here), Bouyer provides a Catholic context for taking up the sophiological intuitions he found in Bulgakov, a very real (though imaginative) gesture toward receiving Bulgakov (or at least his theology) into the Catholic Church.

Pierre Teilhard de Chardin

The Jesuit Pierre Teilhard de Chardin (1881–1955) may be one of the most misunderstood—and vilified—figures of twentieth-century Catholicism. Both a scientist (he was a paleontologist) and a mystic as well as a priest, Teilhard has found more admirers outside of the Catholic Church than inside of it. His holistic worldview of creation as an integral whole and eventually arriving at what he called the "Omega point" unfortunately found a willing reception (and distortion) among a number of New Age "thinkers"—but Orthodox theologians tend to read Teilhard sympathetically and consider his ideas in terms of *theosis* and not as a baptized version of pantheism. Even in some Catholic circles, the anxiety Teilhard once provoked has diminished, and Benedict XVI has expressed admiration for him,[3] though he is still viewed as a heretic by some arch-conservative Traditionalists. Nevertheless, Teilhard's is a commitment to a thoroughly Catholic (in every sense of the word) vision of the cosmos.

Teilhard is represented in this collection by his extraordinary prose poem *L'Éternel Féminin* ("The Eternal Feminine"), written early in his career while he served as a stretcher-bearer during World War I.

---

2. On Bouyer's life and involvement in Vatican II see his memoir, published in English as *The Memoirs of Louis Bouyer*, trans. John Pepino (Kettering, OH: Angelico Press, 2015).

3. Among other places, in Joseph Cardinal Ratzinger [Pope Benedict XVI], *The Spirit of the Liturgy* (San Francisco, CA: Ignatius Press, 2000), 28–9.

Valentin Tomberg

Our last selection comes from a figure virtually unknown in Catholic theological circles, Valentin Tomberg (1900–1970). A Russian esotericist who had been for a time a leading figure in the Anthroposophical Society, Tomberg, a cradle Lutheran, entered the Catholic Church while in a Dutch camp for displaced persons toward the end of World War II. Tomberg was the author of what is, arguably, one of the more remarkable contributions to Catholic thought of the last fifty years: a work originally written in French (Tomberg was a polyglot) but known to readers of English as *Meditations on the Tarot: A Journey into Christian Hermeticism*. It is a book like no other book. Rather than a manual of cartomancy, what the reader finds in this remarkable text is a series of what the author calls "spiritual exercises," profound meditations reaching into the iconography of the Marseilles Tarot, images, like those of the Dance of Death, with roots reaching deep into medieval Catholicism. Due to its unique and idiosyncratic nature (as is all too obvious from its title), the book has proved problematic for some. For others, however, it has provided an otherwise unexpected gateway into the eternally new Catholic mystery.

Tomberg's meditation here—as with all of his meditations—ranges far and wide along the scope of Western and Eastern religions and esotericism. Tomberg identifies himself as a "Hermeticist"—not as a mystic and certainly not as an occultist—and places himself at the service of the Catholic Church:

> The way of Hermeticism, solitary and intimate as it is, comprises authentic experiences from which it follows that the Roman Catholic Church is, in fact, a depository of Christian spiritual truth, and the more one advances on the way of free research for this truth, the more one approaches the Church. Sooner or later one inevitably experiences that spiritual reality corresponds—with an astonishing exactitude—to what the Church teaches: that there are guardian Angels; that there are saints who participate actively in our lives; that the Blessed Virgin *is* real, and that she is almost precisely such as she is understood, worshipped and portrayed by the Church; that the sacraments *are* effective, and that there are seven of them—and not two, or three, or even eight; that the three sacred vows—of obedience, chastity and poverty—constitute in fact the very essence of all authentic spirituality; that prayer is a powerful means of charity, for beyond as well as here below; that the ecclesiastical hierarchy reflects the celestial hierarchical order; that the Holy See and the papacy represent a mystery of divine magic; that hell, purgatory and heaven *are* realities; that, lastly, the Master himself—although he loves everyone, Christians of all confes-

sions as well as all non-Christians—abides with his Church, since he is always present there, since he visits the faithful there and instructs his disciples there. The Master is always findable and meetable there.[4]

He clearly brings a different perspective to the notion that "in my Father's house there are many mansions" (John 14:2).

4. *Meditations*, 282. Emphasis in source.

Hans Urs von Balthasar

from *The Glory of the Lord: Volume I: Seeing the Form*

The Aesthetic Measure

As a first attempt to survey the scope of our inquiry, we proceeded from below, without heeding the warning sounded when we crossed the boundary between the realm of nature and that of grace—the boundary between philosophy and theology. The form of the beautiful appeared to us to be so transcendent in itself that it glided with perfect continuity from the natural into the supernatural world. *Charis* refers to the attractive "charm" of the beautiful, but it also means "grace." "*Charis* is poured out upon your lips," sings the nuptial psalm (44:3). We believe that what is beautiful in this world—being spirit as it makes its appearance—possesses a total dimension that also calls for moral decision. If this is so, then from the beautiful the way must also lead into the religious dimension which itself includes man's definitive answer to the question about God and, indeed, his answer to the question God poses to *him*. It will be objected that the Word which comes from God places everything human under judgment, no matter how transcendent this human reality may be in itself. Such judgement must necessarily mean condemnation, but may well be more of a saving act of taking up and transfiguring what is human. But, in any case, the judgement is above all a free declaration on the part of God, not to be eschewed by worldly beings, especially when they are in danger of forgetting the sovereignty of God's freedom of judgment. Crossing these boundaries so forgetfully, however, belongs to the essence of the beautiful and of aesthetics almost as a necessity. More than either metaphysics or ethics, aesthetics tends toward an immanental self-transfiguration on the part of the world, even if it is only for the moment when the beautiful first catches the eye. And an aesthetic sensibility and its standards will come into play precisely where metaphysics and ethics attempt to achieve a final reconciliation and harmony. Revelation must unmask these incursions by judging them and directing them to their rightful place, and theology will obediently reflect the judgement passed by revelation.

But does this judgment imply for aesthetics nothing but a limitation, perhaps even the demolition of the bridge between natural and supernatural beauty? Let us first grant that our former approach from below was, on the whole, not incorrect, since the moment does exist in which the spirit that beams forth from within and that is fashioning a form for itself must submit, as "spiritual matter" ($ὕλη\ νοητή$), to a higher shaping hand in order to find its own interior law which is to be expressed; and that this in no way violates its spiritual autonomy, but is rather what makes it possible for the spirit to attain such autonomy in the first place. Let us also grant that in the phenomenon of inspiration there exists a moment which the heathen has always sensed but which only the Christian can grasp with all the preciseness of faith. This is the moment when one's own inspiration mysteriously passes over into inspiration through the genius, the *daimon*, or the indwelling god, a moment when the "spirit that contains the god" (*en-thusiasmos*) obeys a superior command which as such implies form and is able to impose form. If all this is granted, then an inner analogy between both forms or stages of beauty ought not to be immediately dismissed. It must, then, be one of our axioms that from inspiration as principle of self-formation and—determination to inspiration as the state of being indwelt by a higher spirit there exists a genuine connecting step. In Christian language we may say that this step leads on into the realm of faith—faith in a supremely personal and freely sovereign Spirit-God. It is a matter of faith that we should not simply give ourselves over to God mystically, as to an Absolute that transcends all worldly forms and relativizes them, not only as to a primal Ground that destroys all of these forms, but that we should at the same time entrust ourselves with the confidence of faith to the *Creator Spiritus*, to the Spirit who from the beginning is a Creator and who, in the end, aims not at a Hindu dissolution of the world through mystical dance, but at creative form, regardless of how much in the form of man and of the world remains to be burnt away as dross. Such creative form, then, is God's work, and the work of man only in so far as he makes himself available to the divine action without opposition, acceptingly, allowing God to act, concurring in his work.

Such "art" becomes visible in the Christian sphere in the life-forms of the chosen. In its exact sense, prophetic existence is the existence of a person who in faith has been divested of any intent to give himself shape, who makes himself available as matter for the divine action. From Abraham, Isaac, Jacob, Joseph, Moses, the charismatic Judges, the Prophets and the Martyrs of faith, all the way to the forerunner and to the "Handmaid of the Lord," in whom the feminine and bridal plasticity of the Daughter of Zion is totally recapitulated and who presents to us the highest paradigm of what is meant by the "art of God" and by "well-structured sanctity": in each of these cases we confront life in the Holy Spirit, hidden life which is inconspicuous, and yet *so* conspicuous that its situations, scenes, and encounters receive a sharp, unmistakable profile and exert an archetypal power over the whole history of faith. This is the opposite of what would be expected if a limited individual surrendered himself wholly—to the very core of his person—to that which is essentially Unbounded and Unformed. What we perceive here is a new spiritual form, chiseled on the very stone of existence, a form which unmistakably derives from the form of God's Incarnation. Now, admittedly the divine principle of form must in many ways stand in sharp contrast to the beauty of this world. This contrast notwithstanding, however, if God's will to give form really aims at man as God truly wants to shape him—aims, that is, at the perfecting of that work begun by God's "hands" in the Garden of Eden—then it appears impossible to deny that there exists an analogy between God's work of formation and the shaping forces of nature and of man as they generate and give birth.

We can post as many question marks and warning signs as we will along the length and breadth of this analogy, but they will only apply to the ever-present possibility of misusing the analogy, and not to its rightful use. Misuse of analogy consists in simply subjugating and subordinating God's revelation with its own form, to the laws not only of metaphysics and of private, social, and sociological ethics but also of this-worldly aesthetics, instead of respecting the sovereignty which is manifested clearly enough in God's work. Such misuse occurs the more frequently and extravagantly in aesthetics because worldly aesthetics appears more engaging and compelling than worldly metaphysics or ethics, which both remain inherently problematical. Most people dare not make strong affirmations about the ultimate nature of the world's essence or about the ultimate justice of human actions. But all those who have been once affected inwardly by the worldly beauty of either nature, or of a person's life, or of art, will surely not insist that they have no genuine idea of what beauty is. The beautiful brings with it a self-evidence that en-lightens without meditation. This is why, when we approach God's revelation with the category of the beautiful, we quite spontaneously bring this category with us in its this-worldly form. It is only when such a this-worldly aesthetics does not fit revelation's transcendent form that we suddenly come to an astonished halt and conscientiously decline to continue on the path. At that point, the application to the sphere of revelation of what we think and know to be beauty will seem to us either a merely "rhapsodic," unchecked use of the beautiful, which at best betrays a naive enthusiasm—a misunderstanding which may perhaps be tolerated because of its edifying effects—or, what basically amounts to the same thing, we will forbid ourselves every kind of falsifying and minimizing application of aesthetic categories out of reverence of God's Word, for its awesomeness and its, literally, in-comparable pre-eminence.

There may well have been an historical *kairos,* as Gerhard Nebel felt justified in believing, when human art and Christian revelation met in an encounter which saw the creation of icons, basilicas and Romanesque cathedrals, sculptures and paintings. But since then too many misunderstandings and too many terrible things have occurred for us still to be in a position to insist more on the similarity of the two spheres than on their dissimilarity. Man's habit of calling beautiful only what strikes *him* as such appears insurmountable, at least on earth. And therefore, at least practically speaking, it seems both advisable and necessary to steer clear of the theological application of aesthetic concepts. A theology that makes use of such concepts will sooner or later cease to be a "theological aesthetics"—that is, the attempt to do aesthetics at the level and with the methods of theology—and deteriorate into an "aesthetic theology" by betraying and selling out theological substance to the current viewpoints of an inner-worldly theory of beauty.

Regardless of how conspicuously the warning signals against such dangers may be posted—and in this realm they must be written in bold print—the element of danger must not be here allowed to prejudice our theoretical reflections in advance. Even a dangerous road remains a road, perhaps one requiring special equipment and expertise, but one which does not for all that become impassable. The prior theoretical decision which must be made is the following: Are we objectively justified in restricting the beautiful to the area of inner-worldly relationships between "matter and form," between "that which appears and the appearance itself," justified in restricting it to the psychic states of imagination and empathy which are certainly required for the perception and production of such expressional relationships? *Or:* May we not think of the beautiful as one of the transcendental attributes of Being as such, and thereby ascribe to the beautiful the same range of application and the same inwardly analogous form that we ascribe to the one, the true, the good? The traditional theology of the Church Fathers and even that of high Scholasticism did this unhesitatingly, prompted by a double impulse. First, they possessed a theology of creation which, likewise unhesitatingly, attributed creation's aesthetic values *eminenter* to the creating principle itself. Second, they had a theology of redemption and of creation's perfecting which ascribed to God's highest work the eminent sum of all of creation's values, particularly as concerns the eschatological form of God's work. But this form already begins with the Lord's Resurrection, which for its part pours out its "sublime splendour" (*kabod, doxa, gloria*) over the whole sphere of the Church and of the bestowal of grace. Should this not prompt us to question the theologies which view the veiled form of the economy of the Cross as the only form appropriate for understanding the whole course of salvation-history? Many Fathers, particularly Augustine, were deeply concerned with this question. For the time being, however, we are not concerned with whether they dealt with the problem in the right way. The moot point at the moment is to determine the angle from which to approach our problem, not the particular details of the methodology to be followed. For the reasons mentioned, the Fathers regarded beauty as a transcendental and did theology accordingly. This presupposition left a most profound imprint on the manner and content of their theologizing, since a theology of beauty may be elaborated only in a beautiful manner. The particular nature of one's subject-matter must be reflected first of all in the particular nature of one's method. This holds for the commentaries on the creation and paradise narratives of Theophilus, Irenaeus, Basil, Gregory of Nyssa, Ambrose, and Anastasius of Sinai. It also holds for the understanding of *conservatio* as the enduring presence and eventual incarnation of the divine Word in his creation, as we see in Clement, Origen, Methodius, Athanasius, Jerome, Victorinus, and Augustine. And, finally, it may also be said of the economy of the flesh and of the Cross as represented by Ignatius, Hermas, Tertullian, Gregory of Nazianzen, Anthony, Cassian, and Benedict. The happy congruence of subject-matter and methodology is particularly true of the Fathers' doctrine of contemplation, from Origen to Evagrius, Macarius and Augustine, and down to Gregory the Great and Maximus the Confessor, all of whom teach an inward and upward ascent that reaches the point where the eternal light transfigures the still veiled earthly forms of salvation. Contemplation here is the flashing anticipation of eschatological illumination, the presaging vision of transparent glory in the form of the Servant. But there are also those Fathers who see the beauty of salvation-history radiating objectively through the veiled form. In this way, Origen sees the Spirit blazing through the letter. Irenaeus recognizes God's highest art in the *oikonomia*: the rightful sequence of the epochs within salvation-history. Cyprian and Hilary see the splendor of love in the moral as well as sacramental and institutional unity of the Church. Leo the Great sees the highest harmony in the choral dance of the Church's feasts, and Evagrius sees the eternal light shining through the purified soul that knows God. Whatever the particular aspects each Father may select and whatever the method he may follow, they are all at one in the explicit recognition and emphasis they give to the aesthetic moment within contemplation, a contemplation indeed that is attentive to just this moment.

Such contemplation, which necessarily contains within itself an "enthusiastic" moment, is all too often and too easily traced back to the unwarranted influence of Hellenistic spiritual attitudes,[5] and those who dismiss contemplation as a "Hellenistic corruption of the Gospel" rejoice that our more modern theology has rid itself of this "foreign intrusion." A more serious objection comes from those who point to the anti-artistic currents running through the whole of the Patristic period and breaking out openly in Byzantium's iconoclastic controversies from the time of the Edict of Emperor Leo III (730) to the establishing of the "Feast of Orthodoxy" under Theodora II (843). We cannot say that the theological arguments proposed in favor of icons always sound very convincing. One such argument draws on Basil the Great's theology of the Trinity, especially on its doctrine concerning the Son's character as image or likeness and the necessary relationship and distinction between original image (*Urbild*) and its likeness (*Abbild*).[6] Another argument follows Denys the Areopagite in affirming the necessity of religious symbols for sense-endowed humanity (Denys the Areopagite, who is, after all, the father of the strictest negative theology). Still another of these arguments says that by despising the image one also despises what is being imaged. A fourth argument gives Christ's Incarnation as the basis for the cult of images, since God's humanity in Christ excludes every kind of Docetism. A final and especially unconvincing argument conceives of a mysterious "indwelling" of the original reality in its image, and then goes on to point to the miracles occurring in and through icons by reason of their *acheiropiia*—their "having fallen from Heaven," their origin as "not having been made by hands." All of these justifications scarcely measure up to the Old Testament's ban on images, a ban which was never expressly revoked in the New Testament, or to the marked restraint and dearth of images of the early Christian period. By contrast, we are given much food for thought by the argument of the iconoclast Constantine V, which says that a merely human representation of Christ—unavoidable, since the divine side of his being remains irrepresentable—constitutes an assault upon Christology and must eventually lead to Nestorianism. Constantine's argument is valid at least by way of permanent warning against allowing the Image of himself that God made appear in the world—the Image that is his Son—to be extended without any critical distance whatever into other images which, regardless of all their religious relevance, nonetheless belong to the sphere of aesthetics. In this way iconoclasm may be seen as a corrective to Patristic theology, one which must always come into con-

---

5. E.g., Ronald Knox's *Enthusiasm*.

6. See F.X. Funk, "'Ein angebliches Wort Basilius' des Grossen uber die Bildverehrung." *TQ* 70 (1888): 297f.

sideration not, of course, simply as a thesis, but precisely as a warning corrective, particularly when it takes milder forms in the course of the Church's history. In a more moderate form, iconoclasm played a role in the Carolingian period and in the Cistercian reform and its sharp reaction against Romanesque extravagances, to say nothing of its role in the Reformation. Even today it is again making itself felt in church architecture and in every realm of church art.

Nevertheless, even such a historical reminder cannot go beyond a theoretical and practical call to the constant vigilance required to keep the transcendental beauty of revelation from slipping back into equality with an inner-worldly natural beauty.

Before we broach the question of whether the Fathers spoke adequately concerning the beauty of revelation, and also the question of what form such a discourse would properly have to take, we must, by way of preamble, briefly consider Sacred Scripture, the very source of theology, which, if not in its entirety, for the most part is a poetical book. Here we ought not to insist greatly on the Bible's external poetic form, since weighty historical arguments could be produced against the theological import of such a form. For instance, it could be argued that the greater part of the Biblical writings derive from an age and a cultural context in which prose in the later sense (such as that of the Greek historians) does not yet even exist. At this time, not only are songs, hymns, parables, Wisdom sayings, cultic formulas, and prophetic discourse the ordinary manner of handing down a tradition, but so too are juridical pronouncements and poetically sophisticated historical saga, legend, story, and so forth, all of which in the earliest times were governed primarily by mnemotechnical needs. The poetical character of Scripture would, accordingly, have to be interpreted historically in the first place, something which would have surprised neither Hamann nor Herder or their disciples. According to them, poetry was mankind's first and oldest language and expressive form, and the Bible must therefore be considered to be the most reliable and "most ancient document of the human race." Another consideration is more serious. We see that, in the general historical sequence and in the divisions of the Hebrew Bible, the "writings" follow the "Law" and the "Prophets" as a third category. Among the writings we have the Psalms, Job, Proverbs, the Song of Solomon, and Ecclesiastes, and, in the canon of the Catholic Church, we also have Ben-Sirach and the Wisdom of Solomon. In this third group of writings there emerges spontaneously an unmistakable aesthetic element which is not consciously present in the first two groups. But here it emerges in the context of the objective stance of the "wise man" as he meditates on the dramatic religious-political history which the Heptateuch, with its appended books, and also the Prophets—wholly integrated into the forgoing histories—unfurl before the beholder. Doubtless the contemplation of the Wisdom literature belongs to a late period for which the powerful drama of the earlier heroic phase and the tragic events of the ripe middle period have definitively entered "the past." And we may add that Hellenistic influences surely awakened and fostered the contemplative attitude, as well as the sense for aesthetic values that comes with it. From the Protestant side, one may look somewhat deprecatingly on the documents of this period, even though important ones have been kept in the Protestant canon. From the Jewish side, a Martin Buber may consider them, in so far as they were written in Greek, as but an insignificant addendum to Scripture. Nevertheless, they form an organic part of the canon of the Catholic Church and she, therefore, considers them to be inspired in an unqualified sense. Indeed, because of the contemplative "caesura" which these books insert between the great action of the Old Testament and the coming action of the New, the Church treasures them as a wholly indispensable link in the economy of revelation.

In the Wisdom books, the Holy Spirit of Scripture reflects on himself. But he takes not only the deeds of the past as the object of his praise (Wis 10–19; Sir 44–50), but also the splendour of natural creation (Wis 13; Sir 42:15–43; Psalms 8, 104, etc.; Job 38f.), the conditions and attitudes of mortal man (Eccl, Job), and above all Wisdom herself, who is conscious of "praising herself" explicitly (Prov 8:12f.; Sir 24:1f.). The self-contemplation of Sophia is "glorious praise" (*Rühmung*), and, therefore, in its own way it is just as prophetic and poetical as God's revelation in history, nature, and human life, which she likewise extols. And here the claim that the poetic form of the first two sections of the Old Testament can be explained in purely historical and cultural terms in no longer tenable. This argument now in retrospect becomes questionable. The specifically Biblical form of inspired contemplation casts an aesthetic light backwards (and also forwards) over salvation-history, a light that allows the unique and supernatural dimensions of the "Law" and the "Prophets" to shine forth along with their natural poetic form. We are not dealing here with a feeble, belated, and romantic transfiguration of a long-past and heroic "golden era." We are witnessing the radiant drawing out into consciousness of the aesthetic dimension which is inherent in this unique dramatic action, a dimension which is the proper object of a theological aesthetics.

"God needs prophets in order to make himself known, and all prophets are necessarily artists. What a prophet has to say can never be said in prose."[7] But if all prophets are artists, then surely not all artists are prophets, although all of them may be such in another, more general sense. Thus, the analogy between natural and supernatural aesthetics again emerges, an analogy which gives the divine Spirit the freedom of space to place all human forms of expression at the service of *his* kind of poetics. Scholars are right in their concern for the different literary genres in Scripture and in paying due regard to the general principles of these genres in their interpretations of the texts. But this activity by no means exhausts the question concerning the particular poetics of Scripture. In fact, this question may really be raised only when the other more general considerations have been concluded, and when for the interpretation of *this* inspiration—a particular inspiration, even though it is integrated into the general forms of inspiration—the interpreter himself enjoys an inspiration in accordance with the inspiration of his subject, analogous to the way the divine Sophia interprets and praises herself in the Wisdom books. We must, then, always see clearly where the competence of the philological and archaeological method really lies and where it must be complemented and even surpassed by a special method suited to the uniqueness of its object. The Fathers frequently exhibit this second element, while the first is often painfully absent; among modern scholars the first element may be found either with or without the second.

The problem may, indeed, be further sharpened by again relativizing historically the complementarity of Biblical sophiology and the sophiology of the Patristic and classical scholastic periods. One would, in this case, relate them both to the common cultural atmosphere of late antiquity, an influence extending at most to the outgoing Middle Ages and which must be expurgated from both the Bible and the history of theology by means of de-mythologization, in a determined effort to transcend it. But we will then ask: Transcend it in favour of what? In favour, perhaps, of a Harnackian "essence of Christianity" or of a Bultmannian "understanding of existence"? But note that from the sophiology of the late Old Testament connecting lines lead directly to Paul, to the author of the Letter to the Hebrews, and to John, all of whom exhibit with regard to Jesus' life and sufferings a transfiguring contemplative stance which is similar to the stance of the Wisdom books with regard to the Law and the Prophets. The two late groups in either Testament are in many ways connected by subterranean bond, a current of Biblical "*gnosis*" which is steeped in the same diffuse atmosphere of late antiquity as are Philo, the early Gnostic mystery texts, hermetic literature, and the

7. F. Medicus, *Grundfragen der Ästhetik* (Jena, 1907), 14.

beginnings of what would eventually produce Alexandrian Christianity. To excise all this from Scriptural revelation would leave only a certain moralism which was non-historical and, therefore, however existential, ultimately ineffective.

Louis Bouyer

from *The Seat of Wisdom: An Essay on the Place of the Virgin Mary in Christian Theology*

Wisdom and the Assumption

The considerations adduced in the last chapter bring us to the last of the mysteries concerning our Lady with which we have to deal, namely, that of the relations between her and the Wisdom of God. In the light of this mystery, as we hope to show, the full meaning of the Assumption becomes manifest.

As we have already seen, Wisdom appears in Scripture as an order imposed on the course of events in the world, and on man's history in particular. At first, it is something purely human, being the fruit of a human experience both extensive and profound, which has been subjected to a process of conscious reflection, itself the highest activity of the human mind.

Yet Wisdom is not simply contemplation, but leads naturally to the most sublime form of action, action of a royal nature, inasmuch as it, more than any other, sets its stamp on the course of the world's history. Wisdom is, essentially, architectonic; it is the art whereby man comes to such knowledge of the world, and so to adapt himself to it by an experience, manifold but unified on a superior plane, that he is enabled to mold history to his own purposes, and, ultimately, to give the world itself its final form.

In Israel, however, precisely in the degree in which it strove to realize consciously this boundless ambition, Wisdom came to be seen as unattainable by man, except as a gift of God; so that, in the end, the subject of this gift disappeared from the scene, as did the kingship of David's house in the course of sacred history, and it was seen, in the end, that God alone was wise, as he alone was king. At this point, however, Wisdom was not equated simply with God, but appeared, in him, another self, as a work achieved before all his works, and one by which they were all accomplished. In one aspect, it appeared as a daughter, in another as a spouse, as the architect and final end of the universe.

We have already noticed the presence, among early Christian writers, of some uncertainty in regard to the scriptural passages where this image occurs, and their hesitation is very instructive. Many see in it a prefiguration of the Son, the Word, the living Thought of the Father, his creative Word; whereas others are more impressed with other aspects which would seem to point to its identity with the Holy Ghost, for it is "the spirit of understanding, holy, one, manifold, subtle, eloquent, active, undefiled, sure, sweet, loving that which is good, quick, which nothing hindereth, beneficent, gentle, kind, steadfast, assured, secure, having all power, overseeing all things, and containing all spirits intelligible, pure, subtle" (Wisdom 7:22–23). It is easy to understand how Theophilus and Irenaeus take it as an image of the Holy Ghost, although, a few verses later, there is a passage where this image is spoken of in terms applied formally, in the epistle to the Hebrews, to the Son— "She is a vapor of the power of God and a certain pure emanation of the almighty God; and therefore no defiled thing cometh into her. For she is the brightness of eternal light, and the unspotted mirror of God's majesty, and the image of his goodness" (Wisdom 7:25–26; Heb 1:3).

On the other hand, there are elements in this image which seem to make it strictly applicable to created beings. This was strongly insisted upon by the Arians, and their arguments could not be conclusively refuted. The fact that the feminine elements were brought out so emphatically would, surely, rule out its complete identification with any of the divine Persons, even with that of the Holy Ghost.

What is there, then, which could correspond to this image of a being apparently inseparable from God in himself, bearing, undoubtedly, a quite special relation both to the Son and the Spirit, yet inseparable, too, from a certain reference to the creation, under the aspect of the chosen one, the Elect destined to become the Spouse of the Lord?

In this connection, the mind turns naturally to the Virgin Mary, especially when she has already been identified with the woman clothed with the sun and crowned with stars shown to us in the Apocalypse. The application to her seems particularly appropriate at this, the final, stage of our study, after the conclusions reached on her union with Christ and the Church, and on her mysterious, intimate relation with the Holy Ghost.

Nonetheless, a simple identification of the image with our Lady would, also, be difficult to sustain. Mary is not presented to us as a divine person made incarnate in the course of history, as is her Son, but as a person wholly comprised in a historical framework. Certainly, she holds a unique place in history, placed, as she is, at its central point, where all is focused and whence all takes its course of development. Yet, surely, it is not possible to transpose her absolutely to the plane, at once pre-cosmic and eschatological, of the Wisdom who is the architect of the universe, of that other self who is the Spouse God finds for himself in history, who was not to be found in eternity, but who, nevertheless, in some aspects, overflows and anticipates the world of time.

We will leave, for the moment, these questions unresolved, and begin by noticing that Wisdom, even in its later developments, is always related to the world and its historic course. At the final stage of a long process of elaboration in the religious thought of Israel, Wisdom becomes, as it were, raised up above the earth and carried up into God. But, even in God, it continues to be related to the creation, and, in particular, to the history of the people of God. It is the figure of God's condescension in seeking to reunite to himself his creature alienated by sin, just as, to draw it from nothingness, he had stooped to this nothingness. If, then, Wisdom, in God, is related to the world, and, particularly, to man, it leads our minds directly to man and the world as God wills them to be, as he sees them from all eternity, and as he will realize them at the end of time.

So it is that, in Wisdom, it is always the creature as God will realize it at the end of time, and as contained in his thought from all eternity.

Here we come upon the mystery of God's unity and infinity. How, within this unity, can there be any place for the multiplication of the world? How can the finite exist within the infinite and not be absorbed?

A possible answer might be that it is precisely in God's vision of the world and its history that the multiplicity of creatures is, finally, recapitulated in the inner unity of the divine life, their finiteness opened to his infinity to be taken into it. This, however, would be no solution to the problem, but simply a different formulation of it, more illuminating, because more profound, but no less mysterious. Wisdom is in God, is of God, and nothing can be that without being God himself. Wisdom, then, in its first aspect, appears impossible to distinguish really from the divine essence; but, in another aspect, it is that in God which leads to the distinction of creature and Creator, but to this distinction as surmounted, if not abolished, by the divine love. Wisdom is identical with the divine essence, but as participable by creatures, as comprising the possibility, realized by the divine mind and will, of their distinct existence. At the same time, it comprises this existence of theirs as merged again in the divine life, taken hold of again, in its distinctness, by the divine love.

The extent to which the distinctness, even the liberty, of the creature is comprised within the divine Wisdom is shown, most of all, in that Wisdom assumes and includes the fact of sin, its permission by God, its actual commission. But it comprises it as within the framework of redemption, of reintegration in love, of the reconciliation and recapitulation of all things.

Whatever is, in this way, brought to pass in the course of the historical process cannot possibly be looked on as something added on, from the outside, to what is in God, unchangeably, from all eternity. On the contrary, all that is real in history, and especially that full communication and participation of life in which history will culminate, is nothing else than a participation in the very life of God. This explains the close relations binding the Wisdom of God to the Son and to the Holy Ghost. For it is in the act of conceiving, bringing forth, the Son, and, as it were, intrinsically to that act, that God conceives and brings forth the divine Wisdom; and it is within the recapitulation of the Son in the Father by the Holy Ghost that Wisdom itself recapitulates in God the whole of history which it takes into itself. It is, therefore, the Son made flesh, identified with fallen man and all his weaknesses, who will bring about the Wisdom of God. That is why Christ, more particularly Christ crucified, is the great Mystery. He is the secret hidden in God, but revealed in the fullness of time, the final word of the divine Wisdom. That, too, is why the pouring out of the Spirit upon all flesh will bring the historical process, fallen away from the divine Wisdom, into ultimate accord, at the end of time, with the eternal plan of God. In this way, human history, being taken back into God, will be, as it were, brought into the very movement of the interior life of the Trinity.

This is the general standpoint according to which Wisdom is presented as the Spouse of the Word, his other self that he seeks out lost in the abyss of sin, the prostitute whose wretched state he came to share, but brought back to life through his death, and restored to virginal splendor by his own purity.

Then it is that the Spirit, after having, by its "unspeakable groanings," brought to fulfilment the mute yearning of all things in travail for a mysterious birth, will unite the spouse to her Spouse, and bring to pass the marriage of the Lamb, in the painful and resplendent re-birth at the end of time.

Thus, she who goes up from the earth, who rises from the desert towards heaven "as a pillar of smoke of aromatical spices," will be the same as she who will come down from heaven, at the end of all things, like a bride adorned for her husband (Cant 3:6; Rev 21:2). She is the new creation whose life now is hidden with Christ in God, and will appear, when Christ, her life, will appear (Col 3:3–4).

From all this we can see how it is that Wisdom is, at one and the same time, personal and impersonal. In God himself, Wisdom has no transcendent and independent actuality, but is realized only in the person of the Son, the Word, the living Thought of the Father, inasmuch as the Son himself is recapitulated in the Father through the Spirit. Wisdom, therefore, in its eternal actuality, is Wisdom of the Father, but wholly filial and bearer of the Spirit. Yet, since Wisdom is not simply the divine essence subsisting in the three Persons, but this essence as comprising the plan of creation and redemption together with its realization, we may say that Wisdom tends towards another personal realization, one which is feminine, which accepts the fact of plurality, even that arising from sin, and so evil, but transcends it, too, in the final recapitulation. Therein consists it eschatological realization in the Spouse of the Lamb, of the incarnate Word, when bought to sonship in her union with the only Son, the Only Beloved, of the Father, a union crowned and sealed by the gift of the Spirit.

But since the Incarnation and Redemption are not processes forcibly imposed on the world of multiplicity and sin, and still less involve its simple reabsorption in God, Wisdom is not confined to a single personal realization in history. It will comprise, while preserving their distinctness, all those who are saved in the actual course of history, all who have attained to the filial status shared by so many brethren in the Only Beloved. More particularly, the Spouse, along with their husband himself, is to be, as it were, made ready and brought into being within time, in view of eternity. Her filial realization as Virgin and Spouse, at the end of time, is, therefore, not only prefigured but pre-contained in an antecedent realization, in the middle of time, as Virgin Mother. It is strictly in this aspect that Mary is, not the final or complete realization of Wisdom, but its supreme realization on the plane of history. Mary is truly the Seat of Wisdom, of the uncreated Wisdom shown forth as a creature in her Son who is, at the same time, Son of the Father; and she is, thereby, the source, within history, of the eschatological Wisdom, created in time to espouse in time its eternal realization in the Son who is the Word.

It cannot, therefore, be said, without qualification, that Mary herself is Wisdom. In eternity, as we have already pointed out, Wisdom has but a single personal realization, namely, the Son. Likewise, in time, or rather at the end and consummation of the ages, it will also have only one, namely, the Spouse, the Church made perfect, wherein all the predestined will have been gathered together in the Son, and the whole of creation made new, set free from the power of the enemy and brought into the glory of the sons of God, to be totally absorbed in it. However, this realization of the Spouse comes about, wholly, through the first realization of Wisdom in the Virgin Mother; for it was in Mary that the creation, accepting in faith the fullest abnegation of self—the state in which the Son himself came down to rejoin and seek it out—was made rich by his poverty (2 Cor 8:9), the poverty of the Cross, the supreme token of the divine love, of the super-abundant riches of God communicated, without reserve, to his creation.

We see the history of the world and of man directed by God to this final end and consummation by means of other realizations of Wisdom. Though not themselves personal, their purpose is to prepare these two great personal realizations—one, in faith, that of the Mother of God; the other, in glory, that of the Spouse of God. The first of these impersonal, or rather inter-personal, realizations, between God and man, is the Torah, the divine Law, the revelation of the Old Covenant; for behind this it is the eternal Word which moves onwards to its own self-revelation, and, through it, preparing and bringing to pass the appearance, on the stage of history, of her who, in her own person, is the acceptance and response to the divine advances, being the Mother of the new man, of the last Adam, in whom all the dispersed sons of the first Adam are to be gathered in one and restored to life, in the Eve of the end of time.

In the birth of Christ from Mary, Wisdom revealed itself to her, in her perfect faith, as Grace (cf. Eccl 24:12). Thus, it prepared the way for its final revelation in that Glory which will leave no more room for faith, since it will fulfil all that faith hopes for. The divine Glory, as investing all flesh, is, then, the final revelation of Wisdom, as wholly divine, wholly realized in the Son. But this revelation will be effected only when the time comes for the revelation of the Spouse of the Son, so that these will be, not two different revelations, but one, that of the marriage of the Lamb. Ultimately, then, Grace will be fulfilled in Glory, and their unity will be revealed inasmuch as they are one and the same participation which, through time, leads us to eternity.

This is why Scripture comes, finally, to assimilate and even to identify Glory—the splendor shining forth from the divine countenance, uncreated but destined to be reflected by the creature—with Wisdom itself. But even more significant is the assimilation of Wisdom to the Shekinah, that mysterious Dwelling of God himself, the God of heaven, sovereign, incomprehensible, inaccessible, with men, in a determined place on earth. This localized and temporary presence of the eternal, transcendent God is necessarily hidden. It is veiled in a cloud; yet this cloud shines with a dazzling light, which, at first, blinds any mortal sight. A day, however, will come when all flesh will see the God whom no man can see without dying. The flame of the burning bush (Exodus 3:2–6), the light of Tabor, will fill the whole universe, and transfigure it, as the human countenance of Christ transfigured. Then it is that the Presence, veiled at first in that Ark, alone holy, which was the virginal flesh of Mary, will fill and make immortal all flesh. "We shall be like to him, because we shall see him as he is" (1 John 3:2).

When that time comes, "Wisdom will be justified of all her children" (Lk 7:35). Its mystery, its secret, which the powers of this world had been made unable to penetrate, otherwise "they would never have crucified the Lord of glory" (1 Cor 2:8), delivered to men in Christ, proclaimed to the world in the Church, will be revealed, not only to all flesh, but to every power in heaven, on the earth, and under the earth (Col 1:24–2:3; Eph 3:8–11). Then every tongue will confess that Christ is the Lord, to the glory of God the Father (Phil 2:10–11); and all flesh seeing, at last, the salvation of God (Lk 3:6; Is 40:5), God will be all in all (1 Cor 15:28).

We are now in a position to make clear the exact place of our Lady, the Church, and each predestined soul, respectively. As we have already said, Wisdom, God's eternal plan for history, the great design he brings to pass with the unfolding of history, is not a kind of fourth person in God. The only personal realization of Wisdom within God is brought about in the generation of the Son, which is recapitulated in the production of the Holy Ghost. But it does not reach out towards a personal realization of itself in its prolongation outside the divinity. The divine Wisdom will be fully shown forth in history only by a creature perfectly conformed to its divine model, united to this model as it is forever realized in the Son, and, in virtue of this union, bearing in itself the presence of the Spirit, which will make this creature no static image, but a living image of the living God, living, that is, by God's own love by which it loves God in return.

The final realization of the person of the Spouse, as we have seen, does not infringe the individual existence of persons formed in the course of history, any more than these cease to be through their union with the eternal person of the Word, their Spouse. On the contrary, what constitutes it is the fullness of the new life they gain by becoming united to him. Made one with Christ, and one with each other in Christ, the individuals thereby are freed from the state of being shut off and irredeemably divided which belonged to them originally by nature. Living all together a new life in Christ, the life of *Agape*, which is the life the divine Persons have in common, they become, so to speak, open to one another. Since they all have one heart and soul in Christ, what each possesses must, necessarily, be common to the rest. The personality of the Spouse that makes its appearance at the end of time, for the marriage of the Lamb, consists of this harmony of so many hearts and souls filled with Christ, all having attained together to the fullness of Christ. At the same time, it is a revelation, in and by the creature, of all that God bore within himself from eternity; so that God will be all in all.

Each one of these souls, these living members of Christ and his Spouse who make but one flesh in one and the same Spirit, will remain distinct, all the more so in that each brings its own indispensable element to the harmony of universal charity. But, if there is one distinguished forever from all the rest by a role, a quality, a gift of grace of incomparable excellence, it is Mary herself. For Mary will forever remain the person through whom the Word was born into the world, and the one through whom his Spouse was born for him, by means of his death. Mary will ever express, within Christ's Spouse, the Church, what, in her, transcends even the quality of Spouse, namely, the divine Motherhood. The incomparable dignity, which, in and for the Church, belongs personally to Mary alone, will be invested with so great splendor because it shows forth the greatest condescension of grace, the most amazing token of the divine love for the creature, namely, the *kenosis* of the eternal Son who made his creature child of God.

In this way, Mary is the realization in a single person, at the center and, we might say, the culmination of history, of all that is most noble and perfect to be realized by the whole world at the end of history. All the graces given to each person, just as, before her, they led up to the grace which was hers, so, from now on, flow from her. In her grace as Mother of God, she is full of grace in an absolute sense. She prefigures, and, as it were, pre-contains all the graces the Church will ever receive; and the supreme grace, uniquely transcendent, of mother of grace itself in its divine source, belongs to the Church and testifies, within it, to its quality of Spouse, only because it belongs forever to Mary, the first and surpassing realization of the Church whose collective personality is realized only in individual persons.

All this has, perhaps, never been more felicitously expressed than by Issac de Stella:

> Indeed, the only Head and the whole Body of Christ is one, one from a single God in heaven and a single mother on earth, many sons, and yet one single son. And, as the Head and the members are one Son and many sons, so Mary and the Church are one Mother and many, one Virgin and many. Both the one and the other are mothers; one and the other are virgins; one and the other conceive of the same Spirit without fleshly union; one and the other give the Father a sinless progeny. The former brought forth, sinless herself, the Head for the body; the latter brought forth, in the remission of all sins, a body for the Head. Both the one and the other are mothers of Christ; but neither brings him to the whole world without the other. So it is that, in the divinely inspired Scriptures, whatever is said, in a universal, of the Virgin Mother who is the Church is, rightly understood, singularly, of the Virgin Mary; and what is said specially of Mary, the Virgin Mother, is said generally of the Church; and as the words of Scripture are compounded of each of them, they are to be understood, almost always

and indifferently, of both. Each soul that believes may, too, be considered as, in its way, spouse of the Word of God, mother, daughter and sister of Christ, Virgin and fruitful. So, then, what applies universally to the Church, applies specially to Mary, and individually to the faithful soul, by the very Wisdom of God which is the word of the Father.[8]

It is on these lines that we may interpret the traditional belief in the Assumption of our Lady. As the recent definition of Pope Pius XII says, it is the traditional belief of the Church that Mary, after reaching the end of her life on earth, was reunited with her risen Son, and glorified both in her body and her soul. Just as in Mary was first effected that perfect union with Christ on the Cross that the whole Church is to realize in the course of its history, so the perfect union with Christ in glory was also accomplished in Mary, as soon as her earthly history was ended, as it will be accomplished for the whole Church at the end of history.

Mary, therefore, should be looked on as the living pledge of Christ's promises to the Church: that where he is, we also shall be (John 14:3); then the glory given him by the Father he will give to us, as he received it (John 17:22).

Consequently, it goes without saying that Mary's Assumption is, by no means, a kind of apotheosis dispensing her from the common human destiny, any more than the Immaculate Conception was an abnormal privilege designed to emancipate her from the conditions of human life. But, as Mary, by the grace of redemption brought by her Son, a grace to which, in opening herself, she opened the whole of mankind, was the first to be saved, and that more perfectly than any other person, as regards sin, so she is seen as saved the first and more perfectly than anyone else, as regards death, the result of sin. Her Immaculate Conception was the pledge of the perfect and wholly virginal purity to which, one day, the creature, sullied by sin, has to attain, in order to become the Spouse of Christ. Likewise, her Assumption is the pledge of the glory Christ will give to his Spouse, as he has already given it to his Mother. As St. John says: "It hath not yet appeared what we shall be. We know that, when he shall appear, we shall be like to him, because we shall see him as he is" (1 John 3:2). For Mary, this condition is already realized. Her perfect faith passed, as it were without any intermediate stage, to sight. In the Mother of Christ and our Mother, we are given the pledge of his promise; seeing him as she sees him, we shall be like to her, who is already like to him. As St. Paul says: "We shall be taken up together to meet Christ, and so we shall always be with the Lord" (1 Thess 4:6).

---

8. Sermon 51, *On the Assumption.*

How, then, are we to represent, as far as possible, this state of glory, of eschatology already realized, to which Mary has entered in the train of her Son?

Christ's Ascension does not mean that he has left us to our present condition, since he has gone only to prepare a place for us, that where he is we also may be; no more does Mary's Assumption mean her separation from us. As her Son is represented in the epistle to the Hebrews as *semper vivens ad interpellandum pro nobis* (7:25),[9] so she remains, as the constant belief of the Church assures us, at his side, the interceder *par excellence*. Already, her blessedness is perfect, present, as she is, with God who has placed in her his delight. But, more than ever, the contemplative prayer which raises her above the angels, in the bliss of an eternal Eucharist, carries an irresistible intercession, on her part, that sinners, all of us countless children of hers, may come to be united to her in her Son. To her more than any other may be applied what one of the Blessed says in a poem of Newman's, "A Voice from afar" (1829):

> Weep not for me;—
> Be blithe as wont, nor tinge with gloom
> The stream of love that circles home,
> Light hearts and free!
> Joy in the gifts Heaven's bounty lends;
> Nor miss my face, dear friends!
>
> I still am near;—
> Watching the smiles I prized on earth,
> Your converse mild, your blameless mirth;
> Now too I hear
> Of whisper'd sounds the tale complete,
> Low prayers, and musings sweet.
>
> A sea before
> The Throne is spread;—its pure still glass
> Pictures all earth-scenes as they pass.
> We, on its shore,
> Share, in the bosom of our rest,
> God's knowledge, and are blest.

If Pascal's saying is true, that Christ, though risen and ascended into heaven is still "in agony till the end of the world" for sinners, surely his Mother, united to him in glory, is still in the pangs of childbirth, till the marriage of the Lamb is consummated, and the last of the elect is born from the Cross to glory.

---

9. "Seeing he ever liveth to make intercession for [us]."

And the spirit and the bride say: Come. And he that heareth, let him say: Come. And he that thirsteth, let him come. And he that will, let him take of the water of life freely. (Rev 22:17)

Pierre Teilhard de Chardin

The Eternal Feminine

I

Ab initio creata sum

When the world was born, I came into being. Before the centuries were made, I issued from the hand of God—half-formed, yet destined to grow in beauty from age to age, the handmaid of his work.

Everything in the universe is made by union and generation—by the coming together of elements that seek out one another, melt together two by two, and are born again in a third.

God instilled me into the initial multiple as a force of condensation and concentration.

In me is seen that side of beings by which they are joined as one, in me the fragrance that makes them hasten together and leads them, freely and passionately, along their road to unity.

Through me, all things have their movement and are made to work as one.

I am the beauty running through the world, to make it associate in ordered groups: the ideal held up before the world to make it ascend.

I am the essential Feminine.[10]

In the beginning I was no more than a mist, rising and falling: I lay hidden beneath affinities that were as yet hardly conscious, beneath a loose and tenuous polarity.

And yet I was already in existence.

In the stirring of the layers of the cosmic substance, whose nascent folds contain the promise of worlds beyond number, the first traces of my countenance could be read.

Like a soul, still dormant but essential, I bestirred the original mass, almost without form, which hastened into my field of attraction; and I instilled even into the atoms, into the fathomless depths of the infinitesimal, a vague but obstinate yearning to emerge from the solitude of their nothingness and to hold fast to something outside themselves.

I was the bond that thus held together the foundations of the universe.

For every monad, be it never so humble, provided it is in very truth a

---

10. 1 Eccl. 24:14.

158

center of activity, obeys in its movement an embryo of love for me:
The universal Feminine.

With the coming of life, I began to be embodied in beings that had been chosen to be in a special way my image.

Step by step, I became individualized.

At first I was ill-defined and elusive, as though I could not make up my mind to be contained in a tangible form:

But then, as souls became more ready to enter into a richer, deeper, more spiritualized union, I became more differentiated.

And thus, patiently and in secret, was developed the archetype of bride and mother.

During this transformation I did not surrender any of the lower charms that marked the successive phases of my appearance—just as the heart of the olive-tree holds firm and sound when, with each new spring, it grows green once more.

I still held them within me, and taught them to bear the burden of a greater consciousness. Thus, as living beings approached greater perfection on earth, so (and yet always outdistancing their growth) I was able to stand before them, matching, circle for circle, the concentric zones of their desires, as the proper form of their beatitude.

Follow with your eye the vast tremor that runs, from horizon to horizon, through city and forest.

Observe, throughout all life, the human effervescence that works like leaven in the world—the song of the birds and their plumage—the wild hum of the insects—the tireless blooming of the flowers—the unremitting work of the cells—the endless labors of the seeds germinating in the soil.

I am the single radiance by which all this is aroused and within which it is vibrant.

Man, nature's synthesis, does many things with the fire that burns in his breast. He builds up power, he seeks for glory, he creates beauty, he weds himself to science. And often he does not realize that, under so many different forms, it is still the same passion that inspires him—purified, transformed, but living—the magnetism of the Feminine.

It was within life that I began to unveil my face.

But it was man who was the first to recognize me, in the disquiet my presence brought him.

When a man loves a woman he thinks at first that his love is given simply to an individual like himself whom he envelops in his power and freely associates with himself.

He is very conscious of a radiance, haloing my countenance, which sensitizes his heart and illuminates all things.

But he attributes this radiation of my being to a subjective disposition of his entranced mind, or to a mere reflection of my beauty in nature's countless facets.

Soon, however, he is astonished by the violence of the forces unleashed in him at my approach, and trembles to realize that he cannot be united with me without inevitably becoming enslaved to a universal work of creation.

He thought that it was simply a partner who stood by his side: and now he sees that in me he meets the great hidden force, the mysterious latency, that has come to him in this form in order to lead him captive.

For the man who has found me, the door to all things stands open. I extend my being into the soul of the world—not only through the medium of that man's own sensibility, but also through the physical links of my own nature—or rather, I am the magnetic force of the universal presence and the ceaseless ripple of its smile.

I open the door to the whole heart of creation: I, the Gateway of the Earth, the Initiation.

He who takes me, gives himself to me, and is himself taken by the universe.

In the knowledge of me, alas, there is both good and evil.

Man's initiation has proved too strong meat for him.

When he saw that I was for him the universe, he thought to encompass me in his arms.

He wished to shut himself up with me in a closed world for two, in which each would be sufficient to the other.

At that very moment, I fell apart in his hands.

And then it could have seemed as though I were the rock on which mankind foundered—the Temptress.

Why, O men, why do you halt in the task of hard-won purification as a summons to which my beauty was made?

I am essentially fruitful: that is to say my eyes are set on the future, on the Ideal.

The moment you try to pin me down, to possess me in some complete form, you stifle me.

What is more, you distort, you reverse—as you would a geometric pattern—my nature.

Since the true balance of life forces you continually to ascend, you cannot set me up as a lifeless idol to cling to, without falling back; instead of becoming gods, you revert to matter.

As soon as you fold your wings around me, you follow matter in its descent: for what drives matter down is the sterile union of its elements in which each neutralizes the other.

What you are grasping is no more than matter: for matter is a tendency, a direction—it is the side of Spirit that we meet as we fall back.

And your fall accelerates at a terrifying speed—as fast as the widening of the gap between your real appetites and the ever lower forms in which you seek for me.

And, when you, who are but dust, reach the term of your efforts, it is but dust that you embrace.

The more, O men, you seek me in the direction of pleasure, the farther will you wander from my reality.

The flesh, in truth, which operates as the pull of evil between you and the lower multiple (that reversed image of God) is no more than my inverted semblance, floating over an abyss of endless dissociation, that is, of endless corruption.

For a long time man, lacking the skill to distinguish between the mirage and the truth, has not known whether he should fear me or worship me.

He loved me for the magic of my charm and my sovereign power; he feared me as a force alien to himself, and for the bewildering riddle I presented.

I was at once his strength and his weakness—his hope and his trial. It was in relation to me that the good were divided from the wicked.

Indeed, had Christ not come, man might well have placed me for ever in the camp of evil.

II

Et usque adfuturum saeculum non desinam[11]
Christ has given me salvation and freedom.

When he said: *Melius est non nubere*, men took it to mean that I was dead to eternal life.

In truth, by those words he restored me to life, with Lazarus—with Magdalen—and set me between himself and men as a nimbus of glory:

In making manifest that great virtue he defined, in fact, my true essence, and guided men, who had lost track of me, back to the true road I had trodden.

11. Ecclesiasticus 24:14.

In the regenerated world I am still, as I was at my birth, the summons to unity with the universe—the world's attractive power imprinted on human features.

The true union, however, is the union that simplifies, and to simplify is to spiritualize.

The true fertility is the fertility that brings beings together in the engendering of Spirit.

If, in the new sphere into which created being entered, I was to remain Woman, I was obliged to change my form without impairing my former nature.

While my deceptive image continues to lure the pleasure-seeker towards matter, my reality has risen aloft, drawing men to the heights: it floats between the Christian and his God.

My charm can still draw men, but towards the light. I can still carry them with me, but into freedom.

Henceforth my name is Virginity.

The Virgin is still woman and mother: in that we may read the sign of the new age.

The pagans on the Acropolis blame the Gospel for having disfigured the world, and they mourn for beauty. These men are blasphemers.

Christ's message is not the signal for a rupture, for an emancipation: as though the elect of God, rejecting the law of the flesh, could break the bonds that tie them to the destiny of their race, and escape from the cosmic current in which they came to birth.

The man who hearkens to Christ's summons is not called upon to exile love from his heart. On the contrary, it is his duty to remain essentially a man.

Thus he has an even greater need of me, to sensitize his powers, and arouse his soul to a passion for the divine.

For the Saint, more than for any other man, I am the maternal shadow leaning over the cradle—and the radiant forms assumed by youth's dreams—and the deep-seated aspiration that passes through the heart like some undisputed alien force—the mark, in each individual being of Life's axis.

Christ has left me all my jewels.

In addition, however, he has sent down upon me from heaven a ray that has boundlessly idealized me.

It seemed good to him, in the first place, to give a new zest to the natural impetus of my development.

Faced by a mankind that never ceases to ascend, the part I have to play insists on my withdrawing to an ever higher level—held aloft, over the earth's growing ambition, as a lure and a prize—almost grasped, but never held. By its very nature, the Feminine must continue unremittingly to make itself progressively more felt in a universe that has not reached the term of its evolution: to ensure the final blossoming of my stock, will be the glory and bliss of chastity.

Countless are the new essences handed over by nature, from age to age, to life!

Under the influence of Christianity, I shall combine, until creation is complete, their subtle and dangerous refinements in an ever-changing perfection which will embrace the aspirations of each new generation.

Then, so long as the world endures, there will be seen reflected in the face of Beatrix the dreams of art and of science towards which each new century aspires.

Since the beginning of all things, Woman has never ceased to take as her own the flower of all that was produced by the vitality of nature or the art of man.

Who could say in what climax of perfections, both individual and cosmic, I shall blossom forth, in the evening of the world, before the face of God?

I am the unfading beauty of the times to come—the ideal Feminine.

The more, then, I become Feminine, the more immaterial and celestial will my countenance be.

In me, the soul is at work to sublimate the body—Grace to divinize the soul.

Those who wish to continue to possess me must change as I change.

Behold!

The center of my attraction is imperceptibly shifting towards the pole upon which all the avenues of Spirit converge.

The iridescence of my beauties, flung like a mantle over creation, is slowly gathering in its outlying folds.

Already the shadow is falling upon the flesh, even the flesh purified by the sacraments.

One day, maybe, it will swallow up even art, even science—things loved as a woman is loved.

The beam circles: and we must follow it round.

Soon only God will remain for you in a universe where all is virgin.

It is God who awaits you in me!

Long before I drew you, I drew God towards me.

Long before man had measured the extent of my power, and divinized the polarity of my attraction, the Lord had conceived me, whole and entire, in his wisdom, and I had won his heart.

Without the lure of my purity, think you, would God ever have come down, as flesh, to dwell in his creation?

Only love has the power to move being.

If God, then, was to be able to emerge from himself, he had first to lay a pathway of desire before his feet, he had to spread before him a sweet savor of beauty.

It was then that he caused me to rise up, a luminous mist hanging over the abyss—between the earth and himself—that, in me, he might dwell among you.

Now do you understand the secret of the emotion that possesses you when I come near?

The tender compassion, the hallowed charm, that radiate from Woman—so naturally that it is only in her that you look for them, and yet so mysteriously that you cannot say whence they come—are the presence of God making itself felt and setting you ablaze.

Lying between God and the earth, as a zone of mutual attraction, I draw them both together in a passionate union.

—until the meeting takes place in me, in which the generation and plenitude of Christ are consummated throughout the centuries.

I am the Church, the bride of Christ.

I am Mary the Virgin, mother of all human kind.

It might be thought that in this conjunction of heaven and earth I am destined to disappear as a useless handmaid, that I will have to vanish like a shadow before the reality.

Those who love me should dismiss this fear.

Just as participated being is not lost when it attains its principle

—but, on the contrary, finds fulfilment in melting in God—

Just as the soul, once it is formed, does not completely exclude the countless elements from which it emerged—but retains, as essential to it, a potency for and a need for flesh in which to contain itself—

So the Cosmos, when divinized, will not expel my magnetic influence by which the ever more complex and more simplified fascicle of its atoms is progressively more closely—and permanently—knit—

I shall subsist, entire, with all my past, even in the raptures of contact with God—

What is more, I shall continue to disclose myself—as inexhaustible in my development as the infinite beauties of which I am always, even if unseen, the raiment, the form, and the gateway.

When you think I am no longer with you—when you forget me, the air you breathe, the light with which you see—then I shall still be at hand, lost in the sun I have drawn to myself.

Blessed elect, you have only (think: is this not true?) to relax for one moment the tension that impels you towards God, or to let your glance fall the least distance short of the center that enchants you, in order once again to see my image playing over the surface of the divine fire.

—And at that moment you may see with wonder how there unfolds, in the long web of my charms, the ever-living series of allurements—of forces that one after another have made themselves felt ever since the borderline of nothingness, and so brought together and assembled the elements of Spirit—through love.

I am the Eternal Feminine.
Verzy, 19–25 March 1918

Valentin Tomberg

from *Meditations on the Tarot:*
A Journey into Christian Hermeticism

Letter XIX

One could also say, in the symbolical language of the Bible, that yoga attains to union (= yoga) of the two luminaries—the moon (or intelligence) and the sun (or spontaneous wisdom of the transcendental Self)—and halts there, whilst Sankya also attains this, but it takes account of still a further kind of "luminary": the "stars" (higher entities of the spiritual world). Sankya, whilst leaving the door open to that which transcends the "transcendental Self," does not occupy itself with it, it is true, in an explicit manner—which has given it the qualification "atheistic." However, its "atheism" does not amount to its denying the existence of a universal *Purusha* higher than all individual *purushas* (it professes to know nothing of this with certain knowledge), but rather to its denying the affirmation of yoga and Vedanta, i.e., that the "transcendental Self" *is* God.

In contrast, Judaeo-Christian Hermeticism, which ranges itself on the side of Sankya with respect to the negation of the identification of the "transcendental Self" with God, is intensely occupied with the third "luminary"—the "stars"—in the three aspects of astrology, angelology and trinitarian theology, which aspects correspond to the body, soul and spirit of the third "luminary." Judaeo-Christian Hermeticism is thus the sustained effort across the centuries to know and understand the *three* luminaries in their *unity*, i.e., to know and understand the "great portent which appeared in heaven—a woman clothed with the sun, with the moon under her feet, and on her head a crown of twelve stars" (Revelation 12:1). It is the woman in this apocalyptic vision who unites the three "luminaries"—the moon, the sun and the stars, i.e., the luminaries of night, day and eternity.

It is she—the "Virgin of light" of the *Pistis Sophia,* the Wisdom sung of by Solomon, the *Shekinah* of the Cabbala, the Mother, the Virgin, the pure celestial Mary—who is the soul of the light of the three luminaries, and who is both the source and aim of Hermeticism. For Hermeticism is, as a whole, the aspiration to participation in knowledge of the Father, Son and Holy Spirit, and the Mother, Daughter and Holy Soul. It is not a matter of seeing the Holy Trinity with human eyes, but rather of seeing with the eyes—and in the light—of Mary-Sophia. For just as no one comes to the Father but by Jesus Christ (John 14:6), so does no one understand the Holy Trinity but by Mary-Sophia. And just as the Holy Trinity manifests itself through Jesus Christ, so *understanding* of this manifestation is possible only through intuitive apprehension of what the virgin mother of Jesus Christ understands of it, who not only bore him and brought him to the light of day, but who also was present—present as mother—at his death on the Cross. And just as Wisdom (Sophia)—as Solomon said—was present at the creation ("when he established the heavens, I was there, when he drew a circle on the face of the deep . . . then I was at work beside him"—Proverbs 8:27–31) and "built her house . . . set up her seven pillars" (Proverbs 9:1), so Mary-Sophia was present at the redemption and "was at work beside him," and "built her house . . . set up her seven pillars," i.e., she became Our Lady of the seven sorrows. For the seven sorrows of Mary correspond, for the work of the redemption, to the seven pillars of Sophia for the work of creation. Sophia is the queen of the "three luminaries"—the moon, the sun and the stars—as the "great portent" of the Apocalypse shows. And just as the *word* of the Holy Trinity became flesh in Jesus Christ, so did the *light* of the Holy Trinity become flesh in Mary-Sophia—the *light*, i.e., threefold receptivity, the threefold faculty of intelligent reaction, or *understanding*. Mary's words: *mihi fiat secundum verbum tuum* ("let it be to me according to your Word"—Luke 1:38) are the key to the mystery of the relationship between the pure act and pure reaction, between the word and understanding—lastly, between Father, Son and Holy Spirit on the one hand and Mother, Daughter and Holy Soul on the other hand. They are the true key to the "seal of Solomon" —the hexagram: ✡

The hexagram is not at all the symbol of good and evil, but rather a is that of the threefold pure act or "fire" and the threefold pure reaction (the threefold *mihi fiat secundum verbum tuum*) or "light of fire," i.e., "water." "Fire" and "water" signify that which acts spontaneously and creatively on the one hand, and that which reacts reflectively on the other hand—the latter being the conscious "yes" or light of *mihi fiat secundum verbum tuum*. This is the elementary meaning of the "seal of Solomon"—elementary in the sense of the *elements* "fire" and "water," taken on their highest level.

But the still higher meaning that this symbol hides—or rather reveals—is that of the *luminous Holy Trinity*, i.e., that of *understanding* of the Holy Trinity.

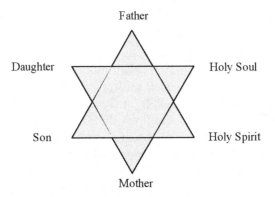

Then it is the hexagram comprising the two triangles: Father-Son-Holy Spirit; Mother-Daughter-Holy Soul (see figure). And these two triangles of the luminous Holy Trinity are revealed in the work of redemption accomplished through Jesus Christ and conceived through Mary-Sophia. Jesus Christ is its agent; Mary-Sophia is its luminous reaction. The two triangles reveal the *luminous Holy Trinity* in the work of creation accomplished by the creative Word and animated by the "yes" of Wisdom-Sophia. The luminous Holy Trinity is therefore the unity of the triune Creator and the triune *natura naturans*, i.e., the unity of the threefold *Fiat* and the threefold *mihi fiat secundum verbum tuum* which reveals itself in *natura naturata*, in the world created before the Fall; and it is the triune divine *spirit* and the triune *soul* of the world manifesting in the *body* of the world—in *natura naturata*.

The *Zohar* puts forward the idea of the luminous Holy Trinity. It teaches that the great name of GOD YHVH reveals the Father (Y = י), the supreme Mother (H = ה), the Son (V = ו), and the Daughter (the second HÉ of the divine name YHVH). Such is the eternal name YHVH. But in the history of the created world there are also revealed: the *Shekinah* (identified with the "community of Israel")—the true "Rachel weeping for her children" (Matthew 2:18), who weeps in exile and who is the "beautiful virgin who has no eyes";[12] the *Messiah-king* who "descends and reascends through all the heavens in order to exercise, with all the prophets who are to be found, the universal function of salvation";[13] and the *Ruah hakodesch* (the "holy breath" or Holy Spirit), of which Saadya speaks, through the intermediary of which the thirty-two

12. *Mishpatim* 95a; *The Zohar*, trans. Sperling-Simon-Levertoff, 5 vol. (London-Bournemouth: The Soncino Press, 1949), 3:285.

13. L. Schaya, *L'homme et l'absolu selon la Kabbale* (Paris: Editions Buchet/Castel, 1958), 96.

ways of wisdom are incorporated in the air that one breathes—the "holy breath" by means of which God is revealed, to the prophets, at the foundation of the secret of creation and which is called the "breath of the living God" (רוּחַ הָאֱלֹהִים חַיִּים).[14] The Messiah is the seventh term or principle of the hexagram Father, Son, Holy Spirit; Mother, Daughter, Holy Soul (= *Shekinah,* or the "community of Israel"). He is the *agent* of all, the active summary of the bi-polar Trinity or, as we have called it, the *luminous Holy Trinity.*

With respect to the concrete manifestation of the *Shekinah,* "it is as a woman that she now appears to the visionaries among the Cabbalists, like Abraham Halevi, a disciple of Luria, who in 1571 saw her at the wailing wall in Jerusalem as a woman dressed in black and weeping for the husband of her youth."[15] The weeping Lady of La Salette also wept at the foot of a wall no less real than the wailing wall in Jerusalem—the wail of universal sin which is placed between humanity and divine grace—but she differs from the *Shekinah* of the visions of the Cabbalists and Hassidim in that she is not the personification of a principle, i.e., she is not solely an *aspect* of the Divine, but rather is a human person who existed in the flesh at the bosom of the visible community of Israel twenty centuries ago. Similarly, the Messiah, whom many have seen and met during the last twenty centuries, is no more only a spirit who "descends and reascends through all the heavens in order to exercise, with all the prophets who are to be found, the universal function of salvation," but rather is a human person who existed at the bosom of the visible community of Israel twenty centuries ago. For just as the Word became flesh in Jesus Christ, so did the *Bath-Kol,* the "Daughter of the Voice," become flesh in Mary-Sophia. The Church worships her as the Virgin, as the Mother and as the celestial Queen, corresponding to the Mother, the Daughter and the "Virgin of Israel" of the Cabbala, and to the Sophianic Trinity—Mother, Daughter and Holy Soul—mentioned above.

The Athenians, also, had an analogous feminine triad, which played the principal role in the mysteries of Eleusis: Demeter—the Mother, Persephone—the Daughter, and "Athena the bringer of salvation"[16]— where Athena was at the same time the "community of Athens" or the "soul of Athens" as it were, analogous to the "Virgin of Israel."

14. Cf. Henri Sérouya, *La Kabbale: Ses origines, sa psychologie mystique, sa métaphysique,* nouvelle edition (Paris: Grasset, 1957), 136.

15. Gershom G. Scholem, *Major Trends in Jewish Mysticism* (London: Thames and Hudson, 1955), 230.

16. Cf. Olympiodorus, *In Platonis Phaedonem commentaria,* ed. W. Norvin (Leipzig: Teubner, 1913), 111.

Historical analogies and metaphysical parallels alone, however, do not suffice to attain the complete certainty of intuition: it is for the heart to say the last decisive word. Thus the following "argument of the heart" proved to be decisive, twenty-five years ago, to the one who writes these lines.

There is nothing which is more necessary and more precious in the experience of human childhood than parental love; nothing more necessary, because the human child, alone, is not viable if it is not taken from the first moments of its life into the circle of care of parental love or, lacking parental love, its substitute—charity; nothing more precious, because the parental love experienced in childhood is moral capital for the whole of life. In childhood we receive two dowries for life, two assets from which we can draw during the whole of life: the vital biological asset which is the treasure of our health and vital energy, and the moral asset which is the treasure of health of soul and its vital energy—its capacity to love, to hope and to believe. The moral asset is the experience of parental love that we have had in childhood. It is so precious, this experience, that it renders us capable of elevating ourselves to more sublime things—even to divine things. It is thanks to the experience of parental love that our soul is capable of raising itself to the love of God. Without it the soul could not truly enter into a living relationship with the living God, one of loving God—being unable to pass beyond the abstract conception of God as the "Architect" or the "First Cause" of the world. For it is the experience of parental love—and it is above all this—which renders us capable of *loving* the "Architect" or "First Cause" of the world as *our Father* who is in heaven. Parental love bears in itself true senses of the soul for the Divine—which are, by analogy, eyes and ears of the soul.

Now, the experience of parental love consists of two elements: the experience of maternal love and that of paternal love. The one and the other are equally necessary and equally precious. The one and the other render us capable of raising ourselves to the Divine. The one and the other signify to us the means of entering into a living relationship with God, which means to love God, who is the prototype of all paternity and all maternity.

Now, love teaches in its own way—with a certainty which excludes all doubt—that the divine commandment, "Honour thy father and thy mother," is truly *divine*, i.e., that it is significant in heaven as well as on earth. "Honour thy father and thy mother" is applicable therefore not only to transitory things but also to eternal things. Such is the commandment revealed to Moses on Mt. Sinai, and such is also the commandment emanating from the depths of the human heart. One should honour the Father who is in heaven *and* the celestial Mother. This is why practising believers of the traditional Church, i.e., the Roman Catholic Church and the Orthodox Church, caring little for the difference stated in dogmatic theology between the celestial Father and Mother, love and honour—in their practice of prayer—the celestial Mother no less than the Father who is in heaven.

Dogmatic theologians may well put believers on their guard against "exaggeration" in the domain of Mariology and Protestant critics may well advance criticism of the cult of the Virgin Mary as "idolatry," but practising believers of the traditional Church continue and will always continue to honour and love their celestial Mother as the eternal Mother of all that lives and breathes. If one says that "the heart has its own reasons, which the intellect does not know," one can also say that "the heart has its own dogmas, which theological reasoning docs not know." Indeed this "dogma" of the heart, although as yet not formulated—being generally confined to the domain of the unconscious—nonetheless exercises a growing influence on the guardians of dogmatic orthodoxy of a kind such that the latter are constrained to give way, through the centuries, one position after another to this irresistible impulse: in liturgical forms and in the practice of prayer sanctioned by ecclesiastical authorities, the role accorded to the Virgin Mary does not stop growing. The Queen of the Angels, the Queen of the patriarchs, the Queen of the apostles, the Queen of martyrs, confessors, virgins, and saints, the Queen of peace, is, in the texts of liturgical prayers, also the Mother of God, the Mother of divine grace, and the Mother of the Church. In the churches of the Greek Orthodox Church one sings: "More honoured than the Cherubim, more glorious than the Seraphim—thou who art the true Mother of God, we honour thee." Now, the Cherubim and Seraphim are the first celestial hierarchy and the Holy Trinity alone is above them. This "dogma" of the heart is so powerful that the time will come when it will result in official recognition from the Church and will be formulated. For it is thus that all Church dogmas have arrived, in the past, at their promulgation: they live first of all in the hearts of the believers, then influence more and more the liturgical life of the Church, in order—lastly—to be promulgated as formulated dogmas. Dogmatic theology is only the last stage of the "way of dogma" which begins in the depths of the life of souls and results in ceremonious promulgation. This way is exactly what is understood by "the direction of the Church by the Holy Spirit." The Church knows it and has the patience to await—even for centuries—the time when the work of the Holy Spirit will have attained to maturity.

Be that as it may, whatever the duration of time for the mysterious process of the birth of the dogma raising maternal love to the level of the Holy Trinity may be, it is already well formulated and is at work across the centuries. All the same, it is a matter, whilst respecting the law of patience and abstaining from all attempts to force things, of cultivating feelings and ideas relating to divine maternal love and of meditating on the ancient Hermetic doctrines which reveal the mystical, gnostic and magical meaning of this aspect of divine love. In other words, it is a matter of meditating on the mystery of the luminous Holy Trinity, whose symbol is the "seal of Solomon": ✡ —or again, on the symbol of the Trinity alongside that of the luminous Holy Trinity: △ ✡

This symbol of the development from the Holy Trinity to the luminous Trinity, i.e., from the triangle to the hexagram, is at the same time the divine meaning—or the highest that I know—of the number nine. Ten further spiritual exercises were necessary for us, after the meditation on the ninth Arcanum of the Tarot, in order to dare to touch on the theme of the development of the Holy Trinity into the luminous Holy Trinity, symbolised by the triangle alongside the hexagram.

We have indicated above that it is the practice of prayer and the liturgical life of the Church where the great truths anticipate their promulgation as dogmas. Now, the mystery of the number nine, that of the development of the Trinity into the luminous Trinity, also lives in the practice of prayer and ritual within the Church.

I have in mind the practice, universally diffused in the Catholic Church, of the novena—the most practised form of which is the act of prayer consisting of one *Pater Noster* and three *Ave Marias*, to which one devotes oneself for nine days. One makes a novena by appealing to the paternal love of the Father (*Pater Noster*) and to the maternal love of the Mother (the three *Ave Marias*) simultaneously for nine days, for the sake of a person or a cause. What depth there is underlying this practice that is so simple! In truth—in any case for the Hermeticist—the direction of the superhuman wisdom of the Holy Spirit is manifested here!

Similarly, it is so with the rosary prayer, where appeal to the two aspects of divine paternal love in the prayer addressed to the Father and the Mother is made during meditation on the mysteries of the Joy, Suffering and Glory of the Blessed Virgin. The rosary prayer is—in any case for the Hermeticist—again a masterpiece of simplicity, containing and revealing things of inexhaustible profundity . . . a masterpiece of the Holy Spirit!

PART II

The Poetry of Sophia

St. Patrick (*fifth century*)

Patrick's Breastplate (The Deer's Cry)

I arise today
Through a mighty strength, the invocation of the Trinity,
Through belief in the threeness,
Through confession of the oneness
Of the Creator of Creation.

I arise today
Through the strength of Christ's birth with His baptism,
Through the strength of His crucifixion with His burial,
Through the strength of His resurrection with His ascension,
Through the strength of His descent for the judgement of Doom.

I arise today
Through the strength of the love of the Cherubim,
In the obedience of angels,
In the service of archangels,
In the hope of the resurrection to meet with reward,
In the prayers of patriarchs,
In prediction of prophets,
In preaching of apostles,
In faith of confessors,
In innocence of holy virgins,
In deeds of righteous men.

I arise today
Through the strength of heaven;
Light of sun,
Radiance of moon,
Splendour of fire,
Speed of lightning,
Swiftness of wind,
Depth of sea,
Stability of earth,
Firmness of rock.

I arise today
Through God's strength to pilot me:
God's might to uphold me,
God's wisdom to guide me,
God's eye to look before me,
God's ear to hear me,

God's word to speak to me,
God's hand to guard me,
God's way to lie before me,
God's shield to protect me,
God's host to save me,
From snares of devils,
From temptation of vices,
From every one who shall wish me ill,
Afar and anear,
Alone and in a multitude.

I summon today all these powers between me and those evils,
Against every cruel merciless power that may oppose my body
    and soul,
Against incantations of false prophets,
Against black laws of pagandom,
Against false laws of heretics,
Against craft of idolatry,
Against spells of women and smiths and wizards,
Against every knowledge that corrupts man's body and soul.

Christ to shield me today,
Against poisoning, against burning,
Against drowning, against wounding,
So there come to me abundance of reward.
Christ with me, Christ before me, Christ behind me,
Christ in me, Christ beneath me, Christ above me,
Christ on my right, Christ on my left,
Christ when I lie down, Christ when I sit down,
Christ when I arise, Christ in the heart of every man who thinks
    of me,
Christ in the mouth of every one who speaks of me,
Christ in the eye of every one who sees me,
Christ in every ear that hears me.

I arise today
Through a mighty strength, the invocation of the Trinity,
Through belief in the threeness,
Through confession of the oneness
Of the Creator of Creation.
   Translated by Kuno Meyer

St. Hildegard of Bingen (1098–1179)

Hymn: O most noble greening power

O most noble greening power
Rooted in the sun,
Who, in dazzling serenity,
Shine in a wheel
That no earthly excellence
Can comprehend.
You are enfolded
In the embrace of divine offices,
You blush like the dawn
And burn like a flame of the sun.
   Translated by Michael Martin

St. Francis of Assisi (c. 1181–1226)

The Canticle of Creatures

Most high omnipotent, good Lord,
Yours are praise, glory and honor and all benediction,
To you alone, Most High, do they belong:
And there is no man worthy to name you.

Praise be to you, my Lord, with all your creatures,
First of all to Brother Sun who is our day,
And through whom you give light:
He is beautiful and radiant, with great splendor:
And of you, Most High, he is a true revealer.

Praise be to you, my Lord, for Sister Moon and for the stars;
In heaven you have formed them, bright, precious and fair.

Praise be to you, my Lord, for Brother Wind,
For the air and for the cloudy or clear sky and all weathers,
By which you give nourishment to all your creatures.

Praise be to you, my Lord, for Sister Water;
She is most useful and humble, precious and pure.

Praise be to you, my Lord, for Brother Fire;
By whom you illuminate the night:
He is fair and merry, mighty and strong.

Praise be to you, my Lord, for our Sister, Mother Earth,
For she sustains and keeps us:
She brings forth diverse fruits, the colorful flowers and grass.

Praise be to you, my Lord, through those who forgive for love of you;
Through those who endure sickness and trial.
Happy those who endure in peace,
For by you, Most High, they will be crowned.

Praise be to you, my Lord, through our sister Bodily Death,
from whose embrace no living person can escape.
Woe to those who die in mortal sin!
Happy those she finds doing your most holy will.
The second death cannot harm them.

O Creatures all! Praise and bless my Lord, and be grateful!
Serve Him with deep humility.

Dante Alighieri (1265–1321)

St. Bernard's Prayer to the Virgin
(*Paradiso*, Canto XXXIII)

O, Virgin Mother, daughter of thy Son,
Humblest and greatest of all creatures;
The eternal counsel's predestined end;

Thou hast brought such glory to human nature
That its divine Creator did not scorn
To make Himself the creature of His creature.

The Love that was in Thy womb enflamed
Sends forth the warmth of the eternal peace
Within which this flower has bloomed.

Here to us, thou art the meridian face
Of charity; and among mortal men,
The living fountain of hope.

Lady, so great are thy power and worth
That who seeks grace without recourse to thee
Would have his wish fly without wings.

Thy sweet benignity not only brings relief
To those who seek, but, indeed, oftentimes
It graciously anticipates the plea.

In thee is mercy, in thee is kindness,
In thee munificence, in thee unites
All that creation knows of goodness.
  Translated by Michael Martin

Robert Herrick (1591–1674)

The Argument of his Book

I Sing of *Brooks*, of *Blossomes*, *Birds*, and *Bowers*,
Of *April*, *May*, of *June*, and *July*-Flowers.
I sing of *May-poles*, *Hock-carts*, *Wassails*, *Wakes*,
Of *Bride-grooms*, *Brides*, and of their *Bridall-cakes*.
I write of *Youth*, of *Love*, and have Accesse
By these, to sing of cleanly-*Wantonnesse*.
I sing of *Dewes*, of *Raines*, and piece by piece
Of *Balme*, of *Oyle*, of *Spice*, and *Amber-gris*.
I sing of *Time's trans-shifting*; and I write
How *Roses* first came *Red*, and *Lillies White*.
I write of *Groves*, of *Twilights*, and I sing
The court of *Mab*, and of the *Fairie-King*.
I write of *Hell*; I sing (and ever shall)
Of *Heaven*, and hope to have it after all.

Henry Vaughan (1621–1695)

Regeneration

A Ward, and still in bonds, one day
          I stole abroad;
It was high-spring, and all the way
      Primros'd, and hung with shade;
      Yet, was it frost within,
          And surly winds
Blasted my infant buds, and sinne
      Like Clouds eclips'd my mind.

2.

Storm'd thus, I straight perceiv'd my spring
          Meere stage and show,
My walke a monstrous, mountain'd thing,
      Rough-cast with Rocks, and snow;
      And as a Pilgrims Eye,
          Far from reliefe,
Measures the melancholy skye,
      Then drops and rains for griefe,

3.

So sigh'd I upwards still; at last
               'Twixt steps and falls
I reach'd the pinnacle, where plac'd
      I found a pair of scales;
      I took them up and layd
              In th'one late pains;
The other smoake, and pleasures weigh'd,
      But prov'd the heavier grains;

4.

With that, some cryed, *Away*; Straight I
Obey'd, and led
Full East, a faire, fresh field could spy
      Some call'd it, *Jacob's Bed*,
      A Virgin-soile, which no
Rude feet ere trod,
Where (since he stept there,) only go
      Prophets and friends of God.

5.

Here I repos'd; but scarse well set,
A grove descryed
Of stately height, whose branches met
      And mixt on every side;
      I entered, and once in
(Amazed to see't,)
Found all was chang'd, and a new spring
      Did all my senses greet;

6.

The unthrift Sunne shot vitall gold,
A thousand peeces,
And heaven its azure did unfold,
      Checqur'd with snowie fleeces;
      The aire was all in spice,
And every bush
A garland wore; Thus fed my Eyes,
      But all the Eare lay hush.

7.

Only a little Fountain lent
Some use for Eares,
And on the dumbe shades language spent

The Musick of her teares;
    I drew her neere, and found
The Cisterne full
Of divers stones, some bright, and round,
    Others ill-shap'd and dull.

8.

The first (pray marke,) as quick as light
Danc'd through the floud,
But th'last more heavy then the night,
    Nailed to the Center stood;
    I wonder'd much, but tyr'd
At last with thought,
My restless Eye that still desir'd
    As strange an object brought;

9.

It was a bank of flowers, where I descried
(Though 'twas mid-day,)
Some fast asleepe, others broad-eyed
    And taking in the Ray;
    Here musing long, I heard
A rushing wind
Which still increas'd, but whence it stirr'd
    No where I could not find;

10.

I turn'd me round, and to each shade
Dispatch'd an Eye
To see, if any leafe had made
    Least motion, or Reply,
    But while I listening sought
My mind to ease
By knowing where 'twas, or where not,
    It whisper'd, *Where I please.*

    Lord, then said I, *On me one breath,*
    And let me dye before my death!

Cant. chap. 5. ver. 17

Arise O North, and come thou South-wind and
blow upon my garden, that the spices thereof may flow out.

Cock-Crowing

Father of lights! what Sunnie seed,
What glance of day hast Thou confin'd
Into this bird? To all the breed
This busie Ray Thou hast assign'd;
      Their magnetism works all night,
      And dreams of Paradise and light.

Their eyes watch for the morning-hue;
Their little grain expelling night,
So shines and sings, as if it knew
The path unto the house of light.
      It seems their candle, howe'r done,
      Was tinn'd and lighted at the sun.

If such a tincture, such a touch,
So firm a longing can impowre,
Shall thy own image think it much
To watch for thy appearing hour?
      If a mere blast so fill the sail,
      Shall not the breath of God prevail?

O thou immortal light and heat!
Whose hand so shines through all this frame,
That by the beauty of the seat,
We plainly see, who made the same.
      Seeing thy seed abides in me,
      Dwell thou in it, and I in thee!

To sleep without thee, is to die;
Yea, 'tis a death partakes of hell:
For where thou dost not close the eye,
It never opens, I can tell.
      In such a dark, Ægyptian border,
      The shades of death dwell and disorder.

If joys, and hopes, and earnest throws,
And hearts, whose Pulse beats still for light
Are given to birds; who, but thee, knows
A love-sick soul's exalted flight?
      Can souls be track'd by any eye
      But his, who gave them wings to flie?

Onely this Veyle which thou hast broke,
And must be broken yet in me,
This veyle, I say, is all the cloke
And cloud which shadows thee from me.

This veyle thy full-ey'd love denies,
    And onely gleams and fractions spies.

O take it off! make no delay;
But brush me with thy light that I
May shine unto a perfect day,
And warme me at thy glorious Eye!
        O take it off! or till it flee,
            Though with no Lilie, stay with me!

The Knot

Bright Queen of Heaven! Gods Virgin Spouse!
        The glad worlds blessed maid!
Whose beauty tyed life to thy house,
        And brought us saving ayd.

Thou art the true Loves-knot; by thee
        God is made our Allie,
And mans inferior Essence he
        With his did dignifie.

For Coalescent by that Band
        We are his body grown,
Nourished with favors from his hand
        Whom for our head we own.

And such a Knot, what arm dares loose,
        What life, what death can sever?
Which us in him, and him in us
        United keeps for ever.

Thomas Traherne (1636?–1674)

The Improvement

I

'Tis more to recollect, than make. The one
Is but an accident without the other.
We cannot think the world to be the Throne
Of God, unless His Wisdom shine as Brother
    Unto His Power, in the fabric, so
    That we the one may in the other know.

II

His goodness also must in both appear,
And all the children of His love be found
In the creation of the starry sphere,
And in the forming of the fruitful ground;
  Before we can that happiness descry
  Which is the Daughter of the deity.

III

His wisdom shines in spreading forth the sky,
His power's great in ordering the Sun,
His goodness very marvellous and high
Appears, in every work His hand hath done:
  And all His works in their variety
  United or asunder please the eye.

IV

But neither goodness, wisdom, power, nor love,
Nor happiness itself in things could be,
Did they not all in one fair order move,
And jointly by their service end in me:
  Had He not made an eye to be the Sphere
  Of all things, none of these would e'er appear.

V

His wisdom, goodness, power, as they unite,
All things in one, that they may be the treasures
Of one enjoyer, shine in the utmost height
They can attain; and are most glorious pleasures,
  When all the universe conjoined in one,
  Exalts a creature as if that alone.

VI

To bring the moisture of far-distant seas
Into a point, to make them present here,
In virtue, not in bulk; one man to please
With all the powers of the Highest Sphere
  From East, from West, from North and South, to bring
  The pleasing influence of every thing.

VII

Is far more great than to create them here
Where now they stand; His wisdom more doth shine
In that His might and goodness more appear
In recollecting; He is more divine
  In making every thing a gift to one
  Than in the sev'ral parts of all His spacious Throne.

VIII

Herein we see a marvellous design,
And apprehending clearly the great skill
Of that great Architect, whose love doth shine
In all His works, we find His life and Will:
  For lively counsels do the Godhead shew,
  And these His love and goodness make us know.

IX

By wise contrivance He doth all things guide,
And so dispose them, that while they unite
For man He endless pleasures doth provide,
And shows that happiness is His delight,
  His creatures' happiness as well as His:
  For that in truth He seeks, and 'tis His bliss.

X

O rapture! wonder! ecstastie! delight!
How great must then His glory be, how great
Our blessedness! How vast and infinite
Our pleasure, how transcendent, how complete,
  If we the goodness of our God possess,
  And all His joy be in our blessedness.

XI

Almighty power when it is employed
For one, that He with glory might be crown'd;
Eternal wisdom when it is enjoyed
By one whom all its pleasures do surround,
  Produce a creature that must, all his days,
  Return the sacrifice of endless praise.

XII

But Oh! the vigour of mine infant sense
Drives me too far: I had not yet the eye,
The apprehension, or intelligence
Of things so very great, divine, and high.
  But all things were eternal unto me,
  And mine, and pleasing which mine eye did see.

XIII

There was enough at first: eternity,
Infinity, and love were silent joys;
Power, wisdom, goodness, and felicity;
All these which now our care and sin destroys,
  By instinct virtually were well discern'd,
  And by their representatives were learn'd.

XIV

As sponges gather moisture from the earth
Whereon there is scarce any sign of dew;
As air infecteth salt: so at my birth
All these were unperceive'd, yet near and true:
  Not by reflexion, and distinctly known,
  But by their efficacy all mine own.

My Spirit

I

My naked simple Life was I,
    That Act so strongly shin'd
Upon the earth, the sea, the sky,
It was the substance of my mind;
    The sense itself was I.
I felt no dross nor matter in my Soul,
No brims nor borders, such as in a bowl
We see. My essence was capacity,
    That felt all things;
    The thought that springs
Therefrom's itself. It hath no other wings
  To spread abroad, nor eyes to see,
    Nor hands distinct to feel,

Nor knees to kneel.
But being simple like the Deity
  In its own centre is a sphere
  Not shut up here, but everywhere.

II

It acts not from a centre to
    Its object as remote,
But present is when it doth view,
Being with the Being it doth note
    Whatever it doth do.
It doth not by another engine work,
But by itself; which in the act doth lurk.
Its essence is transformed into a true
    And perfect act,
    And so exact
Hath God appeared in this mysterious fact,
  That 'tis all eye, all act, all sight,
    And what it please can be,
    Not only see,
Or do; for 'tis more voluble than light:
  Which can put on ten thousand forms,
  Being cloth'd with what itself adorns.

III

This made me present evermore
    With whatsoe'er I saw.
An object, if it were before
My eye, was by Dame Nature's law,
    Within my soul. Her store
Was all at once within me; all Her treasures
Were my immediate and internal pleasures,
Substantial joys, which did inform my mind.
    With all she wrought
    My soul was fraught,
And every object in my heart a thought
  Begot, or was; I could not tell,
    Whether the things did there
    Themselves appear,
Which in my Spirit truly seem'd to dwell;
Or whether my conforming mind
Were not even all that therein shin'd.

IV

But yet of this I was most sure,
    That at the utmost length,
(So worthy was it to endure)
My soul could best express its strength.
    It was so quick and pure,
That all my mind was wholly everywhere,
Whate'er it saw, 'twas ever wholly there;
The sun ten thousand legions off, was nigh:
    The utmost star,
    Though seen from far,
Was present in the apple of my eye.
  There was my sight, my life, my sense,
   My substance, and my mind;
    My spirit shin'd
Even there, not by a transient influence:
    The act was immanent, yet there:
    The thing remote, yet felt even here.

V

O Joy! O wonder and delight!
    O sacred mystery!
My Soul a Spirit infinite!
An image of the Deity!
    A pure substantial light!
That Being greatest which doth nothing seem!
Why, 'twas my all, I nothing did esteem
But that alone. A strange mysterious sphere!
    A deep abyss
    That sees and is
The only proper place of Heavenly Bliss.
  To its Creator 'tis so near
   In love and excellence,
    In life and sense,
In greatness, worth, and nature; and so dear,
    In it, without hyperbole,
    The Son and friend of God we see.

VI

A strange extended orb of Joy,
    Proceeding from within,

Which did on every side, convey
Itself, and being nigh of kin
   To God did every way
Dilate itself even in an instant, and
Like an indivisible centre stand,
At once surrounding all eternity.
    'Twas not a sphere,
    Yet did appear,
One infinite. 'Twas somewhat everywhere,
  And tho' it had a power to see
   Far more, yet still it shin'd
   And was a mind
Exerted for it saw Infinity.
    'Twas not a sphere, but 'twas a might
    Invisible, and yet gave light.

VII

O wondrous Self! O sphere of light,
   O sphere of joy most fair;
O act, O power infinite;
O subtile and unbounded air!
   O living orb of sight!
Thou which within me art, yet me! Thou eye,
And temple of His whole infinity!
   O what a world art Thou! A world within!
   All things appear
   All objects are
Alive in Thee! Supersubstantial, rare,
  Above themselves, and nigh of kin
   To those pure things we find
   In His great mind
Who made the world! Tho' now eclipsed by sin
   There they are useful and divine,
   Exalted there they ought to shine.

THE HEAVENLY COUNTRY

Johann Wolfgang von Goethe (1749–1842)

from *Faust, Part II*

Mountain Gorges
Forest, Rocks, Desert

Holy anchorites scattered up the mountain-side, dwelling among the clefts.

Chorus and Echo.

> Forests are swaying here,
> Rocks weight them downward sheer,
> Roots clutching rocks appear,
> Trunk close by trunk is near.
> Wave dashes after wave,
> Shelter hath deepest cave.
> Lions, soft-footed, dumb,
> Friendly around us come,
> Honouring the sacred place,
> Refuge of love and grace.

Pater Ecstaticus hovering up and down.

> Endless ecstatic fire,
> Glow of pure love's desire,
> Pangs of the yearning breast,
> Rapture in God to rest.
> Arrows, pierce through me here,
> Lances, subdue me here,
> Bludgeons, come, batter me,
> Lightnings, come, shatter me,
> That my mortality
> Flee from reality,
> Endless star shine above,
> Core of eternal love.

Pater Profundus, Lower Region.

> As chasms at my feet descending
> Burden the chasms more profound,
> As a thousand radiant streams are wending
> To foaming cataracts' awesome bound,
> As, by its own strong impulse driven
> The tree mounts upward, straight and tall,
> So to Almighty Love 'tis given

To fashion all, to cherish all.
 All round me is a savage roaring
As if swayed wood and rocky steep;
Yet plunges, lovely in its pouring,
The wealth of water to the deep,
Summoned below, the vale to brighten,
The bolt that fell with sudden flare,
The atmosphere to cleanse and lighten
Which in its bosom poison bare,
 Heralds of love are they, proclaiming
Creative powers that us enfold.
May they, my inner self inflaming,
Quicken my soul confused and cold,
Its blunted senses galled unceasing,
Bound fast in chains that cramp and smart.
O God! these thoughts of mine appeasing,
Illumine Thou my needy heart!

Pater Seraphicus, Middle Region.

 What a morning cloudlet hovers
Through the pine trees' tossing hair!
Do I guess what life it covers?
They are spirits young and fair.

Chorus of Blessèd Boys.

 Tell us, father, whither go we?
Tell us, kind one, who are we?
Happy are we all, that know we;
Sweet, oh, sweet it is to be.

Pater Seraphicus.

 Boys! At midnight born, with only
Halfway opened sense and brain,
Straightway lost to parents lonely,
For the angels sweetest gain.
If ye feel that in this place is
One who loves, then hither fare;
But of earth's rude ways no traces
Do ye happy spirits bear.
In mine eyes descend, pray choose them,
Organs meet for earthly sphere;
As your own eyes ye can use them,
Gaze upon this landscape here.
 He receives them into himself.

Those are trees, and cliffs are yonder,
There a stream that downward leaps,
Rolling with the voice of thunder
Down its short way to the deeps.

Blessèd Boys, from within.

Grand the scene to which we're waking,
But too full of gloom and woe;
We're from fright and terror quaking,
Noble, kind one, let us go!

Pater Seraphicus.

On to higher spheres ascending,
Unawares grow endlessly,
As in fashion pure, unending,
God's high presence strengthens thee.
That is spirits' sustentation,
In free ether all effecting,
Endless loving's revelation,
To beatitude perfecting.

Chorus of Blessèd Boys, circling round the highest peaks.

Hand in hand clinging,
In a glad ring unite,
Soaring and singing,
Feeling a pure delight.
Godlike the yearning,
Confident be;
For whom we're yearning,
Him shall ye see.

Angels, soaring in the higher atmosphere, bearing Faust's immortal part.

Lo! rescued is this noble one
From evil machination;
"Who e'er aspiring, struggles on,
For him there is salvation."
And if to him Celestial Love
Its favouring grace has given,
The Blessed Host comes from Above
And welcomes him to Heaven.

The Younger Angels.

Roses sainted women spended,
Penitent through mercy glorious,

Helped to make the fight victorious,
That the lofty work be ended,
That be won this spirit-treasure.
Demons shrank in sore displeasure,
Devils fled the roses' flinging.
Not with wonted hell-pangs stinging,
Love-pangs brought them to disaster
Even the old Satan-Master
By sharp pain was penetrated.
Shout with joy! It's consummated!

The More Perfected Angels.

Still earthly rests remain
Which have oppressed us;
They'd not be pure of stain,
Though of asbestos.
When every element
Strong spirit-forces
Have borne away and blent,
No angel divorces
The natures two in one,
So close they weave them;
Eternal Love alone
Can ever cleave them.

The Younger Angels.

Mist-like round yonder height,
I'm just discovering
Where in approaching flight
Spirit-life's hovering.
The clouds are growing clear,
I see a host draw near
Of Blessèd Boys,
Freed from the stress of earth,
Circling, united!
They taste the joys
Of spring in their new birth,
Therein delighted.
Let him at once begin
Perfected joy to win,
With these united!

The Blessèd Boys.

> Glad we're receiving now
> Him as a chrysalis,
> Thereby achieving now
> Pledge of angelic bliss.
> Loosen all earthly flakes
> That cling around him;
> Fair and great now he wakes,
> Divine life has crowned him.

Doctor Marianus in the highest, purest cell.

> Here is the outlook free,
> The soul uplifting.
> Women I yonder see,
> Heavenward drifting,
> And glorious, midway seen,
> Star-crowned, yet tender,
> Heaven's own lofty Queen!
> It is Her splendour.
>> *Enraptured.*
>> Highest mistress of the world,
> Let me, of Thy pleasure,
> See Thy mystery unfurled
> In the vaulted azure.
> Look with grace on what doth move
> Human hearts to greet Thee
> And with holy bliss of love
> Bears them up to meet Thee.
>> All invincible we feel
> When supreme Thou willest,
> Swiftly tempered is our zeal
> When its glow Thou stillest.
> Virgin, pure in fairest sense,
> Mother sweet, supernal,
> Chosen Queen of our defence,
> Peer of gods eternal!
>> Little clouds circle
> Around Her splendour:
> Penitent women,
> Of natures tender,
> Ether respiring,
> At Her knees pleading,
> Her mercy needing.

O Thou of immaculate ray,
From Thee 'tis not taken
That those lightly led astray
Come with trust unshaken.
　　Rapt away, to weakness prone,
It is hard to save them.
Who by their own strength alone
Rend the lusts that slave them?
Whose foot does not slip awhile
On steep, slippery places?
Whom befool not glance and smile,
Flattery's breath and phrases?
　　The Mater Gloriosa soars into view

Chorus of Penitent Women.

To heights art soaring
Of realms eternal,
Hear our imploring,
Matchless, Maternal,
Of grace supernal!

Magna Peccatrix (St. Luke, 7:36).

By the love that ever glowing
For Thy Son, the Heaven-born,
Shed warm tears to balsam flowing
Spite of Pharisaic scorn;
By the box whose ointment precious
Dropped its perfume rare and sweet;
By the locks whose gentle meshes
Dried the Saviour's holy feet.

Mulier Samaritana (St. John 4).

By the well to which were driven
Abram's herds in days of yore;
By the pitcher once 'twas given
Our dear Saviour to restore;
By the spring, rich and supernal,
Whence flow waters far and wide,
Overflowing, bright, eternal,
Pouring through the worlds their tide—

Maria Aegyptiaca (Acta Sanctorum).

By the sacred place where mortals
Our dear Master's body laid;

By the arm which at the portals
Warningly my entrance stayed;
By the forty years' repentance
Truly passed in desert-land;
By the blessèd farewell sentence
That I wrote upon the sand—

All Three.

Thou who women greatly sinning
Grantest to come nigh to Thee,
By sincere repentance winning
Bliss through all eternity,
Grant to this good soul Thy blessing,
Who but once herself forgot,
Who knew not she was transgressing,
Pardon meet refuse Thou not!

Una Poenitentium, formerly named Gretchen, drawing closer.

Bend, oh bend now,
Matchless, attend Thou,
Thy radiance spend now,
Look on my bliss in charity.
My early lover,
His troubles over,
Comes back to me.

Blessèd Boys hovering in a circle.

Mighty of limb, he towers
Already above us;
Soon for this care of ours
Richly he'll love us.
Early were we removed,
Life did not reach us;
But he has learned and loved
And he will teach us.

The One Penitent formerly named Gretchen.

Girt by the noble choir of Heaven,
Himself the new-come scarcely knows,
Scarce feels the fresh life newly given
Ere like the holy throng he grows;
See! how each earthly bond he's riven,
From that old vesture freed at length,
Now in ethereal garb of Heaven

Appears his pristine, youthful strength,
Oh, grant that I may now instruct him,
Since blinds him still the new-born day.

Mater Gloriosa.

Come, rise to higher spheres! Conduct him!
If he feels thee, he'll go thy way.

Doctor Marianus prostrate, adoring.

Penitents, look up, elate,
Where ye see salvation;
Grateful, to you blessed fate
Grow through re-creation.
May each better sense be keen
In Thy service precious;
O Thou Virgin, Mother, Queen,
Goddess, be Thou gracious!

Chorus Mysticus.

All earth comprises
Is symbol alone;
What there ne'er suffices
As fact here is known;
All past the humanly
Wrought here in love;
The Eternal-Womanly
Draws us above.

Finis.
Translated by George Madison Priest

William Blake (1757–1827)

Jerusalem (Preface to *Milton, a Poem*)

And did those feet in ancient time
Walk upon Englands mountains green:
And was the holy Lamb of God,
On Englands pleasant pastures seen!

And did the Countenance Divine,
Shine forth upon our clouded hills?
And was Jerusalem builded here,
Among these dark Satanic Mills?

Bring me my Bow of burning gold:
Bring me my arrows of desire:
Bring me my Spear: O clouds unfold!
Bring me my Chariot of fire!

I will not cease from Mental Fight,
Nor shall my sword sleep in my hand:
Till we have built Jerusalem,
In Englands green & pleasant Land.

William Wordsworth (1770–1850)

Ode: Intimations of Immortality from Recollections of Early Childhood

The child is father of the man;
And I could wish my days to be
Bound each to each by natural piety.

I

There was a time when meadow, grove, and stream,
The earth, and every common sight,
To me did seem
Apparelled in celestial light,
The glory and the freshness of a dream.
It is not now as it hath been of yore;—
Turn wheresoe'er I may,
By night or day.
The things which I have seen I now can see no more.

II

The Rainbow comes and goes,
And lovely is the Rose,
The Moon doth with delight
Look round her when the heavens are bare,
Waters on a starry night
Are beautiful and fair;
The sunshine is a glorious birth;
But yet I know, where'er I go,
That there hath past away a glory from the earth.

III

Now, while the birds thus sing a joyous song,
    And while the young lambs bound
        As to the tabor's sound,
To me alone there came a thought of grief:
A timely utterance gave that thought relief,
        And I again am strong:
The cataracts blow their trumpets from the steep;
No more shall grief of mine the season wrong;
I hear the Echoes through the mountains throng,
The Winds come to me from the fields of sleep,
        And all the earth is gay;
        Land and sea
   Give themselves up to jollity,
        And with the heart of May
Doth every Beast keep holiday;—
        Thou Child of Joy,
Shout round me, let me hear thy shouts, thou happy Shepherd-boy!

IV

Ye blessèd Creatures, I have heard the call
    Ye to each other make; I see
The heavens laugh with you in your jubilee;
    My heart is at your festival,
      My head hath its coronal,
The fulness of your bliss, I feel—I feel it all.
        Oh evil day! if I were sullen
        While Earth herself is adorning,
          This sweet May-morning,
        And the Children are culling
          On every side,
      In a thousand valleys far and wide,
      Fresh flowers; while the sun shines warm,
And the Babe leaps up on his Mother's arm:—
        I hear, I hear, with joy I hear!
        —But there's a Tree, of many, one,
A single field which I have looked upon,
Both of them speak of something that is gone;
        The Pansy at my feet
        Doth the same tale repeat:
Whither is fled the visionary gleam?
Where is it now, the glory and the dream?

V

Our birth is but a sleep and a forgetting:
The Soul that rises with us, our life's Star,
        Hath had elsewhere its setting,
          And cometh from afar:
      Not in entire forgetfulness,
      And not in utter nakedness,
But trailing clouds of glory do we come
      From God, who is our home:
Heaven lies about us in our infancy!
Shades of the prison-house begin to close
      Upon the growing Boy,
        But He
Beholds the light, and whence it flows,
      He sees it in his joy;
The Youth, who daily farther from the east
      Must travel, still is Nature's Priest,
      And by the vision splendid
      Is on his way attended;
At length the Man perceives it die away,
And fade into the light of common day.

VI

Earth fills her lap with pleasures of her own;
Yearnings she hath in her own natural kind,
And, even with something of a Mother's mind,
      And no unworthy aim,
      The homely Nurse doth all she can
To make her Foster-child, her Inmate Man,
      Forget the glories he hath known,
And that imperial palace whence he came.

VII

Behold the Child among his new-born blisses,
A six years' Darling of a pigmy size!
See, where 'mid work of his own hand he lies,
Fretted by sallies of his mother's kisses,
With light upon him from his father's eyes!
See, at his feet, some little plan or chart,
Some fragment from his dream of human life,
Shaped by himself with newly-learned art

A wedding or a festival,
A mourning or a funeral;
        And this hath now his heart,
        And unto this he frames his song:
        Then will he fit his tongue
To dialogues of business, love, or strife;
        But it will not be long
        Ere this be thrown aside,
        And with new joy and pride
The little Actor cons another part;
Filling from time to time his "humorous stage"
With all the Persons, down to palsied Age,
That Life brings with her in her equipage;
        As if his whole vocation
        Were endless imitation.

VIII

Thou, whose exterior semblance doth belie
        Thy Soul's immensity;
Thou best Philosopher, who yet dost keep
Thy heritage, thou Eye among the blind,
That, deaf and silent, read'st the eternal deep,
Haunted for ever by the eternal mind,—
        Mighty Prophet! Seer blest!
        On whom those truths do rest,
Which we are toiling all our lives to find,
In darkness lost, the darkness of the grave;
Thou, over whom thy Immortality
Broods like the Day, a Master o'er a Slave,
A Presence which is not to be put by;
Thou little Child, yet glorious in the might
Of heaven-born freedom on thy being's height,
Why with such earnest pains dost thou provoke
The years to bring the inevitable yoke,
Thus blindly with thy blessedness at strife?
Full soon thy Soul shall have her earthly freight,
And custom lie upon thee with a weight,
Heavy as frost, and deep almost as life!

IX

        O joy! that in our embers
        Is something that doth live,

THE HEAVENLY COUNTRY

That Nature yet remembers
What was so fugitive!
The thought of our past years in me doth breed
Perpetual benediction: not indeed
For that which is most worthy to be blest;
Delight and liberty, the simple creed
Of Childhood, whether busy or at rest,
With new-fledged hope still fluttering in his breast:—
Not for these I raise
The song of thanks and praise;
But for those obstinate questionings
Of sense and outward things,
Fallings from us, vanishings;
Blank misgivings of a Creature
Moving about in worlds not realised,
High instincts before which our mortal Nature
Did tremble like a guilty Thing surprised:
But for those first affections,
Those shadowy recollections,
Which, be they what they may,
Are yet the fountain-light of all our day,
Are yet a master-light of all our seeing;
Uphold us, cherish, and have power to make
Our noisy years seem moments in the being
Of the eternal Silence: truths that wake,
To perish never;
Which neither listlessness, nor mad endeavour,
Nor Man nor Boy,
Nor all that is at enmity with joy,
Can utterly abolish or destroy!
Hence in a season of calm weather
Though inland far we be,
Our Souls have sight of that immortal sea
Which brought us hither,
Can in a moment travel thither,
And see the Children sport upon the shore,
And hear the mighty waters rolling evermore.

X

Then sing, ye Birds, sing, sing a joyous song!
And let the young Lambs bound
As to the tabor's sound!
We in thought will join your throng,

> Ye that pipe and ye that play,
> Ye that through your hearts to-day
> Feel the gladness of the May!
What though the radiance which was once so bright
Be now for ever taken from my sight,
>> Though nothing can bring back the hour
Of splendour in the grass, of glory in the flower;
>> We will grieve not, rather find
>> Strength in what remains behind;
>> In the primal sympathy
>> Which having been must ever be;
>> In the soothing thoughts that spring
>> Out of human suffering;
>> In the faith that looks through death,
In years that bring the philosophic mind.

XI

And O, ye Fountains, Meadows, Hills, and Groves,
Forebode not any severing of our loves!
Yet in my heart of hearts I feel your might;
I only have relinquished one delight
To live beneath your more habitual sway.
I love the Brooks which down their channels fret,
Even more than when I tripped lightly as they;
The innocent brightness of a new-born Day
>> Is lovely yet;
The Clouds that gather round the setting sun
Do take a sober colouring from an eye
That hath kept watch o'er man's mortality;
Another race hath been, and other palms are won.
Thanks to the human heart by which we live,
Thanks to its tenderness, its joys, and fears,
To me the meanest flower that blows can give
Thoughts that do often lie too deep for tears.

The Virgin

> Mother! whose virgin bosom was uncrost
> With the least shade of thought to sin allied.
> Woman! above all women glorified,
> Our tainted nature's solitary boast;
> Purer than foam on central ocean tost;
> Brighter than eastern skies at daybreak strewn

With fancied roses, than the unblemished moon
Before her wane begins on heaven's blue coast;
Thy image falls to earth. Yet some, I ween,
Not unforgiven the suppliant knee might bend,
As to a visible Power, in which did blend
All that was mixed and reconciled in thee
Of mother's love with maiden purity,
Of high with low, celestial with terrene!

Johann Christian Friedrich Hölderlin (1770–1843)

When I was a boy...

When I was a boy
  A god often rescued me
    From the shouts and the rages of men.
      Then, safe and well, I played
        With the flowers of the grove,
         And the winds of heaven
          With me played.

And as you delight the hearts
Of the plants when they meet you,
When they stretch their
Tender arms towards you,

So you delighted my heart,
Father Helios! And, like Endymion,
I was your beloved,
Sacred Moon!

O all you faithful
Friendly gods!
Would that you knew
How my soul loved you!

Although I could not call you
Then with a name, nor did you
Call me, as men do (as if they
Really knew one other) by name.

But I knew you better than
I ever knew men.
I understood the silence of the Æthers,
But never understood human words.

The rustling meadow
Taught me music,
And I learned to love
Among the flowers.

I grew in the arms of the gods.
Translated by Michael Martin

As when on a holiday[1]

As when on a holiday, to see the field
A countryman goes out, at morning, when,
Out of the hot night the cooling lightning had fallen
The whole time and the thunder still sounds in the distance,
The river trips into its banks once more,
And the fresh ground becomes green
And with the gladdening rain from heaven
The grapevine drips, and gleaming
In quiet sunlight stand the trees of the grove:

So in favourable weather they stand,
Whom no master alone, but wonderfully
[All-present] [Now] she educates in a light embrace
The powerful, divinely beautiful nature.
So when she seems to be sleeping at times of the year
Up in the heavens or among plants or the peoples
The poets' faces also are mourning,
They seem to be alone, yet are always divining.
For divining too she herself is resting.

But now day breaks! I waited and saw it come,
And what I saw, may the holy be my word.
For she, she herself, who is older than the ages
And above the gods of Occident and Orient,
Nature is now awakening with the clang of arms,
And from high ether down to the abyss
According to firm law, as once, begotten out of holy chaos,
Inspiration, the all-creative,
Again feels herself anew.

And as a fire gleams in the eye of the man,
Who has conceived a lofty design; so

---

1. The poem is unfinished. Brackets represent the alternate word choices of Hölderlin.

THE HEAVENLY COUNTRY

Once more by the signs, the deeds of the world now
A fire has been kindled in the souls of the poets.
And what came to pass before, though scarcely felt,
Only now is manifest,
And they who smiling tended our fields for us,
In the form of servants, they are known,
The all-living, the powers of the gods.

Do you ask about them? In the song their spirit blows
[When from the sun of day and warm earth]
[That also the sun, like flowers, and darkest earth]
[It awakens] [Grows], and storms that are in the air, and others
That more prepared in the depths of time,
And more full of meaning, and more perceptible to us
Drift on between heaven and earth among the peoples
The thoughts of the communal spirit they are,
Quietly ending in the soul of the poet.

So that quickly struck, for a long time known
To the infinite, it quakes
With recollection, and kindled by the holy ray
Its fruit conceived in love, the work of gods and men
The song, so that it may bear witness to both, succeeds.
So, as poets say, when she desired to see
The god, visible, his lightning fell on Semele's house
And ashes [mortally] [divinely] struck gave birth,
To the fruit of the thunderstorm, to holy Bacchus.

And hence the sons of earth now drink
Heavenly fire without danger.
Yet us it behoves, you poets! to stand
Bareheaded beneath God's thunderstorms,
To grasp the father's ray, itself, with our own hands
And to offer to the people
The heavenly gift wrapped in song
For only if we are pure in heart,
Like children, are our hands innocent.

The [higher] sphere
that is higher than that
of man that is the god

[The father's ray, the pure, does not sear it]
[Then pure does not kill it, does not sear it] *The [higher]*
And deeply shaken, sharing the suffering *sphere that is*
Of the stronger, remaining in the [down-rushing] *higher than that of*
[unstoppable] storms of *man that is the god*
God when he nears, the heart still holds.
But oh my shame! (when of
a self-inflicted wound my heart is bleeding, and

deeply lost is peace and freely-modest contentment,
and unrest and lack drive me to the abundance
of the gods' tables, when round about me)

[My shame!]
                              and let me say at once,
That I approached to see the heavenly,
And they themselves cast me down below the living
The false priest that I am, into the dark
To sing for those who can learn the warning song.
There
    Translated by William S. Allen

Novalis (*Georg Philipp Friedrich Freiherr von Hardenberg,* 1772–1801)

from *Hymns to the Night* (*Hymnen an Die Nacht*)

1

What living person, gifted with any sense, doesn't love, more than all the wonderful appearances of spread-out space around him, the all-joyful Light—with its colors, beams, waves; its gentle presence, as waking day. As life's inner soul it's breathed by the Giant-world of countless stars, and swims dancing in its blue tide—the glittering, ever-peaceful stone breathes it, the sensuous sucking plant, the wild and burning so many formed beast—but above all that splendid stranger with sense-filled eyes, with gliding gait and gently-closed, rich-toned lips. Like an earthy nature king, it summons each force to uncounted changes, makes and dissolves each force joinings without end, hangs its heavenly picture on each earthy being.—Its presence alone opens up the wonder, the splendor of the earth's kingdom.

Away I turn to the holy, the unspeakable, the secretive Night. Over there, far, lies the world—sunken in a deep pit—desert, its place lonely. In the heart's strings, deep sadness blows. In dewdrops I'll sink and mix with the ashes.—Memory's distances, a young man's wishes, childhood's dreams, the whole long life of short joys and hopeless hope comes grey-clad, like evening mist after the sun has set. In other places Light's pitched happy tents. Should It never come back to Its children, who've waited for it with simple faith?

What wells up so menacingly under the heart and gulps down the soft air's sadness? Are you teasing us, dark Night? What're you holding under your cloak, that grabs so unseen at my soul? Costly balm drips from your hand, from a bundle of poppies. You raise up the soul's heavy wings. Darkly, unspeakably we feel moved—I see a serious face startled with joy, it bends to me softly, reverently, and under the endlessly tangled hair of the Mother a lovely youth shows. How poor and childish the Light seems now—how happy and blessed the day's departure—So now, since Night makes its servants strangers, you'd sow gleaming spheres in the far spaces to show your own omnipotence—your return—in the times of your distance. More heavenly than those flashing stars the endless eyes seem, which Night opens up in us. They see farther than those palest of all countless hosts—no need for Light to look through the depths of a loving soul—which a higher space fills with unspeakable delight. Praise the world queen, the higher messenger of a holy word, a nurse of blessed love—she sends me you—tender, loved—Night's lovely sun,—now I wake—for I'm yours and mine—you called the Night to life for me,—humanized me—tear my body with spirit fire, so I can mix with you inwardly, airily, and then the wedding night will last forever.

Translated by Dick Higgins

6

"Longing for Death"

Down into the earth's womb,
Away from Light's kingdom,
Pain's raging and wild force
Ensigns the happy departure.
We've come in from a little boat
Swiftly to heaven's shore.

Blessed be the endless Night to us,
Blessed by the endless sleep.
Truly the day has made us hot,
And long care's withered us.
The wish for strange things is gone away,
And now we want our Father's home.

What should we do in this world now,
With our own love and faith?
The old things have been set aside,
What use could any new ones be?

O! There stands alone and in despair
Whoever calls on and misses times gone by.

Those times gone by, where the senses' light
Burned brightly with high flames,
Where the Father's hand and countenance
Were still recognized by humanity,
And high sense, in simplicity,
Many still matched to His former image.

The past, where still blood-rich
And primeval races walked abroad,
And children yearned for heaven's kingdom
After their affliction and their death,
And if also desire and life spoke,
Still many a heart broke from love.

The past, where with youthful ardor
God showed himself to one and all,
And with love's strength committed
His sweet life to an early death,
Did not avoid the fear and pain
So He would be even dearer to us.

With anxious longing we see them now,
Shrouded in the dark of Night,
And in this temporality
Never will thirst be quenched.
For we must go away to home
To know and see the holy time.

What holds us back from this trip home,
From our loved ones so long laid to rest?
Their graves closed down on our lives' course,
We are sad, we are afraid.
We have no more to search for here—
The heart is full, the world is empty.

Endless and full of mystery
Sweet trembling courses through us—
To me it seems an echo sounds
Out of the deep distance of our grief.
Our loved ones are longing too for us,
And sent to us this yearning breath.

Down now to the sweet bride, on
To Jesus, to the beloved—
Comfort, evening's darkling greys

THE HEAVENLY COUNTRY

To the loving, to the grieving.
A dream will break our fetters off,
And sink us forever in our Father's lap.
Translated by Dick Higgins

John Ruskin (1819–1900)

La Madonna dell' Acqua

Around her shrine no earthly blossoms blow,
No footsteps fret the pathway to and fro;
No sign nor record of departed prayer,
Print of the stone, nor echo of the air;
Worn by the lip, nor wearied by the knee,—
Only a deeper silence of the sea:
For there, in passing, pause the breezes bleak,
And the foam fades, and all the waves are weak.
The pulse-like oars in softer fall succeed,
The black prow falters through the wild seaweed—
Where, twilight-borne, the minute thunders reach
Of deep-mouthed surf, that bays by Lido's beach,
With intermittent motion traversed far,
And shattered glancing of the western star,
Till the faint storm-bird on the heaving flow
Drops in white circles, silently like snow.
Not here the ponderous gem, nor pealing note,
Dim to adorn—insentient to adore—
But purple-dyed, the mists of evening float,
In ceaseless incense from the burning floor
Of ocean, and the gathered gold of heaven
Laces its sapphire vault, and, early given,
The white rays of the rushing firmament
Pierce the blue-quivering night through wreath or rent
Of cloud inscrutable and motionless,
Hectic and wan, and moon-companioned cloud!
Oh! lone Madonna—angel of the deep—
When the night falls, and deadly winds are loud,
Will not thy love be with us while we keep
Our watch upon the waters, and the gaze
Of thy soft eyes, that slumber not, nor sleep?
Deem not thou, stranger, that such trust is vain;
Faith walks not on these weary waves alone,

Though weakness dread, or apathy disdain
The spot which God has hallowed for His own.
They sin who pass it lightly—ill divining
The glory of this place of bitter prayer;
And hoping against hope, and self-resigning,
And reach of faith, and wrestling with despair,
And resurrection of the last distress,
Into the sense of heaven, when earth is bare,
And of God's voice, when man's is comfortless.

George MacDonald (1824–1905)

I Know What Beauty Is

I know what beauty is, for Thou
　　Hast set the world within my heart;
　　Its glory from me will not part;
I never loved it more than now.

I know the Sabbath afternoon:
　　The light lies sleeping on the graves;
　　Against the sky the poplar waves;
The river plays a Sabbath tune.

Ah, know I not the spring's snow-bell?
　　The summer woods at close of even?
　　Autumn, when earth dies into heaven,
And winter's storms, I know them well.

I know the rapture music brings,
　　The power that dwells in ordered tones,
　　A living voice that loves and moans,
And speaks unutterable things.

Consenting beauties in a whole;
　　The living eye, the imperial head,
　　The gait of inward music bred,
The woman form, a radiant soul.

And splendours all unspoken bide
　　Within the ken of spirit's eye;
　　And many a glory saileth by,
Borne on the Godhead's living tide.

But I leave all, thou man of woe!
   Put off my shoes, and come to Thee;
   Thou art most beautiful to me;
More wonderful than all I know.

As child forsakes his favourite toy,
   His sisters; sport, his wild bird's nest;
   And climbing to his mother's breast,
Enjoys yet more his former joy—

I lose to find. On forehead wide
   The jewels tenfold light afford:
   So, gathered round thy glory, Lord,
All beauty else is glorified.

Gerard Manley Hopkins (1844–1889)

God's Grandeur

The world is charged with the grandeur of God.
   It will flame out, like shining from shook foil;
   It gathers to a greatness, like the ooze of oil
Crushed. Why do men then now not reck his rod?
Generations have trod, have trod, have trod;
   And all is seared with trade; bleared, smeared with toil;
   And wears man's smudge and shares man's smell: the soil
Is bare now, nor can foot feel, being shod.

And for all this, nature is never spent;
   There lives the dearest freshness deep down things;
And though the last lights off the black West went
   Oh, morning, at the brown brink eastward, springs—
Because the Holy Ghost over the bent
   World broods with warm breast and with ah! bright wings.

The Blessed Virgin compared to the Air we Breathe

Wild air, world-mothering air,
Nestling me everywhere,
That each eyelash or hair
Girdles; goes home betwixt
The fleeciest, frailest-flixed
Snowflake; that's fairly mixed

212

With, riddles, and is rife
In every least thing's life;
This needful, never spent,
And nursing element;
My more than meat and drink,
My meal at every wink;
This air, which, by life's law,
My lung must draw and draw
Now but to breathe its praise,
Minds me in many ways
Of her who not only
Gave God's infinity
Dwindled to infancy
Welcome in womb and breast,
Birth, milk, and all the rest
But mothers each new grace
That does now reach our race—
Mary Immaculate,
Merely a woman, yet
Whose presence, power is
Great as no goddess's
Was deemèd, dreamèd; who
This one work has to do—
Let all God's glory through,
God's glory which would go
Through her and from her flow
Off, and no way but so.

    I say that we are wound
With mercy round and round
As if with air: the same
Is Mary, more by name.
She, wild web, wondrous robe,
Mantles the guilty globe,
Since God has let dispense
Her prayers his providence:
Nay, more than almoner,
The sweet alms' self is her
And men are meant to share
Her life as life does air.

    If I have understood,
She holds high motherhood
Towards all our ghostly good
And plays in grace her part
About man's beating heart,

Laying, like air's fine flood,
The deathdance in his blood;
Yet no part but what will
Be Christ our Saviour still.
Of her flesh he took flesh:
He does take fresh and fresh,
Though much the mystery how,
Not flesh but spirit now
And makes, O marvellous!
New Nazareths in us,
Where she shall yet conceive
Him, morning, noon, and eve;
New Bethlems, and he born
There, evening, noon, and morn—
Bethlem or Nazareth,
Men here may draw like breath
More Christ and baffle death;
Who, born so, comes to be
New self and nobler me
In each one and each one
More makes, when all is done,
Both God's and Mary's Son.
    Again, look overhead
How air is azurèd;
O how! nay do but stand
Where you can lift your hand
Skywards: rich, rich it laps
Round the four fingergaps.
Yet such a sapphire-shot,
Charged, steepèd sky will not
Stain light. Yea, mark you this:
It does no prejudice.
The glass-blue days are those
When every colour glows,
Each shape and shadow shows.
Blue be it: this blue heaven
The seven or seven times seven
Hued sunbeam will transmit
Perfect, not alter it.
Or if there does some soft,
On things aloof, aloft,
Bloom breathe, that one breath more
Earth is the fairer for.
Whereas did air not make

This bath of blue and slake
His fire, the sun would shake,
A blear and blinding ball
With blackness bound, and all
The thick stars round him roll
Flashing like flecks of coal,
Quartz-fret, or sparks of salt,
In grimy vasty vault.

　　So God was god of old:
A mother came to mould
Those limbs like ours which are
What must make our daystar
Much dearer to mankind;
Whose glory bare would blind
Or less would win man's mind.
Through her we may see him
Made sweeter, not made dim,
And her hand leaves his light
Sifted to suit our sight.

　　Be thou then, O thou dear
Mother, my atmosphere;
My happier world, wherein
To wend and meet no sin;
Above me, round me lie
Fronting my froward eye
With sweet and scarless sky;
Stir in my ears, speak there
Of God's love, O live air,
Of patience, penance, prayer:
World-mothering air, air wild,
Wound with thee, in thee isled,
Fold home, fast fold thy child.

Vladimir Solovyov (1853–1900)

All in azure did my empress

All in azure did my empress
Appear today before me.
My heart beat in sweet rapture
And my soul began to shine
With quiet light in rays of the dawning day.
But in the distance, burning low,

THE HEAVENLY COUNTRY

The cruel flame of the earthly fire still glowed.
(*End of November 1875, Cairo*)
Translated by Boris Jakim

My empress has a lofty palace

My empress has a lofty palace
With seven golden pillars.
My empress has a seven-pointed crown,
Inlaid with countless precious stones.

In my empress's green garden
Fair roses and lilies bloom,
And a silvery stream catches the reflection
Of curls and brow in its transparent waters.

But my empress does not hear what the stream whispers.
She does not so much as glance at the flowers:
Sorrow beclouds the light of her azure eyes,
And all her reverie is full of grief.

She sees: far off in a midnight land
Amidst the freezing mists and blizzards,
Her beloved, whom she has forsaken, is perishing
In solitary combat with dark and evil powers.

She casts aside her diamond crown,
Abandons the golden palace, and, arriving,
An unexpected guest, at her faithless beloved's door,
She knocks upon it, her hand full of grace.

And bathed in light, she bends down over him
Like youthful springtime over somber winter
And, full of quiet tenderness,
Covers him with her radiant veil.

And the dark powers are stricken to the ground.
His whole being burns with a pure flame,
And with eternal love in her azure eyes
She softly speaks to her beloved: "I know

Your resolve is more inconstant than sea waves:
You vowed to keep fidelity to me. You have
Betrayed your vow—but could your betrayal
Really have caused my heart to change?"
(*between the end of November 1875 and 6 March 1876, Cairo*)
Translated by Boris Jakim

Three Meetings

(Moscow–London–Egypt, 1862–75–76)

Triumphing beforehand over death
And through love having overcome the chain
Of aeons, eternal beloved, I will not name you,
But my tremulous song will reach your ears.
Not believing the deceitful world,
Beneath the rough crust of matter
I have touched the incorruptible royal purple
And recognized the radiance of divinity. . . .
Have you not thrice appeared to my real sight?
You have not been a figment of the mind,
O no! As portent, help, or as reward,
Your image has come to answer my soul's call.

1

The first time—but how long ago that was!
Thirty-six years have passed since my soul,
Then childish, unexpectedly felt love's longing
Together with the anxiety of dark dreams.

I was nine years old, and she . . . she was nine too.
"It was a day in May in Moscow," as Fet wrote.
I then confessed my love. Silence. O God!
I have a rival. He will answer to me!

A duel! A duel! At the Ascension Feast service
A stream of passionate torments coursed through my soul.
Let us lay aside . . . all earthly cares: drawn out,
These words of the hymn faded gradually and stopped.

The sanctuary was open . . . But where were priest and deacon?
Where was the crowd of praying people? Suddenly,
The stream of passions dried up without a trace.
Azure was all around; azure was in my soul.

Suffused with a golden azure, and your hand
Holding a flower that came from other lands,
You stood there smiling a smile of radiance.
You nodded to me, and vanished in the mist.

With that the childish love grew far removed
From me, my soul grew blind to earthly things…
My German nurse kept on repeating sadly:
"Volodinka, ach, how he has stupid become!"

2

Years passed by. A docent and a master,
I rushed abroad for the first time... Berlin,
Then Hanover, Cologne all glimmered past,
In rapid motion hiding from my sight.

Not the world's center, Paris, not Spain,
Nor the Orient's bright multicolored splash—
Rather, the British Museum was my dream.
Nor did this place at all deceive my hopes.

Will I ever forget you, blissful half-year?
Fleeting beauty's phantoms meant nothing to my soul,
Nor did people's lives here, passions, nature.
All my soul was possessed by you alone, beloved.

Despite people's scurrying back and forth in droves
Under the din of fire-breathing machines,
Despite massive soulless edifices all around,
I am immersed in sacred quiet. I am here alone.

Cum grano salis, to be sure: I was
Alone, but surely not a misanthrope.
For people still did find their way to me.
And whom among these people should I mention?

A pity. I do not know how to put
Their names or foreign talk into my meter.
Among them were two or three British scholars
And two or three docents from Moscow. Still,

I was often alone in the reading room,
And, credit this or not, God is my witness
That mysterious powers led me to choose for reading
Everything possible concerning her.

Whenever some sinful whim suggested to me
To open up a book "from another opera,"
Such trouble would ensue from this
That, quite confused, I'd leave for home.

But once—it was in autumn—I said to her:
"O blossoming of divinity! I feel
Your presence here. But why have you not revealed
Yourself to my eyes since I was a child?"

Hardly had I thought these words
When all around was filled with golden azure
And before me she was shining again—
But only her face, it was her face alone.

That instant was one of happiness much prolonged.
My soul again became blind to things of earth.
And if I spoke, any "sober" ear
Would consider my speech incoherent and stupid.

3

I said: "Your face has been revealed to me.
But I would still wish to see all of you.
You were not stingy with the child, and so
Why is it that you should refuse the youth?"

"Go then to Egypt!" sounded a voice inside me.
To Paris! And then steampower bore me southward.
Feeling did not have to fight with reason:
Reason remained quite silent—like an idiot.

To Lyons, Turin, Piacenza, and Ancona,
To Fermo, Bari, then to Brindisi.
Behold: across the shimmering deep-blue
I found myself being sped by a British steamer.

Credit and lodging were offered to me in Cairo
By Hotel Abbat—alas, no longer there!
A cozy, modest hotel, best in the world…
Russians were staying there, even some from Moscow.

A retired general entertained us there
With memories of his old Caucasus days.
It does no harm to name him—he's long dead.
And I have only good things to say about him.

He was the well-known Rostislav Faddeev,
Retired soldier, good man with a pen.
Excellent at remembering names of coquettes.
Knowledgeable, too, about the local cathedrals.

Twice daily we sat together at the table d'hôte.
He was loquacious, he spoke merrily,
Was ever ready with some dubious anecdote,
And, in his limited way, philosophized.

THE HEAVENLY COUNTRY

I waited, meanwhile, for the promised meeting,
And suddenly, one night when all was still,
I heard, just like the wind's cool breath, these words:
"I am there in the desert. Go to meet me."

I had to walk. (For one is not transported
From London to the Sahara for nothing.
A marble might have rolled round my empty pocket—
For days on end I had been living on credit.)

God alone knew whither, without provisions
And without money, one fine day, I went,
Like Uncle Vlas, composed without revisions
By Nekrasov. (There, I've somehow found a rhyme.)

Surely, you must have been laughing at me when I,
Attired in tall top-hat and warm overcoat in the desert,
Was taken, by sturdy bedouins, for a demon,
Provoking a shiver of fear in them and thus

Was nearly killed. When, in the Arab manner, noisily,
Sheiks of two tribes held a council to decide
My fate, then later tied my hands together
Like a slave's and without mincing words

Led me some distance off, and generously
Untied my hands—and then departed. Now
I'm laughing with you, my beloved: gods and men alike
Can laugh at troubles once they've passed.

By that time the mute night had descended
Directly to the earth. Around me I heard
Only the silence, and saw the darkness
Between the little starry flames.

Lying upon the ground, I looked and listened...
I heard the sinister wailing of a jackal,
Who was dreaming, most likely, of devouring me,
And I'd not brought even a stick to ward him off.

Yet worse than the jackal was the piercing cold...
It now was zero perhaps, and yet the day had been hot.
The stars shined mercilessly clear.
Their shining and the cold warred with my sleep.

Long I lay there in a frightened slumber, till
At last, I heard a gentle whisper: "Sleep, my poor friend."

Then I fell into a deep sleep; and when I waked
The fragrance of roses wafted from earth and heaven.

And in the purple of the heavenly glow
You gazed with eyes full of an azure fire.
And your gaze was like the first shining
Of universal and creative day.

What is, what was, and what will be were here
Embraced within that one fixed gaze… The seas
And rivers all turned blue beneath me, as did
The distant forest and the snow-capped mountain heights.

I saw it all, and all of it was one,
One image there of beauty feminine…
The immeasurable was confined within that image.
Before me, in me, you alone were there.

O radiant one! I'm not deceived by you.
I saw all of you there in the desert…
And in my soul those roses shall not fade
Wherever it is the billows of life may rush me.

A single instant! Then the vision was hidden
And into heaven's dome the solar sphere began its rise.
The desert was silent, but my soul was praying
And church bells kept on ringing in my soul.

My spirit was strong! But for two days I'd fasted
And visions of higher things began to fade.
Alas! However sensitive one's soul,
Starvation never can be a friend, they say.

Toward the Nile I followed the sun's westward path,
And in the evening I returned to Cairo.
Though my soul preserved the traces of your rosy smile,
Many holes had worn their way into my boots.

Viewed from the outside it was all quite stupid.
(I gave the facts but I concealed the vision.)
After he ate his soup quite wordlessly,
The general, gaze fixed at me, grandly began:

"While intelligence gives one the right to be stupid,
It's surely better not to abuse the privilege:
All told, people's obtuseness isn't quite adept
At drawing distinctions between types of madness.

And therefore, if it would offend you
If anyone considered you demented
Or merely a fool, then make no further mention
Of this inglorious adventure to anyone."

His witty utterances flowed on, but before me
The azure mist kept sending out its radiance,
And, defeated by the mysterious beauty,
The ocean of humdrum life receded far away.

****

Still slave of this vain world, this then was how
Beneath the rough crust of matter, I came to see
The incorruptible royal purple
And felt the radiance of divinity.

Overcoming death by premonition,
Through dreams having triumphed over the chain
Of aeons, eternal beloved, I will not name you,
But pardon, for your part, my feeble song!
(*26–29 September 1898*)
   Translated by Boris Jakim

William Butler Yeats (1865–1939)

To the Secret Rose

Far-off, most secret, and inviolate Rose,
Enfold me in my hour of hours; where those
Who sought thee in the Holy Sepulchre,
Or in the wine-vat, dwell beyond the stir
And tumult of defeated dreams; and deep
Among pale eyelids, heavy with the sleep
Men have named beauty. Thy great leaves enfold
The ancient beards, the helms of ruby and gold
Of the crowned Magi; and the king whose eyes
Saw the pierced Hands and Rood of elder rise
In Druid vapour and make the torches dim;
Till vain frenzy awoke and he died; and him
Who met Fand walking among flaming dew
By a grey shore where the wind never blew,
And lost the world and Emer for a kiss;

And him who drove the gods out of their liss,
And till a hundred morns had flowered red
Feasted, and wept the barrows of his dead;
And the proud dreaming king who flung the crown
And sorrow away, and calling bard and clown
Dwelt among wine-stained wanderers in deep woods:
And him who sold tillage, and house, and goods,
And sought through lands and islands numberless years,
Until he found, with laughter and with tears,
A woman of so shining loveliness
That men threshed corn at midnight by a tress,
A little stolen tress. I, too, await
The hour of thy great wind of love and hate.
When shall the stars be blown about the sky,
Like the sparks blown out of a smithy, and die?
Surely thine hour has come, thy great wind blows,
Far-off, most secret, and inviolate Rose?

Lapis Lazuli
(for Harry Clifton)

I have heard that hysterical women say
They are sick of the palette and fiddle-bow,
Of poets that are always gay,
For everybody knows or else should know
That if nothing drastic is done
Aeroplane and Zeppelin will come out,
Pitch like King Billy bomb-balls in
Until the town lie beaten flat.

All perform their tragic play,
There struts Hamlet, there is Lear,
That's Ophelia, that Cordelia;
Yet they, should the last scene be there,
The great stage curtain about to drop,
If worthy their prominent part in the play,
Do not break up their lines to weep.
They know that Hamlet and Lear are gay;
Gaiety transfiguring all that dread.
All men have aimed at, found and lost;
Black out; Heaven blazing into the head:
Tragedy wrought to its uttermost.
Though Hamlet rambles and Lear rages,
And all the drop-scenes drop at once

THE HEAVENLY COUNTRY

Upon a hundred thousand stages,
It cannot grow by an inch or an ounce.

On their own feet they came, or on shipboard,
Camel-back, horse-back, ass-back, mule-back,
Old civilisations put to the sword.
Then they and their wisdom went to rack:
No handiwork of Callimachus
Who handled marble as if it were bronze,
Made draperies that seemed to rise
When sea-wind swept the corner, stands;
His long lamp chimney shaped like the stem
Of a slender palm, stood but a day;
All things fall and are built again
And those that build them again are gay.

Two Chinamen, behind them a third,
Are carved in Lapis Lazuli,
Over them flies a long-legged bird
A symbol of longevity;
The third, doubtless a serving-man,
Carries a musical instrument.

Every discolouration of the stone,
Every accidental crack or dent
Seems a water-course or an avalanche,
Or lofty slope where it still snows
Though doubtless plum or cherry-branch
Sweetens the little half-way house
Those Chinamen climb towards, and I
Delight to imagine them seated there;
There, on the mountain and the sky,
On all the tragic scene they stare.
One asks for mournful melodies;
Accomplished fingers begin to play.
Their eyes mid many wrinkles, their eyes,
Their ancient, glittering eyes, are gay.

Æ (*George Russell, 1867–1935*)

By the Margin of the Great Deep

When the breath of twilight blows to flame the misty skies,
All its vaporous sapphire, violet glow and silver gleam,
With their magic flood me through the gateway of the eyes;
    I am one with the twilight's dream.

When the trees and skies and fields are one in ducky mood,
Every heart of man is rapt within the mother's breast:
Full of peace and sleep and dreams in the vasty quietude,
    I am one with their hearts at rest.

From our immemorial joys of hearth and home and love
Strayed away along the margin of the unknown tide,
All its reach of soundless calm can thrill me far above
    Word or touch from the lips beside.

Aye, and deep and deep and deeper let me drink and draw
From the olden fountain more than light or peace or dream,
Such primeval being as o'erfills the heart with awe,
    Growing one with its silent stream.

Paul Claudel (*1868–1955*)

The Second Great Ode

Argument

The poet in captivity of the Pekin walls, dreams of the Sea. Exhilaration of the water that is the infinite and liberation. But the spirit is still superior in penetration and liberty. Desire toward the absolute God who only liberates us from the contingent. But in this life we are separated from him. Nevertheless he is there even though invisible and we are tied to him by that fluid element, the spirit or the water, where all things are penetrated. Vision of Eternity in the transitory creation. The voice that is at the same time spirit and water, the figure and will that imposes itself, is the expression of this joyful union. The spirit in all things clears the water, illumines and clarifies. He demands of God to be himself and clear of mortal darkness. The water that purifies when it springs to the call of God, those are the tears that come out of a penitent heart. Remembrance of past mistakes. Everything is finished now and the poet hears in a profound silence God's Spirit that whispers this voice of Wisdom which is addressed to every man.

The Spirit and the Water

After the long smoky silence
After the great civil silence of many days all smoking of rumors and
smoke
Breath of cultivating earth and warbling of great golden cities
Suddenly the Spirit again, suddenly the breath again
Suddenly the blow in the heart, suddenly the given word, suddenly the
breath of the Spirit, the dry abduction, suddenly the possession of the Spirit!
As when in the night's sky before the crack of the first lightning fire,
Suddenly the wind of Zeus in turbulence full of hay and dust with all the
laundry of the village!

My God, who at the beginning separated the upper waters from the lower
waters,
And who again separated these humid waters that I have mentioned
before,
The arid, like a child divided from the abundant maternal body,
The earth heated, leaf-tender and nourished by the rain's milk,
And who during the time of sorrow like the day of creation you hold in
your hand all powerful
The human clay and spirit from all sides you glide between your fingers,
Again after the long terrestrial roads,
Here is the Ode, here this great Ode presents itself anew,
Not like a thing that starts, but piece by piece like the sea that was here,
The sea of all the human words with the surface of its diverse places
Recognized by a breath under the fog and the eye of the matronly Moon!

But, now, near a palace the color of concern among
Trees of many roofs shading a rotten throne,
I live within an old empire the principal ruins.
Far from the free and pure sea, more than the earth I saw yellow,
Where the earth itself is the element one breathes, staining immensely of
its substance the air and the water,
Here converge the filthy canals and the old used roads and the tracks of
donkeys and camels,
Where the Emperor traces his furrow and lifts his hands to the useful sky
from whence come times good and bad.
And as in the days of grain along the coast one sees the lighthouses and
the points of rocks all enveloped in mist and pulverized foam,
That is how in the ancient wind of the Earth, the square city raises its
entrenchments and its doors,
Terraces lay out in tiers its colossal doors in the yellow wind, three times
three doors like elephants,

In the wind of ash and dust, in the great gray wind of powder that was Sodom, and the empires of Egypt and Persia, and Paris and Tadmor, and Babylon.

But what do I care now about your empires, and all that dies,
And you others that I have left, your ugly way of life over there!
Because I am free! what do I care about your cruel arrangements? because at least I am free! because I have found! because at least I am outside!
Because I no longer have a place among created things, but my part with the one who created them, the spirit liquid and lustful!
Does one scorn the sea? Do you smoke it like a patch of peas?
Do you choose its rotation, alfalfa or wheat or cabbage or beets yellow or purple?
Though it is life itself without which all is dead, ah! I want life itself without which all is dead!
Life itself and all the rest which is mortal kills me!
Ah, I do not have enough! I look at the sea! All this fills me to completion.
But here and where I turn my face and from that other corner
There is more and again and there also and always and similarly and more! Always, dear heart!
Do not fear that my eyes use it up! Ah, I have had enough of your drinkable waters.
I do not want your arranged waters, reaped by the sun, passed through the filter and the still, distributed by the machine of the mountains,
Corrupt, streaming.
Your headwaters are not springs. The element itself!
The prime matter! It is the mother, I say, that I am missing!
Let's possess the eternal and salty sea, the great grey rose! I lift one arm toward paradise! I advance toward the sea with bowels of grape!
I sailed eternally! I am like the ancient sailor who only knows land by its fires, the green or red star systems given by the map and the portolan.
One moment at the dock between bales and barrels, documents at the consulate, a handshake from a stevedore;
And again the rope cast off, a stamp to the machines, the break-water that one doubles, and underneath my feet
Again the swelling of the wave!

Nor
The sailor, nor
The fish that follows another fish to eat,
But the same thing and all the barrel and the living grain,
And the water itself, the element itself, I play, I shine! I share the omnipresent freedom of the sea!
The water

Always comes to find the water,

Composing one singular drop.

If I were the sea, crucified by a million arms on these two continents,

A full belly feeling the rude pull of the circular heaven, stationary sun as the wick lighted under the suction cup,

Knowing my own quantity,

It is me, I pull, I call upon all my roots, the Ganges, the Mississippi,

The thick tuft of the Orinoco, the long thread of the Rhine, the Nile with its double bladder,

And the nocturnal lion drinking, and the marshes, and the subterranean mud, and the full and round heart of men that last their instant.

Not sea, but I am spirit! and like water

Of the water, the spirit recognizes spirit,

The spirit, the secret breath,

The creative spirit that makes you laugh, spirit of life and the great pneumatic breath, the release of spirit

That whispers and intoxicates and makes you laugh!

Oh, that is full of life and agile, do not fear being left to dry! Far as I push, I cannot defeat the elasticity of the abyss.

From the bottom of the water one sees at the same time a dozen goddesses with beautiful limbs

Mount green in a rush of air bubbles,

They play at the divine daybreak in the great white lace, in the cold and yellow fire, in the airy and sparkling sea!

What

Door will stop me? what wall? The water

Odore the water, and me, I am even more liquid!

As it dissolves the earth and the cemented rock I have the intelligences everywhere!

The water that has made earth a delight, the spirit that has made the door open the lock.

And what is the inert water next to the spirit, its power

Next to its activity, the matter at the price of the worker?

I feel, I smell, I arrange, I detect, I breathe with a sure sense

How the thing is made! And I am also full of a god, I am full of ignorance and the genius!

Oh working forces around me,

I know as much as you do, I am free, I am violent, I am free your way that teachers do not understand!

Just like the tree in spring new each year—

Invented, worked by its soul

The green, the same that is eternal, creates out of nothing its pointy leaf,

Me, the man,

I know what I do,

Of the thrust and of the power itself of birth and of creation
I wear out, I am master,
I am in the world, I exercise in all places my knowledge,
I know all things and all things know themselves in me.
I bring to everything its deliverance.
By me
Nothing more stays alone but I associate it to another in my heart.

It is not yet enough!

What do I care about the open door, if I do not have the key?
My liberty, if I am not its master?
I regard all things, and you see that I am not its slave, but the ruler.
Everything
Undergoes less than it imposes, forcing that one improves it, all is new
A victory over the beings who were here before!
And You who art the perfect Being, You did not prevent that I may also
be!
You see this man that I make and this being that I take in You.
Oh, my God, my being sighs for yours!
Deliver me from myself! Deliver the being from the condition!
I am free, deliver me from freedom!
I see many ways of not being, but there is only one way
Of being, that is in You, who is Yourself!
The water
Grasp the water, the spirit *odore*, the essence.
My God, who separated the lower waters from the higher waters,
My heart moans for You, deliver me from myself because You are!
What is this liberty, and what have I to do somewhere else?
I must sustain you.
My God, I see the perfect man on the cross, perfect on the perfect Tree.
Your Son and ours, in Your presence and in ours nailed by feet and hands
of four nails,
The heart broken in two and the great Waters penetrated to his heart!
Deliver me from time and take my miserable heart, take, my God, this
heart that beats!
But I cannot force this life
Towards you because of my body and Your glory is like the resistance of
salty water!
The surface of your light is invincible and I cannot find
The failure of your radiant darkness!

You are here and I am here.
You prevent me from passing and I also prevent You from passing.

And you are my end, and I also am Your end.

And as the puniest of worms uses the sun to live and the machine of the planets,

So not a breath of my life may I take from Your eternity.

My liberty is limited by my position in your captivity and by my burning part in the game!

So that one of those rays of your life-creating light that was destined for me does not escape.

And I extend my hands to the left and right

So that no gap in the perfect enclosure of your creatures subsists by me!

There is no need that I die so that you live!

You are in this visible world just as in the other.

You are here.

You are here and I cannot be anywhere else than with You.

What is happening to me? it is as if this old world were now closed.

As in olden days when the head above brought the temple from the sky,

The keystone came to capture the pagan forest.

Oh my God, I see it, the key now that delivers,

It is no longer the one that opens, but the one that closes! are here with me!

It closed by your will like a wall and by your power as if by a very strong belt! and here just as in the past Ezekiel with a reed of seven and a half cubits,

I could meet at the four cardinal points the four dimensions of the City.

It is closed, and here suddenly that everything in my eyes

Acquired proportion and distance.

Here is that Jerusalem and Sion kissing like two sisters, those of Heaven

And the exiled woman that in the river Khobar washes the laundry of sacrifices

And that the earthly Church toward her royal Consort raises its towering crowned head!

Greetings, new world in my eyes, world now total!

O creed complete of visible and invisible things, I accept you with a catholic heart!

Where I turn my head

I envisage the immense octave of Creation!

The world opens and, no matter how broad the span, my view traverses it from one end to the other.

I weigh the sun like a large sheep that two strong men suspend on a pole between their shoulders.

I have taken inventory of the Heaven's army and I have trained it,

After the great figures that hang on the old man Ocean

Until the rarest fire swallowed the deepest abyss.

As the dark blue Pacific or the whaler spies a wind's event like white down.

You are caught and from one end of the world to the other around You I have stretched the immense net of my knowledge.

Like the phrase that takes the brass wins the wood and gradually invades the depths of the orchestra,

And like the eruptions of the sun

Affect the earth in water crisis and tidal wave,

So, from the greatest Angel who sees you to the pebble in the path, and from one corner of your creation to the other,

There shall not cease continuity, neither the soul to the body;

The ineffable movement of the Seraphim spreads to the Nine orders of the Spirits,

And here the wind that rises in turn on the earth, the Sower, the Harvester!

Thus the water continues the spirit, and supports it, and feeds it,

And between

All your creatures until unto You there is a liquid link.

I salute you, oh liberal world in my eyes!

I understand by what you are present,

It is because the Eternal is with you, and where the Creature is, the Creator shall no longer abandon it.

I am in you and you are in me and your possession is mine.

And now in us finally

Bursts the beginning,

Bursts the new day, bursts in the possession of the source I do not know what kind of angelical youth!

My heart no longer beats in time, it is the instrument of my endurance,

And the imperishable spirit considering the passing things.

But did I say passing? Here they begin again.

And mortal? There is no longer death with me.

All being, as it is one

Work of Eternity, it is this how it is an expression.

She is present and all things pass through her.

It shall not be the text naked of light: look, all is written from one end to the other:

You can appeal to the funniest detail: not a syllable missing.

The earth, the blue sky, the river with its boats and three trees carefully on the bank,

The leaf and the insect on top of the leaf, this rock that I weigh in my hand,

The village with all the people with two eyes at the same time talking, weave, shop, make fire, carry loads, complete like an orchestra that plays,

All of that is eternity and the liberty of not being is withdrawn,

I see them with the eyes of my body, I produce them in my heart!

With the eyes of my body, in paradise I will not use any other eyes than those!

Do we say that the sea has perished because already another wave, and the third, and the large wave, has triumphantly resolved in the foam?

It is contained in its shores and the

World with its limits, loses nothing in this place that is closed,

And freedom is contained in love,

Frolic

In all invented things the most exquisite approximation, all beauty in its insufficiency.

I do not see you, but I am uninterrupted with these beings that you see.

One returns only what has been given.

And like with all things of yours

One received being, in time they return the eternal.

And me also

I have a voice, and I listen, and I hear the noise it makes.

And I make water with my voice, like the water that is pure water, because it nourished all things, all things brush in it.

So the voice with which I make of your eternal words! I cannot name anything other than the eternal.

The leaf yellows and the fruit falls, but the leaf in my verses does not perish,

Nor the mature fruit, nor the rose among roses!

She perished, but her name in the spirit who is my spirit no longer perishes. Here is what escapes time.

And I who make things eternal with my voice, make me be complete

This voice, a totally incomprehensible word!

Free me from the bondage and weight of this inert matter!

Clarify me then! strip me of this vile darkness and make it that I may finally be

All this in me obscurely desired.

Vivify me, as the air that breathes by our machine makes our intelli gence shine like an ember!

God who breathed over the chaos, separating the dry from the humid,

Over the Red Sea, and it divided in front of Moses and Aaron,

Over the wet earth, and here the man,

You command also my waters, you have placed in my nostrils the same creation spirit and figure.

It is no longer the impure that ferments, it is the pure that is seed of life.

What is water but the need to be liquid

And perfectly clear in God's sun like a translucent drop?

What do you talk to me about this blue and the air that you liquefy? Oh the human soul is the most precious elixir!

If the dew turns red in the sun

How much more human carbuncle and substantial soul within the intelligible ray!

God who baptized the chaos with your spirit

And who the day before Easter exorcises by the mouth of the priest the pagan fountain with the letter psi,

You sow with the baptismal water our human water

Agile, glorious, impassive, imperishable!

The water that is clear and seen by our eye and sound heard by our ear and taste

By the vermilion mouth drunk from the sextuple spring

And colors our skin and makes our plastic body.

And like the seminal drop fertilizes the mathematic, divesting figure

The abundant elements of his theorem primer,

So the body of glory desires under the body of mud, and the night

To be dissolved in visibility!

My God, have pity on these desiring waters!

My God, you see that I am not only spirit, but water! have pity on these waters that die of thirst!

And the spirit is desiring, but the water is the thing desired.

O my God, you have given me this minute of light to see,

Like the young man thinking in his garden in the month of August that sees all the sky by intervals and the earth in one go,

The world in one go all filled by a great golden lightning strike!

O strong sublime stars and what just-perceived fruit in the dark abyss! O sacred bend of the long branch of the Little Bear!

I do not die,

I do not die, but I am immortal!

And everything dies, but I believe like a more pure light!

And, since they make death of death, of its extermination I make my immortality.

That I entirely cease to be obscure! Use me!

Squeeze me in your paternal hand!

Bring out finally

All the sun that there is in me and the capacity of your light, that I see you

Not only with the eyes, but with all my body and my substance and the sum of my sound and radiant quantity!

The divisible water that makes the man

Does not lose its nature which is to be liquid

And perfectly pure by whatever is reflected on it.

Like these waters that carry God at the beginning,

So these hypostatic waters in us

Do not cease to desire it, there is no desire than of him only!

But what is desirable in me is not ripe.
The night, then, waits for the part where my soul slowly composes itself,
The drop ready to fall into its greater heaviness.
Let me make you a libation in the darkness,
Like the mountain spring that gives the Ocean to drink with its little shell!

My God who knows each man by his name before he is born,
Remember me as I was hidden in the fissure of the mountain,
There where the sources gush boiling water and my hand on the colossal wall of white marble!
Oh my God when the day is extinguished and Lucifer alone appears in the Orient,
Our eyes alone, it is not our eyes alone, our heart, our heart cheers the inextinguishable star,
Our eyes toward its light, our waters towards the glare of this glorified drop!
My God if you have put this rose in the sky, endowed
With so much glory this golden capsule in the ray of the created light,
How much more the immortal man animated by the eternal intelligence!
So the vine under its trailing clusters, so the fruit tree in its blessing day
So the immortal soul to whom this disappearing body is no longer enough!
If the extenuated body desires the wine, if the adoring heart welcomes the recovered star,
how much more is the desiring soul not worth any other human soul?
And I, too, found at the end, the death I so needed! I met this woman. I knew the woman's love.
I possessed the interdiction. I knew this spring of thirst!
I wanted the soul, namely, this water that no longer knows death! I held in my arms the human star!
O friend, I am not a god,
And my soul, I cannot share it with you and you cannot take me or contain me or possess me.
And so, like someone who turns away, you betrayed me, you are no longer anywhere, o rose!
Rose, I will no longer see your face in this life!
And here I am all alone at the stream's edge, the face against the earth,
Like a penitent at the feet of God's mountain, arms in cross in the thunder of the roaring voice!
Here the great tears that come forth!
And I am there like someone who dies, who is smothered and heartbroken, and all my soul springs out of me like a great jet of clear water!
My God,
I see myself and I judge myself, and I don't have any price for myself.

You have given me life: I give it back to You; I prefer that you take all.

I see myself at last! And I have desolation, and the pain inside me opens everything like a liquid eye,

O my God, I don't want anything, and I return everything to You, and nothing has any value for me,

And I only see my misery, and my nothingness, and my privation, and that at least is mine!

Now gush

The deep springs, gush my dirty soul, burst with a great shout the deep pocket of the seminal purity!

Now I am perfectly clear, all bitterly clear, there is nothing more in me Than a perfect privation of You alone!

And now again after the course of a year,

Like Habakkuk the reaper that the Angel brought to Daniel without him letting go of his basket's handle,

Suddenly, the spirit of God's ravishes me over the wall and here I am in this unknown country.

Where is the wind now? where is the sea? where is the route that brought me here!

Where are the men? there is nothing but the always pure sky. Where is the ancient storm?

I pay attention: there is nothing but the shivering tree.

I listen: there is nothing but this insistent leaf.

I know that the fight is over. I know that the storm is finished!

There was the past, but it is no longer. I feel on my face a most cold breath.

Here again the Presence, the frightening solitude, and suddenly again the breath on my face.

Lord, my vineyard is in my presence and I see my deliverance can no longer escape me.

He who knows deliverance, he does not laugh now at all the ties, and who would understand the laughter in his heart?

He regards all and laughs.

Lord, it is nice for us in this place, so that I do not return to the view of men.

My God, undress me in view of all men, that I may not be recognized by any of them,

And like the eternal star

Its light, may there be nothing left of me but the voice only.

The understandable verb and the *expressed* word and the voice that is the spirit and the water!

Brother, I cannot give you my heart, but where matter no longer serves comes and goes the subtle word

That is myself with an eternal intelligence.

Listen, my child, and lean your head on me, and I will give you my soul.

There are many voices in the world and meanwhile the lover with the broken heart hears only on top of the tree the trembling of the sibylline leaf.

So among the human voices which is it that is not softer or louder?

Why are you the only one that hears it? Because only submissive to a divine measure!

Because it is an entirely free measure!

The saintly, free, all-powerful, creative measure!

Ah, I feel it, the spirit no longer ceases to be carried by the waters!

Nothing, my brother, and yourself,

Does not exist but by an inexpressible proportion and the right number on the infinitely divisible waters!

Listen, my child, and do not close your heart, and welcome

The invasion of the reasonable voice, who is the liberation of the water and of the spirit by which are

Explained and resolved all ties!

It is no longer the master's lesson, or the homework given for learning,

It is the invisible food, it is the measure that is above all word,

It is the soul that receives the soul and all things in you become clear.

Here is in the ground of my house, the Word that is like an eternal young woman.

Open the door! And the Wisdom of God is in front of you like a tower of glory and like a crowned queen!

O friend, I am no longer a man or a woman, I am the love that is above all word!

I salute you, my beloved brother.

Do not touch me! Do not seek to take my hand.

Pekin, 1906

Translated by Lourdes I. Torres-Monaghan

Rainer Maria Rilke (1875–1926)

[I find you in all these myriad things]

I find you in all these myriad things
I love and care for like a brother.
As seed, you sun yourself in the smallest
and in the greatest, spread generously abroad.

That is the wondrous play of powers
that move selflessly, upward and down:
rising in the roots, dwindling in the bough
and blooming like resurrection in the crown.

Translated by Daniel Polikoff

Oscar Vladislas de Lubicz Milosz (1877–1939)

Canticle of Spring

The Spring is returned from its distant voyages,
And it brings us peace of heart.
Lift yourself, dear head! Behold, the beautiful visage!
The mountain is an island in the middle of the mist: it has recovered its
cheerful color.
O youth! O viburnum of the leaning house!
O season of the prodigal wasp!
The foolish virgin of summer
Sings in the heat.
All is confidence, charm, repose.
How beautiful is the world, beloved, how beautiful is the world!
A heavy and pure cloud is come from a dark kingdom.
A silence of love has fallen over the gold of noon.
A sleepy nettle bends his purpled head
Beneath the beautiful crown of the Queen of Judea.
Do you hear? The rain is here.
It comes… it is fallen.
All love's kingdom has the scent of a waterflower.
The young bee,
Daughter of the sun,
Flies to uncover the mystery of the orchard;
I hear the bleating herds;
The echo answers the shepherd.
How beautiful is the world, beloved, how beautiful is the world!
We will follow the bagpipe to the forsaken places.
Down there, in the shadow of the cloud, at the foot of the tower,
The rosemary counsels sleep; and there is nothing so beautiful
As the child of the sheep the color of day.
The tender moment beckons us from the shrouded hill.
Arise, proud love, lean upon my shoulder;
I will thrust aside the willow's tresses,
We will gaze into the valley.
The flower bends itself, the tree shivers: they are drunk with scent.
Already, already the grain
Is rising in silence, as in the dreams of sleepers.
And the city, she, too is beautiful in the blue of the time; the towers
Are like women who, from afar
Come to watch their loves.
Puissant love, my eldest sister,

Let us rush to where the garden's hidden bird calls.
Come, cruel heart,
Come, gentle face;
The breeze with the cheeks of a child blows upon the cloud
Of jasmine.
The dove with beautiful feet comes to drink at the fountain;
How white she appears in the new water!
What does she say? Where is she?
It seems she sings in my new heart.
And here away...
How beautiful is the world, beloved, how beautiful is the world!
Come, follow me! I know the confines of solitude.
The woman of the ruins calls my name from the high window:
See how her hair of wildflowers and the wind
Is spread over the crumbling eaves
And I hear the striped bumblebee,
Ancient bell-ringer of innocent days.
The time has come, mad one, for us
To adorn ourselves with the berries that breathe in the shade.
The oriole sings in the most secret alley.
He awaits us in the dew of solitude.
O beautiful dark face, long and soft,
Midnight lamp of July,
Illumined depths of the tulip in flower!
I behold you: all of my soul is drowned
In tears.
Come, my love, come my July,
Come, o my night!
Do not fear me: my heart cuts the rain
Offered by the storm to the migrating bird!
There was a vein on thy temple during calm,
Sleepy one.
It is my grass-snake from the hearth,
Fed bread and white honey for another year.
There in your eyes the secret of the night,
The charm of the water. As in the night, as in the water,
There are many dangers.
Tell me, does your heart also go there, does yours, also, change?
You laugh; and to laugh, my sister,
You incline the head, you extend the neck,
Black swan, tame swan, swan of great beauty;
And the sloping shoulder widens a fold of water.
How beautiful is the world, beloved, how beautiful is the world!
Now you lift the head and the shade of eyelashes

A turning circle
Comes to me as from the depths
Of the arbor;
And this is the way to read in the heart.
Whether you are a dream that we touch…
—Listen! Echo has joined his hands of bark over his mouth,
He calls us. And the forest is vested in genius.
Come! I want to show you my brothers, my sisters,
To the pomegranates of the South, to the mountain of vines;
"Here my sister, here my companion,
Here is my love adorned in colors.
He brought me to the kingdom of childhood;
My poor head was at the bottom of the dark river of science:
He is come, he opens the door of the tomb!"
How beautiful is the world, beloved, how beautiful is the world!
O sister of my thought! what is this mystery?
Enlighten me, awaken me, for these are things seen in a dream.
Oh! most certainly I sleep.
How beautiful is life! no more lies, no more remorse
And the flowers lift themselves from the earth
As a pardon from the dead.
O month of love, O voyager, O day of joy!
Be our guest, stay,
You shall rest yourself beneath our roof.
Your grave projects will be lulled by the winged murmur of the alley.
We will feed you with bread, with honey and with milk.
Do not flee.
What have you to do over there?
Are you not well here?
We will hide you from worries.
There is a beautiful secret bedroom
In our house of repose;
There, the green shadows enter through the open window
On a garden of enchantment, of solitude and water.
It listens… it lingers…
How beautiful is the world, beloved, how beautiful is the world!
    Translated by Michael Martin

THE HEAVENLY COUNTRY

Alexander Blok (1880–1921)

from Ante Lucem

17

I was walking toward bliss. My path was shining
With the red light of the evening dew,
And in my heart a tremulous distant voice
Sang a song of dawn. It sang
A dawn song as the sunset was fading,
The stars were glowing,
And the high seas of the sky
Were burning with the evening purple!...
My soul was burning and my voice was singing
Of the dawn at the evening hour.
I was walking toward bliss. My path was shining
With the red light of the evening dew.
(*18 May 1899*)
Translated by Boris Jakim

from Verses about the Beautiful Lady

17

The heavenly is not measurable by the mind,
The azure is hidden from minds.
Only rarely do seraphim bring
Holy dreams to the chosen of the worlds.
And I imagined the Russian Venus,
Entwined in a heavy tunic,
Passionless in her purity, joyless without measure,
The features of her face expressing a tranquil dream.
She has come down to earth not for the first time
But crowding round her for the first time
Are her new heroes and champions...
And strange is the gleam of her deep eyes...
(*29 May 1901, Shakhmatovo*)
Translated by Boris Jakim

54

Your image appears spontaneously
Amid the familiar banal days.

Sometimes it's easy, sometimes painful,
Not to bow down to the ground before You.
In my forgetfulness without sadness
I cannot forget sometimes
How inconsolably my constellations
Sorrowed over You.
You lived not in my agitation
But in that land native to us—
And in solitary veneration
I came to know Your truth.
(*22 September 1900*)
    Translated by Boris Jakim

56

Smoke rises from the altars and incense from the censers
        Of the children of earth.
The goddess of life, the mysterious heavenly body,
        Is in the distance.
They sing solemnly and triumphantly glorify
        The mute firmament.
They grasp at the desolate air with their hands,
        Receiving death.
Ungraspable, she is not among us;
        She is beyond the earth,
While we, calling with triumphant words,
        Lie in dust.
(*29 September 1900*)
    Translated by Boris Jakim

85

Over there, in the half-darkness of the cathedral,
In the light of an icon's lamp,
The living night will soon gaze
Into your sleepless eyes.
In the speeches about heavenly wisdom
You sense earthly currents.
Up there, beneath the arches, you find unknown darkness,
While here you have the coldness of a stone bench.
The intense heat of an accidental meeting
Breathed from the church heights
Onto these slumbering candles,
Onto the icons and the flowers.
The silence is inspiring,

Your thoughts are hidden,
And you obscurely sense the knowledge
And the trembling of the dove and of the serpent.
(*14 January 1902*)
  Translated by Boris Jakim

86

We bowed down before the scriptures
And were taken aback by the silence of the temple.
In the rays of the divine light
The smile of the Woman was remembered.
Souls united and silent,
In the same rays and within the same walls,
We perceived the solar waves
Above—on the dark cupolas.
And from that ancient gilding,
From those terrible depths,
Onto my holiday descended Someone
With the smile of the tender Woman.
(*18 January 1902, St. Isaac's Cathedral*)
  Translated by Boris Jakim

111

I seek strange and new things on the pages
Of old and familiar books;
I dream of white vanished birds
And sense the isolated instant.
Agitated rudely by the commotion of life
And dismayed by whispers and shouts,
I am anchored securely by my white dream
To the shore of the recent past.
White You are, imperturbable in the depths,
Stern and wrathful in life,
Mysteriously anxious and mysteriously loved,
Maiden, Dawn, Burning Bush.
The cheeks of golden-haired maidens fade,
Dawns are not as eternal as dreams.
Thorns crown the humble and wise
With the white fire of the Burning Bush.
(*4 April 1902*)
  Translated by Boris Jakim

Guillaume Apollinaire (*1880–1918*)

Clair de Lune

The moon honeys the lips of madmen
The orchards and the villages this night are greedy
The stars figure well the bees
Of this luminous honey which drips from trellises
For here soft and falling from the sky
Each ray of the moon is a ray of honey
Hidden gold I perceive the very soft adventure
I fear the fiery dart of that bee Arcturus
Who set in my hands the deceiving rays
And took his lunar honey from the rose of the winds
Translated by Michael Martin

Eleanor Farjeon (*1881–1965*)

A Morning Song (for the First Day of Spring)

Morning has broken,
Like the first morning,
Blackbird has spoken
Like the first bird;
Praise for the singing,
Praise for the morning,
Praise for them springing
Fresh from the Word.

Sweet the rain's new fall,
Sunlit from heaven,
Like the first dewfall
On the first grass;
Praise for the sweetness,
Of the wet garden,
Sprung in completeness
Where His feet pass.

Mine is the sunlight,
Mine is the morning,
Born of the one light
Eden saw play;

Praise with elation,
Praise every morning,
God's re-creation
Of the new day.

The World's Amazing Beauty

The world's amazing beauty would make us cry
Aloud; but something in it strikes us dumb.
Beech-forests drenched in sunny floods
Where shaking rays and shadows hum,
The unrepeated aspects of the sky,
Clouds in their lightest and their wildest moods,
Bare shapes of hills, June grass in flower,
The sea in every hour,
Slopes that one January morning flow
Unbrokenly with snow,
Peaks piercing heaven with motions sharp and harsh,
Slow-moving flats, grey reed and silver marsh,
A flock of swans in flight
Or solitary heron flapping home,
Orchards of pear and cherry turning white,
Low apple-trees with rosy-budded boughs,
Streams where young willows drink and cows,
Earth's rich ploughed loam
Thinking darkly forward to her sheaves,
Water in Autumn spotted with yellow leaves,
Light running overland,
Gulls standing still above their images
On strips of shining sand
While evening in a haze of green
Half-hides
The calm receding tides—
What in the beauty we have seen in these
Keeps us still silent? something we have not seen?

James Joyce (1882–1941)

From *Ulysses*

I love flowers Id love to have the whole place swimming in roses God
of heaven theres nothing like nature the wild mountains then the sea
and the waves rushing then the beautiful country with the fields of oats
and wheat and all kinds of things and all the fine cattle going about
that would do your heart good to see rivers and lakes and flowers all
sorts of shapes and smells and colours springing up even out of the
ditches primroses and violets nature it is as for them saying theres no
God I wouldnt give a snap of my two fingers for all their learning why
dont they go and create something I often asked him atheists or whatever they call themselves go and wash the cobbles off themselves first
then they go howling for the priest and they dying and why why
because theyre afraid of hell on account of their bad conscience ah yes
I know them well who was the first person in the universe before there
was anybody that made it all who ah that they dont know neither do I
so there you are they might as well try to stop the sun from rising
tomorrow the sun shines for you he said the day we were lying among
the rhododendrons on Howth head in the grey tweed suit and his
straw hat the day I got him to propose to me yes first I gave him the bit
of seedcake out of my mouth and it was leapyear like now yes 16 years
ago my God after that long kiss I near lost my breath yes he said I was a
flower of the mountain yes so we are flowers all a womans body yes
that was one true thing he said in his life and the sun shines for you
today yes that was why I liked him because I saw he understood or felt
what a woman is and I knew I could always get round him and I gave
him all the pleasure I could leading him on till he asked me to say yes
and I wouldnt answer first only looked out over the sea and the sky I
was thinking of so many things he didnt know of Mulvey and Mr Stan-
hope and Hester and father and old captain Groves and the sailors
playing all birds fly and I say stoop and washing up dishes they called it
on the pier and the sentry in front of the governors house with the
thing round his white helmet poor devil half roasted and the Spanish
girls laughing in their shawls and their tall combs and the auctions in
the morning the Greeks and the jews and the Arabs and the devil
knows who else from all the ends of Europe and Duke street and the
fowl market all clucking outside Larby Sharons and the poor donkeys
slipping half asleep and the vague fellows in the cloaks asleep in the
shade on the steps and the big wheels of the carts of the bulls and the
old castle thousands of years old yes and those handsome Moors all in
white and turbans like kings asking you to sit down in their little bit of

a shop and Ronda with the old windows of the posadas 2 glancing eyes
a lattice hid for her lover to kiss the iron and the wineshops half open
at night and the castanets and the night we missed the boat at Algeciras
the watchman going about serene with his lamp and O that awful
deepdown torrent O and the sea the sea crimson sometimes like fire
and the glorious sunsets and the figtrees in the Alameda gardens yes
and all the queer little streets and the pink and blue and yellow houses
and the rosegardens and the jessamine and geraniums and cactuses
and Gibraltar as a girl where I was a Flower of the mountain yes when I
put the rose in my hair like the Andalusian girls used or shall I wear a
red yes and how he kissed me under the Moorish wall and I thought
well as well him as another and then I asked him with my eyes to ask
again yes and then he asked me would I yes to say yes my mountain
flower and first I put my arms around him yes and drew him down to
me so he could feel my breasts all perfume yes and his heart was going
like mad and yes I said yes I will Yes.[2]

Charles Williams (1886–1945)

Mater Dei

> Who hath heard my title?
>   Who hath known my name?
> While all loves' recital
>   Rumours but my fame,
> Mine, when young doves' cooing
>   Through the land is heard.
> When by my renewing
>   All the spring is stirred!
>
> Follow, lovers mortal,
>   To the heart of Love,
> Where through me the portal
>   Fleets the holy Dove,
> Where through me the Eternal
>   Flashes into times.
> And the still Supernal
>   Multitudinous chimes.
>
> Love, on journey faring
>   Through infinity,

---

2. Taken from the 1st edition. Public domain.

Wrought me for his bearing,
　And the worlds for me.
None but my white sinless
　Virgin arms enmesh
Him, the sole, the kinless,
Archetypal flesh!

Lovers all, behold him:
　To one end ye move!
In my arms I fold him,
　Archetypal Love.
Diverse love-ways haunting,
　To one end ye throng,
All your wills a chanting,
　All your blood a song!

Have ye seen the vestal
　Glory, swift and clear,
Where upon the quest all
　Hailed the huntress spear?
Know your mouths the voicing
　First, of love's delight,
While the eyes rejoicing
　Darken with the night?

Light of vestals massèd
　In my light arose,
I the unsurpassèd
　Dian of the snows;
In my arms was nursèd
　Love's too mortal bliss,
I the unprecursèd
　Eve of heavenly kiss!

Lo with me imploring
　All your manhoods rise:
Lo on me adoring
　Flame the God-filled skies!
Daring all the thunder,
　Mighty, unafraid,
I unite and sunder,
　Mother yet a maid!

Follow, mortal lovers,
　Love through me the gate.
Each whose touch discovers
　Her, immaculate!

Turn, behold, and grasp her,—
    Mighty, unafraid!
See and spring and clasp her,
    The maternal maid!

David Jones (1895–1974)

The Tutelar of the Place

She that loves place, time, demarcation, hearth, kin, enclosure, site, differentiated cult, though she is but one mother of us all: one earth brings us all forth, one womb receives us all, yet to each she is other, named of some name other...

          ...other sons, beyond hill, over strath, or never so neighbouring by nigh field or near crannog up stream. What co-tidal line can plot if nigrin or flaxhead marching their wattles be cognate or german of common totem?

Tellus of the myriad names answers to but one name: From this tump she answers Jac o' the Tump only if he call Great-Jill-of-the-tump-that-bare-me, not if he cry by some new fangle moder of far gentes over the flud, fer-goddess name from anaphora of far folk wont woo her; she's a rare one for locality.

Or, gently she bends her head from far-height when tongue-strings chime the name she whispered on known-site, as between sister and brother at the time of beginnings . . . when the wrapped bands are cast and the worst mewling is over, after the weaning and before the august initiations, in the years of becoming.
When she and he 'twixt door-stone and fire-stane prefigure and puppet on narrow floor-stone the world-masque on wide world-floor.
When she attentively changes her doll-shift, lets pretend with solemnity as rocking the womb-gift.
When he chivvies house-pet with his toy *hasta*, makes believe the cat o' the wold falls to the pitiless bronze.
        Man-travail and woman-war here we see enacted are.
      When she and he beside the settle, he and she between the
        trestle-struts, mime the bitter dance to come.
Cheek by chin at the childer-crock where the quick tears drop and the quick laughter dries the tears, within the rim of the shared curd-cup each fore-reads the world-storm.
Till the spoil-sport gammers sigh:

Now come on now little children, come on
now it's past the hour. Sun's to roost, brood's in pent, dusk-star tops
mound, lupa sniffs the lode-damps for stragglers late to byre.
Come now it's time to come now for tarry awhile and slow
                              cot's best for yeanlings
                              crib's best for babes
here's a rush to light you to bed
here's a fleece to cover your head
against the world-storm
                brother by sister under one *brethyn*[3]
kith of the kin warmed at the one hearth-flame
(of the seed of far-gaffer? fair gammer's wer-gifts?)
cribbed in garth that the garth-Jill wards.

Though she inclines with attention from far fair-height outside all
boundaries, beyond the known and kindly nomenclatures, where all
names are one name, where all stones of demarcation dance and interchange, troia[4] the skipping mountains, nod recognitions.
As when on known-site ritual frolics keep bucolic interval at eves and
divisions when they mark the inflexions of the year and conjugate with
trope and turn the seasons' syntax, with beating feet, with wands and
pentagons to spell out the Trisagion.
Who laud and magnify with made, mutable and beggarly elements the
unmade immutable begettings and precessions of fair height, with
halting sequences and unresolved rhythms, searchingly, with what's to
hand, under the inconstant lights that hover world-flats, that bright by
fit and start the tangle of world-wood, rifting the dark drifts for the
wanderers that wind the world-meander, who seek some hidden gram-
mar to give back anathema its first benignity.
Gathering all things in, twining each bruised stem to the swaying trellis
of the dance, the dance about the sawn lode-stake on the hill where the
hidden stillness is at the core of struggle, the dance around the green
lode-tree on far fair-height where the secret guerdons hang and the
bright prizes nod, where sits the queen *im Rosenhage* eating the honey-
cake, where the king sits, counting-out his man-geld, rhyming the
audits of all the world-holdings.
Where the marauder leaps the wall and the wall dances to the marauder's leaping, where the plunging wolf-spear and the wolf's pierced
diaphragm sing the same song…

Yet, when she stoops to hear you children cry
                from the scattered and single habitations

---

3. Welsh for "cloth."
4. "meander."

or from the nucleated holdings
> from tower'd *castra*
> paved *civitas*
> treble-ramped *caer*[5]
> or wattled *tref*[6]
>> stockaded *gorod* or
>> trenched *burh*

from which ever child-crib within whatever enclosure
demarked by a dynast or staked by consent
wherever in which of the wide world-ridings
> you must not call her but by that name

which accords to the morphology of that place.
Now pray now little children pray for us all now, pray our
gammer's prayer according to our *disciplina* given to us
within our labyrinth on our dark mountain.
> Say now little children:

Sweet Jill of our hill hear us
bring slow bones safe at the lode-ford
keep lupa's bite without our wattles
make her bark keep children good
save us all from dux of far folk
save us from the men who plan.
Now sleep on, little children, sleep on now, while I tell
out the greater suffrages, not yet for young heads to understand:

Queen of the differentiated sites, administratrix of the demarcations,
let our cry come unto you.
> In all times of imperium save us

when the *mercatores* come save us
> from the guile of the *negotiatores* save us

from the *missi*, from the agents
> who think no shame

by inquest to audit what is shameful to tell
> deliver us.

When they check their capitularies in their curias
> confuse their reckonings.

When they narrowly assess the *trefydd*[7]
> by hide and rod
> by *pentan*[8] and pent

---

5. "fort."
6. "hamlet."
7. "hamlets."
8. "hob."

by impost and fee on beast-head
              and roof-tree
and number the souls of men
              notch their tallies false
disorder what they have collated.
When they proscribe the diverse uses and impose the
rootless uniformities, pray for us.
              When they sit in *Consilium*
to liquidate the holy diversities
              mother of particular perfections
              queen of otherness
              mistress of asymmetry
patroness of things counter, parti, pied, several
protectress of things known and handled
help of things familiar and small
              wardress of the secret crevices
              of things wrapped and hidden
mediatrix of all the deposits
              margravine of the troia
empress of the labyrinth
              receive our prayers.
When they escheat to the Ram
              in the Ram's curia
the seisin where the naiad sings
              above where the forked rod bends
or where the dark outcrop
              tells on the hidden seam
pray for the green valley.
When they come with writs of oyer and terminer
                      to hear the false and
                      determine the evil
according to the advices of the Ram's magnates who serve
the Ram's wife, who write in the Ram's book of Death.
In the bland megalopolitan light
              where no shadow is by day or by night
 be our shadow.
Remember the mound-kin, the kith of the *tarren*[9] gone from this
mountain because of the exorbitance of the Ram... remember them in
the rectangular tenements, in the houses of the engines that fabricate
the ingenuities of the Ram...
Mother of Flowers save them then where no flower blows.
              Though they shall not come again

---

9. "knoll."

because of the requirements of the Ram with respect to the world plan, remember them where the dead forms multiply, where no stamen leans, where the carried pollen falls to the adamant surfaces, where is no crevice.

In all times of *Gleichschaltung*, in the days of the central economies, set up the hedges of illusion round some remnant of us, twine the wattles of mist, white-web a Gwydion-hedge

like fog on the *bryniau*[10]

against the commissioners and assessors bearing the writs of the Ram to square the world-floor and number the tribes and write down the secret things and take away the diversities by which we are, by which we call on your name, sweet Jill of the demarcations

arc of differences
tower of individuation
queen of the minivers

laughing in the mantle of variety
belle of the mound

for Jac o' the mound
our belle and donnabelle

on all the world-mountain.
In the December of our culture ward somewhere the secret seed, under the mountain, under and between, between the grids of the Ram's survey when he squares the world-circle.
Sweet Mair devise a mazy-guard
in and out and round about
double-dance defences
countermure and echelon meanders round
the holy mound

fence within the fence
pile the dun ash for the bright seed

(within the curtained wood the canister within the canister the budding rod)
troia in depth the shifting wattles of illusion for the ancilla for the palladia for the kept memorials, because of the commissioners of the Ram and the Ram's decree concerning the utility of the hidden things.

When the technicians manipulate the dead limbs of our culture as though it yet had life, have mercy on us. Open unto us, let us enter a second time within your stola-folds in those days—ventricle and ref-

---

10. "hills."

uge both, *hendref*[11] for world-winter, asylum from world-storm,
Womb of the Lamb the spoiler of the Ram.

Czesław Miłosz (1911–2004)

Rivers

Under various names, I have praised only you, rivers!

You are milk and honey and love and death and dance.

From a spring in hidden grottoes, seeping from mossy rocks

Where a goddess pours live water from a pitcher,

At clear streams in the meadow, where rills murmur underground,

Your race and my race begin, and amazement, and quick passage.

Naked, I exposed my face to the sun, steering with hardly a dip of the
paddle—

Oak woods, fields, a pine forest skimming by,

Around every bend the promise of the earth,

Village smoke, sleepy herds, flights of martins over sandy bluffs.

I entered your waters slowly, step-by-step,

And the current in that silence took me by the knees

Until I surrendered and it carried me and I swam

Through the huge reflected sky of a triumphant noon.

I was on your banks at the onset of midsummer night

When the full moon rolls out and lips touch in the rituals of kissing—

I hear in myself, now as then, the lapping of water by the boathouse

And the whisper that calls me in for an embrace and for consolation.

We go down with the bells ringing in all the sunken cities.

Forgotten, we are greeted by the embassies of the dead,

While your endless flowing carries us on and on;

And neither is nor was. The moment only, eternal.

Berkley, 1980

Translated by Renata Gorczynski and Robert Hass

11. "ancestral dwelling."

Rivers

"So lasting they are, the rivers!" Only think. Sources somewhere in the mountains pulsate and springs seep from a rock, join in a stream, in the current of a river, and the river flows through centuries, millennia. Tribes, nations pass, and the river is still there, and yet it is not, for water does not stay the same, only the place and the name persist, as a metaphor for a permanent form and changing matter. The same rivers flowed in Europe when none of today's countries existed and no languages known to us were spoken. It is in the names of rivers that traces of lost tribes survive. They lived, though, so long ago that nothing is certain and scholars make guesses which to other scholars seem unfounded. It is not even known how many of these names come from before the Indo-European invasion, which is estimated to have taken place two thousand to three thousand years BC. Our civilization poisoned river waters, and their contamination acquires a powerful emotional meaning. As the course of a river is a symbol of time, we are inclined to think of a poisoned time. And yet the sources continue to gush and we believe time will be purified one day. I am a worshipper of flowing and would like to entrust my sins to the waters, let them be carried to the sea.

Translated by Czeslaw Milosz and Robert Hass (1998)

William Everson (Brother Antoninus, 1912–1994)

A Canticle to the Great Mother of God

Now all good things came to me together with her, and innumerable riches through her hands, and I rejoiced in all these; for this wisdom went before me, and I knew not that she was the mother of them all. Which I have learned without guile, and communicate without envy, and her riches I hide not.   The Book of Wisdom

I dream I am on a hill overlooking San Francisco. I stand to the east across the bay, the light falling forward out of the west and north as it does toward sunset in summer. I see the merging lines of traffic, usually reminiscent of scurrying ant trails, but now transforming into processions, perhaps religious processions in solemn chant intent upon the source of their life and vitality, slowly descending from the long bridges and the winding freeways beneath me, out of the latency of the darkening world behind. At last I see the outline of the city recede, until in its place only a sublime presence persists, a mysterious feminine implication, evocative and potent, like the memory of the Beloved, evading definition or the strictness of analysis, but haunting and omnipresent. Across the void of that awareness one gull, white-bodied and agile, wheels toward the sinking sun. In the coming of the night, touched by a perfect peace, I stand a long time until, far out in the Pacific, the light drops, and on the darkened west the crescent moon emerges. Then I go down, but neither the crash of traffic, nor the threat of whatever predatory violence menaces the slums through which I wander, can dispel from my mind the reality of that moment, which persists, like a permanent bestowal, and which, I cannot doubt, will change my life forever.

Sometimes I dream you measured of bright walls, stepped on a hill and diademed with rose, Sea-cinctured, the black wave-haunted wharves radialed round your hems, and the nuzzling tugs Shunted like suckling
    spaniels at your piers.

All the resplendent bridges of your bays converge upon your heart to
    there deploy,
Dilated into streets, fanned to the outmost sectors, bloodlines of
    pulsant use that throbbing flow,
Serving the induct of all crafts and hallowed skills.

Trending into your colonnades at dawn, down from those airgirthed
    arches of the sky,
We pause in tremble, sleep-cozened but reprieved, stirred to the
    richening diastole.
Soaring on noon we sense it loudly replete, swelled to the stately
    tempo, augmented to the day-drummed dance,
Pace of the proudness, an opulence subsumed, the strident fluting and
    the resonance of blare.
Sinking toward dusk we drink a slowed, more moded music, muted, a
    hushed convergence, a deep relapsed repose.
In all the hinterlands about the trains come nosing home, mallowed of
    late light,
Shrilling their long crescendos, creaming with racing lamps the fast
    ingathered gloom.
Night is your nuance. Listening we hear the wild seabirds, flittered like
    intuition through your coolest thought,
Falter and then fly on, seeding steep sky, the beacon-raftered verge,
South-sought, mewling one plaintive meed, a tremulance of plight,
    before they pass,
Reflashing on pale tips the birth-reverted instinct of all trek.

Hidden within the furlongs of those deeps, your fiery virtue impreg-
    nates the sky, irradiant with wisdom.
You are Byzantium, domed awesomeness, the golden-ruddy richness
    of rare climes, great masterwork of God.
Kneeling within thy moskey naves, seized in the luminous indult of
    those dusks,

THE HEAVENLY COUNTRY

We hold the modal increase, subsumed in chant, ransomed of the
 balsam and the myrrh.
Keeping an immost essence, an invitational letting that never wholly
 spends, but solemnly recedes,
You pause, you hover, virtue indemnable, at last made still, a synthesis
 unprobed.
Checked there, we tremble on the brink, we dream the venue of those
 everlapsing deeps.

But always there is a somethingness eludes us, Mother, city and citadel,
Proud battlement and spire, croft, granary, and the cool, sky-thirsting
 towers.
Obscure behind those nodes, those many-mingled lights, that wink
 and then well up,
Pale opals on the movement of your breasts, or the navel-cuspèd
 moonstone at your womb,
Always your essence hovers. The flashing glances of the sea belt you
 about with brightness, blind our eyes,
And the famished senses swoon of that vaunted spicery.

For how could we ever know you wholly as you are, thou who are
clearly here so manifest of God?
Our coarseness keeps us pinioned of our nerves, while you, immaculate, conceived simplicity,
Subsume the inviolable instance. We are unworth, who shunt in stupor
 whelming at your breasts,
Rude shoulderers who sully what we seek, foul our sole good.

But you, that which you have, you give, and give it graced, not as it is
 but as we use it of you,
Dimensioned down to our foreboded taste, our thirst of need, filtered
 to our mereness and our plight.
We suck through sin. Our boon is that you are subsistent of the light,
 bringing the Light to us,
whose darkness dams out grace.
Confirmed unto the kindness, gaped mouths of thirst, we tongue a
 milk like honey,
And know from whence it sprung, being yours, who never could taste
 the heaven-nurtured nectar that you use.

Believe us when we seek, Mother and Mercy, who in our lives are
 unbelievable,
All faithlessness of the flesh wrought flaccid, the stunt will burdened in
 the bone.
That need we nurse is sharper than our cry.
Through you alone, the Wisdom and the Womb, keen-creeps the child,

The visionary life fast-set against the acrid element, deaths factual
zone.

Clearly you are to us as God, who bring God to us.
Not otherwise than of those arms does grace emerge, blessing our
birth-blank brow.
Wombed of earth's wildness, flank darked and void, we have been
healed in light,
Traced to the sweet mutation of those hands, a touch closing the
anguish-actual stripe,
Whip-flashed the sin, lip-festered on our soul.

This is all plain. But plainness drowns in everything you are, the
presence you proclaim,
That mystery in which achieves all you are meant.
Squinting our eyes we cannot comprehend.
You we behold, but never what makes you be, the Allness you relate to,
The Finalness you keep, and which we ache to touch.
This thing neither can you say, because of us, lacking your whole
capacity to know.

But see: out of this too redounds your deepest motherhood;
As one unable to yield the child that utterness no child can spell,
She yet *subsumes* the truth, is the grave wisdom of her wakeful eyes.
Or else the child, callow-stumped and closed, never grows up to what
deep knowledge is,
completes its mode.
Our spirits, watchful, tenacious on their term, see to it only as it
gleams in you, because of what you are,
The radiance on which the world's blunt might is closed, sharp in a
singleness simple as any star,
Bright-bought, sheer as one nexus-seeding coal.

Hive of the honey, city and citadel, cathedral and cloister and the cool
conventual keeps,
Receive us in. The anchorhold of heaven helms us on.
Hungered of that pledge we trample up the ramps limned of
a vision,
Questing for what you smile of veiled in rapture mirrored in your eyes,
A solace deeper you said than all such clustered balms,
Pierced to a presence totaled on all truth, vaster than the Prophet's
dream descried,
And larger, if we believe you, even than your love.

THE HEAVENLY COUNTRY

Thomas Merton (1915–1968)

Hagia Sophia

I. *Dawn. The Hour Lauds.*

There is in all visible things an invisible fecundity, a dimmed light, a meek namelessness, a hidden wholeness. This mysterious Unity and Integrity is Wisdom, the Mother of all, *Natura naturans*. There is in all things an inexhaustible sweetness and purity, a silence that is a fount of action and joy. It rises up in wordless gentleness ad flows out to me from the unseen roots of all created being, welcoming me tenderly, saluting me with indescribable humility. This is at once my own being, my own nature, and the Gift of my Creator's Thought and Art within me, speaking as Hagia Sophia, speaking as my sister, Wisdom.

I am awakened, I am born again at the voice of this my Sister, sent to me from the depths of the divine fecundity.

Let us suppose I am a man lying asleep in a hospital. I am indeed this man lying asleep. It is July the second, the Feast of Our Lady's Visitation. A Feast of Wisdom.

At five-thirty in the morning I am dreaming in a very quiet room when a soft voice awakens me from my dream. I am like all mankind awakening from all the dreams that ever were dreamed in all the nights of the world. It is like the One Christ awakening in all the separate selves that ever were separate and isolated and alone in all the lands of the earth. It is like all minds coming back together into awareness from all distractions, cross-purposes and confusions, into unity of love. It is like the first morning of the world (when Adam, at the sweet voice of Wisdom, awoke from nonentity and knew her), and like the Last Morning of the world when all the fragments of Adam will return from death at the voice of Hagia Sophia, and will know where they stand.

Such is the awakening of one man, one morning, at the voice of a nurse in the hospital. Awakening out of languor and darkness, out of helplessness, out of sleep, newly confronting reality and finding it to be gentleness.

It is like being awakened by Eve. It is like being awakened by the Blessed Virgin. It is like coming forth from primordial nothingness and standing in clarity, in Paradise.

In the cool hand of the nurse there is the touch of all life, the touch of Spirit.

Thus Wisdom cries out to all who will hear (*Sapientia clamitat in plateis*) and she cries out particularly to the little, to the ignorant and the helpless.

Who is more little, who is more than the helpless man who lies asleep in his bed without awareness and without defense? Who is more trusting than he who must entrust himself each night to sleep? What is the reward of his trust? Gentleness comes to him when he is most helpless and awakens him, refreshed, beginning to be made whole. Love takes him by the hand, and opens to him the doors of another life, another, day.

(But he who has defended himself, fought for himself in sickness, planned for himself, guarded himself, loved himself alone and watched over his own life all night, is killed at last by exhaustion. For him there is no newness. Everything is stale and old.)

When the helpless one awakens strong at the voice of mercy, it is as if Life his Sister, as if the Blessed Virgin, (his own flesh, his own sister), as if Nature made wise by God's Art and Incarnation were to stand over him and invite him with unutterable sweetness to be awake and to live. This is what it means to recognize Hagia Sophia.

II. *Early Morning. The Hour of Prime.*

O blessed, silent one, who speaks everywhere!

We do not hear the soft voice, the gentle voice, the merciful and feminine.

We do not hear mercy, or yielding love, or non-resistance, or non-reprisal. In her there are no reasons and no answers. Yet she is the candor of God's light, the expression of His simplicity.

We do not hear the uncomplaining pardon that bows down the innocent visages of flowers to the dewy earth. We do not see the Child who is prisoner in all the people, and who says nothing. She smiles, for though they have bound her, she cannot be a prisoner. Not that she is strong, or clever, but simply that she does not understand imprisonment.

The helpless one, abandoned to sweet sleep, him the gentle one will awake: Sophia.

All that is sweet in her tenderness will speak to him on all sides in everything, without ceasing, and he will never be the same again. He will have awakened not to conquest and dark pleasure but to the impeccable pure simplicity of One consciousness in all and through: one Wisdom, one Child, one Meaning, one Sister.

The stars rejoice in their setting, and in the rising of the Sun. The heavenly lights rejoice in the going forth of one man to make a new world in the morning, because he has come out of the confused primordial dark into consciousness. He has expressed the clear silence of Sophia in his own heart. He has become eternal.

III. *High Morning. The Hour of Tierce.*

The Sun Burns in the sky like the Face of God, but we do not know his countenance as terrible. His light is diffused in the air and the light of God is diffused by Hagia Sophia.

We do not see the Blinding One in black emptiness. He speaks to us gently in ten thousand things, in which His light is one fullness and one Wisdom.

Thus He shines not on them but from within them. Such is the loving-kindness of Wisdom.

All the perfections of created things are also in God; and therefore He is at once Father and Mother. As Father He stands in solitary might surrounded by darkness. As Mother His shining is diffused, embracing all His creatures with merciful tenderness and light. The Diffuse Shining of God is Hagia Sophia. We call her His "glory." In Sophia His power is experienced only as mercy and as love.

(When the recluses of fourteenth-century England heard their Church Bells and looked out upon the wolds and fens under a kind sky, they spoke in their hearts to "Jesus our Mother." It was Sophia that had awakened in their childlike hearts.)

Perhaps in a certain very primitive aspect Sophia is the unknown, the dark, the nameless Ousia. Perhaps she is even the Divine Nature, One in Father, Son and Holy Ghost. And perhaps she is in infinite light unmanifest, not even waiting to be known as Light. This I do not know. Out of the silence Light is spoken. We do not hear it or see it until is spoken.

In the Nameless Beginning, without Beginning, was the Light. We have not seen this Beginning. I do not know where she is, in this Beginning. I do not speak of her as a Beginning, but as a manifestation.

Now the Wisdom of God, Sophia, comes forth, reaching from "end to end mightily." She wills to be also the unseen pivot of all nature, the center and significance of all the light that is *in* all and *for* all. That which is poorest and humblest, that which is most hidden in all things is nevertheless most obvious in them, and quite manifest, for it is their own self that stands before us, naked and without care.

Sophia, the feminine child, is playing in the world, obvious and unseen, playing at all times before the Creator. Her delights are to be with the children of men. She is their sister. The core of life that exists in all things is tenderness, mercy, virginity, the Light, the Life considered as passive, as received, as given, as taken, as inexhaustibly renewed by the Gift of God. Sophia is Gift, is Spirit, *Donum Dei*. She is God-given and God Himself as Gift. God as all, and God reduced to Nothing: inexhaustible nothingness. *Exinanivit semetipsum.* Humility as the source of failing light.

Hagia Sophia in all things is the Divine Life reflected in them, considered as a spontaneous participation, as their invitation to the Wedding Feast.

Sophia is God's sharing of Himself with creatures. His outpouring, and the Love by which He is given, and known, held and loved.

She is in all things like the air receiving the sunlight. In her they prosper. In her they glorify God. In her they rejoice to reflect Him. In her they are united with him. She is the union between them. She is the Love that unites them. She is life as communion, life as thanksgiving, life as praise, life as festival, life as glory.

Because she receives perfectly there is in her no stain. She is love without blemish, and gratitude without self-complacency. All things praise her by being themselves and by sharing in the Wedding Feast. She is the Bride and the Feast and the Wedding.

The feminine principle in the world is the inexhaustible source of creative realizations of the Father's glory. She is His manifestation in radiant splendor! But she remains unseen, glimpsed only by a few. Sometimes there are none who know her at all.

Sophia is the mercy of God in us. She is the tenderness with which the infinitely mysterious power of pardon turns the darkness of our sins into the light of grace. She is the inexhaustible fountain of kindness, and would almost seem to be, in herself, all mercy. So she does in us a greater work than that of Creation: the work of being in grace, the work of pardon, the work of transformation from brightness to brightness *tamquam a Domini Spiritu.* She is in us the yielding and tender counterpart of the power, justice and creative dynamism of the Father.

IV. *Sunset. The Hour of Compline. Salve Regina.*

Now the Blessed Virgin Mary is the one created being who enacts and shows forth in her life all that is hidden in Sophia. Because of this she can be said to be a personal manifestation of Sophia, Who in God is *Ousia* rather than Person.

Natura in Mary becomes pure Mother. In her, *Natura* is as she was from the origin from her divine birth. In Mary *Natura* is all wise and is manifested as an all-prudent, all-loving, all-pure person: not a Creator, and not a Redeemer, but perfect Creature, perfectly Redeemed, the fruit of all God's great power, the perfect expression of wisdom in mercy.

It is she, it is Mary, Sophia, who in sadness and joy, with the full awareness of what she is doing, sets upon the Second Person, the Logos, a crown which is His Human Nature. Thus her consent opens the door of created nature, of time, of history, to the Word of God.

God enters into His creation. Through her wise answer, through her obedient understanding, through the sweet yielding consent of Sophia, God enters without publicity into the city of rapacious men.

She crowns Him not with what is glorious, but with what is greater than glory: the one thing greater than glory is weakness, nothingness, poverty.

She sends the infinitely Rich and Powerful One forth as poor and helpless, in His mission of inexpressible mercy, to die for us on the Cross.

The shadows fall. The stars appear. The birds begin to sleep. Night embraces the silent half of the earth.

A vagrant, a destitute wanderer with dusty feet, finds his way down a new road. A homeless God, lost in the night, without papers, without identification, without even a number, a frail expendable exile lies down in desolation under the sweet stars of the world and entrusts Himself to sleep.

David Gascoyne (1916–2001)

Pietà from Miserere

Stark in the pasture on the skull-shaped hill,
In swollen aura of disaster shrunken and
Unsheltered by the ruin of the sky,
Intensely concentrated in themselves the banded
Saints abandoned kneel.

And under the unburdened tree
Great in their midst, the rigid folds
Of a blue cloak upholding as a text
Her grief-scrawled face for the ensuing world to read,
The Mother, whose dead Son's dear head
Weighs like a precious blood-encrusted stone
On her unfathomable breast:

Holds Him God forsaken, Word made flesh
Made ransom, to the slow smoulder of her heart
Till the catharsis of the race shall be complete.

Robert Kelly (b. 1935)

The Heavenly Country

Once I thought it was the place my father brought me and my mother to, between the rivers up north. The near river was full of white stones bleached in the sun, and the banks on the far side were red clay. At night it was almost cold, so we slept with blankets or walked out in sweaters early morning to see deer or whatever else might reveal itself to us. That it is a matter of It willing to reveal to Us I have never doubted.

Later I thought it was England. Perhaps only tonight, in my thirty-ninth year, have I been able to bear up under a sort of intellectual scrutiny and realize that it is not England. Till now, all the paradises seemed green places in which words like weir and scream and wood and moor and fell and rain and sheep and cloud and hill might accurately be spoken. It was Tolkien's England after it was De la Mare's England after it was Chesterton's England after it was Kipling's England after it was Doyle's England after it was Kilvert's England, Hopkins' England, Wordsworth's England, Blake's England. Always the shire and the sure, the comfortable man-sized landscapes, cool summers, a shimmer of rainy light to hold us closer in the known.

What I am writing is a confession. I saw those vistas with the wilful eye of protracted Innocence. Winne the Pooh was closer to my heart than *Christabel*, and to say so is to confess myself not a child but a divided man who has trifled with visions of degradation and visions of exaltation without admitting either to the center of my heart. So I suppose now that center to be not known, and I flounder as I floundered thirty years ago, in shy love of a country innocent and personal as a piece of bread in my mouth, and like it silent, comforting, warm and selfish.

When Blake spoke of Satanic mills, I refused to think of the Manchester my great-grandfather came from, that Engels so passionately atomized: I thought instead of mythologies, and ahrimanic intensities lathing cogwheels for the heart. I thought always outside of town, except for Baker Street, which was alive (remember) with rain and fog and wind, but only one person at a time. The sexy women of actual England, Mollies and Nell Gwynnes and Christine Keelers, inhabited a different chamber of my thought, along with the Rochesters and Aretinos and Sades: an international of the flesh that, for all my concerns with it, had nothing to do with any England at all. There were no Scarlet Women among Owl's relations.

It hardly troubled me that the men who seemed to know the place best were troubled by a lust or dread that wormed their hearts: I took the summer glow of Machen's garden and left his ægipans and troglodytes alone, left Hardy's anguish and Lawrence's need to be answered, and contented myself with the storms and trees and birds and small furry animals hardly consequential to their histories.

Certainly I needed the place. Perhaps I even used it well, husbandman of a land I've never entered. I think those intimate landscapes lie behind my perceptions and registrations of nearer or 'realer' country; sometimes they show through, when yearning or demand overpowers me looking at, say, the big field down Barrytown with the mountains low beyond it. Not this field, the mind whispers, but a field just like it somewhere else, no lovelier at all, but *there*.

Now tonight I give the mind its *there*, but force it to its work. Not England, not even England at another time (some May morning between Robin Hood and Malory). Not the sheep and not the rock, not the richness of that well-watered grass, the grey sky perfecting all the colors of earth. Not that, but what *that* in turn resembles or shadows. Now, mind, do your work. Find the country whose present nearby shadows I have so long mistaken for no better thing than its shadows somewhere else. Find the there to which all I have ever known or dreamt or fantasized is here.

This night that unlocks England, and keeps me from worshipping the shadow of a shadow, may it unlock too all the chambers of my heart, all the places I've too long protected from reality. By that word I mean whatever that true country or condition is this field puts me in mind of.

David Craig (b. 1951)

The Prophecy of Simeon
—Luke: 2:25–35

Her suffering has always been quietly
beyond me: the barest ripple
across her face—each like a breeze
over water. Her spaces deepen
while I pose, a feint in the direction
of strength I do not possess.

I've learned to sit close by,
like a shepherd, staff alongside,
close enough to accept correction—
the ancient voices which move her.
I do what men do: fetch wood, move furniture,
try to be a place she can count on.
But I cannot reach her—the her
who moves with other times, peoples.

She likes my jokes,
because they amuse me.

When she sighs, my soul deepens,
shifts like shelves of rock. This prophecy
is like that. What does it portend?
Whose heart moves in hers,
what sorrow? Is she God's breastplate,
the only candle in that wind?

This temple is beyond me—and my kin.

She is wife, yes, always, but more,
because she is a grace, a white room
I seem to move around in:
a speech already written, a yes
which will mark us all.

I walk alongside, alone in my folly.

THE HEAVENLY COUNTRY

Franz Wright (1953–2015)

Rosary

Mother of space,
inner

virgin
with no one face—

See them flying to see you
be near you,

when you
are everywhere

Artur Grabowski (b. 1967)

Sun Shines in Between

The more luminous (I like the word) it is (it sounds
so clear), the more it's lucid (I like the sound)
for all its soundless
efforts—in highlighting high waves
    (chasing each other
    over the darker side
    of their hide).
   Translated by Artur Sebastian Rosman

PART III

Critical Essays

Theotokos:
Sophiology and Christological Overdetermination of the Secular

Aaron Riches

ACCORDING TO John Milbank, the genius of the Russian sophiological tradition lies in its encounter with the post-secular aspect of German idealism and specifically in a two-fold apprehension of it. In the first place, Russian sophiology was keenly aware that the nihilist problematic underpinned *tout court* the various projects of German idealism and in this sense could see that German idealism represented itself a "theological turn" of sorts. In the second place, the Russians fully grasped that, in making this turn, German idealism had restored the integral unity of faith and reason—and so grace and nature, spirit and history—through a positing of reason *over* faith, and so in a heretical and Gnostic variant that needed to be both critiqued and recapitulated from an orthodox and theological point of view. In this way, on Milbank's reading, the sophiological tradition from Solovyov to Bulgakov should be understood as simultaneously extending the German idealist attempt to think rationally after Jacobi, while overdetermining its heretical residuals. And herein lies what is truly radical of the sophiological tradition.

In the first place the sophiological tradition is radical in the sense of the Latin "radix"—it represents a return to sources, patristic and biblical, underdeveloped or forgotten in tradition, by which the tradition can be marshaled from its source to enter into a profound dialogue with (and critique of) modernity. Armed with the old "newness" of the wisdom literature and patristic commentary on it, the sophiologists were able to confront the new questions thrown up by modernity with a fresh boldness, that was both in tandem with the German idealist critique of modernity, but also recapitulating the German idealist "solution." According to Milbank, the inexorable anthropological insight raised by modernity and grasped by German idealism coalesces around the heretofore-unimaginable realization that—far from possessing a static nature—the human being is constitutively and basically dynamic and creative in character. The human creature is, by nature, the possessor of what de Lubac called an "unstable ontological constitution" (*constitution ontologique instable*).[1] And if the human being is constitutively dynamic, his being is radically rooted in the temporal unfolding of his experience, which is bound in the historical experience of a wider community. A series of questions arise from this. Milbank lists the following:[2]

(1) Why, philosophically and theologically, is there life in time?

(2) Why are there successive human generations?

(3) Is human collective existence primary over individual existence?

(4) What exactly is it that binds together the human collectivity that composes human nature?

(5) If human creativity possesses a seemingly unlimited and potentially catastrophic power to transform non-human nature, then what exactly is our role within nature and what is the meaning of nature for us?

According to Milbank, in the face of this new understanding, the genius of the Russian sophiologists was their ability, first, to discriminate between what was in the ineluctable in modernity and what is ideological and problematic, and second, to forge a Christian response that attempted to meet the challenges of modernity head on through a contemplative fusion of biblical sophianic literature, the writings of the Fathers, and the popular Russian devotion to the feminine figure of Sophia. The result is a paradoxical recapitulation of the insights of modernity, now understood within a theological vision, of which Milbank highlights three:[3]

(1) To take better account of the dynamism of nature, appeal is made to a nontemporal heart of nature which is created Sophia as the world-soul.

(2) In order to take better account of human historicity and collectivity, appeal is made to some sort of ahistorical [or perhaps better, eternal] Adam-Kadmon figure.

1. Henri de Lubac, *Le Mystère de surnaturel*, in *Oeuvres complètes*, vol. 12 (Paris: Les Éditions de Cerf, 2006), 149.

2. John Milbank, "Sophiology and Theurgy: The New Theological Horizon," in Adrian Pabst and Christoph Schneider (eds.), *Radical Orthodoxy and Eastern Orthodoxy* (Basingstoke: Ashgate, 2009), 48.

3. Milbank, "Sophiology and Theurgy," 49.

(3) In order to come to terms with evolutionary struggle [and seeming flux of life towards death], the primacy of life and the unreality of death is invoked.

Dogmatic aporias that result from the seemingly ineluctable insights of modernity, which would appear to contradict outright the traditional doctrinal formulations of the Church, are now freshly reinterpreted through a sophianic lens. Critically, the dogmatic impetus here is rooted, first of all, in Trinitarian theology: between the persons of the Trinity, defined as substantive relations, there can be no third term. This concerns the classical doctrine of the mutual penetration, *circumincedere* of the Trinitarian persons on account of the undivided divine essence.[4] The doctrine is based on the words of Jesus himself: "I am *in* the Father and the Father is *in* me" (John 14:10); "I and the Father are one" (John 10:30). This principle of divine filiation applies, moreover and equally, to the indwelling of the Holy Spirit, who also is wholly *in* the Father and Son, who in turn are equally *in* the Spirit, since the Spirit abides, knows and searches "even the depths of God" himself (1 Cor 2:10). Trinitarian mediation, then, involves not middle terms but a paradoxical abiding of each term in the other.

The Trinitarian principle of mediation applies, as Milbank points out, equally to at least four other relations, each different from the others but alike insofar as they are realized by the mediatory possibilities of Trinitarian circumincession. The first relation is that between God and creation: we have mediation with no *tertium quid* because between created and uncreated being there is precisely "nothing." At once there is a perfect intimacy of being coupled with a maximal difference of being: created being is so related to uncreated being so as to exist wholly constituted in relation to the latter, while the latter impossibly has no need of created being in order to be *the Creator*. As Milbank puts it: "if God were related to the creation and not just the Creation constitutively related to God, there would be a greater than God and God would not be God."[5] And so: God is more intimate to creation than creation is to itself.

The second relation in which the principle of Trinitarian mediation is at work is that of the hypostatic union: it is axiomatic of orthodox Christology that Christ is both fully human and fully divine, while no *tertium quid* results from this unity. In Jesus there is nothing "between" divinity and humanity; rather, he simply *is* the eternal Son who is wholly *in* the

---

4. Cf. Council of Florence: "Because of this unity the Father is entirely in the Son and entirely in the Holy Spirit; the Son is entirely in the Father and entirely in the Holy Spirit; the Holy Spirit is entirely in the Father and entirely in the Son" (DS 704).

5. Milbank, "Sophiology and Theurgy," 49.

Father and in whom the Father wholly is. This Christological truth is formulated in the Chalcedonian *Definitio* and forms also the basis of the patristic doctrine of *communicatio idiomatum*, but it receives its most powerful and provocative articulation in the axiom of Dionysius the pseudo-Areopagite who specifies that Jesus does not do divine things divinely and human things humanly, but rather does human things divinely and divine things humanly.[6] There is a perfect interpenetration, a perfect circumincession of divinity and humanity in the "one" Jesus.

The third relation of third-term-less mediation applies to the Holy Spirit in relation to the infallible Church and the inerrant Scriptures. The former is of course composed of exceedingly fallible human beings and institutionally led by fallible priestly ministers and bishops, while the latter, the Scriptures, are texts that are entirely human (in composition and interpretation). Nevertheless, both the Church and the Scriptures, by the indwelling of the Spirit, are simultaneously otherwise: the Church is the spotless bride of Christ and the Scriptures are inbreathed to be Holy Writ.

Perhaps most daringly and mysteriously, but really the total sum of relations (1), (2) and (3), is the fourth relation, which is that of the human being to God. The human being is "the only creature on earth that God has willed for its own sake," as *Gaudium et spes* put it (no. 22), and as such his relation to God is so intimate as to make of his being a question in relation to the divine answer. Only God saves the human being. All this is entailed by the fact that, again as *Gaudium et spes* taught and as John Paul II loved to repeat, Christ "reveals man to himself and brings to light his most high calling" (no. 24). And so between the God who is able in Christ to become man and the human being whose destiny is revealed in that theandric fact, there is again no *tertium quid*. The patristic axiom according to which God became man that man might become God could as easily be rephrased: God became man that man might become human.

According to Milbank, sophiology is best understood as the most remarkable twentieth-century attempt to think through this unique mediation of difference with no "middle," where mediation appears at once as seemingly impossible (because not enabled by a "thing" that one can point to), while at the same time arising from the very source of being, the Trinitarian fact that is God himself. Sophia designates the *metaxu* that does not lie "between" the two terms of difference, nor on one side or the other, but rather abides simultaneously *within* both poles at once. This means, as Milbank puts it, that Sophia "does not

6. Denys the Areopagite, *Epistula* 4 (PG 3.1072b–c).

subsist before the two poles," but rather she "co-arises with them such that they can only exist according to a mediated communication which remains purely occult, a matter of utterly inscrutable affinity."[7]

Sophia and Divine-Humanity

As much as we can retrospectively "define" Sophia as the *metaxu*, the mysterious "co-arising" that gives expression to the intimacy of theological mediation, for Bulgakov Sophia was less a figure that could be "defined" and was more a figure that had to be intuited and seen. Andrew Louth offers that Bulgakov's evocative and poetic description of Hagia Sophia is, for this reason, his most precise statement of the nature of Sophia.[8] Bulgakov writes:

> Human tongue cannot express the lightness, the clarity, the simplicity, the wonderful harmony which completely dispels all sense of heaviness—the heaviness of the cupola and the walls. A sea of light pours from above and dominates all this space, enclosed and yet free. The grace of the columns and the beauty of their marble lace, the royal dignity—not luxury, but regality—of the golden walls and the marvellous ornamentation: it captivates and melts the heart, subdues and convinces. It creates a sense of inner transparency; the weightiness and limitations of the small and suffering self disappear . . . the soul is healed. . . . It becomes the world: I am in the world and the world is in me. . . . This is indeed Sophia, the real unity of the world in the Logos, the co-inherence of all with all, the world of divine ideas. . . . Truly, the church of Hagia Sophia is the artistic, tangible proof and manifestation of Hagia Sophia—of the Sophianic nature of the world. . . . How true was our ancestors' feeling in this temple, how right they were in saying that they did not know whether they were in heaven or on earth! Indeed they were neither in heaven nor on earth, they were in Hagia Sophia—between the two: this is the *metaxu*. . . . O Lord, how holy, how marvellous, how precious is this manifestation![9]

The clarity of the description lies in its mood. Bulgakov is not trying to "define" Sophia, much less to "defend" her. Rather he is *intuiting* the sophianic, evoking her, which would seem to be the most precise and correspondent way to approach her. Sophia is best understood, then, not

7. Milbank, "Sophiology and Theurgy," 50.

8. Andrew Louth, "Father Sergii Bulgakov on the Mother of God," *St. Vladimir's Theological Quarterly* 49 (2005): 145–64, 151.

9. Sergei Bulgakov, *Avtobiograficheskiye zametki*, as translated and quoted in Louth, "Father Sergii Bulgakov on the Mother of God," 150–1; italics are mine, and I have modified the spelling of "metaxuv" to "metaxu."

as a doctrine but as a liminal reality that can only be approached or seen in the most aesthetic of ways. Sophia is apprehended, not with the rigor of the scientific lens, but with the eyes of the heart that senses her and feels she is at the deepest mystery of reality. What is key is the metaxological mode of her being; she is "the co-inherence of all with all."

Keeping this invocation of Sophia in mind, we can now turn to a more technical explication of Sophia. Bulgakov begins with the *Quicumque vult*, the so-called "Athanasian Creed." The key passage concerns the Trinitarian third-term-less mediation we touched on above: *ut unum Deum in Trinitate, et Trinitatem in unitate veneremur.*[10] What "one God in Trinity and Trinity in unity" signifies is the paradoxical status of perfect unity and difference as mutually internal to one another and not exclusive. If God is truly "one," he is perfect unity, the simple oneness to which every unity gestures; while if God is truly "many" (triune), then it follows that he contains within himself perfect difference, and so the interval of every distinction. God, then, embraces within himself—within his simple oneness—the perfect intimacy of otherness and total dissimilitude, in which the maximality of difference must be equally as great as the simplicity of divine "oneness." According to Bulgakov this paradoxical coincidence of unity and difference was unevenly probed in the development of Trinitarian thought. While the trihypostatic reality of God was clearly grasped and contemplated in the three persons of the Trinity (Father, Son, and Spirit), the face of the theological consubstantiality of their difference in unity remained, he thought, obscure in the mainline tradition. The face of consubstantiality Bulgakov sought to discover, he caught a glimpse of in the biblical figure of Sophia.

Drawing on the wisdom literature of the Old Testament, especially Proverbs 8:22–31, Bulgakov suggests that Sophia herself is the *ousia* of God, the principle of "oneness" which is the unity of the trihypostatic life of God. She is the "personal" face of the principle of unity (*ousia*) correspondent to the concretely different "persons" of Father, Son, and Spirit (*hypostasis*). From this, Bulgakov goes on to argue that the *ousia*-Sophia of God is the principle of God's "self-revelation," such that the unity of God's life, which is a genuine other in relation to God's trihypostatic reality, is paradoxically the condition of the possibility of God's extra-divine self-positing (first in creation, then in the Incarnation).[11] In other words, in God it is not only that difference is mediated by unity, but also that unity in relation to difference is itself an alterity that

---

10. Serge Boulgakov, *La Sagesse de Dieu: Résumé de sophiologie*, trans. Constantin Andronikof (Lausanne, Suisse: L'Age d'homme, 1983), 19–26.

11. Ibid., 37.

both *is* the unity of divine difference and *is* the openness of the divine life to what is not divine. Here, indeed, Bulgakov stretches the bounds of traditional orthodox Trinitarian theology narrowly conceived. Whether he does so to the breaking point is contestable. (To what extent "sophiology" represents a linguistic innovation more distracting than useful is again another issue.) What, however, is indubitable is the fact that the whole of Bulgakov's sophiology, on the strictly theological level, is at pains to articulate something rather convertible with a basic insight of classical Augustinian theology: the principle of "otherness" in God is the principle of his self-communication in love.

God is Love (1 John 4:16). For Bulgakov, as for Augustine, this is the most basic thing we can say about God.[12] "Love" specifies God's Trinitarian being; it is the basis of his inner life and of his going-out-from-himself in creation and in the Incarnation. As soon as we affirm that God is Love we affirm the mystery of unity and difference in God, since the God who "*is* Love" must *actively love* "love."[13] "God is love, and it is proper for love to love and to expand in love."[14] Because God is Love, God is paradoxically *both* "inside" and "outside" himself. Sophia is precisely the term or name of this "inside-out" loving of divine Love, both eternally *in* God (as God's *ousia*) and *outside* God in the primeval divine idea that is the economy of creation and Incarnation, what we call the "world soul."[15] The Sophia of God's own life, then, the economy of love that interpenetrates the divine persons and constitutes both their unity and difference, is also the ground of the being of the world. Sophia is both created and uncreated, inside and outside, not as "two discrete things," but rather as the differentiation of *coincidentia oppositorum*. Sophia is the identity in distinction and differentiation in union of the created and uncreated realms of interpenetrating love that is the Love of God himself.[16]

For Bulgakov all of this means that Sophia is neither "divine nature" nor a mythological "person." This is crucial to emphasize. The persons of God are three. The divine nature does not exist apart from the three divine persons, as a fourth "thing." Rather, as Rowan Williams clarifies,

---

12. Ibid., 25.

13. Sergii Bulgakov, "The Unfailing Light," trans. Rowan Williams, in Rowan Williams, *Sergii Bulgakov: Towards a Russian Political Theology* (Edinburgh, UK: T&T Clark, 1999), 113–62, at 134.

14. Sergius Bulgakov, *The Lamb of God*, trans. Boris Jakim (Grand Rapids, MI: Eerdmans, 2008), 120.

15. Williams, *Sergii Bulgakov*, 128.

16. Boulgakov, *La Sagesse de Dieu*, 50.

Bulgakov's Sophia is an "aspect of the divine nature *in action*."[17] This reality of Sophia as "action" (*energia*) is the crux of the essential clarification Bulgakov made in his crucial 1925 essay, "Ipostas' i ipostasnost'."[18] Moved to defend himself from the accusation of heresy, Bulgakov was forced to clarify that, in contradistinction to an infamous and unfortunate formulation of Pavel Florensky, Sophia is in no way a "fourth hypostasis." Sophia, Bulgakov clarified, is rather "hypostaticity" or "hypostasizing energy," a personalization that reaches the depth of all being in the act of love. The hypostasizing energy of divine love, the uncreated life of God, is that out of which creation is drawn; while it is not a person or hypostasis, it is somehow "personalizing," it is the capacity of all being to be enfolded in love. Here an interpretation of Milbank is helpful:

> Sophia [for Bulgakov] is the Creation in God; Sophia is also God in the Creation. [*But*:] There is not one Sophia, hovering onto-theologically between God and the Creation; there are two Sophias on two sides of the chasm, yet somehow their deep-beyond-deep affinity renders them after all but one. But not "one" in the sense of an hypostasis; one rather in the sense of a shared essence or character or power-to-personify.[19]

A "deep-beyond-deep affinity," Sophia is the "co-inherence" of reality in the act of love, which is not only a personal act but also an act that personalizes. And herein lies the distinction for Bulgakov between Sophia and humanity on the one hand, and the Christological accomplishment of humanity on the other. As Williams explains:

> God as personal (hypostatic) love, love in action, loves also the *fact* that self emptying love is *what* God is. And that "what," which is not simply conceptually identical with any or all of the Trinitarian hypostases, that eternal object of divine love, is Sophia. As object of eternal love, it is the prototype of the created world, or, speaking boldly, the prototype of *humanity*—because humanity is the perfection of the world's being as object of divine love; what is loved is always love itself, but love cannot exist without loving *agents*, and so when God loves the world he cannot but love in it the capacity of the world to be "hypostatic," a world of

17. Williams, *Sergii Bulgakov*, 165.

18. Sergii Bulgakov, "Ipostas' i Ipostasnost' (*Scholia k Svetu Nevechernemu*)," in *Sbornik statei posviashchennykh Petru Berngardovichu Struve ko dniu tridtsatipiatiletiia ego nauchno-publitsisticheskoi deiatel'nosti*, 1890–1925 (Prague: Legiografie, 1925), 353–71; and "Protopresbyter Sergii Bulgakov: Hypostasis and Hypostaticity: Scholia to the Unfading Light," revised trans., ed. and intro. of A. F. Dobbie Bateman by Anastassy Brandon Gallaher and Irina Kukota, *St. Vladimir's Theological Quarterly* 49 (2005): 5–46.

19. Milbank, "Sophiology and Theurgy," 65.

agents and subjects. Thus what God loves is the directedness of the world towards the human; God loves the heavenly image or idea of humanity, the "Heavenly Adam." And that reality is fully actualised when Christ, the divine person, brings created humanity to perfection because he introduces into humanity the action of the perfect other-directed hypostatic life that belongs to the Holy Trinity.[20]

Drawing together these strands of interpretation of Bulgakov by Williams and Milbank, we begin to see how the hominization of creation is the perfection of created being, since the human person is the hypostatic realization of the sophianic reality of creation as such. The human creature is creation capable of love; creation, that is, capable of receiving and giving the "I" of love that is at the source of all reality, created and uncreated. In this way, the human being is the still point at which created being and triune being cohere.

Christology and Sophia

With the forgoing in mind, I want now to turn to the Christological heart of Bulgakov's theology. I want to do so, ultimately, in order to offer Bulgakov's Christology as the basic touchstone of the irreducible "co-"entailed by his sophiological *metaxu*, and so the secret source of his post-secular theological vision.

For the Fathers, from Ignatius of Antioch to Maximus the Confessor, from Irenaeus of Lyon to Cyril of Alexandria, the Incarnation of the Son of God is not only *the* unrepeatable metaphysical exception of human history, it is also ultimate and definitive illumination of the enigma of human being.[21] From its origin, then, Christology entails a double focus: it concerns the transcendent revelation of Wholly-Other in the face of the only begotten Son of the Father made flesh, while at the same time it concerns the most intimate unveiling of the interior mystery of universal human experience.

For Bulgakov, the interface between Christology and anthropology is based on the three principle modalities of "image" posited by John of Damascus: (1) the Son as the *Imago Dei perfecta*; (2) the "divine ideas" (*paradigmata*) of creation in the mind of God; and (3) the human being, the created *imago Dei*.[22] The *Imago Dei perfecta* is the Son, which

20. Williams, *Sergii Bulgakov*, 166.

21. Cf. Joseph Ratzinger, "Concerning the Notion of the Person in Theology," trans. Michael Waldstein, *Communio* 17 (1990): 439–54, at 450.

22. John of Damascus, *De imaginibus, Oratio* III, 18–20 (PG 94.1337C–1341A). Cf. Boulgakov, *La Sagesse de Dieu*, 51, n. 38.

means that he is the *ens realissimum* of the human creature, the creature God created according to the divine image, *ad imaginem Dei*. This means that the human being—created according to the image of the Son, and "as the created image" of the eternal "divine ideas" of God—is himself the "hinge" of the relation of creation to the Creator. For Bulgakov three things entail this: (1) the "divinity" of the human being created in the image of God; (2) the "microcosmic" reality of the human as the imaging unity of the "divine ideas"; and (3) the "humanity" of God according to the apostle Paul's notion of humanity as the offspring of God (cf. Acts 17:29).[23] There is thus, for Bulgakov, an internal relation between "divinity" and "humanity," the uncreated and the created, nature and grace, the natural and the supernatural, all of which converge on the human being, on the one hand, and the divine person of the Son on the other. The trajectories of human experience (of the desire that sets the human being on the path to his divine destiny) and of divine love (that sets God ultimately outside himself in the path of descent of the Son of God) overlap in the life of divine-humanity, a life which is ultimately sophiological. Central to the life of divine-humanity is the hypostatic nature of the human being, the mode by which he is a "created person," a created being capable of giving personal voice to the sophiological depth of the cosmic reality.

The personal being of the human creature is rooted in the fact that he is created in the image of God, which is his "divine origin," the locus of his reception of the "spirit" or "breath" of God (cf. Gen 2:7).[24] The human being is thus an "incarnate spirit."[25] This is both what makes him a creature capable of being a "partaker of the divine nature" (2 Pet 1:4) and what makes him a "person." Personhood is thus, for Bulgakov, convertible with "spirit" such that the human "person" is supernatural, the embodiment of a divine principle of "spirit" breathed into creation out of God's own life. In *Agnets Bozhiy* (1933),[26] the first volume of his trilogy on divine-humanity, Bulgakov clarifies how the pneumatic and personal core of anthropology interlocks with Christology through a creative rereading of Apollinaris of Laodicea (d. 390), the "first to pose the problem of divine-humanity."[27]

Condemned at Constantinople I (381), according to Bulgakov, Apollinaris's opponents wholly misunderstood his Christological proposal.

23. Boulgakov, *La Sagesse de Dieu*, 51.
24. Ibid., 57.
25. Ibid., 38.
26. Bulgakov, *The Lamb of God*.
27. Ibid., 3.

While Apollinaris was taken to have suggested that Christ's human "mind" (*nous*) was replaced with the Logos such that the natural faculty of the human "rational soul" would have to be found lacking in Jesus, according to Bulgakov this was not Apollinaris's doctrine properly understood. According to Bulgakov, Apollinaris in no way meant to suggest that in Jesus the faculty of human soul was absent; but, to the contrary, that Jesus is fully a human being, with all the faculties of human nature, though he is, as Chalcedon would clarify latter, *not a human person*, but rather the divine person of the Logos. For Bulgakov, that this is Apollinaris's doctrine is clarified when we understand the Pauline tripartite anthropology Apollinaris presumed. On this scheme, the human is not a mere composite of "soul" and "body"; rather, he is "spirit" (*pneuma-nous*), "soul" (*psyche*) and "body" (*soma*). While "soul" and "body" are faculties of human nature, "spirit" (*pneuma-nous*) is not a faculty of nature but rather the principle of personal being, the hypostatic term.[28] When Apollinaris is reread in this light, he is understood to have said, not that Jesus lacks some infrastructure of human nature, but rather that the Logos in Jesus took the place of human personhood: that Jesus was not a human hypostasis, but the divine hypostasis of the Son. According to this rereading Apollinaris is made to fully anticipate Chalcedonian orthodoxy, which of course holds that the hypostasis/person of Jesus simply *is* the divine Son, such that Jesus is not a "human person" but rather is a "divine person." Moreover, according to Bulgakov, by this method "Apollinaris . . . understood the christological problem also as an anthropological one and indissolubly linked these two problems."[29]

Leaving aside the question of whether Bulgakov's rereading of Apollinaris is historically justifiable, the key dogmatic point he wants to make concerns the recovery of the Pauline trichotomy as internal to the sophiological vision of divine-humanity. The Pauline trichotomy is, in a sense, the hinge on which Christology and anthropology turn. On Bulgakov's scheme it allows that "the postulate of the Incarnation" involves a "primordial identity" between the Logos, the divine hypostasis of the Second Person, and human personhood ("spirit").[30] Moreover, his personal "primordial identity" establishes a correlate identity between human being in general and the filiation of the Son: humanity aims at the divine life, which is to say that human personhood internally tends to its personal perfection in the life of God. The "man from heaven" is the personal *link* that binds creation to God and God to creation, while

---

28. Cf. ibid., 8–9.
29. Ibid., 12.
30. Ibid., 186.

the flesh of human being is the soil of inner-penetration (*circumince-dere*) of the cosmos in God and God in the cosmos. In this way, Bulga-kov specifies the Christological nature of how human nature is wholly correlative, a relation to the supernatural that is unthinkable apart from it. Moreover, he specifies what is at stake in the claim that the human is the "microcosm," the "world soul," the created face of Sophia. Bulgakov writes:

> The human hypostatic spirit, which lives in man and which funda-mentally distinguishes him from the animal world, has a divine, uncreated origin from "God's breath" [cf. Gen 2:7]. This spirit is a spark of Divinity that is endowed by God with a creaturely hypostatic face in the image of the Logos and, through Him, in the image of the entire Holy Trinity.... Through his spirit, man communes with the Divine essence and is capable of being "deified." Being united with and living by the divine nature, man is not only man but also potentially—by predestination, by his formal structure—a god-man. At the same time, in his nature, as the soul of the world, as "flesh" (i.e., through his animate body), man unites in himself the entire world, which in this sense is his humanity. Man consists of an uncreated, divine spirit, hypostatized by a creaturely I, and of a created soul and body.[31]

In this passage we see how the Damascene's three modes of "image" converge on the human being. First, the human is the summary of the "divine ideas," he "unites in himself the entire world, which in this sense is his humanity." Second, he is uniquely a created image of God, the "image of the entire Holy Trinity" who is endowed with "hypostatic spirit," a "spark" of the divine life itself. Finally, the human is "by his formal structure" predestined to be "a god-man" because his "hypo-static face" is the created "image of the Logos."

Created according to the image of the *Imago Dei perfecta*, the Logos is thus the proto-Image according to which the human is created and hypostatically perfected.[32] "The Logos is the eternal man, the prototype of humanity; he is the Lamb slain from the foundation of the world [cf. Rev 13:8], who is predestined to become the earthly man."[33] This per-sonal destiny of Logos to become human corresponds to the destiny of human personhood to perfect creation through becoming a participant of the divine nature. This means that there is both a "divinity" of human being and a "humanity" of God. All of this comes together when we rec-ognize how the Logos is the proto-Image of humanity, and thus "the

31. Ibid., 186.
32. Ibid., 113.
33. Boulgakov, *La Sagesse de Dieu*, 52.

eternal Man," the "Man from Heaven," the Man who "comes down" from above.[34] Thus:

> Man is created in the image of God but this means that he is created in the image of Christ; for man, Christ is the revelation and accomplishment of this image. The image of the coming Christ is imprinted in the first man not only in his body, which is an image of the sophianic world [i.e., the "divine ideas"], and not only in his spirit, which in a certain sense is sent from heaven. It is also imprinted in the structure of man in the union of two natures (spiritual and psycho-corporeal) in one hypostasis.[35]

The destiny of the human being to deification is constitutive: "He desires to become a son of God and to enter into the glory of creation, for he is predestined to this."[36] Anthropology in this light must be unfolded in concretely Christological terms: "Man bears within himself the coming Christ; and prior to Christ's coming, man does not have the power to become himself (i.e., the true man)."[37] To heal the world and deify human flesh, Christ cannot merely "assume" humanity, he must bring it "down from above."

Divine-Humanity and the Man Who "Came Down" from Above

The Bulgakovian ideas we have explored thus far establish two interrelated anthropological premises: (1) the human being bears within himself the coming of Christ, the True Man who is the "Heavenly Man" who "came down" from above; and (2) the human person is the hypostatic realization of the wisdom of God, Sophia, the created act of receiving the personal Love of the uncreated God and responding in turn with a love that likewise is fully personal, but now wholly created. On the one hand this thesis is strictly Christocentric, while on the other hand it is (as we shall see) a Mariological opening of Christology through which the *metaxu* of Sophia is incarnated in the double gaze of love loving love. This expansion is rooted in the primordial pneumatological fact that while the Logos is the "hypostasis" proper to the theanthropic truth of humanity, it is the Holy Spirit who is the "principle" of divine-humanity.[38]

For Bulgakov, the dyadic relation of the Son and Spirit is crucial to

---

34. Bulgakov, *The Lamb of God*, 113.
35. Ibid., 139.
36. Ibid., 187.
37. Ibid., 187.
38. Boulgakov, *La Sagesse de Dieu*, 52.

economy of the Incarnation. In the first place this means recognizing that the Father is revealed—not by the Logos alone—but by the interrelation of the Logos with the Spirit.[39] The dyadic descent of the Logos and the Spirit in the Incarnation is attested to in the Creed: *Et incarnatus est de Spiritu Sancto ex Maria Virgine*.[40] Bulgakov finds the crucial patristic resource to the dyadic interrelation of the Logos and the Spirit in the Trinitarian theology of John of Damascus, outlined in his *De fide orthodoxa*.

According the Damascene, the Spirit is the "breath" of the Father's utterance: "for the Word there must be breath (*pneuma*), for our word too is not without breath."[41] Accordingly, the Spirit is the power of the Logos's annunciation, apart from which the Logos does not sound. A one-sided theology that forgets the Spirit, then, ends by silencing the Logos. The uncreated sophiological life of the Trinity is rooted here, in the way the Son is un-abstractable from the Spirit. The Damascene fuses his Trinitarian understanding of the Spirit-Logos dyad with the narrative characterization of their interrelation in the Gospel, where the Spirit is characterized repeatedly as "resting" on the Son (in the overshadowed womb of Mary, at the baptism in the Jordan, on Mount Tabor, in the resurrected body in the tomb). This "rest" of the Spirit constitutes, for the Damascene, the Spirit's procession: the Spirit proceeds from the Father to "rest" upon/in the Logos in order that the Logos might sound.[42] The Son's revelation of the Father always implies this fundamental interrelation with the Spirit. This interrelation is precisely the intimation of uncreated Sophia, the life of Love that loves love. And this means, for Bulgakov, that just as the Father is revealed by the dyadic reciprocity of the Logos and the Spirit, so the sophianic reality of humanity/creation must be revealed in a correspondent dyadic rationality: the *divine* hypostasis of Logos, the God-Man, the Heavenly Man, must sound in relation to a genuine *human* hypostasis, in whom the Spirit, the principle of divine-humanity, has descended and become transparent.

The co-constitutive nature of divine-humanity in the dyadic relation of the Logos and Spirit is, moreover, reflected in the creation of the human being, "male" and "female." The reciprocal correlation that ani-

---

39. See Sergei Bulgakov, *The Comforter*, trans. Boris Jakim (Grand Rapids, MI: Eerdmans, 2004), 177–218.

40. Bulgakov, *The Lamb of God*, 177.

41. John of Damascus, *De fide orthodoxa*, 1.7 (PG 94.804C), quoted in Bulgakov, *The Comforter*, 49.

42. John of Damascus, *De fide orthodoxa*, 1.7 (PG 94.805B), quoted in Bulgakov, *The Comforter*, 84.

mates the human experience from the beginning, thus, analogically intimates the dyadic revelation of the Father in the Son and the Spirit.[43] Just as the reciprocity of the Son and the Spirit reveals the Father, so the reciprocity of the "masculine" and the "feminine" together achieves the *similitudo Dei* of humanity created according to the image of God.[44] This points to the mystical logic of the unity of Christ and the Church, which is the concrete instantiation of divine-humanity. Accordingly, it entails that divine-humanity is only achievable within a relation of mutual union between God and the human, where the divine hypostasis of the God-Man is put in dyadic relation to a created-feminine hypostatic representative of the Church, that is to say a human hypostasis that perfectly bears the Spirit, the principle of divine-humanity. Precisely this interrelation of divine-humanity is personified in the love of Jesus and Mary, which corresponds in their mutuality to the Logos and the Spirit.

The meaning of the dyadic relation of Jesus and Mary for Bulgakov is based, first of all, on a reread of the Annunciation that is mindful of the co-descent of the Spirit with Logos. Mary becomes the Theotokos when she receives the overshadowing Spirit who incarnates her Son. Thus the pattern of divine-humanity unfolds as a two-fold event:

> The Second Person is incarnate and becomes the hypostatic God-Man, while the Third Person is not himself incarnate but rather impregnates human nature, to abide in it and deify it. The dyadic descent of these Hypostases from heaven aims to achieve divine-humanity, the unity of the divine life with human life, to establish the communion of created humanity with the uncreated humanity of heaven.[45]

Crucially, the Holy Spirit—the "principle" of divine-humanity—is not hypostatically incarnated, but rather "impregnates" and "abides" in the flesh and heart of a created hypostatic spirit. In this way, the Spirit enables a created spirit to personally correspond to the uncreated hypostasis of the Logos, the Heavenly Man. The Logos "alone," then, does not hypostatically accomplish the human vocation: there is a genuine sophianic/created "response" to God uttered by a created person. This is crucial for Bulgakov since (1) the Logos himself—even while he is the Heavenly Man—is nonetheless a "divine" person/hypostasis, and (2) he is dependent on a creature to prepare a body for him, he is humanly dependent on the "Yes" of a human "spirit." Mary's hypostatic

---

43. Boulgakov, *La Sagesse de Dieu*, 52.
44. Ibid., 52.
45. Ibid., 69.

response—enabled by the Holy Spirit—is thus internal to the becoming human of the divine hypostasis of the Son, and so to the full manifestation of divine-humanity.[46]

In Bulgakov's theology the correlation between Mary and the Spirit is thereby intimately linked to the hypostatic union. Mary is "the human manifestation of the Holy Spirit."[47] Just as the divine Son is the God-Man, the human Mother is the "Spirit-bearer."[48] Mary is the "epiphany" of the Holy Spirit.[49] In being the "epiphany" of the Spirit, Mary is fulfilled as a created person in such a way that she truly fulfills the "hypostaticity" of sophianic creation as such. Thus, "in her person, [Mary] represents the whole of humanity."[50] "Mary is creation."[51]

The dyadic reciprocity of Logos and Spirit is thereby "incarnated" in the mother-child reciprocity of Jesus and Mary. The God-Man and the Spirit-bearer together realize the internality of the Logos (the principle of humanity) with human nature (the capacity for deification, the "hypostaticity" capable of personal response). The Son alone is not the image of divine-humanity, but rather it is the Son *with* the Mother. This is the icon of Sophia; she is an act of love that loves love flowing between the Son and the Mother; she is revealed in the divine-humanity of these two faces gazing upon each other: the face of the divine person of Son become flesh, and the face of the human person of the Mother become Theotokos.

---

46. Ibid., 76.

47. Bulgakov, "Hypostasis and Hypostaticity," 34.

48. Bulgakov, *The Comforter*, 187; *Lamb of God*, 140.

49. Alexander Schmemann, *The Virgin Mary*, trans. John A. Jillions (Crestwood, NY: St. Vladimir's Seminary Press, 1995), 75.

50. Sergius Bulgakov, *The Orthodox Church*, trans. Lydia Kesich (Crestwood, NY: St. Vladimir's Seminary Press, 1988), 177.

51. Bulgakov, "Hypostasis and Hypostaticity," 34.

On Understanding, Wisdom, and the Son of Man

Gregory Yuri Glazov

This article presents insights into wisdom realized by Anthony Opisso, M.D., a medical doctor of Jewish ancestry who died in 2001 on the grounds of a Trappist Monastery in Canada where he lived as a tertiary Carmelite hermit for several decades. Loved by many for his wisdom, understanding, and counsel, he authored, with the help of people who prayed for his work, a number of remarkable books, the last of which, The Revelation of the Son of Man, *argued that the "Son of Man" title identifies Jesus as God's Understanding. The work completed an earlier attempt (in* The Book of Understanding) *to explain the range of symbols associated with Understanding in the Scriptures and to map out its relationship to the other sapiential entities, such as wisdom, knowledge, and counsel. It is hoped that this summary of the insights in these works will provide an original scripture-based perspective to reflection on the meaning and role of Sophia.*

CRUCIAL in all Brother Anthony's works is the anthropology presented by Jesus's Parable of the Sower. Brother Anthony emphasized this in his writings by drawing attention to Jesus's asking the disciples, "Do you not understand this parable? How then will you understand all the parables?" (Mark 4:13).[1] Brother Anthony understood this to mean that the parable explains (Jesus' understanding of) the fundamental mystery of human destiny, lot and calling. Accordingly, the parable draws two fundamental analogies, the first between the human heart and earth, facilitated by the homophony allowed by the Hebrew words for *man, 'Ādām,* and *earth/ground, ădămâ,* respectively, emphasizing that man is literally an "earthman," and the second between God's word and seed, emphasizing that as a living seed that transforms the earth that keeps it, and raises it up into an upright, fruit-bearing plant filled with seeds that are

---

1. All translations from scriptural and extra-scriptural sources are the author's.

children to the implanted seed, so the Word of God can transform the heart that receives it in meekness and raise it up to a new life (Isa 55:10; Luke 8:11; Mark 13:19; Jam 1:12; 4 Ezra 4:30). As the "Word" of God given for such keeping is called a commandment, its keeping is identifiable with performing it, and with righteousness (Pro 3:9, LXX; Hos 10:12; 2 Bar 32:1; PsSol 15:5; OdesSol 17:14 Syr), while the "fruit-bearing tree" stage would be identifiable with the attainment of a capacity to dispense wisdom as counsel, echoed in the homophony of the Hebrew terms for *tree*, "*ēṣ*," and *counsel*, "*ēṣâ*," and by metaphoric descriptions of a person attaining this stage as an "oak of righteousness" (Isa 61:3), "tree of life" (Pro 11:30; cf. Gen 2:9; 3:22; Pro 3:18, 1:30, 12:12, 15:4; 4 Macc 18:16; Rev 22:14), "Paradise of the Lord" (PsSol 14:2.3). The "fruit" of this righteousness is called the "peaceable fruit of righteousness" (Heb 12:11; Jam 3:18; Phil 1:11), because it is also the "fruit" of "wisdom," "understanding," and "knowledge" (cf. Sir 24:19, 6:19, 37:22 M.T. and LXX), and because those who have acquired these possessions are able to give "sweet counsel" (Pro 27:9; Psa 55:14). The analogy can be seen to inform the imagery of Psalm 1, and St. James's description of divine, heavenly Wisdom as a "wheel of generation" which begins with the chaste and meek keeping of the seed and results in the yield of the peaceable fruit of righteousness (Jam 3:3–18).

Since the themes and imagery of the Parable of the Sower and of Psalm 1 strongly echo the Garden of Eden story, the sapiential lesson of the Parable and the Psalm can be applied to the Story to suggest that when God "commanded upon Adam" not to eat of the fruit of the tree of the knowledge of good and evil (Gen 2:16), He was not doing so out of selfish jealousy, but in fact providing the means by which Adam could organically enter into divine life and become, as it were, a Tree of Life, from whose fruit he would be able to see and know the goodness of God.

By building on the Garden of Eden story, the Law, the Prophets and the Wisdom Writings serve to depict and explain the divine plan by which Man and his children, exiled into the field from which he was taken, are called, and given the means to return to God and fulfil their original calling. The two books of Brother Anthony, *The Book of Understanding* and *The Revelation of the Son of Man*, explain the role played by Wisdom and Understanding in this plan.

I. The Relationship of Wisdom and Understanding

In *The Book of Understanding*, Brother Anthony explains and sequences a number of sapiential terms by representing them as rungs on the Ladder of Understanding. The reason why the Ladder is of Understanding rather than Wisdom will be clarified in *The Revelation of the Son of Man*. The foundation of the "rungs" is the Fear of the Lord; the summit of the Ladder is Truth and its rungs are: 1) Wisdom [*ḥokmâ*]; 2) Basic Understanding (the human capacity "to understand" [denoted by forms of the Hebrew verb *bîn*]); 3) Insight [*bînâ*]; 4) Skillful Understanding and capacity to Teach [*sekel*]; 5) Great Understanding [*tᵉbûnâ*]; 6) Knowledge [*da'at*]; 7) Divine or Holy Knowledge [*dē'â*]; 8) Counsel ['*ēṣâ*]; and 9) Powerful Counsel [*taḥbulôt*]. The lack of perfect correspondence with the list of what seem to be seven spiritual gifts in Isaiah 11:2–3 raises questions about the subjectivity of this arrangement.[2]

1. The Fear of the Lord may be identified as the foundation on the basis of a) injunctions in the Law and the Prophets to walk after the Lord by fearing Him and doing His commandments (Deut 5:29, 10:12, etc.), and b) strategically placed declarations in the Wisdom books that it is Wisdom's "beginning" (Ps 111:10; Pro 1:7, 9:10 [the conclusion of the first section of Proverbs]; 15:33 [the center of the book]; 31:30 [the end of the book]; Job 28:28 [the heart of the discourse on Wisdom]), "root" (Sir 1:20, 6:36), and prerequisite (Sir 32:14; cf. also Pss 34:11–12, 145:19; Sir 6:36 [Hebrew text], 21:11). The affirmation that it also crowns wisdom (Sir 1:11, 16, 18; 23:27) underscores that every higher stage must always be grounded upon it.

There are several reasons why the Fear of the Lord is foundational. Its association with humility and meekness, an argument for conflating it with the spirit of piety in LXX Isa 11:2, means that it fosters a teachable disposition, an eagerness to be taught, a capacity to listen, keep silence, ponder, and thus receive wisdom (Ps 25:9; Job 13:5, 33:33; Pro 2:1–2, 8:33, 11:12, 17:28, 23:19, 12:15; Sir 1:27, 14:20–21, 51:16; Wis 6:15; Mat 11:25; Jam 3:12). This is corroborated by the principle that wisdom will not come to the proud, rebellious and scornful (Jer 17:23; 2 Bar 51:4; Pro 14:6; Sir 15:7–8).

2. Wisdom, *ḥokmâ*, involves the capacity to fasten, join, weave, coordinate and guide beautifully and skillfully (Exod 31:6–9 [M.T.], 35:25, 36:1 and 8; Pro 9:1, 14:1, 24:3; Job 38:36, LXX; Sir 6:28–29 [Syriac Text men-

---

2. The M.T. of Isa 11:2–3a reads: "and shall rest upon him the spirit of the LORD, the spirit of *ḥokmâ*, and *bînâ*, the spirit of '*ēṣâ* and *gebûrâ*, the spirit of *da'at* and the fear of the LORD, and his delight shall be in the fear of the Lord." The Targum interprets the initial "spirit of the Lord" as the Spirit of Prophecy, and repeats both occurrences of the "fear of the Lord." By contrast, the LXX and the Vulgate render the "spirit of the Lord" as such and then seemingly see the remaining spirits as subdivision of it, reading the first "fear of the Lord" as *eusebeia, pietas.*

tioning the "net of wisdom"]; Wis 10:17; 2 Bar 28:2; 2 Esd 13:54). Observing then that she was the first of God's creative works (Pro. 8:22; Sir 1:4, 24:9), and the instrument by which He founded and established the earth (Ps 104:24; Pro 3:19; Jer 10:12, 51:15; 1 QH 1:7; 11 QPs^a XXVI.7), Brother Anthony makes her the first rung, assuming that she is instrumental in the construction of the rest. I find this argument unconvincing because such a power reflects the acquisition of skills acquired higher up the ladder, especially the gift of skillful understanding. More persuasive is the argument based on Solomon's request, at the start of his reign, for God to grant him an "understanding heart to judge his people," a request that pleased God and prompted him to give Solomon "a wise and understanding heart" (1 Kgs 3:8–12, 4:29, 5:12). This example is important because it corroborates that Wisdom is a) a treasure (Pro 3:15, 8:11, 16:16; Job 11:6, 28:12–21, 38:36; Ps 51:6; Wis 7:8–9, 8:5 and 18); b) hidden and concealed; but c) obtainable via the gift of divine inspiration and revelation, owing to the fact that God, being alone truly wise (Jer 10:7; Dan 2:20; Job 12:13; Sir 15:18–19), must be her ultimate source. Her presentation as a treasure leads to her representation as "a beautiful woman whom God loves and wants us to love and long for" (Pro 3:18, 4:6 and 8, 8:12 and 17; Sir 1:22, 2:3, 4:14, 6:26–27, 14:22, 24:19, 51:19–26; Wis 6:13–16, 7:8–10 and 28, 8:2–21), but chastely (Sir 51:20; Wis 7:24 and 26), since Wisdom will not dwell in a deceitful and corrupt soul (Wis 1:4). Here, too, I pause to ask why, if Wisdom will only enter and take residence in a good and understanding heart, it is not understanding that is the first rung on the Ladder, prerequisite to the reception of Wisdom, as a closer reading of Solomon's request and God's response might indicate:

> "Give thy servant therefore *a hearing heart* to govern thy people, that I may *discern* [*lᵉhābîn*] between good and evil. . . ." It pleased the Lord that Solomon had asked this. And God said to him, "Because you have asked this, and have not asked for yourself long life or riches or the life of your enemies, but have asked for yourself understanding to discern what is right, behold, I now do according to your word. Behold, I give you a heart, wise and understanding, so that none like you has been before you and none like you shall arise after you." (1 Ki 3:9–12)

Here a heart that discerns and understands precedes and makes way for the acquisition of wisdom. Consequently, I would read a proverb such as 4:7 ("Wisdom is the first thing [you must get], therefore get wisdom, and with all your getting get understanding") not as proof that Wisdom is the first of the sapiential gifts, but that she must be the first thing desired (which is what God highlighted in 2 Ki 3:11 above), while understanding must be essential for acquiring her (Sir 18:28).

The reflection implicitly defines Wisdom as a spirit (Exod 28:3; Deut 34:9; Isa 11:2; Wis 1:6, 7:7 and 22 [Vulg]). Its portrayal as feminine seems to be a metaphoric function of a) the intention to make her desirable to a male audience and b) the high degree of presence in women of the gifts associated with her (Pro 31). The most concrete definition of her is in Wisdom of Solomon where she is characterized as eternally radiant, luminous, and unfading (6:12, 22, 23 [Vulg]; 7:10), "fairer than the sun and above all the order of the stars, superior to light . . . the brightness of eternal light, the unspotted mirror of the working of God, and the image of His goodness" (7:29–30). This links to earlier texts about her making a man's face shine (Pro 17:24 [Vulg]; Eccl 8:1; Sir 27:1 [Vulg]), and the prophecy in Dan 12:3 that those who turn others to righteousness through her will be exalted and shine like the stars of heaven. However, the saying that "light is sown for the righteous" (Ps 97:11) suggests that the agricultural metaphor must also be brought into play whereby if wisdom brings radiance at the end of the journey, in the fruit stage, this is so because the journey begins with the acquisition of light in the very beginning, at the seed stage. Consequently, my question about the point at which Wisdom is to be acquired on the ladder may best be resolved by the agricultural metaphor. As Jam 3:17–18 teaches, Wisdom is a cycle of generation, which begins with her coming as a seed, a seed that generates the rest of the plant (organizes the Ladder), proceeds through the stage of reasoning or understanding, and concludes with her manifestation in various good fruits, including that of peacemaking.

3. Brother Anthony associates the next four rungs of the Ladder with four grades of understanding, the first being *bînâ*, which he in turn subdivides into a) the basic, innate human faculty of understanding, essentially the power to draw distinctions or divide (Pro 17:2, LXX; Job 39:17; Sir 33:8, 11; 1 QH 13:13) and make connections between things, as represented by forms of the verb *bîn* (cf. the preposition "between," *bên*), and thus the power to examine, scrutinize, and search out counterfeits (Pro 28:11; Job 12:11, 34:3; Sir 36:19); and b) the spiritual perfection of this faculty which grants the power to understand divine words, parables, and secrets in ways exceeding natural human understanding (Pro 1:2; Sir 6:35; 9:15 [Hebrew text]), as represented by the noun *bînâ* (Isa 11:2; cf. Dan 1:17, 8:15–16, 9:22, 10:1; 1 QH 1:21; 1 QM 10:16). I find this distinction somewhat problematic, first, on grammatical grounds, since *bîn* and *bînâ* are the verb and noun forms of the same root, whereby the Hebrew would not support that verbal forms are secular and the noun form is spiritual; and, secondly, because of the aforementioned contention that all of the dispositions presuppose the Fear of the

Lord, which requires recognition of the principle that "the wicked do not understand" (a verbal form; Pss 28:3 and 5, 82:4–5; Pro 29:7; 1 QH 5:25–26; Jer 4:22; Sir 21:15 [Vulg]; Jam 3:15). Real understanding therefore comes with "departing from evil," which testifies to taking God's counsels and commandments to heart and following them (Deut 4:6; Pro 9:6; Job 28:28). Like Wisdom, it is also rooted in the fear of the Lord (Sir 6:36, Hebrew text) and reflects a renewal of the faculty of understanding (Ps 119:27, 33, 34, 73, 104, 125, 144, 169), which, as Brother Anthony notes, involves the awareness of the possibility of unseen or unconscious faults and a prayerful desire to avoid them (Ps 91:12; Job 1:5; 6:24; Pro 20:24). The seat of understanding is the heart (Exod 36:2; Isa 6:10; Sir 17:6; Enoch 14:2; T. Naph. 2:8; MR Psalm 103.3f.), and the two are virtually synonymous (cf. Greek translations of the Hebrew "heart" as "understanding" at Exod 28:3, 36:1; Deut 6:5; Job 7:17, 9:4; Pro 2:10, 6:32, 7:7, 9:4, 11:12, 11:29, 19:8). Moreover, since wisdom "will not enter into a deceitful soul, nor dwell in a body enslaved to sin" (Wis 1:4), but "rest in the heart of him who has understanding" (Pro 14:33; cf. Pro 2:8–10), the good "heart/understanding" must be *the* place where Wisdom is to be found. Having noted the challenges facing the attempt to differentiate natural from renewed phases of understanding, I would also observe that the argument overall tends to support it inasmuch as it emphasizes the importance of associating the "sons of man" with "understanding" (see next section). I would resolve the problem by correlating the innate, natural understanding with the soil and ground into which the seed of wisdom is sown and then proceed to identify the Fear of the Lord as the foundation of the Ladder, whose first rung would be the Understanding grounded on this Fear, i.e., the Understanding that departs from evil.

4. As understanding grows, it becomes more skillful and practical, bringing the ability to teach and make others understand (2 Chr 30:22, Neh 8:8, Sir 50:27, Hebrew Text), to be sensitive to their needs (Ps 41:1), to carry out actions that lead to success and prosperity (cf. translations of Deut 29:9; Josh 1:7; 1 Kings 2:3), and, being a gift from God (1 Chr 22:12; 1 QS 2:3), to compose and sing praises to him (Ps 47:7). The ability is reflected by forms of the root *sākal*. Since these skills are involved in "shepherding" people (Jer 3:15, 10:21), the power of *sekel* is valuable to kings (Jer 23:5), and brings into favor servants who possess it (Isa 52:13; Pro 1:1–3, 14:35, 17:2; Sir 7:21; 10:23, 25, 30, Hebrew text). Wisdom, too, is loved for her bestowal of the "bread of understanding" (Sir 15:3, Hebrew text) like an understanding woman or wife (Sir 25:8, 7:19, 40:23, Hebrew text) whereby such understanding is a fountain of life to those who have

it (Pro 16:22). Such passages corroborate that this stage of understanding is possessed by those who have taken hold of Wisdom.

5. Eagerness to keep the commandments and please the Lord (Sir 15:15, Hebrew text) from whose mouth comes great understanding, *tᵉbûnâ* (Pro 2:6), brings the ability to maintain a cool spirit in times of great stress and to reflect this great understanding (Pro 11:12, 14:29, 17:27). Those who keep it are in turn kept by it (Pro 2:11). *Tᵉbûnâ*'s greatness is evident in the fact that God used it to make, stretch out, and establish the heavens (Ps 136:3 and 5; Jer 10:12, 51:15; Pro 3:19) and crush Rahab (Job 26:12). When God showed Moses "patterns of things in the heavens" to make a glorious tabernacle for Himself, he sent Bezaleel, a man "filled with the Spirit of God, in wisdom, and in *tᵉbûnâ* and in knowledge" to perform the task (Exod 31:3, 35:31, 36:1). This example supplies an important clue to the relationship between wisdom and understanding, since if something is constructed very wisely and intricately, as are the heavens, it is only a great understanding that can make this wisdom intelligible (Wis 7:21, 22). Hence, while wisdom "cries" outside, from the heavens, on top of the walls, and in noisy places to get attention (Pro 1:20–21, 8:1 and 4), *tᵉbûnâ* "puts forth the voice," low down, at the gate, in the streets, where the people are, to explain wisdom. This, too, is why "Wisdom is known by the word, but *tᵉbûnâ* by the reply of the tongue" (Sir 4:24, Hebrew text A), for the capacity to explicate a wise word lies in the power of drawing out its wisdom, as stated by Proverbs 20:5: "Counsel in the heart of man is like deep water, but a man of *tᵉbûnâ* will draw it out." The connection between the power of understanding and answering (Sir 4:24b, Hebrew text; Heb, 8:9, 11:7) highlights that the reason why Jesus astonished his hearers by his "replies" was that these revealed his "understanding" (Luke 2:47), in which "are hid all the treasures of wisdom and knowledge" (Col 2:3). This Understanding explains what Jesus must have been referring to when he claimed to make present "something greater than the wisdom of Solomon" (cf. Mat 12:42, Luke 11:31), inasmuch as Solomon's wandering into evil in his old age (Sir 47:13–21) betokened a failure of understanding and therefore a failure to hold on to Wisdom.

6. The rungs of understanding are succeeded by two rungs of knowledge: "(holy) knowledge," *daʿat* (the verb being *yādaʿ*), and the "Lord's knowledge," *dēʿâ*. Understanding acquires knowledge and is the means or key to it (Pro 14:6, 18:15a, 21:11; Ps 119:125; Hos 14:9), because God gives knowledge to those who understand (Dan 2:21) and men know according to the measure of their understanding (1 QH 1:21, 31).

One of the most important things to know is the time of one's judgment, since "God will bring every action to judgment along with every secret thing" (Eccl 8:5–6, 12:14; Rom 14:10). Since this knowledge is often lacking (Jer 8:7; Eccl 9:12), the Psalms direct us to pray for it (Pss 39:4, 90:12). Hence knowledge too begins with the fear of the Lord (Pro 1:7), and demands departure from evil. The corollary of this is that the wicked "have no knowledge" (Dan 12:10; Isa 44:18, LXX; Jer 4:22; Pro 13:19, LXX; 29:7; Pss 14:4, 53:4), because wickedness blinds one to the mysteries of God (Wis 2:21, 22). The thing that the wicked do not see and know is that no one can hide from God's knowledge (PsSol 9:5–6) because God sees and knows all (Isa 29:15), and can reveal all that is deep, dark, and hidden by the light that dwells with Him (Dan 2:22), since by "His knowledge the depths are broken up" (Pro 3:20), including the secrets of the heart (Ps 4:21; Sir 42:17–19, Hebrew text, Masada Scroll) which is deep beyond all things (Jer 17:9, LXX). For God's "light of knowledge" (T. Levi 4:L3, 18:3; T. Benj 11:2, B Text; Hosea 10:12, LXX) is given to dispel the darkness of ignorance, and bring truth to light (Isa 42:3; Sir 24:27 [LXX, Ms 248]; Sir 24:37 [Vulg]).

As knowledge is given to the upright to perfect them, it is acquired by correction, i.e., through rebukes, scourges, and suffering (Pro 15:5, 17:10, 19:25; Sir 22:19), which the brutish hate (Pro 12:1; Jer 10:8, 14; 51:17) but those who love knowledge receive quietly (Sir 10:25, LXX, Cursives 248, 70, 106, 307), knowing about the "disciplines of knowledge" (1 QS 3:1) and counting discipline a source of knowledge and a good (Pss 94:12, 119:71 and 75; Jer 31:18–19; Wis 11:9, 16:16 and 18; 2 Mac 9:9 and 11). Consequently, trials and suffering are the price for acquiring perfect knowledge (Sir 34:10, LXX Sinaiticus; 11 QPs 19:13–15; Eph 4:12, 13; Phil. 3:8 and 10; Hebrews 2:10, 5:8–9). The greatest knowledge is knowledge of God, which Moses knew must be attained by the knowledge of His ways (Exod 33:12–13), which lead to love of God (Hos 6:6) and a zeal that His will be done and His Truth upheld (Rom 3:7, 2 Thess 2:10).

7. The rare term $D\bar{e}'\hat{a}^3$ seems to connote a lofty form of knowledge (1 Sam 2:3; Isa 11:9, 28:9; Jer 3:15; Ps 73:11) that God dispenses piecemeal as food to a child (Jer 3:15) and which will one day fill the earth as the waters cover the sea to bring about a great peace (Isa 11:6–9; cf. 54:13; Targ. Isa 53:5). The wicked cannot know (Isa 48:22, 57:21) this peace since it surpasses all understanding (Phil 4:7), but it is the end of the upright (Ps 37:37), since peace accompanies the fruit of righteousness

---

3. Perhaps not to be confused with $d\bar{e}'a$, which seems to be exclusively associated with the suspicious claims of Elihu in Job 32:6–10, 36:3–4, 37:16.

(Ps 85:10; Isa 32:17, 48:18; Baruch 5:4), attained in the fullest measure through the knowledge of God and of Jesus our Lord (2 Pet 1:2).

8. Those who have learned to plan and establish everything on the reception of wisdom, understanding and counsel in the form of dispensed counsel (Pro 15:22, 20:18; Sir 32:19, 37:16; Acts 20:17)[4] gain the ability themselves to give good counsel, '*eṣâ* (cf. Ps 16:7, MT and LXX; Pro 7:4 [Syr], 12:15, 13:10, 19:20; 1 Chr 26:14; Sir 32:22, Vulgate text; PsSol 17:42; Tob 4:18), and so become "guides" and "leaders" (Sir 44:3). Divine counsel is important because it leads to life (Pro 3:21, 23, LXX), because it grants the heart's desire (Ps 20:1, 4), and because people are lost without it (Deut 32:28; Jer 49:7; Mic 4:9; Ezek 7:26). Those who attempt to resist it by evil counsel will be exposed and caught in the traps of their own counsel (Isa 29:15; 31:6, LXX; Sir 42:18, Hebrew Masada text; Wis 6:3; 1 Cor 4:5), for God's counsel is not to be moved or resisted (Rom 9:19; Hebrews 6:17), but will be accomplished and stand forever (Isa 44:26; Ps 33:11; Pro 19:21). God works everything according to the "counsel of his will," reveals His will and way through His counsel (Ps 73:20 and 24), and delivers by it those who commit themselves to it (Pro 1:3; 1 Kgs 3:11 and 28; Isa 16:3; Sir 25:4).

Even though God's good counsel is plain in the commandments, exhortations, and counsels of the Scriptures, He hides them in it to make us search for it as for hidden treasures, as evident in the exhortations to seek Him (Deut 4:29; Isa 55:6; Pss 27:8, 105:4; 1 Chr 16:11). Though the task seem impossible (Job 23:3; Psa 42:2), the assurance is given that He will be found if sought with all of one's heart and soul (Deut 4:29; 1 Chr 28:9). Hence the most important counsel of all is to "set one's heart and soul to seek the Lord" (1 Chr 22:19), or to love the Lord "with all of one's heart, soul, strength" (Deut 6:5; Isa 26:9; Pss 42:1–2, 63:1). Since, however, he would not be recognized unless He first revealed Himself, every heart pursuing Him must be drawn to do so by such a revelation, which must be associated with the desire to see Him, and the necessity of purifying the heart to do so (2 Chr 15:12 and 15, 30:18–19; Sir 24:19, 51:26; Wis 6:13; Mt 5:8; John 7:37).

9. What *Tᵉbûnâ* is to *Bînâ*, and *Dēʿâ* to *Daʿat*, that *Taḥbûlôt* is to '*eṣâ*.

---

4. One can hear here echoes of the beginning, end and middle of the Lord's Prayer (Matt 6:9–12), inasmuch as it ends with the petitions to be not led into temptation but be delivered from evil, voices the aspiration to yoke one's will to the accomplishment of God's will almost at the beginning, and requests midway the sustenance of daily bread, which could be a metaphor for counsel and the "bread of understanding."

Etymologically related to the skill of handling ropes on a ship, i.e., to steersmanship (Job 37:10, 11–13), it is associated with the power of marshalling plans in warfare (Pro 20:18) so essential to saving people from destruction (Pro 11:14). Consequently, although the term itself can carry a neutral or even a negative meaning (Pro 12:5), it is the term chosen to denote God's mighty counsel (Jer 32:19). It is obtainable through understanding (Pro 1:5) and bestows the ability to bring deep things to light (Sir 32:16 [Hebrew text, E; LXX and Vulgate read "kindle righteous deeds"]).

10. The last rung of the Ladder is *Tûsîyyâ*, a word translated as "good counsel," "wise judgment," "sound policy," "ability," "resourcefulness," "success," "victory," "salvation," and a host of other terms. A comparison of its occurrence in Isa 28:29: "The Lord of Hosts is wonderful in counsel and great in *Tûsîyyâ*," with Jeremiah 32:19: "The Lord of Hosts is great in counsel and mighty in *'alîlîyyâ*," suggests an equivalence with *'alîlîyyâ*, a unique term deriving from *'alîlâ*, whose use in Isa 12:4, Pss 9:12, 77:13, 78:11, 103:7, 105:1, and 1 Chr 16:8 refers to the "marvelous deeds" of God, suggesting that *Tûsîyyâ*, in turn, denotes a marvelous feat of deliverance and salvation (Pro 2:7, LXX), which God hides within the righteous as a seed in the ground (Jer 31:33; Isa 51:7).

Tûsîyyâ also involves the ability to see, bring forth, and grasp the truth because a) it is *Tûsîyyâ* to see the Name of God (Mic 6:9), which is Truth, since God is Truth (Jer 10:10), and His Seal is Truth (OdesSol 12:13, 17:8; cf. 1 Ki 21:8; Est 8:8); and b) the speaking-forth of truth is the goal and perfection of understanding and knowing wisdom (Ps 15:2; Pro 12:17; Jam 3:2). The reasons for this are organic. The ascent into the Truth is ascent into the light, the light that was hidden in the righteous as a seed (Psa 97:11; Eph 1:13; James 1:18, 21; Clement of Alexandria, *Strom* I.c.1) but arose for the upright (Pss 43:1 and 3, 112:4) via the way of uprightness, i.e., in the "plant of righteousness" (Psa 85:11) unto the bearing of the "fruit of light" (Col 1:10 and 12; Eph 5:9; 4 Ezra 6:28; 1 QM 13:9, 10). Thus, since God is Truth and Light (1 John 1:5), those who believed and held His Word of Truth in their hearts allowed it to act on their hearts (1 Pet 1:23; James 1:18; Heb 4:12; 1 Thess 2:13) to bring forth from them the fruit of light and Truth (John 17:19). This transpires through the Spirit within the Word, the Spirit of Truth (1 John 5:6), which guides them into all the Truth (John 16:13; 1 Pet 1:22) and makes them "children of God" (Rom 8:14), "children of light" (John 12:36; Luke 16:8; 1 Thess 5:5) and "children of Truth" (1 QS 4:5–6).

II. Knowledge, Understanding, and the Revelation of the Son of Man

This summary of *The Ladder of Understanding* highlights that Understanding is prerequisite to securing Wisdom and that Wisdom cannot be attained without Understanding. Since Understanding is so crucial to finding the way to Wisdom and embracing her, and must therefore be obtained first, the way towards obtaining "it" must also be identified. This is the goal of Brother Anthony's work, *The Revelation of the Son of Man*, which, by focusing on the relationship of Understanding to Knowledge, identifies Understanding with Jesus as Son of Man.

1. Seeing and Hearing

The argument begins by emphasizing the near-synonymity of "seeing" and "knowing," and of "hearing" and "understanding." The linkage between seeing and knowing is evidenced in short phrases such as "see now and know" (Jer 5:1; 1 Sam 18:28) and its contraries, "neither see, nor know" (Isa 44:9). That the two are virtually synonymous is underscored by the LXX translation of the Hebrew phrase "saw and knew" in 1 Sam 18:28 by means of the sole Greek term *eiden*, "he saw," since this term is a past-tense form of the obsolete verb *eidō*, "to see," the perfect of which, *oida*, "I have seen," is used in Greek as the present "I know" on the grounds that what has been seen is known.

In the meantime, understanding's linkage to hearing may be illustrated by the idiomatic use of "to hear" to connote understanding a language (2 Ki 18:26), by phrases such as "hearing with understanding" (Neh 8:2), in reminders that it takes understanding to hear (Job 34:10 and 16), in admonitions to understand by applying the ear (Pro 5:1; Ps 5:1), and in declarations that to hear with the ear is to understand (Job 13:1). The hardening oracle of Isa 6:9, "Hear and hear but not understand and see and see but do not know" underscores the perversity of hearing and not understanding (and seeing and not knowing), while the reference to "understanding with the heart" in the following verse, 6:10, explains that the heart is the true seat of understanding.

Awareness of these relationships allows one to see how they inform biblical parallelism in delightful ways, as for instance at Isa 1:3, which declares that a) "The ox knows his owner, and the ass his master's crib," b) "while Israel does not know, my people does not understand." The parallelism between strophes *a* and *b* contrasts the ox who knows in strophe *a* with Israel who does not know in strophe *b*, and the people who do not understand in strophe *b* with the donkey in strophe *a*. The parallelism between what the animals do and the people do not do shows that the verb which should explain what the ass does in the second part of strophe *a* but which is omitted (a phenomenon called ellipsis) should be "understands." Consequently, knowledge, a concept associated with seeing, is associated with the ox, a creature with large eyes, while understanding, a concept associated with hearing, is associated with the donkey, a creature with large ears.

Accordingly, understanding and hearing are discursive and more lowly and servile than seeing and knowing, which, by contrast, are more immediate and higher, and lordly. These differences may also be appreciated in the parallelisms which correlate knowing to the processes of beholding, being mindful, and remembering, on the one hand, and understanding to the processes of counting or accounting, scrutinizing, thinking, or testing on the other. Such can be seen for example in the following verses: "What is man, that thou art mindful of him? and the son of man, that thou take account of him? (Ps 8:4, 144:3), and "The Lord . . . his eyes behold, his eyelids test the sons of men" (Ps 11:4). The parallelisms in these verses correlate man/men with knowing, being mindful, and beholding on the one hand, and the sons of man with taking account, scrutinizing (through the narrowing of the eyelids), and testing on the other.

2. The West and the East

Knowledge is the result of understanding. *The Revelation of the Son of Man* unpacks the parallelistic representation of the symbols of this relationship. One set of such symbols relates to the path of the sun, whereby understanding is correlated to sunrise in the east and knowledge to sunset in the west. A clear correlation of the two is evident in Jer 2:10: "Pass over the isles of Kittim [in the West], and see; and send unto Kedar [in the East], and understand [LXX: 'observe accurately']." Psalm 104:19 links sunset to knowledge: "the sun knows his going down." Isa 45:6 indicates that knowledge results from beholding what has happened by the time the sun sets, while Eccl 2:19, 6:5 and 6:12 relativize this knowledge. The relationship of the dawn to understanding is evident in the LXX's translating the messianic term "Branch" in Jer 23:5 and Zech 3:8 with the name "The East," *anatolē*. Philo explicates that "understanding is truly a thing of the dawn, all radiancy and brightness" (*Plant* 40), while Isaiah's linkage of the dawn and the east to the Messiah is taken up by Mat 2:1–2 ("we have seen his star in the east"), Luke 1:78 ("the East/ Dawn [*anatolē*] from on high shall visit us"), and 2 Pet 1:19 ("pay attention to this [prophetic word] as to a lamp shining in a dark place, until the day dawns and the morning star rises in your hearts").

3. The Understanding of the Almighty and the Knowledge of the Most High

Not to be missed in the preceding reflection is the relationship of the messianic "Branch" of Jer 23:5 and Zech 3:8–9 to the "tender plant" (*yônēq*) and the Arm of the Lord in Isa 53:1–2:

> Who has believed what we have heard? And to whom has the arm of the LORD been revealed? For he grew up before him like a tender plant [LXX: "child"], and like a root out of dry ground; he had no form or comeliness that we should look at him, and no beauty that we should desire him. (Isa 53:1–2)

Seeing a relationship between the plant and God's Arm depends upon a couple of parallel verses which equate God's "great understanding," *tebûnâ*, with His "right hand." As was noted, God's *tebûnâ* is great because it stretched out the heavens in Jer 10:12 and smote Rahab in Job 26:12. But these declarations find matching verses in Isaiah 48:13 and 51:9, except that these replace God's *tebûnâ* with His "right hand" and "arm," respectively; and the latter passage, Isa 51:9, addresses God's arm as the agent of redemption. This suggests that the "tender plant," or "child," and suffering servant of Isa 53:2ff. is the arm of the Lord of Isa 53:1 whose agency has not been understood and requires revelation (cf. Acts 7:25). Further biblical witnesses linking the divine right hand to the power of understanding are implicit in Dan 10, where angelic beings (vv. 5, 16, 18) strengthen Daniel's understanding (vv. 12, 14) by the touch of a hand (vv. 10, 16, 18), an association made explicit in 4 Ezra 10:30. Further linkages may be noted in passages which relate God's "might" to the strength of his heart or understanding (Job 36:5), declare that "it is the breath of the Almighty that makes men understand" (Job 32:8; cf. Job 11:7 and 11) and speak of the "understanding of the Almighty" (Jud 8:13, Code 58 and Old Latin and Syriac texts; Sir 42:17, 18, LXX Codex Sinaiticus and Alexandrinus).

If understanding comes from the spirit of the Almighty, the spirit of Knowledge must come from the "God of Knowledge" (1 Sam 2:3). The association of knowledge and sight also suggests that God knows all because he sees all, and does so because of his vantage point, i.e., height, for divine knowledge is described as being wonderfully and unattainably high (Ps 139:6), so high as to reduce to absurdity the denials of those who question his omniscience (Ps 73:11; Job 22:12–13). Consequently, the scriptures identify him as the Most High (Sir 42:18), and speak of the "knowledge of the Most High" (Num 24:16; Ps 73:11).

The distinction between the Most High and the Almighty may be noted to inform the parallelism at Ps 91:1: "He that dwells in the secret place of the Most High shall abide under the shadow of the Almighty." Similar distinctions may be noted in the association of God Most High with the God of Abram/Abraham, as indicated by Abraham being distinctively blessed by God Most High via Melchizedek (Gen 14:18–19; cf. 14:22), and in the special relationship between Abraham's grandson Jacob and the "Mighty One of Jacob," who strengthened Jacob's hands (Gen 48:3; 49:24; Ps 132:2, 5; Isa. 49:26, 60:16), and, as symbolized by their wrestling, purified him of guile, to reform him as Israel (Gen 32:24–29; John 1:47).

If the Mighty One of Jacob is the Almighty, who is such because of the power of his arm and Right Hand or Understanding, one activity that he may be expected to do with His "hands" is "forming," as made explicit at Jer 10:16, which states that "the portion of Jacob formed [yāṣar, plassō] all things." That "forming" correlates with "understanding" is corroborated by Isa 29:16b, which highlights the folly of saying that the God who forms does not understand. By attributing the things that are formed to the right hand and understanding of the Almighty, these verses prompt one to wonder whether a distinction is to be made between the agencies responsible for formed things such as dry land and formless things like the sea. The sensibility of the question is confirmed by the parallelism of Ps 95:5: "The sea is his, and he made it, and his hands formed the dry (land)." This parallelism is also evident at Isa 22:11: "Ye have not looked unto its maker, neither had respect unto him who formed it long ago."

If this discussion suggests the existence of "two powers" in God, the first called the Most High and the second the Almighty, the first associated with Knowledge and the second with Understanding; the first with seeing, the second with hearing; the first with great height above the heavens, the second with the hands that stretched them out broadly; the first with creation, the second with formation; the first with the West, the second with the East; it follows that the mysterious question asked at Pro 30:4, "Who has ascended up into heaven, or descended? who has gathered the wind in his fists? who has bound the waters in a garment? who has established all the ends of the earth? what is his name, and what is his son's name, if thou canst tell?," may be answered by naming the Most High as the name of the first question, and the Almighty as name of the second. But this would further imply that the Most High is Father to the Almighty.

4. The Father and the Son of Man

The last inference can be corroborated by noting the attribution of fatherhood to the Most High in the scriptures. Thus Psalm 82:6 declares that "all of you are children of the most High," while Sir 4:10 exhorts: "Be like a father to orphans . . . you will then be like a son of the Most High." Later texts show this to be a scribal tradition, as illustrated by T. Levi. 4:2: "Therefore the Most High hath heard thy prayer, To separate thee from iniquity, and that thou should become to Him a son, and a servant, and a minister of His presence," and by Jubilees 22:11: "Blessed be my son Jacob and all the sons of God Most High" (cf. 22:19 and 23). The New Testament also picks up on the pattern at Luke 1:32: "He shall be great, and shall be called the Son of the Highest," and also at Luke 6:35: "But love ye your enemies, and . . . lend, hoping for nothing again, and your reward shall be great, and ye shall be children of the Highest. . . ." John 8:28 and 10:15 describe the Father as a teacher and knower of the Son, and OdesSol 23:18 echoes this conception: "the Son of Truth from the Most High Father."

Supports for the inference that the Most High is Father of the Almighty come from the indications that this relationship also applies to that between Knowledge and Understanding when one begins to note the word pairs associated with these terms in biblical parallelism. Thus, observing that understanding is linked to hearing and counting in time, while knowledge comes either instantaneously through seeing or is the culmination of understanding over time (memory), one may note that understanding is associated with the sons of man, since these understand, count, take account, or are the objects of such activities, while (adult) men know and remember. This may be elegantly illustrated by the famous question of Ps 144:3: "Lord, what is man, that you know him or the son of man, that you take account of him!" (cf. Ps 8:4). In several variations on this theme, for instance at Job 4:17 and 15:14, "Man" is called to purity and blamelessness, while the "sons of man" are called to righteousness, a correlation also evident at Ps 72:1: "Give the king thy judgments, O God, and thy righteousness unto the king's son" (cf. Pss 72:3, 103:17). In all these verses the "son of man" is associated with "righteousness" and "man" with judgment, mercy, and peace. This makes sense since, as may be remembered from Part I, "righteousness" pertains to the stage of keeping the seed-word, while "judgment," "mercy," and "peace" pertain to fruit-bearing stages. The patterns in the parallelism indicate that the "son of man" travels through righteousness towards perfection so that keeping graduates to giving, righteousness to mercy and loving-kindness, and the son of man becomes a son of God, as may be corroborated by matching up counsels such as Mat 5:48: "Be ye therefore perfect, even as your Father which is in heaven is perfect" and Luke 6:36: "Be ye therefore merciful, as your Father also is merciful" (cf. Mat 19:21; Phil. 2:5).

5. The Fruit of Knowledge and the Bread of Understanding

The use of agricultural metaphors to describe the role of wisdom, understanding and knowledge in God's plan for sharing his life with humanity, as explained in Brother Anthony's *The Book of Understanding*, is developed in *The Revelation of the Son of Man* to clarify the destiny of Man, the lot of the sons of Man and the calling of both. Accordingly, Man, beginning his life in the garden, had the destiny of becoming "a tree of knowledge," and was called to bring forth the fruit of this knowledge from the ground of his heart. As he disobeyed, he and his children, the sons of man, were exiled into the field from which he was taken, so that the field became the world of the sons of man (Mat 13:38). In this field, the sons of man do not have any knowledge to begin with, but do begin life with what is innate to them, understanding, and, being in a field rather than in a garden, are meant to become not fruit-bearing trees, but wheat and vines, bearing the smaller, wheat- and grape-like "fruits of understanding," to produce the bread and wine of understanding, which takes much toil and suffering but which brings much joy in the end. Thus it is that as bread and wine are the primary symbols of the life of the sons of man, the Son of Man, who sits at the "right hand of power" (Mark 14:61) and declared himself to be the "bread which came down from heaven" (John 6:41), being the "true Bread" (John 6:32) and the "true Vine" (John 15:1) gave himself to us as Bread and Wine.

It is to the credit of Brother Anthony and those who prayed for him that by "holding on to the form of sound words" of Scripture (2 Tim 1:13) they have illuminated how and where Wisdom is to be found. Thus, having highlighted in *The Book of Understanding* that Understanding is the means to Wisdom, being the way (Bar 3:20, 21; Job 28:20, 23), instrument and means, the "silver" by which the "gold" of Wisdom and Knowledge are acquired (Pro 2:3 and 4, 3:13 and 14, 8:10, 16:16, 17:16; Eccl 10:19), and the Place where Wisdom is to be found, and secured (Job 28:12, 20, 23; Bar 3:14, 15, 20, 21), and having highlighted there also that what Wisdom wants and longs for is to be loved, embraced, and known by (and within the mighty arms of) Understanding, while Understanding burns to embrace and know Wisdom (Pro 4:8, 8:12 and 17; Sir 1:22, 6:26–27, 51:21; Wis 6:13–14, 7:10, 8:2), they, in *The Revelation of the Son of Man*, have shown as well that this way and place have also been made accessible to us by the Incarnation of God's Understanding and Right Hand, the Agent of His Redemption and Salvation, in the Person of Jesus Christ, in whose heart/understanding are hidden all the treasures of wisdom and knowledge.

BIBLIOGRAPHY

Opisso, Anthony (pseudonomously authored by A Monk who prayed for a Hermit who wrote). *The Bread of God.* New York: Vantage Press, 1975.

———— (pseudonymously authored by Two Hermits). *The Secret Joy of Repentance.* Boston, MA: St. Paul Editions, 1985.

———— (pseudonymously authored by Two Hermits). *The Revelation of Bethlehem.* Petersham, MA: St. Bede's Press, 1985.

———— (pseudonymously authored by Levi Khamor). *The Revelation of the Son of Man.* Petersham, MA: Ben Yamin Press and St. Bede's Press, 1989.

———— (pseudonymously authored by Michael Anthony). *The Book of Understanding.* Geneva, NY: Ben Yamin Press, 1994.

References and Abbreviations

Biblical Versions

LXX Greek Septuagint Text
Vulg. Latin Vulgate Text
M.T. Hebrew Masoretic Text
Targ. Aramaic Targum (as specified)

Deuterocanonical & Apocryphal Texts

Enoch Either 1 Enoch (Ethiopic) or 2 Enoch (Slavonic), as indicated
3 Ezra 1 Esdras
4 Ezra 2 Esdras (Greek, Syriac or Latin)
Jub Jubilees
Macc1, 2, 3, 4 Maccabees as indicated
OdesSol Odes of Solomon (Syriac & Coptic)
PsSol Psalms of Solomon
SirLXX or Syriac text of Sirach or Hebrew text of Ben Sira, as indicated
T.X. Testament of the Twelve Patriarchs, where X stands for Simeon, Levi, Judah, Dan, Naphtali, Issachar, Zebulon, Joseph, Benjamin
Wis Wisdom of Solomon

Dead Sea Scrolls

1 QH Hymn of Thanksgiving Scroll
1 QM War Scroll
1 QS Scroll of Community Rule
1 QSPs^a Cave 11 Psalms Scroll

Rabbinic Texts
MR Midrash Rabbah (on a biblical book as specified)

Philo
Plant *De Plantatione*

Early Christian Writings
Clement of Alexandria *Strom Stromata*

John Pordage
and Sophianic Mysticism

Arthur Versluis

ALTHOUGH he is one of the most prolific mystics of the past few centuries, and arguably the most important of the Sophianic tradition, very few people are familiar with the work of John Pordage (1607–1681). Nonetheless, Pordage is author of thousands of pages on his visionary experiences and on metaphysics, and while his work is in the tradition of the great German mystic Jacob Boehme (1575–1624), Pordage's work is strikingly original and lucid in style. Pordage only published some short writings in English, however, and it seems that all his manuscripts in English were lost after they were translated into and published in German.[1] Only in the next few years will Pordage's work again be available in English, once again because of a monumental translation project.[2] In what follows, we will look more closely at Pordage's mysticism more broadly, as well as at the role that Sophia plays in this mystical tradition.

Pordage was born in 1607, the son of a London merchant family, and entered Pembroke College, Oxford, in 1623.[3] He may have received a

1. Pordage's extant works include *Innocencie appearing through the dark mists of pretended guilt* (London, 1655); *Göttliche und wahre metaphysica* (Frankfurt, 1715); *Ein gründlich philosophisch Sendschreiben* (Amsterdam, 1698); *Sophia: das ist die holdseelige ewige Jungfrau der Göttlichen Weissheit* (Amsterdam, 1699); *Theologia Mystica, or the Mystic Divinitie of the Aeternal Invisibles, viz. the Archetypous Globe* (London, 1683); *A Treatise of Eternal Nature with Her Seven Eternal Forms* (London, 1681); and *Vier Tractätlein* (Amsterdam, 1704).

2. Robert Faas is currently sponsoring the translation of all of Pordage's German works into English, to be published under the Grailstone Press imprint associated with New Cultures Press. The following account of Pordage's work is that of this author, as the new, complete translations are not yet available. There are some excerpts translated in Arthur Versluis, ed., *Wisdom's Book: The Sophia Anthology* (Minneapolis: Paragon House, 2000).

3. Works that refer to Pordage include Brian Gibbons, *Gender in Mystical and Occult Thought: Behmenism and its Development in England* (Cambridge: Cambridge University Press, 1996); Bernard Gorceix, *Flambée et Agonie, Mystiques du XVII siècle allemand*

diploma of a doctor of medicine at Oxford in 1640, but some scholars doubt this.[4] Pordage did practice medicine, but his primary calling was to the inner or contemplative life. We cannot be certain of all his schooling, but we know Pordage entered into the holy orders of the Anglican Church and was made vicar of the parish of St. Lawrence's at Reading in 1644. Soon, under the auspices of Elias Ashmole, he was made rector of the rather wealthy parish at Bradfield, a position he held until 1654.

Pordage married a young woman, Mary Freeman, who was gifted with second sight, and during their time at Bradfield he, Mary, and their children experienced visions, some terrifying. During this period Pordage and Mary witnessed angelic apparitions, and these were seen by others belonging to a small group of theosophers who gathered around them in a prayer group. This group was eventually to include men like Thomas Bromley and Edmund Brice (both Oxford-educated, themselves authors of significant theosophical works), and women like Anne Bathurst and Mrs. Joanna Oxenbridge, both of high society and who wrote memoirs of their spiritual journeys.

Early in his clerical career, Pordage was tried before the local Anglican commission as a heretical minister of the faith. Against him were arrayed a whole range of charges, including that he had made provocative statements and had engaged in immoral conduct. Pordage was able to defend himself well against all these charges: the supposedly provocative or heretical statements imputed to him he proved to have been taken out of context and misinterpreted; the charge that he had kept a mistress in London he demonstrated to be quite false. Thus he was able to exonerate himself from the accusations and was allowed to continue as a minister from 1649 to 1654. But, in 1654, Pordage was tried again on the same charges and, despite his eloquent rebuttal, he was removed from his ministerial position at Bradfield.[5]

(Sisteron: Présence, 1977), and *Johann Georg Gichtel, Théosophe D'Amsterdam* (Paris: L'Age d'Homme, 1975); Serge Hutin, *Les Disciples anglais de Jacob Boehme aux XVIIe et XVIIIe siécles* (Paris: Editions Denoël, 1960); Rufus Jones, *Studies in Mystical Religion* (London: Macmillan, 1909) and *Spiritual Reformers in the Sixteenth and Seventeenth Centuries.* (London: Macmillan, 1914); Nils Thune, *The Behmenists and the Philadelphians: A Contribution to the Study of English Mysticism in the 17th and 18th Centuries* (Uppsala: Almquist and Wiksells, 1948); Arthur Versluis, *Theosophia: Hidden Dimensions of Christianity* (Hudson: Lindisfarne, 1994) and *Wisdom's Children: A Christian Esoteric Tradition* (Albany: SUNY, 1999); Versluis, ed., *Wisdom's Book: The Sophia Anthology*; and Versluis, ed., *The Wisdom of John Pordage* (St. Paul: New Grail, 2004).

4. See Serge Hutin, *Les Disciples anglais de Jacob Boehme aux XVIIe et XVIIIe siécles* (Paris: Editions Denoël, 1960), 82.

5. See John Pordage, *Innocencie appearing through the dark mists of pretended guilt.*

Although Pordage was deprived of his livelihood, and although he found himself in extremely difficult circumstances for the remainder of his life, these outward difficulties only served to intensify his, and his group's, convictions and inward life. Of course, their persecution did mean that for some years they lived spiritually in the "outer darkness" surrounded by wrath, suffering something akin to what St. John of the Cross called the "dark night of the soul." But eventually they were restored to angelic communications and to the spiritual light.

For the remainder of his life, Pordage and his small group kept themselves out of public view and therefore censure. During this time—from the early 1670s until his death in 1681—Pordage wrote most of his elaborate, lucid, and concisely expressed metaphysical treatises. All these treatises were based wholly and directly on his own spiritual experience, exemplary of which is the treatise *Sophia*, probably written in 1675. Pordage's magnum opus, *Göttliche und Wahre Metaphysica* [*Holy and True Metaphysics*], was also written during this time, probably completed in the year of his death, 1681.

Pordage has only two works originally published in English—*A Treatise of Eternal Nature with Her Seven Essential Forms* (1681) and *Theologia Mystica, or the Mystic Divinitie of the Aeternal Invisibles, viz. the Archetypous Globe* (1683). *The Treatise of Eternal Nature* offers a general introduction to the concept of Eternal Nature, the "first original and true ground of all created beings and so of all true knowledge."[6] The physical cosmos, for Pordage, has its origin in Eternal Nature, which is akin to the Platonic realm of Ideas. Eternal nature is hidden in the nature that we see, like a jewel in a cabinet, and in turn has its origin in the Abyssal Nothing, which is "ground of all Essences, and yet no Essence to be seen in it," the "fruitful Mother of all Things." In the *Treatise on Eternal Nature*, Pordage introduces us to a kind of visionary ascent from physical to eternal nature, at the heart of which is the transcendent Abyss.[7]

Jane Lead wrote the preface to *Theologia Mystica*, where she confirmed that the entire time she knew him "*until the Time of his Death*, he was ever more imployed and busied in an internal contemplative Life." And she remarks on "those wonderful Transportations he had (or rather they had him) for the space of three weeks together. . . . His outward Body lay in passive Stillness in this visible Orb."[8] It is clear that Pord-

6. See *A Treatise of Eternal Nature with Her Seven Eternal Forms*, preface.
7. Both treatises are available in modern English in Arthur Versluis, ed., *The Wisdom of John Pordage*.
8. *Theologia Mystica, or the Mystic Divinitie of the Aeternal Invisibles, viz. the Archetypous Globe*, 2 and 7.

age's visionary treatises and his writings about Sophia were the result of deep contemplative practice that lasted for exceptional lengths of time.

Pordage emphasizes the image of opening an eye in one's heart in explaining the nature of his visionary spirituality and the process that reveals inner vision:

> The sight of the Holy Trinity from the opening of the Eye, in the inward Court of the Holy Place, is a lively, operative, reviving, and yet amazing and surprising sight. . . . No pen can decipher it, It is only the Spirit of the Eye that can open it self.[9]

This illumination is essentially a vision of the Archetypes of all things:

> This sight of God's Attributes from the opening of the Eye in the Abyssal Globe, is both a ravishing and amazing sight, for you do not behold Ideas or Similitudes of things, but the things themselves intellectually, which causeth most inexpressible joys, and extasies in the Spirit of the Soul, to which nothing in this world can be compared.[10]

This illumination is, even further, beholding God "Face to Face," in the Eye, the Center of the Heart. Pordage then writes of the Virgin Sophia, who is "co-essential" and "co-eternal" with the Holy Trinity, but not "co-equal" with them, for she is but a passive efflux of the Trinity, its glory and mirror. Finally, Pordage writes of the angelic spirits, their nature and qualities. The spirits possess a materiality and senses of their own: "These *Spirits* are endued with a Spiritual kind of materiality from the Love-Essence in the Heart of God." Hence they are "endued with the Spiritual senses of seeing, hearing, smelling, tasting and feeling, whereby they are inabled to discern the object of the still Eternity." The spirits have their own language; they have one ear, one eye, one breath (details that underscore their unity), and their "food and ink" is power from the Trinity.[11] Pordage's treatise thus leads us from the initial vision and cosmology, through the transmuting power of Sophia, into the angelic heavenly realm itself.

The clues that are given in Pordage's treatises in English are developed further in his other books. Pordage's *Sophia* offers many details of his experiential knowledge of Sophianic revelation in a journal form, dated June 21 to July 10, in twenty-two chapters. Pordage begins by explaining the nature of Sophia, or Divine Wisdom, as well as of the Light World, and the soul's hunger and thirst for spiritual truth. He discusses the meaning of the Biblical references to the creation of a "new

---

9. Ibid., 31.
10. Ibid., 37.
11. Ibid., 87 and 92.

heaven and a new earth"; of the harmony of this world below and that above; of the Paradisical Eden in the Soul; and of the Quintessence or Elixir of Life. Pordage explains that the Holy Virgin reveals the New Jerusalem in the heart and soul of the newly reborn man, and discusses in detail the way that the contemplative process unfolds inwardly as a Sophianic revelation and creation in this life of the "magical earth" one can inhabit posthumously.

The treatise *Sophia* could be compared to the work of the twentieth-century author Henry Corbin, who wrote at length and insightfully about Sufi and Isma'ili mysticism, and in particular about the *mundus imaginalis*, or the "imaginal world" that is encountered by the visionary as manifesting in an "external" form the inner life and transmutation of the individual mystic. In other words, one can encounter in an imaginal world (a world of spiritual images and vision) one's own self-transcendence manifesting in visionary form, which later may be related in a spiritual narrative form.

At this point, it is worthwhile noting that in a short work, a "Treatise on the Philosopher's Stone," Pordage discusses an inner contemplative process from a different angle, that of spiritual alchemy. In this treatise, he draws on alchemical terminology and process in order to explain the process in which one purifies one's wrathful energies, awakens love, and transmutes one's fallen nature into its transcendent form. Fallen humanity is under the influence of Mars and Venus, or anger and lust (emotional attraction and repulsion rooted in selfishness).[12] But the contemplative individual moves through the different planetary energies, the feminine planets softening the wrathful male ones, until the process culminates in the "milk and blood of the Virgin," the "Pearl of the Virgin," and ultimately in the unity and harmony of the planetary qualities within the individual, who is suffused with spiritual light. The treatise ends with the "Pearl of the Virgin," which symbolizes purity and Sophianic illumination.

This treatise outlines a path of regeneration in which the individual soul is transmuted by stages through a process symbolized by the planets, and in particular by the "female" planets, the Moon and Venus, which temper the harshness of "male" planets like Mars and Saturn. What's more, the process is symbolized by the gestation, birth, and development of a spiritual child. The symbolism throughout the alchemical treatise turns on the vital importance of the divine feminine joined with the divine masculine through a process of transmutation

---

12. John Pordage, *Ein gründlich philosophisch Sendschreiben*, 7.

both psychological and spiritual. What it offers are keys to the actual process of Sophianic mysticism.

More clues to the nature of the contemplative process are offered in the early sections of *Sophia*. Whereas in his letter on the philosopher's stone Pordage offers a sequential process expressed in symbolic terms, in *Sophia* he offers clues concerning the contemplative inner life. Early on, Pordage writes that the contemplative may often search above or elsewhere to find the Wisdom of God and divine revelation and be caught up in various belief-structures, but eventually the wise learn not to struggle to ascend but rather to allow themselves to "sink" or settle into their own inner Ground. When they do this, then the hidden door of Sophia opens for them, and they experience peace, and the Virgin Sophia appears to them. They then experience the *Abgrund* or *Chaos* in and of which Sophia can create the "new paradise" of a new inner earth.[13] Much of the book centers on the creation and meaning of the hidden new earth that is created or revealed inwardly by and through the power of Sophia.

In *Sophia*, which is arranged in the form of a daily spiritual memoir, Pordage emphasizes that through Sophia is awakened in the contemplative an inner "magical earth" that should not be understood as a mere shadow or copy of this physical world, but rather as a paradisal world with its own materiality and its own nature. It is a "principium" whose limits only God knows and that is accessible anywhere in this earthly world. But this independent magical earth is not comprehensible by "stumplike" or truncated reason; it is not accessible through ratiocination or calculation, and indeed Pordage goes so far as to say that one should not broach its existence with those who belong to the schools or academies of the modern world, because they cannot comprehend it. It is only comprehensible through a different faculty, the inner eye of the contemplative, to which we all have access in addition to our faculty of reason.

Pordage goes on to ask how this inner paradisal world came into being, and he answers that it comes into being through the Trinity along with the creative power of the Holy Sophia, the divine mirror through whom (through Wisdom) creation takes place. Thus, in effect, the Sophianic world of the magical earth, replete with paradisal plants and beings, is the world that came into being before the Fall of man, before the emergence of evil and discord; it is closer to eternity than our mutable world, and exists with its own kind of spiritual materiality. He then

13. John Pordage, *Sophia: das ist die holdseelige ewige Jungfrau der Göttlichen Weisheit* (Amsterdam, 1699), 2–3.

goes on to outline how our posthumous destiny should not be understood as a bifurcation into heaven and hell as the only possibilities, because those who enter heaven must be spotless, and very few answer to that description. But, in fact, drawing on the verse that "in my Father's house are many dwellings" Pordage explains that there are many posthumous possibilities that can manifest in the magical earth, which is a paradise of love, light, and joy.

Pordage also discusses how individual souls may suffer after death, because there also is a "dark magical fire" that came into being with the Fall of the angels. This is a realm of suffering, and it too has its dwellers, but they are those who sucked its principle into themselves and rendered themselves suited to that dark and wrathful world of suffering. Hence it becomes clear that, for Pordage, posthumous destiny is not so much determined by an outside judge or being as by we ourselves, who can come into a paradisal realm with which we are already familiar during life—or we can make our own lives ones of wrath, evil, anxiety, and suffering, which then is what will greet us in eternity after death.

Thus we can see that in *Sophia* Pordage provides something more than a treatise of visionary experiences or narratives. What he is offering, rather, is a sketch of how it is possible in this short human life to open one's eye that sees into eternity, and in so doing experience for ourselves the paradisal earth that after death offers us a "dwelling" in eternity that allows us to grow further spiritually and become transmuted. In other words, Pordage's work offers a radically different kind of Christianity than that with which most of us are familiar. It is a Christianity of the inner life and as such is actually closer to meditative and experiential traditions like those of Tibetan Buddhism than to those forms of Christianity that insist on adherence to dogmatic assertions that are not informed by mystical experience.

There are several aspects of Pordage's work that we should remark upon here. First, Pordage's work, and particularly his Sophianic works, must be understood in the context of Boehme's baroque works. Of course Pordage was his own man; he was not copying Boehme, but rather set out as a visionary into the realms introduced by Boehme, writing from his own direct observation and with hardly any mention of his great predecessor. Pordage was himself a mystic, and his books should be understood as visionary records, not as theological or even philosophical, if one is using those terms in the modern academic sense. And second, Pordage's Sophia exists in a much larger metaphysical context without which her presence and purpose cannot be understood.

This larger metaphysical context can be understood best through Platonic mysticism. As I demonstrated in *Mysticism* (2015), Platonic

mysticism is the line that runs through Western mysticism from Dionysius the Areopagite through Meister Eckhart and many others, right
into the modern period. At the heart of this tradition are the *via nega-
tiva*, or apophatic way of transcendence, and the *via positiva*, or the
kenophatic way that goes through images that reveal the divine nature.
Both of these are represented in the tradition of Boehmean mysticism
that Pordage so well represents. The apophatic heart of mysticism is
expressed by Boehme as the *Nichts*, or the Nothing, which expresses
itself in existence through the *Ungrund* out of which being comes, in
whose nature the divine is reflected as in a mirror as Sophia, the divine
feminine. Sophia thus also is the guide that can bring us back toward
the transcendence that is ultimately beyond being, because her splendor
is the divine splendor, but perceptible to humans who make themselves
worthy of it through contemplative praxis.

It is true that Pordage is not a Platonist in any strict or perhaps even
loose sense, yet his work can be better understood by reference to this
tradition. For Platonism recognizes that there is no contradiction
between the apophatic and the kenophatic ways, that between we
humans here in the material world and pure transcendence there are
other realms and beings that allow us to participate in those eternities,
that are "in between" the physical realm and the *Nichts* or transcendent
divine No-thing. Thus, just as in Platonism the soul is understood to
move toward realization of the transcendent through theurgic contact
with the gods or higher beings and realms, so too in Pordage's Christian
mysticism one can through vision experience eternal realms and their
simpler and purer intelligences.

We need to understand that, for Pordage, what he sees in vision (and
he is clear about this) possesses a kind of spiritual corporeality of its
own; there are bodies, and realms within which they exist. This spiritual
corporeality is timeless by comparison to the material cosmos in which
humans exist, and it can be blissful in ways that we also cannot fully
comprehend without directly experiencing it. And this is in-between
the physical world with which we are familiar and pure transcendence
that is entirely beyond subject and object. Here, subject and object are
not separate, which is why Pordage can narrate what the experience of a
"simplified spirit" is: because he participates in it.

It is also important to recognize that Pordage sees—and to some
extent participates in—these transcendent realms because he has
undergone a process that makes it possible; and here we need to outline
what that process is. It cannot be reduced to the psychological, although
it certainly does have psychological aspects. He indicates, in his treatise
on the philosophical stone, the nature of this process as entailing an

alchemical union of male and female principles, in which the female (Sophianic) aspect has an essential role. This alchemical process is one in which the divine couple pass through a series of stages, symbolically represented by the planets and their traditional characteristics. These stages represent an inner transmutation whereby the two realize their fundamental unity represented by the figure of Sophia, divine Wisdom.

But that is primarily a symbolic expression of the inner contemplative process. In *Sophia*, on the other hand, Pordage offers a different window on aspects of contemplative practice. Here, the focus is on how by engaging in contemplative praxis in this life, that process—because it takes place in eternity—essentially reveals the light-body and "magical earth" in which one lives posthumously in inexpressible joy. Pordage offers again clues to how one realizes this inner life (allowing one's consciousness to "sink" rather than struggle to achieve something or to go somewhere or to grasp some belief system). And again, as in Pordage's treatises in English, we see that the process entails also the opening of the eye of the heart, that is, the eye in us that sees into eternity. However, paramount in *Sophia* is what we may term the metaphysics of our afterlife, the nature of paradise, and how we may enter into it.

Pordage's work, taken as a whole, is one of the more remarkable collections of specific contemplative symbolic "maps" in the entire Christian tradition. He offers instructions on opening the "eye in the heart," a clear symbolic alchemical process, and a developed cosmology and metaphysics of the light-body and the afterlife in paradise (or other posthumous destinations) that, taken together, are uniquely detailed—even in the Boehmean tradition. In many respects, what Pordage outlines in *Sophia* presents parallels to the Buddhist traditions of the Pure Land, that is, paradisal realms into which one can enter after death and continue to awaken. Pordage is deeply Christian, of course, and I am not suggesting otherwise. But what he offers is a Sophianic cosmology and metaphysics that undoubtedly call for more and deeper investigation by both scholars and contemplative practitioners.

In the contemplative processes that Pordage describes, the figure of Sophia or Divine Wisdom is absolutely crucial. Just as creation came about through Sophia, that is, through the divine mirror, so too inward contemplative praxis in Pordage's work has a Sophianic and active dimension. One comes to know Sophia through contemplative "sinking" of the consciousness, quieting and opening oneself to her; but one is also, in knowing Sophia, as Pordage makes clear, enabling the revelation of a new inner creative activity that has all manner of implications for one's afterlife. The Sophianic contemplative process is the awakening of the eye that sees, and the realization of the light-body that participates in eternity, that is, beyond time and space. Thus Sophia, for Pordage, is crucial to awakening to what can indeed be accurately described as eternal life, or life in eternity, or timeless life. Sophianic wisdom is, in the end, perhaps best described neither as outside nor inside us, but as neither and both at once. Sophia, for Pordage, provides nothing less than guidance to and through the door to eternity.

New Organs of Perception:
Goethean Science
as a Cultural Therapeutics

Brent Dean Robbins

The human being knows himself only insofar as he knows the world; he perceives the world only in himself, and himself only in the world. Every new object, clearly seen, opens up a new organ of perception in us.
Johann Wolfgang von Goethe

MOST OF US are familiar with Goethe the poet, but Goethe's approach to natural science is far less known. His work has nevertheless been the subject of some serious scholarship in the history and philosophy of science. Among those who have commented on Goethe's scientific endeavors, there are various opinions about how his method of science relates to the project of "modern science." According to Amrine and Zucker, there are generally three assessments of Goethe's science: (1) a few scholars argue that it is not a genuine scientific approach to the investigation of nature; (2) others assert that it was indeed a modern scientific enterprise, which generated legitimate and important interpretations of natural phenomena; and, finally, (3) there are those scholars—in fact, the majority of Goethe scholars—who argue that Goethe's way of science provides a model for a viable alternative to modern science.[1] I join with the scholars in the latter category. I believe Goethe's science is an approach to natural phenomena that addresses many of the problems raised in contemporary philosophy of science. I go a few steps farther in

---

1. Frederick Amrine and Francis J. Zucker, "Goethe's Science: An Alternative *to* Modern Science or *within* It—or No Alternative at All?," in Frederick Amrine and Francis J. Zucker, eds., *Goethe and the Sciences: A Reappraisal* (Boston: D. Reidel Publishing Company, 1987), 373–88.

saying that Goethe's approach to the study of nature provides a method for what I will call a "cultural therapeutics." As a method for a "cultural therapeutics," I shall argue, Goethe's method provides a bridge between the natural sciences, the human sciences, and the humanities.

Cultural Therapeutics

The term "cultural therapeutics" is one I have borrowed from Robert Romanyshyn and Michael Sipiora, both of whom were inspired by J. H. van den Berg's historical phenomenology (metabletics). According to Sipiora, the aim of a cultural therapeutics is to own up to our obligations to that which is unconscious yet continues to claim us in our technological world.[2] It is a matter of making explicit those responses to the world that are covered over or concealed by layers of culture, but which nevertheless continue to call us and which remain accessible only through careful, critically engaged description of phenomena. The process of owning up to our obligations is one that can be a healing process, a process of coming home to ourselves; hence it is "therapeutic."

Goethe's method of science is a form of "cultural therapeutics" because, arguably, it offers not only a different approach to science than modern science, it offers a style of understanding nature that is *therapeutic*. When I say that Goethe offers a "therapeutic" approach to nature, I mean that his process of studying nature is one that is potentially *transformative* for the scientist. It is a *therapeutic* process because it is one that may potentially restore to health and wholeness those who practice it. It is a "cultural therapeutics" because, if it were taken up as a cultural practice and as a cultural worldview, it might be curative and restorative for our entire culture.

Goethe is quite clear about his belief that science should be transformative of the scientist: "The human being knows himself only insofar as he knows the world; he perceives the world only in himself, and himself only in the world. Every new object, clearly seen, opens up a new organ of perception in us."[3] There is no question that, for Goethe, observation has as its aim the development of the observer, who in the process of careful and clear description of the object under investigation is in the

2. Michael Sipiora, "Obligations beyond Competency: Metabletics as a Conscientious Psychology," in The Simon Silverman Phenomenology Center, *Metabletics: J. H. van den Berg's Historical Phenomenology* (Pittsburgh: The Simon Silverman Phenomenology Center, 1999).

3. J. W. von Goethe, *The Collected Works: Scientific Studies, Volume Twelve*, trans. and ed. D. Miller (Princeton, NJ: Princeton University Press, 1988), 39.

process of schooling his or her faculties of observation.[4] Quite literally, he or she is engaged in a process of realizing nascent possibilities for seeing the world anew.

Modern Science and Substantive Rationality

Goethe's approach to science, with its emphasis on the metamorphosis of the scientist, stands in stark contrast to conventional images of science as a means to gain mastery and control over the natural world. The origins of modern science can be traced back at least to Francis Bacon, who asserted that "the secrets of nature reveal themselves more readily under the vexations of art [i.e., artisanry, technology] than when they go their own way."[5] Bacon implies that nature is best understood in conditions when humans attempt to master and control it.[6] Descartes was more explicit when he asserted that, through his practical philosophy as a basis for the sciences, "we could make ourselves the masters and possessors of nature."[7] Newton's physics—which was the prime target of Goethe's criticisms—was founded on Cartesian principles, including Descartes' project of utilizing the sciences for the purpose of prediction and control.

The problem with the "modern science" of Descartes and Newton is not simply their use of prediction and control. The problem is that they set up a science in which prediction and control become ends in themselves. The sociologist Max Weber pointed out that modern society is characterized by the collapse of "substantive rationality" into "formal rationality."[8] Formal rationality refers to "the calculability of means and procedures," whereas substantive rationality refers to "the value (from some explicitly defined standpoint) of ends or results."[9] In other words, modernity can, in part, be characterized by the subordination of *ends*— that is, values—to mere *means*. The means of calculation and procedure becomes *ends in themselves* rather than a *means to* an extrinsic "good."

---

4. See also Frederick Amrine, "The Metamorphosis of the Scientist," in *Goethe's Way of Science: A Phenomenology of Nature*, ed. David Seamon and Arthur Zajonc (Albany, NY: SUNY Press, 1998), 33–54.

5. Aphorism XCVIII in Francis Bacon, *Selected Writings of Francis Bacon*, ed. H.G. Dick (New York: The Modern Library, 1955).

6. See also Morris Berman, *The Reenchantment of the World* (Ithaca & London: Cornell University Press, 1981).

7. Rene Descartes, *Essential Works of Descartes*, trans. L. Blair (New York: Bantam, 1961), 37.

8. Max Weber, *Economy and Society, Volume 2*, ed. R. Roth and C. Witich (Berkeley: University of California Press, 1978).

9. Rogers Brubaker, *The Limits of Rationality: An Essay on the Social and Moral Thought of Max Weber* (New York: Routledge, 2013), 36.

When prediction and control become ends in themselves rather than means to some other purpose or goal, this means substantive rationality has collapsed into formal rationality. When science loses sight of the purpose of its calculations, and when calculation becomes an end in itself, then science becomes monstrous. It begets the atom bomb and ecological catastrophe. In general, we get an unsustainable technological culture which becomes highly efficient at destroying the earth—and ourselves along with it—in a very short time period.

The Alien in the Machine

The worldview of Descartes and Newton, moreover, is one based on a variety of assumptions that largely remain with us today. Arguably, the most important of these assumptions is the Cartesian view of the universe as a machine separate from the souls of humans, who Descartes thought were distinct from the mechanisms of the world. Descartes's mechanistic view depicts a world in which the human is alien rather than a participant. The universe, like a machine, is understood in an atomistic fashion, through the breakdown of its various parts and through an understanding of the relationship among these parts. Also, the Cartesian-Newtonian view understands the world through a veil of mathematics. The world of human perception is understood to be largely untrustworthy. The truth of the world is discovered not by the qualitative experience of the human, but through the quantitative analysis of phenomena in artificial, experimental conditions that are designed to isolate variables in order to determine cause-and-effect relations. The identification of these cause-and-effect relations, again, serves the purpose of prediction and control.

The discoveries of Newton's science have come to "rape the senses," so that the world that they produce is one that is largely at odds with the world we live as humans. The abstractions of Newton's physics come to replace the concrete experience of our immediate contact with the world. The experience of color, for example, comes to be understood as epiphenomenal—a mere product of the human mind—while the abstract concept of light waves, which we do not directly experience, comes to be the scientific "truth" of color. When there are protests that the modern sciences fail to do justice to immediate experience of the world, the modern scientist asserts that our immediate experience of the world is illusory—that, in effect, it fails to predict and control—and reasserts the value of the Cartesian-Newtonian paradigm as one that produces "truth" in the form of utility. It performs, in other words, what philosophers have come to call "reductionism": it comes to explain the world of human experience by "reducing" its meaning to causal events "behind" the phenomena. For example, what you see are colors, but, in reality, there are "nothing but" waves of light. Reductionism, in this sense, is the disease of "nothing-but-ness." "Nothing-but-ness" is another term for nihilism.[10]

The project of modern science is one that claims it is seeking to discover the truth of a human-independent or human-transcendent world, an "objective" world that exists outside of "subjective" human concerns. Yet, in fact, the worldview of modern science is not "objective," but a peculiar, historically contingent style of seeing the world.[11] It is a world that comes to be increasingly disclosed through a veil of abstractions. For example, content analysis of scientific journals has found that the only variable that distinguishes the supposedly "hard" sciences from the "soft" sciences is the relatively more frequent use of graphs in "hard" science journals.[12] What is remarkable about this trend is the fact that the observation of graphic depictions of a quantified nature has come to replace the direct and immediate observation of the phenomena of nature itself. The map has become increasingly confused with the countryside. As Werner Heisenberg noted, "science sacrifices more and more the possibility of making 'living' the phenomena immediately perceptible to our senses.... [W]e must admit that a blind man may learn and understand the whole of optics and yet he will have not the faintest knowledge of real light."[13] Of course, if we look closely at what the products of modern science depict, they of course depict graphic representations of the causal relationships between objectified and reified units of natural phenomena. In other words, they serve in the project of prediction and control.

Modern psychological science belongs in the tradition of Newton's physics. Like Newton's view of nature, it tends to depict the human being as a mechanism determined by causal forces both within and outside of its organism. In contrast to Descartes, who saw the human soul as distinct from the mechanics of nature, modern psychology rejects the notion of an immaterial soul and injects the human into the Cartesian

10. Viktor Frankl, *Man's Search for Meaning* (New York: Pocket, 1997).

11. See Berman, *The Reenchantment of the World*, as well as two works by Robert D. Romanyshyn, *Technology as Symptom and Dream* (New York: Routledge, 1990) and *Mirror and Metaphor: Images and Stories of Psychological Life* (Pittsburgh: Trivium, 2001).

12. See L.D. Smith, L.A. Best, D.A. Stubbs, A.B. Archibald, and R. Roberson-Nay, "Constructing Knowledge: The Role of Graphs and Tables in Hard and Soft Psychology," *American Psychologist* 57, No. 10 (2002): 749–61.

13. Werner Heisenberg, *Philosophical Problems of Quantum Physics* (Woodbridge, CT: Ox Bow Press, 1979), 36–37.

machine. Thus, when psychologists speak of human values, such as morality or aesthetics, these values are understood to be epiphenomenal—that is, "nothing but" the product of external or internal causal forces. As phenomenologists such as Husserl and Merleau-Ponty have noted, the deterministic view of modern psychology is philosophically untenable, because such a position undermines its own foundations: the very assertion of determinism would not be a reason for human behavior but rather the result of causal forces indifferent to human concerns, including concerns about the reasons for human behavior.[14] If we start from such a deterministic position, the inevitable result is the problem Weber announced: the reduction of the ends of science (substantive rationality) to mere means (instrumental rationality): prediction and control for the sake of prediction and control, with no extrinsic meaning or purpose.

Goethe's Antidote

Goethe's approach to science is an antidote to the resultant nihilism of modern science. The horizon of Goethe's method is one of a participatory stance with regard to nature. His science begins with the assumption that the human being is fundamentally at home in the world. The cosmos is a space of belonging. Goethe's worldview, in this sense, shares an affinity to the contemporary movement of Deep Ecology, where the self is "experienced as integrated with the whole of nature."[15] The self is acknowledged as the "the world knowing itself." As Joanna Macy (1991) celebrates: "We can relinquish our separateness. We can come home again—and participate in our world in a richer, more responsible and poignantly beautiful way."[16] As a participatory approach to nature, Goethe's method stresses that the process of scientific investigation should be a matter of becoming increasingly "at home" with the phenomena.[17]

Goethe's participatory approach to nature is one that is rooted in a sense of nature as sacred. By "sacred," I join with Peter Reason in his

14. Maurice Merleau-Ponty, *Phenomenology of Perception*, trans. C. Smith (London: Routledge and Kegan Paul, 1962).

15. Bill Devall and George Sessions, "The Development of Natural Resources and the Integrity of Nature," *Environmental Ethics* 6 (1984): 302–03.

16. Joanna Macy, *World as Lover, World as Self* (Berkeley: Parallax Press, 1991), 14. See also R.S. Gottlieb, "Ethics and Trauma: Levinas, Feminism, and Deep Ecology," *Cross Currents* 44, No. 2 (1994): 222–40.

17. David Seamon, "Goethe, Nature and Phenomenology: An Introduction," in *Goethe's Way of Science*, 1–14, at 3.

description of sacred inquiry as one that is "based on reverence, in awe and love for creation, valuing it for its own sake, in its own right as a living presence."[18] Sacred inquiry, according to Reason, involves four aspects: 1) giving primacy to experience as sacred, 2) using representations of that experience in such a way that it brings beauty, 3) developing understandings of that experience that are not alienated, and 4) initiating action and forms of engagement that heal ourselves and our planet. Goethe's approach to science includes each of these aspects and so can be considered a form of sacred inquiry. Goethe affirms his perspective of nature as sacred when he asserts that: "Natural objects should be sought and investigated as they are and not to suit observers, but respectfully as if they were divine beings."[19]

Goethe calls his style of sacred inquiry a "delicate empiricism" (*zarte Empirie*), which he contrasts with "the gloom of the empirico-mechanico-dogmatic torture chamber" of Newton's science.[20] There are at least two aspects to Goethe's notion of a "delicate empiricism." First, it is an "empiricism" in the sense that it gives primacy to perception. Secondly, Goethe's empiricism is "delicate" to the extent that it gives itself over to an ethically responsive obligation to the observed.

The Primacy of Perception

Goethe's science grants a "primacy to perception" in the same sense as phenomenology.[21] As Merleau-Ponty wrote, "All consciousness is perceptual. . . . The perceived world is the always presupposed foundation of all rationality, all value and all existence."[22] Consciousness, in this sense, is not an interior realm of meaning, but rather the life-world that surrounds us and sustains us. Consciousness, from the phenomenological perspective, is always "turned primarily toward the world, turned toward things; it is above all a relation to the world."[23] As Gurwitsch notes, "We do not, so to speak, move within a self-contained domain of interiority"; rather, "It is the thing itself that presents itself . . . and with

18. Peter Reason, "Reflections on Sacred Experience and Sacred Science," *Journal of Management Inquiry* 2, No. 3 (1993): 273–83, at 276.

19. J.W. von Goethe, "Cautions for the Observer," in *Goethe's Color Theory*, ed. R. Matthaei (New York: Van Nostrand Reinhold, 1971), 57.

20. Quoted in Erich Heller, *The Disinherited Mind: Essays in Modern German Literature and Thought* (Cambridge: Bowes and Bowes, 1952), 18.

21. Herbert Hensel, "Goethe, Science, and Sensory Experience," in *Goethe's Way of Science*, 71–82.

22. Maurice Merleau-Ponty, *Phenomenology of Perception*, 13.

23. Maurice Merleau-Ponty, *Phenomenology of Perception*, 116–17.

which we are in contact." [24] These sentiments of Merleau-Ponty and Gurwitsch repeat a theme of Goethe's: that, in essence, human perception is not an impediment to scientific investigation but is always already presupposed in every empirical observation. There is no such science capable of rendering nature separate from its own intentionality, that is, its constructions. And, yet, we are not locked in upon ourselves as solipsism would have it; rather, we are in direct, fleshy contact with things of this world and, indeed, have our being only through our intertwining relations with other beings, each of us sustained by the founding soil of the earth.

Because we become who we are in our essence through our relations with the surrounding world and its beings—and, indeed, because our bodies are formed of and by this encompassing earth—our organs can be understood to be the flesh of the world emerging into consciousness of itself, like an infant examining for the first time the back of her own hand and gaining sudden insight that the flailing limb is her own. And so in a certain manner of speaking the beauties of nature which appear through perception—the colors of the rainbow, the pungent scent of the forest after a spring rain, awe before natural disasters and the endless expanse of darkness receding infinitely into the depths of the night sky—are not merely "subjective" phenomena; they are of nature because we are of nature, and they exist only in a relation between the vacancy of consciousness and the plenitude of being. They are gifts of the natural world to itself. And they may even be gratuitous gifts, without reason or purpose beyond the immediate enjoyment and inspiration they engender. Indeed, these meanings cannot be reduced to simpler or more fundamental phenomena—say, atoms or genes—without losing their essence as relational phenomena constituted in the intertwining of nature upon nature in the coming-to-awareness of itself.

In the investigation of color, we do violence to the meaning of color when we consider it epiphenomenal and reduce its ontological meaning to the by-product of something behind the phenomena. "The blue of the sky reveals to us the basic law of color," writes Goethe. "Search nothing beyond the phenomena, they themselves are the theory."[25] When I see the color green, the meaning of the color green is immediate to my perception, and any conceptualization of the color green beyond that perception is not that color precisely *as* it appears within my life-world.

24. Aron Gurwitsch, *Phenomenology and the Theory of Science* (Chicago: Northwestern University Press, 1974), 243 and 236.
25. J.W. von Goethe, "Cautions for the Observer," 76.

Thus, Goethe asserts, in a variety of ways, that science must be based upon a fundamental faith in experience. "The human being himself, to the extent that he makes use of his senses," writes Goethe, "is the most exact physical apparatus that can exist."[26] Elsewhere, he asserts that "We are adequately equipped for all our genuine earthly needs if we will trust our senses, and develop them in such a way that they continue to prove worthy of our confidence."[27] The senses do not deceive us, he argued, judgment does.[28]

To say that Goethe's "delicate empiricism" gives primacy to perception is not to say, however, that the object of investigation will give itself over to us all at once. For Goethe, nature is always in the process of becoming (*natura naturans*) and never a finished product (*natura naturata*).[29] Yet the becoming of nature is a process that cannot be reached only through ideas or mathematical abstractions; it can only be reached by careful observation and, in particular, observation that utilizes what Goethe termed "exact sensorial imagination." The method of "exact sensorial imagination" when observing a phenomenon is a matter of retaining past forms of the phenomenon while anticipating the forms the phenomenon will likely take as it unfolds into the future. It is, in other words, a matter of grasping the temporal structure of the phenomena. Indeed, the method of "exact sensorial imagination" is actually a refinement of the natural process of perception, which is always already infused with memory and the imaginative projection of future possibilities. As Arnheim noted, "Perception turns out to be not a mechanical recording of the stimuli imposed by the physical world upon the receptor organs of man and animal, but the eminently active and creative grasping of structure."[30] By refining our natural predilection for sensorial imagination, Goethe makes it an *exact* sensorial imagination, a move which elevates his "delicate empiricism" to the precision necessary for it to be a science.

The structure grasped by the "exact sensorial imagination" leads eventually to an insight (*aperçu*) into the essential structure of the phenomenon, which Goethe called *the Ur-phenomenon*: "an ultimate which can not itself be explained, which is in fact not in need of explanation,

---

26. J. W. von Goethe, *The Collected Works: Scientific Studies, Volume Twelve*, 311.

27. Quoted in Amrine, "The Metamorphosis of the Scientist," 45.

28. Hensel, "Goethe, Science, and Sensory Experience," 74.

29. Amrine and Zucker, "Goethe's Science," 373–88, at 382.

30. Rudolf Arnheim, *New Essays on the Psychology of Art* (Berkeley: University of California Press, 1986), x.

but from which all that we observe can be made intelligible."[31] When Goethe studied plants, for example, he would examine the plants from the time they were a seedling until they matured. He would also examine them in different contexts. Taking each of these perspectives into consideration, he aimed to disclose the *archetype* of the plant. Grasping the archetype of a plant, as Goethe did in his examination of plant morphology, is not unlike grasping the essential structure of a musical score. A musical score can be produced with great variation: it can be played upon different instruments, at soft or loud volumes, in different settings with different acoustics, introducing various forms of reverberation and echo, and so forth. Yet, amongst all these variations, the musical composition maintains a certain structural necessity, a necessity that would be disturbed if notes were omitted, added or rearranged. Likewise, a plant can be introduced into various environments, but the temporal unfolding of the plant maintains a certain structural necessity—a structure that can only be grasped through careful, meticulous observation of the plant over time and in different environmental conditions.

Goethe's notion of the *Ur-phenomenon* challenges one of the earliest and most fundamental claims of Western metaphysics, namely, Aristotle's claim that actuality is metaphysically prior to possibility. Aristotle's metaphysics, retained in this aspect in the science of Newton, is based on the idea that nature is a standing presence or composed of discrete, isolated and determinate objects. However, as in the existential-phenomenological philosophy of Heidegger, Goethe's *Ur-phenomenon* implies that the phenomenon is an event or happening, a process of becoming, in which actuality and possibility are fused and gathered by the thing as it is revealed to the perceiver within the context of the life-world.[32]

The Cartesian-Newtonian worldview is completely closed off to the experience of the *Ur-phenomenon*. Instead, it remains fixated upon a world abstractly conceived to be composed of discrete, extrinsically related objects, the meanings of which are reducible to the determining forces of prior causal effects. Beginning with such a conception of the world forecloses the possibility of grasping the essential structure of the phenomenon. Such conception relies upon a kind of "judgment" which has distanced itself from the phenomena as they appear in their most immediate contact with us through our participatory engagement with

31. Ernst Lehrs, *Man or Matter: Introduction to a Spiritual Understanding of Matter Based on Goethe's Method of Training, Observation and Thought* (London: Faber & Faber, 1958), 125.

32. Martin Heidegger, *Being and Time*, trans. John Macquarrie and Edward Robinson (New York: Harper and Row, 1962).

them. Yet, when we attend to the phenomena with a fidelity to their givenness to us in our most immediate contact with them, they appear fundamentally as a process of unfolding; a temporal, emergent event which we can honor best through our imaginative capacity to retain past forms and project them into the future. At the best of times such a close attunement to the fidelity of things, and our relation with them, can produce in us a kind of genuine, deeply felt pleasure—the kind of experience common to encounters with the aesthetic.

For the Goethe, the disclosure of the primordial archetype of the phenomenon is fundamentally an aesthetic experience. As Goethe writes:

> The archetypal plant shall be the most marvelous creature in the world, and nature shall envy me for it. With this model and the key to it one can invent plants *ad infinitum* that must be consistent, i.e., that could exist even if they do not in fact, are not just picturesque shadows, but have instead an inner truth and necessity.[33]

In this passage, Goethe expresses his experience of the archetype's profound beauty. The beauty of the archetypal phenomenon can be understood in light of Rudolf Arnheim's theory of aesthetics. The perception of beauty, for Arnheim, is the result of the interaction of two tendencies in the perception of form: on the one hand, a "tendency toward tension-increasing articulation," and, on the other, a "countertendency toward equilibration."[34] The experience of beauty occurs when the meaning of a phenomenon is revealed so that there is a perfect balance between tension reduction and tension enhancement.[35] The Goethean *Ur-phenomenon* is the ideal of beauty in that it reduces tension through its depiction of the essential, harmonious simplicity of a phenomenon as pure possibility while enhancing tension by virtue of its rootedness in the actual, concrete and conditioned nature of the phenomenon in all its particular manifestations. For example, the archetypal plant is the essential structure of all possible plants, and yet this essential structure can only ever be realized in the concrete, individual form of any given plant.

The scientist is transformed through the process of disclosing the archetypal structure of the phenomenon. Indeed, as Amrine notes, the process of Goethean science "is more important than the end result. Experiments must be concentrated, ongoing experiences through which

---

33. Quoted in Amrine, "The Metamorphosis of the Scientist," 39–40.

34. Rudolf Arnheim, "The Two Faces of Gestalt Psychology," *American Psychologist* 41 (1986): 820–24, at 822.

35. Arnheim, "The Two Faces of Gestalt Psychology," 823.

one learns new ways of seeing."[36] Indeed, we are given "new organs of perception." In this sense, Goethean science is closer to the humanities than to Newtonian science. Whereas the Newtonian worldview attempts to "empower what we already are," Goethe provides a means of investigation which permits us to "grow beyond ourselves."[37]

Ethically Responsive Obligation to the Observed

When we open ourselves to become transformed by the phenomenon, then we also enact the second aspect of Goethe's "delicate empiricism." We develop the capacity to become *ethically responsive* to our obligations to the observed. As Shotter has asserted:

> To ignore our own, initial, responsive relations to living phenomena in our inquiries into their nature is to cut ourselves off from the very spontaneous calls and invitations they exert upon us in *their* way of coming-into-being—and thus to deny ourselves the kind of knowledge we need if we are to answer their calls in ways that "they can understand," that are appropriate to *their* nature.[38]

Shotter refers to Goethe's method as a "relationally-responsive understanding," which he contrasts with the "referential-representational understanding" of Descartes and Newton. With a "referential-representational" approach to phenomena, we act as if we are separate from the world, as if we are not called or claimed by the objects of our study, and as if we were not therefore obligated to the phenomena under our investigation. With a "relationally-responsive" attitude, on the contrary, we stay closely attuned to the way the phenomena claim us. When we allow ourselves to be claimed by phenomena, we open ourselves to feel our relational obligation to them. In other words, we become morally engaged with them. Indeed, when we spend time in deep contemplation of the structure of a plant, for instance, we come to appreciate the plant as an end in itself rather than a mere means. We come to better understand ways that we can live harmoniously with the plant. We sensitize ourselves to actions that may violate the value of the plant. And through the wisdom we gain, we create a space not only to improve our own lot, but also ways to improve the plant, which we come to understand as an

---

36. Amrine, "The Metamorphosis of the Scientist," 42.

37. R.H. Brady, "The Idea in Nature: Rereading Goethe's Organics," in *Goethe's Way of Science*, 83–114, at 109.

38. John Shotter, "Seeing Historically: Goethe and Vygotsky's 'Enabling Theory-Method," *Culture and Psychology* 6, No. 2 (2000): 233–52, at 242.

extension of our own existence, indeed, as part of the ground of being that sustains us.

Goethean Science as a Cultural Therapeutics

Clearly, Goethe has given us a powerful method to carry out what I defined above as a "cultural therapeutics." Whether we realize it or not, we continue to be claimed by the natural world around us, but, for a variety of reasons, we are often unconscious of the claims the natural world makes on us. To the extent they remain unconscious, we run the risk of failing to respond to our obligations to the natural world. In our technological world, the call of the natural world can get drowned out by the abstract theoretical concepts that have increasingly come to replace our receptivity to the concrete claims of the phenomena that compose our life-world. Through formal education, we learn to ignore our immediate perception of the world, and we come to forget how to remain relationally-responsive to things. Yet, Goethe provides us with a concrete practice for cultivating the "organs of perception" we will need in order to heal ourselves and the planet.

In contrast to the Cartesian-Newtonian worldview, arguably a symptom of our cultural illness, Goethe offers a viable alternative. In place of an alienated consciousness, he grants us a vision of ourselves "at home" and belonging with the things of the natural world. In contrast to an approach to science that creates a chasm between the world of our conceptions and the world of our perceptions, Goethe offers us a science that gives a primacy to the meaningful world given to our senses. In place of a universe conceptualized abstractly as a vast machine, Goethe offers a more intuitively satisfying description of the world as a vast organism which is constantly in the process of becoming, a process in which we participate and disclose through our careful observation. Through that careful observation, we also come to understand a world composed of beauty which obliges us to moral action to protect and care for it. And, finally, Goethe offers us a way out of the implicit nihilism that results from the collapse of substantive rationality into instrumental rationality. Goethe's method aims not merely to predict and control, but has its end, rather, in the aesthetic and morally responsive obligation to the observed.

These aspects of Goethean science close the gap between natural science and the humanities since both come to share the tasks of schooling our faculties of observation and cultivating wisdom. The natural sciences and the human sciences become united in Goethean science because the observation of nature is always also a process of self-discovery. Through that process of self-discovery, we may come to better realize more sustainable practices of living with nature and with each other. As a cultural therapeutics, Goethean science is an interdisciplinary affair.

Russian Sophiology

Robert F. Slesinski

THE FACT that there is a qualifier to this chapter title indicates that sophiology as a topic is not specifically Russian, but enjoys a wider basis in intellectual circles in the historical domain. This is, indeed, the case.[1] Nonetheless, the chief luminaries and propagators of sophiology were Russians, Vladimir Sergeyevich Solovyov (1853–1900) being not only the first Russian systematic philosopher, but also the founder of the School of Russian Sophiology, his primary and most famous intellectual heirs being the Russian Orthodox priest-philosopher-theologians Pavel Aleksandrovich Florensky (1882–1937) and Sergius Nikolaevich Bulgakov (1871–1944). They were all aware of the writings of Jacob Boehme,[2] but at the same time embarked on their own independent researches. It is this "Russian" stamp on the subject matter at hand that is the focus of the present exposition. The fact that Russian sophiological thought is, indeed, linked to esoteric currents in Western thought has, unfortunately, but not entirely wrongly, held it suspect in ecclesial Orthodox circles, even having it condemned as "heretical," at least in regard to the theological writings of Sergius Bulgakov.[3] As for Solovyov himself, the learned judgment of a sympathetic Catholic theologian, Hans Urs von Balthasar (1905–1988), bears noting:

> But because in reading all these [Western esotericists enamored of Sophia] and many others he fully appropriates them for himself, the muddy stream runs through him as if through a purifying agent and is distilled in crystal-clear, disinfected waters, answering the need of his

---

1. One need only think of the esoteric-mystical writings of the Silesian Lutheran Jacob Boehme (ca. 1575–1624), the "Western Father," as it were, "of sophiology," along with other notables as Johann Wolfgang von Goethe (1749–1832) and Rudolf Steiner (1861–1925), among others, not to mention the influence of the Jewish Kabbalah. For an expansive discussion of this matter, see Michael Martin, *The Submerged Reality: Sophiology and the Turn to a Poetic Metaphysics* (Kettering, OH: Angelico Press, 2015).

2. See Zdenek V. David, "The Influence of Jacob Boehme on Russian Religious Thought," *Slavic Review* 21 (1962): 43–64.

own philosophical spirit, which (in contrast to that of so many of his speculative compatriots) can live and breathe only in an atmosphere of unqualified transparency and intelligibility.[4]

His positive assessment only continues:

Soloviev lived in an habitual state of "baptized Eros" directed toward Sophia. His only desire was to see all things in her light; not only relations with the individual human "Thou," but also relations with human society and this cosmos in general must be "a living relationship of syzygy."[5]

"This Sophia," von Balthasar perceptively remarks, "is Soloviev's 'immortal beloved,'"[6] as intimated in his poems, especially in his late work "Three Encounters," which details his visions of Sophia, first as a child of nine in a Moscow church, then as a young adult at the British Museum in London, and subsequently in the Saharan Desert not far from Cairo.[7]

The poetic accounting of Solovyov's visions of Sophia finds further articulation in his philosophical prose that seeks to justify his fundamental intuition that Divine Wisdom through and through pervades the whole created order, entailing a necessary all-embracing unity at the root of all existence itself. Unfortunately, Solovyov himself never gives a detailed, coherent presentation of his sophiological position, postulat-

---

3. On this matter, see the two decrees of Metropolitan Sergius (Stragorodskii) of Moscow that are respectively dated September 7 and December 27, 1935, issued in brochure format under the title *Ukaz Moskovskoi Patriarkhii preosviashchennomu Mitropolitu Litovskomu i Vilenskomu Elevferiiu* (Decree of the Moscow Patriarchate to the Most Reverend Eleutherius of Vilna and Lithuania). Most important is Bulgakov's response to his own bishop at the time, Metropolitan Evlogii of Paris, who came to Bulgakov's defense. See *Dokladnaia zapiska Mitropolitu Evlogiiu po povodu opredeleniia arkhiereiskogo sobora v Karlovtsakh otnositel'no ucheniia o Sofii Premudrosti Bozhiei* (Memorandum to Metropolitan Evlogii in regard to the determination of the Synod of Bishops in Karlovci concerning the teaching about Sophia, the Wisdom of God) (Paris: YMCA Press, 1936). Cf. also C. Lialine, "Le débat sophiologique," *Irénikon* 13 (1936): 168–205, and V. Losskii, *Spor o Sofii* (The dispute about Sophia) (Paris, 1936).

4. Hans Urs von Balthasar, *The Glory of the Lord: A Theological Aesthetics, Vol. III: Studies in Theological Style: Lay Styles* (San Francisco: Ignatius Press, 1986), 292. For my own treatment of this matter, see "Toward an Understanding of V. S. Solovyov's 'Gnosticism,'" *Diakonia* 31 (1998): 77–88.

5. Ibid., 292ff.

6. Ibid., 292.

7. For a valuable collection of Solovyov's writings on Sophia, see Judith Deutsch Kornblatt, *Divine Sophia: The Wisdom Writings of Vladimir Solovyov* (Ithaca and London: Cornell University Press, 2009). A translation of "Three Encounters" is found in this volume.

ing various theses about Sophia that can leave his reading audience somewhat baffled as to what he is trying to convey. His most extensive elaboration is found in his acclaimed *Lectures on Divine Humanity* (*Chteniia o Bogochelovechestve*) that were attended by the educated elite of Saint Petersburg, including such renowned novelists as Fyodor Dostoevsky and Lev Tolstoy.[8]

Writing between 1877 and 1881, Solovyov sets forth his ideas for a metaphysics of all-embracing unity that can sustain the vital interaction that obtains between the absolute, all-embracing principle that is God and the created order, which includes both humankind and the world itself. In the process, he enlarges upon his two key ideas of *Bogochelovechestvo*, variously translated as "Godmanhood," "Divine humanity," and "the Humanity of God," and Sophia, Divine Wisdom as the prototype of the created wisdom that obtains in the created order in a dynamic process of reintegration with its Eternal Source.[9] An interpolation beyond the explicit Christian dogma of the Incarnation of the Logos in Jesus Christ, the God-Man, the concept of *Bogochelovechestvo* underscores the fact that God is active in humanity, that true communion obtains between God and humankind, and the fact that humanity can come into its own only in God, according to the divine plan. This flowering of humankind finds its fullest expression in the Church, the Body of Christ and supreme exemplification of Sophia on earth.

Characterizing the triadic relation within the Godhead of Father, Son, and Holy Spirit "as being-in-itself, being-for-itself, and being-at-home-with-itself" (*kak v-sebe bytie, dlia-sebia-bytie i u-sebia-bytie*) in his seventh lecture (LDH, 96; SS, 3:103), Solovyov cannot but posit a similar structure in determinate human being that manifests itself in the three human spiritual centers of the will, the mind, and the heart actualized as will, representation, and feeling that enjoy a necessary intentionality directed toward the realization of the good, the true, and the beautiful—all reflective, it must be added, of the absolute goodness, truth, and beauty that is God, constituting, as it were, the all-embracing content or essence of the Divinity. Reduced to inner unity these three transcendentals—goodness, truth, and beauty—are nothing but forms

---

8. See *Sobranie sochinenii*, ed. S.M. Solovyov and E.L. Radlov (Sankt-Peterburg, 1911–14; reprinted with two additional volumes, Bruxelles, 1966–70), 3:1–181. Eng. trans., *Lectures on Divine Humanity*, revised and edited by Boris Jakim (Hudson, NY: Lindisfarne Press, 1995.) Henceforth *SS* and *LDH*, respectively.

9. On this matter and those that will follow see my "Sophiology as a Metaphysics of Creation According to V.S. Solov'ëv," in Wil van den Bercken, Manon de Courten, and Evert van der Zweerde, eds., *Vladimir Solov'ëv: Reconciler and Polemicist* (Leuven: Peeters, 2000), 131–45.

of love.[10] Positings of a single subject, in their interpenetration a new concrete unity is realized. As Solovyov underscores his point, *"the absolute actualizes goodness in beauty, through truth (absoliutnoe osushchestvliaet blago chrez istinu v krasote)."*[11]

Accenting the specifically Christian cast to his argument, Solovyov avers that Christ is "the actualized expression of the absolutely existent God"[12] in the divine organism of Whom "the acting, unifying principle," i.e., unity as a principle in itself, is the Word or Logos, whereas the unity that obtains within Him as a phenomenon or "produced unity" is Sophia, "God's body, the matter of Divinity permeated with the principle of divine unity,"[13] Christ, as the integral divine organism, being both Logos and Sophia. In creation, God speaks his Word, finding its ultimate realization in Christ (the Logos), being the sublime instance of Divine Wisdom (Sophia). In this fashion, all creation partakes of the Logos and Sophia. Summing up his philosophical prose, Solovyov ends his lecture on a poetic note, citing verse from an unnamed poet identified as A. K. Tolstoy:

> That all born of the Word,
> Shedding about the rays of love,
> Yearns to return to Him;
> That every stream of life,
> Subject to love's law,
> Hurries irresistibly to God's bosom by the force of being.
> All is alive with sound, athrob with light,
> And all the worlds have a single principle,
> And there is nothing in nature
> That is not full of love.[14]

In his remaining lectures, Solovyov revisits the theme of Sophia in different contexts, pointing to the wide-range of possibilities in understanding Divine Wisdom in itself and as applied to creation. Thus, in lecture eight, he writes that Sophia as a produced unity is "ideal or perfect humanity, eternally contained in the integral divine being, or Christ"[15] only to venture off on another path in lecture nine, now declaring Sophia to be the "world soul" or "archetypical humankind" occupying "a mediating position between the multiplicity of living enti-

10. *LDH*, 103; *SS*, 3:110.
11. Ibid., 3:111.
12. Ibid., 107; *SS*, 3:114.
13. Ibid., 108; *SS*, 3:115.
14. Ibid., 111; *SS*, 3:118–19.
15. Ibid., 113; *SS*, 3:121.

ties, which constitute the real content of its life, and the absolute unity of Divinity, which is the ideal principle and norm of its life"[16]—only to venture further into murky waters, assigning a defiant will to the world soul, displacing the divine principle with an egotistical one, the root of all evil that can only yield the fruit of suffering.[17] Such a cosmogonic accounting of the evolution of the world and the evil within it is, of course, problematic as it seems to confound spheres, namely, the personal with the impersonal.[18]

Given the polyvalence of the meaning of Sophia in Solovyov's writings, one can well understand the lament of Frederick C. Copleston, S.J., that since sophiology is "in the public domain" it cannot be exempt from "critical examination" and a rational exposition of it should be expected if it is not to be relegated to obscurant esotericism.[19]At the same time, given the complexity of Solovyov's thought, one can readily agree with the more positive assessment of Sergius Bulgakov, namely, that "thanks to the multifaceted nature of his philosophy . . . every person finds *his own* road to him, receives answers to *his own* questions, distinguishes his or her favorite motif within the sonorous chord."[20]

Unlike Solovyov, who grew up in a devoutly Orthodox family, Pavel Florensky was raised in a nonobservant, secular household, the family only observing conventional religious practices. Enthralled by nature, his first religious instincts were admittedly pantheistic in character, but his zeal for truth gradually led him to an express commitment to the Church and religious observance. His magnum opus, *The Pillar and Ground of the Truth*,[21] may well be taken as a sort of an autobiographical study of the stages of his religious conversion. Even in its eclecticism, this hefty and, at times, seemingly unwieldy tome has a clear development of thought, beginning on an epistemological quest, being further given a firm ontological grounding that in short order flowers in sophi-

16. *LDH*, 131; *SS*, 3:140.

17. For the discussion, see *LDH*, 133–34; *SS*, 3:142.

18. In lecture ten, Solovyov expands upon this point, writing that, separated from the divine principle, "the world soul is only an indeterminate tendency toward all-unity, an indeterminate passive possibility (potency) of all-unity" (*LDH*, 136; *SS*, 3:144).

19. Frederick C. Copleston, S.J., *Russian Religious Philosophy: Selected Aspects* (Notre Dame, IN: University of Notre Dame Press, 1988), 81 and 98–99.

20. S. Bulgakov, "Priroda v filosofii Vl. Solov'eva" (Nature in the philosophy of Vl. Solovyov) in *O Vladimire Solov'eve* (Tomsk: Izdatel'stvo "Vodolei," 1997), 6. Also quoted in Kornblatt, 4.

21. *Stolp i utverzhdenie istiny: Opyt pravoslanvoi feoditsei v dvenadtsati pismakh*, Moscow, 1914. Eng. trans. and annotations by Boris Jakim (Princeton: Princeton University Press, 1997). The subtitle of the volume is *An Essay in Orthodox Theodicy in Twelve Letters*. Henceforth, *Stolp* and *PGT*, respectively.

ology. The text, on the other hand, with its *recherché* style, met with stern disapproval in Orthodox circles, the chief opponents being Nicolas Berdyaev and Georges Florovsky, the former bemoaning his "stylized Orthodoxy,"[22] the latter lamenting the fact that Florensky's study "is the book of a Westerner who dreamily and aesthetically seeks salvation in the East."[23] This critical opposition notwithstanding, *The Pillar and Ground of the Truth* has been deemed by other Russian scholars the most characteristic volume of the Russian religious renascence during Russia's Silver Age of cultural flowering.[24]

Florensky notably opens his work postulating "living religious experience as the sole legitimate way to gain knowledge of the dogmas,"[25] thereby framing his epistemological quest in experiential terms, at the same time noting how philosophical inquiry is less a matter of "proving" than of "grasping" ultimate truth as given in a lived contact with reality. For Florensky, one insight is incontrovertible: namely, that the human mind is open to truth and is restless until it grasps it, however gropingly, but in an ever-living and lived fashion, in an unmediated way in contrast to all "schooled," i.e., rationalistic, classifying thought. He aims, in other words, for integral knowledge that arises from the engagement of the human person in his or her cognitive, volitional, and affective faculties *with being* itself. Ultimately, the human person can know truth by entrusting him- or herself to truth, being in constant interaction with being, both as a listening subject and one capable of confiding with the created order that transcends the limitations of the inquiring mind. For Florensky, the human "yes" to being, in the final analysis, cannot but be an *abiding* in truth, in fine, a confiding "yes" to the ultimate source of all being, the Self-Proving Subject that grounds all knowledge and being, the Subject of Truth that "contemplates Itself

22. See his "Stilizovannoe pravoslavie," *Sobranie sochinenii*, 3, *Tipy religioznoi mysli v Rossii* (Collected works, 3, Types of religious thought in Russia) (Paris: YMCA Press, 1989), 543–66, the original being published in *Russkaia mysl'* (Russian thought) 29, no. 1 (1914). An English translation of this review article may be found in Nikolai Berdyaev, *Essays on Russian Thinkers*, trans. Boris Jakim (Kettering, OH: Semantron Press, 2015).

23. *Puti russkogo bogosloviia* (The ways of Russian theology) (Paris: YMCA Press, 1937).

24. See Nicolas Zernov, *The Russian Religious Renaissance of the Twentieth Century* (London: Darton, Longman & Todd, 1963), 101ff. Cf. also the comments of Sergei Bulgakov, *Sophia, The Wisdom of God: An Outline of Sophiology*, revised edition (Hudson, NY: Lindisfarne Press, 1993), 10f, and Nicholas O. Lossky, *History of Russian Philosophy* (New York: International Universities Press, Inc., 1951), 179. Oddly enough, even Florovsky acknowledges this point; *Puti russkogo bogosloviia*, 493.

25. *PGT*, 5; *Stolp*, 3.

through Itself in Itself"; or, as Florensky adds, "Truth is the contemplation of Oneself through Another in a Third: Father, Son, and Spirit."[26]

The inherent drive of the mind to know impels the knower beyond a mere static possession of truth, toward outright communion with Truth, a true being-at-one with Truth. Further elaborating on this point, Florensky directly remarks that "if the mind does not commune with being, then being does not commune with the mind, and, therefore, is a-logical,"[27] thus entailing stances of skepticism, illusionism, and nihilism. He is, indeed, insistent on this point, stressing the *ontological* nature of knowledge beyond a merely gnoseological casting of the problematic, averring that "knowing is a real *giving* of the knower *out* of himself, or (what is the same thing) a real *going* of what is known *into* the knower, a real unification of the knower and what is known."[28]

A realized knowledge of Truth being a true participation *in* Truth, Florensky draws an analogy between knowledge and love, appropriating as the epigraph of his study the words of St. Gregory of Nyssa, "knowledge becomes love,"[29] clearly affirming that "in love and only in love is real knowledge of the Truth conceivable,"[30] expanding upon the ultimate theological dimensions of the matter:

> Essential knowing of the Truth, i.e., communion with the Truth itself, is therefore the real entering into the interior of the Divine Triunity, and not only an ideal touching of the Triunity's outer form. Therefore, true knowledge, knowledge of the Truth, is possible only through the transubstantiation (*presushchestvlenie*) of man, through his deification (*obózhenie*) through the acquisition of love as the Divine essence.

At this juncture, Florensky is in a position to expound upon his fundamental contribution, namely, the metaphysics of consubstantiality (*homoousios*) wherein a dynamic interaction between all the beings in the created order obtains, signifying a real *internal* unity in creation, unlike all metaphysics of similarity, which can only sustain a merely *external* unity among beings governed only by principles of association like resemblance and contiguity, and mechanical causation as in the worldview of the empiricist David Hume (1711–1775). It is Florensky's

---

26. *PGT*, 37; *Stolp*, 48.
27. *Stolp*, 73; cf. *PGT*, 55, with the Eng. trans. lacking the force of the Russian: "For if reason is not associated with being, then being is not associated with reason, is alogical."
28. Ibid.
29. Frontispiece; *PGT*, 65; *Stolp*, 88.
30. *PGT*, 56; *Stolp*, 74.

homoousian, rather than *homoiousian,* metaphysics that gives rise to his sophiological reflections.[31]

If a genuine internal unity obtains within the entire created order, this fact somehow, but unquestionably, must bespeak Divine Wisdom or Sophia at work, as evidently all created reality is nothing but words of the Word in the deemed/spoken act of creation, being *actualizations* of Divine Wisdom wherein the Godhead manifests his *love* for creation, *deigning* to be at One with it. First declaring Sophia to be "the Great Root of the whole creation,"[32] the creative love of God constituting the essence of every creature, it provides the sap of existence without which there can only be death. As conservative of creation, keeping it in being, Sophia is no less "the Guardian Angel of creation" who instills in the world order and not chaos. But since all of creation is but a word of the Word, the Logos, somehow Sophia must be conjoined to this Word; hence Florensky's further determination of Sophia as "the Eternal Bride of the Word of God," receiving from him her creative power, and thus being "one in God, she is multiple in creation."[33] In other words, being one in God she is Divine Sophia, but being multiple in creation she is creatural Sophia, being both *essentially* of the Godhead, but *ever-reflective* of his *goodness* in creation.

Being a *"fourth* hypostatic element"[34] of the Holy Trinity, Sophia partakes of the life of the Trihypostatic Godhead and thus, as Florensky expounds upon the point:

> From the point of view of the Hypostasis of the Father, Sophia is the ideal *substance,* or ground of creation, the power or force of the being of creation. From the point of view of the Hypostasis of the Word, Sophia is the *reason* of creation, the meaning or truth of creation. From the point of view of the Hypostasis of the Spirit, Sophia represents the *spirituality* of creation, its holiness, purity, and immaculateness, i.e., its beauty. This triune idea of *ground-reason-holiness,* becoming fragmented in our rational mind, appears to the sinful mind in three mutually exclusive aspects: *ground, reason,* and *holiness.* Indeed, what does the ground of creation have in common with its

---

31. On this matter and what follows see my chapter "Sophia: An Exigence of Human Thought and Experience" in *Pavel Florensky: A Metaphysics of Love* (Crestwood, New York: St. Vladimir's Seminary Press, 1984), 169–213.

32. *PGT,* 237; *Stolp,* 326.

33. Ibid., 239; *Stolp,* 329.

34. Ibid., 235; *Stolp,* 323.

reason or holiness? For a corrupted mind, i.e., for the rational mind, these ideas can in no wise be united into an integral image. According to the law of identity, they are impenetrable here for one another.[35]

But once grasped integrally, this triadic unity as found in the Godhead renders Sophia as an all-embracing transcendental property of being, conjoining the transcendentals of unity, truth, goodness, and beauty into one principle of being, creatural Sophia essentially being reflective of Divine Sophia.

Thus conceived, creaturely Sophia enjoys a twofold moment. Extensively speaking, Sophia is coterminous with the whole of creation. Intensively speaking, on the other hand, she is subject to progressive deepening or incremental interiority. If Sophia is, indeed, the Great Root of all creation, we can only expect her to manifest herself in ever-outreaching branches. But in the matter of incremental interiority, another image suggests itself, namely, that of ever-decreasing concentric circles. Availing himself of the logical form of sorites, Florensky lyrically expands upon this image, writing:

> If Sophia is all of Creation, then the soul and conscience of Creation, Mankind, is Sophia *par excellence*. If Sophia is all of Mankind, then the soul and conscience of Mankind, the Church, is Sophia *par excellence*. If Sophia is the Church, then the soul and conscience of the Church, the Church of the Saints, is Sophia *par excellence*. If Sophia is the Church of the Saints, then the soul and conscience of the Church of the Saints, the Intercessor for and Defender of creation before the Word of God, Who Judges and divides it in two, the Mother of God, "Purifier of the World," is, once again, Sophia *par excellence*. But the true sign of Mary Full of Grace is Her Virginity, the beauty of Her soul. This is precisely Sophia.[36]

With this passage Florensky's sophianic vision is captured in a nutshell. While he never develops his sophiology further, his brief articulation of it is still no less moving and remains conducive to more systematic treatment, a multilayered task subsequently to be tackled by Sergius Bulgakov.

Like his mentor in philosophy, Vladimir Solovyov, Bulgakov was raised in a devoutly Orthodox family, truly being of the priestly tribe of Levi as a descendent of six generations of priests. Thus, as one born and raised in the provincial town of Livny in Orel Province, he could proudly

35. *PGT*, 252–53; *Stolp*, 349.

36. *PGT*, 253; *Stolp*, 350–51. In this context, consider William Wordsworth's poem "The Virgin" (included in this volume), wherein he calls her "our tainted nature's solitary boast."

proclaim that he was both a Livnian and a Levite.[37] But disenchantment with his seminary studies soon found him professing atheism and giving allegiance to Marxism, later becoming a professor of economics. But, as a consequence of reading Solovyov, this period of his life was short-lived. Not only did Bulgakov return to the Church of his forefathers, but he was in time (1918) to be ordained into the ranks of the Orthodox clergy, thus justifying a quip of Prince E. N. Trubetskoy: "You were born in an epitrachelion."[38]

Bulgakov's first entry into the Sophiological project comes with his 1912 study *Philosophy of Economy: The World as Household*,[39] in which he tries to outline the ontology of the economic process that can only, in turn, bring out the "sophianicity of [the] economy" (*sofiinost' khozaistva*).[40] Characterizing economic process as "the struggle of humanity with the elemental forces of nature," he goes on to stress that economic activity, in fine, is to be understood as the "*humanization of nature*" (*ochelovechenie prirody*),[41] "*the activity of labor*" (*trudovaia deiatelnost'*) constituting "the trademark of economy,"[42] with labor precisely bringing out the richness inherent in nature, herself serving as "man's peripheral body."[43] Bulgakov further expands upon this point, remarking that "nature without labor, without a working culture, is incapable of revealing all its forces, at least, in man."[44] The creative character of the economic order, to his mind, only bespeaks its *sophianic* moment. As he underscores it, "in knowledge, economy, culture, art," human creativity is "*sophic* [sophianic], that is, it partakes of the divine Sophia. Man's participation in Sophia, which brings the divine forces of the Logos to

37. See his *Avtobiograficheskie zametki* (Autobiographical remarks) (Paris: YMCA Press, 1946), 8 and 15.

38. Ibid., 37. An epitrachelion is a priestly Byzantine vestment symbolizing the consecrating grace of the priesthood.

39. *Filosofiia khozaistva: Mir kak khozaistvo* (Westmead, Farnborough, Hants, England: Gregg International Publishers Ltd, 1971), reprint of the Moscow edition, 1912; *Philosophy of Economy: The World as Household*, trans. and ed. by Catherine Evtuhov (New Haven and London: Yale University Press, 2000); henceforth *FKh* and *PE*, respectively.

40. This point and what follows are treated in my prior studies, "Bulgakov on Sophia," *The Journal of Eastern Christian Studies*, 39 (2007): 131–45, and "Bulgakov's Sophiological Conception of Creation," *Orientalia Christiana Periodica*, 74 (2008): 443–54, both of which will be used in my forthcoming monograph, *The Theology of Sergius Bulgakov*.

41. *PE*, 72; *FKh*, 43.

42. Ibid., 75; *FKh*, 46.

43. Ibid., 121; *FKh*, 106.

44. Ibid., 76; *FKh*, 48.

the world and plays the role of *natura naturans* toward nature, makes human creativity possible."[45] In this light, we can grasp how the sophianicity of economics discloses its inherent *transforming* possibilities that, in turn, ultimately render economics "supra-economic"[46] in the sense that it truly, as Bulgakov stresses, "*creates culture*."[47] In sum, for Bulgakov, Divine Sophia and creaturely Sophia work in concert, the former endowing the world with divine forces that render the world a cosmos rather than a chaotic morass, whereas the latter impels humanity to go beyond itself in creative striving in a way that reinforces its being in Divine Truth.

With his *Unfading Light*,[48] Bulgakov's thought is expressly personalist as he articulates the key *a priori* truth of religious experience, namely, that it entails a metaphysics of "Thou art" (*Esi*)[49] in which the essential *gift* character of being is grasped in response to the ultimate Thou or Creator, the Source, in other words, of our being. This intuition of creaturehood is no mere deduction, but a true *prise de conscience* of the fundamental religious experience of the *religio*, the bonding of human being with God, i.e., of creature with Creator. In *The Bride of the Lamb*, Bulgakov returns to this theme, remarking how human being is the "cryptogram of Divinity" and how "humanity in the world presupposes the Divine-Humanity."[50]

In the final volume of his major theological trilogy, *The Bride of the Lamb*, Bulgakov poses the fundamental sophiological question in definitive form: "What is the world in God and what is God in the world?"[51] In answering his own question, Bulgakov notes two cosmological pitfalls, writing that one must eschew the "Scylla of pantheism, in which the world is in danger of sinking in the ocean of divinity," on the one

45. *PE*, 145; *FKh*, 139.
46. Cf. *PE*, 153; *FKh*, 155.
47. Cf. *PE*, 142; *FKh*, 135.
48. *Unfading Light: Contemplations and Speculations*, trans. and ed. Thomas Allan Smith (Grand Rapids, Michigan/Cambridge, UK: William B. Eerdmans Publishing Company, 2012). Rus. original: *Svet nevechernii: sozertsaniia i umozreniia* (Westmead, Farnborough, Hants, England: Gregg International Publishers Ltd, 1971), reprint of Moscow edition, 1912. Henceforth *UL* and *SN*, respectively.
49. *SN*, 15–17; *UL*, 17–19.
50. *The Lamb of God*, trans. by Boris Jakim (Grand Rapids, MI/Cambridge, UK: William B. Eerdmans Publishing Company, 2008), 116. Rus. original: *Agnets Bozhii* (Paris: YMCA-Press, 1948), 139. Henceforth *LG* and *AB*, respectively.
51. *The Bride of the Lamb*, trans. by Boris Jakim (Grand Rapids, MI: William B. Eerdmans Publishing Company/Edinburgh, UK: T&T Clark, 2002), 33. Rus. original, *Nevesta Agntsa* (Paris, 1945); reprint (Westmead, Farnborough, UK: Gregg International Publishers Ltd, 1971), 40. Henceforth *BL* and *NA*, respectively.

hand, and the "Charybdis of abstract cosmism, in which the world's being loses its connectedness with divinity,"[52] on the other. To his mind, a principle of creativity needs formulation in contrast to the principle of causality, the distinguishing mark of traditional Christian philosophy. For him, God is not a cause, impersonally understood, but a Doer (*Deiatel'*), an acting Person.[53] The weakness in Bulgakov's argument lies in his reduction of the principle of causality to a solely mechanical understanding typical of the Modern Age, failing to grasp the key point that a Doer is, indeed, a Causal Agent, one not bearing any relation at all to mechanical, transitive action, but precisely to *intransitive* action, signifying a *relation without motion*, an ultimate Giver of a gift, the very act of donation being utterly *gratuitous*, "from nothing"; in other words, the gift ("creation") mediating the *co-presence* of the giver ("Creator") and the giftee ("the creature"), the glory of the Giver finding an adequate response in a recipient creature, who exemplifies creaturely Sophia preexisting in Divine Sophia as Causal Agent. In this light the fundamental intuition of Bulgakov stands. There is, indeed, a "co-imageness" (*so-obraznost'*) that obtains between Divine Sophia and creatural Sophia, meaning that "the Divine Sophia, as the pan-organism of ideas, is the *pre-eternal Humanity in God*, as the divine proto-image and foundation for man's being."[54]

52. *BL*, 34; *NA*, 41.
53. Ibid., 36; *NA*, 43.
54. *LG*, 113; *AB*, 136.

True and Truer *Gnosis*:
The Revelation of the Sophianic in Hans Urs von Balthasar

Jennifer Newsome Martin

HANS URS VON BALTHASAR has a sophiology in almost exactly the same way that the subject of René Magritte's 1964 painting *The Son of Man* has a face: that is, perhaps he does and perhaps he does not. Magritte's iconic surrealist painting depicts a dapper gentleman in an elegant bowler-style chapeau whose "real" face of flesh is almost wholly obscured by the large green apple suspended directly in front of it. It is impossible to say with absolute certainty that the full features of the face are there in any definitive sense, although scattered intimations of two eyes, a brow, and the cleft of a chin are barely visible. To obscure matters further, as Magritte would certainly have us do (hearkening to the earlier and more well-known painting *The Treachery of Images*, which depicts a brown pipe, under which he has famously written "*Ceci n'est pas une pipe*"), the hidden face of apparent flesh is of course not a face of flesh at all but only its representation in pigment, and somehow an absent representation at that. In much the same way, Balthasar does not have an explicit sophiology, although a case can and will be made that a certain sort of intimated sophianicity characterizes his thinking: his sophiology is the face that both is and is not there, the face which might be, the face that can plausibly be presumed but may certainly not be assured.

There are good reasons for not ascribing an explicit sophiology to Balthasar. Not only does he not announce it as such as central to his theological thinking or formation, he has on the contrary registered concerns about the orthodoxy of sophiology in both its Russian and its Gnostic iterations, insofar as it might jeopardize the ontological gulf between creature and creator and eliminate the need for Christ as mediator.[1] Balthasar's reserve is probably the sharpest in his monograph *Cosmic Liturgy: The Universe According to Maximus the Confessor*:

> The "Sophia" that Bulgakov sees as a remarkable intermediate being, hovering between God and created nature—one face turned toward eternity as everlasting creaturehood, as a superessential yet passive, feminine world of ideas, the other face turned toward the world as its source and root: this "Sophia," to which Böhme, Schelling, Baader, and Soloviev pay their respects, flows down to them, through Byzantium, from ancient Platonic and Gnostic springs. A certain ineradicable mistrust for an autonomous, objective nature, which exists prior to all participation in grace and which is not only spiritual but corporeal—a mistrust, in fact, for the fundamental analogy between God and the creature—has always characterized Eastern thought and has led it to feel primordially related to all forms of self-transcendence, absorption, release of the finite into the infinite.[2]

Balthasar sees Maximus's strong personal Christology as a corrective or antidote to these "Eastern" tendencies; he will later absolve Vladimir Solovyov's sophiology at least partially on the grounds of his "Maximian" pedigree. Balthasar virulently opposes certain strains of speculative thought, including some versions of sophiology which are totally unmoored from a robust Christological interpretation, with allergies particularly to the "misuse" of Christian mysticism in Jacob Boehme.[3] Furthermore, he suggests that his own appropriation of Bulgakov's trinitarian kenosis brackets out the latter's so-called "sophiological excesses."[4]

---

1. See Hans Urs von Balthasar, *The Glory of the Lord: A Theological Aesthetics, Volume VII: Theology: The New Covenant*, trans. Brian McNeil, C.R.V., ed. John Riches (San Francisco: Ignatius Press, 1989), 213; Hans Urs von Balthasar, *Cosmic Liturgy: The Universe According to Maximus the Confessor*, trans. Brian Daley, S.J. (San Francisco: Ignatius Press, 2003), 190; Hans Urs von Balthasar, *Mysterium Paschale: The Mystery of Easter*, trans. Aidan Nichols, O.P. (San Francisco: Ignatius Press, 1990), 46n.69. For secondary comments on this reserve, see Cyril O'Regan, *The Anatomy of Misremembering: Von Balthasar's Response to Philosophical Modernity, Volume I: Hegel* (New York: Crossroads Publishing Company, 2014), 303.

2. Balthasar, *Cosmic Liturgy*, 190.

3. Hans Urs von Balthasar, *The Glory of the Lord: A Theological Aesthetics, Volume I: Seeing the Form*, ed. Joseph Fessio, S.J. and John Riches (San Francisco: Ignatius Press, 1982), 49.

4. Balthasar, *GL VII*, 213–14. Antoine Arjakovsky's "The Sophiology of Father Sergius Bulgakov and Contemporary Western Theology," *St. Vladimir's Theological Quarterly* 49:1–2 (2005), 219–35, which does see a kind of sophiology in Balthasar, explains the "sophiological excesses" comment by indicating that it is reflective of Florovsky's criticism of a gnostic swerve in Bulgakov which Balthasar may have absorbed through P. Henry,

Katy Leamy's recent book, *The Holy Trinity: Hans Urs von Balthasar and His Sources*, takes Balthasar at his word here, rendering a wholly skeptical judgment on Balthasar's adoption—latent or otherwise—of sophiology, arguing that Balthasar eliminates sophiology from his own thought even as he heavily appropriates Bulgakov's trinitarian thinking. Leamy decisively states that "Balthasar acknowledges his dependence on Bulgakov's Trinitarian theology, but *rejects Bulgakov's concept of Sophia.*"[5] He is able to do so, the argument goes, by appealing to Thomas Aquinas's postulate that divine essence is relation, which renders the need for a concept such as sophiology for bridging the metaxic space between God and the world superfluous. It is certainly true that Balthasar expresses nervousness about sophiology, but—especially given Bulgakov's assertion that Sophia is nothing other than the dynamic *ousia* or essence of the divine which is constitutively kenotic self-gift—it may be difficult to "bracket out" something both so ubiquitous to Sergei Bulgakov's kenoticism and so central to Balthasar's own trinitarian theology, which will be taken up in due course.[6] At the very least, a tempering of excess is not necessarily a total erasure.

৵৯

Though evidence of Balthasar's wariness regarding the sophiological is present in his work, these stray comments are somewhat slender against the balance of a more diffuse or suffused presence throughout of what we might call *sophianicity*, which is clear enough in his declared commitment to an intuitive, poetic, and integrative perception of the visible forms of cosmos and creation, nature and art, as well as a thoroughly

---

"Kénose" *DBS* V (1957), 7–61, which Balthasar does cite (*Mysterium Paschale*, 44n.30). See Arjakovsky, 228 n.24. This explanation, however, seems to rest on the claim that Balthasar *only* knew Bulgakov through these secondary sources, which does not seem plausible given the level of engagement in texts like *Theo-Drama IV*.

5. Katy Leamy, *The Holy Trinity: Hans Urs von Balthasar and His Sources* (Eugene, OR: Pickwick Publications, 2015), 3; italics added.

6. John Milbank has argued compellingly that Bulgakov (at least at his best) does not make the mistake of over-literalizing the "between" or bridging capacity of Sophia, and when he does make this "lapse," it coincides with positing "Sophia as too literally a fourth hypostasis, possessing a kind of uniquely independent substantiality" (John Milbank, "Sophiology and Theurgy: The New Theological Horizon," *Encounter Between Eastern Orthodoxy and Radical Orthodoxy*, ed. Adrian Pabst and Christoph Schneider [Burlington, VT: Ashgate Publishing Company, 2009], 71). Also consult Hans Urs von Balthasar, *Theo-Logic: Theological Logical Theory Volume II: Truth of God*, trans. Adrian J. Walker (San Francisco: Ignatius Press, 2004), 128–34, for a selection where Balthasar articulates the limits of Aquinas's Trinitarian thought.

sapiential reading of the Bible. For as analogical, generous, and open a theologian as Balthasar is to a great range of possible non-theological and non-magisterial sources, it is implausible that he would reject such a rich concept as sophiology out of hand, even given his stated reservations. As a general rule, Balthasar affirms rather than rebuffs thinkers who are fundamentally attentive to the blazing glory and ineffable beauty that both is and illuminates divine revelation: surely the twelve "styles" that he selects to populate and give concreteness to his theological aesthetics—figures which by all accounts are strange bedfellows— witness to this fact, as well as his own adoption of Bulgakov in the theo-dramatics.[7] With respect to the twelve styles, readers find alongside the usual suspects of Irenaeus, Augustine, Pseudo-Dionysius, Anselm, Bonaventure, Dante, and others, the Protestant philosopher Johann Georg Hamann, two Catholic poets (Gerard Manley Hopkins and Charles Péguy), and, most apropos here, Russian Orthodox philosopher Vladimir Solovyov, one of the originary "fathers" of Russian Sophiology to whom Balthasar refers as "a thinker of universal genius."[8] Balthasar subsequently devotes a lengthy and unusually laudatory essay to Solovyov, whom he absolves probably with more insistence and hyperbole than consistency.[9] At this point most of the reserve about Sophiology that Balthasar registered in *Cosmic Liturgy* seems to have evaporated altogether, as he refuses to render a judgment on Solovyov's use of "Sophia," a term which, Balthasar says without any compunction, "now becomes necessary"[10] in Solovyov's account.

Other sophiological thinkers are affirmed, more or less dramatically and with more or less reserve, including Teilhard de Chardin, Fr. Louis Bouyer, and Valentin Tomberg, and, to an even greater degree, the Russian Orthodox Sergei Bulgakov. These inclusions and partial affirmations seem certainly to countenance Balthasar's attentiveness to the

---

7. See Hans Urs von Balthasar, *The Glory of the Lord: A Theological Aesthetics, Volume II: Studies in Theological Style: Clerical Styles*, trans. Andrew Louth, Francis McDonagh and Brian McNeil C.R.V. and ed. John Riches (San Francisco: Ignatius Press, 1984), 11–30.

8. Ibid., 19.

9. Hans Urs von Balthasar, *The Glory of the Lord: A Theological Aesthetics, Volume III: Studies in Theological Style: Lay Styles*, trans. Andrew Louth, John Saward, Martin Simon and Rowan Williams, and ed. John Riches (San Francisco: Ignatius Press, 1986), 279–352. See Cyril O'Regan, *The Anatomy of Misremembering*, 313–14 for a persuasive argument that Balthasar reads Solovyov here "as if" he were Bulgakov. Also see Jennifer Newsome Martin, "The Absolution of Vladimir Soloviev," *Hans Urs von Balthasar and the Critical Appropriation of Russian Religious Thought* (Notre Dame, IN: University of Notre Dame Press, 2015), 112–15.

10. Balthasar, *GL III*, 307.

sapiential, if not the straightforwardly sophiological, all of which con-
spires to challenge the view that Balthasar does (or even can) bracket
out sophiology altogether. Consider, for example, Balthasar's reception
of Teilhard and Bouyer. Indeed, in *Test Everything*, Balthasar recom-
mends Teilhard—through the lens of de Lubac's reading and elsewhere
with the qualification that it is Solovyov who can offer a corrective to his
evolutionism[11]—and Bouyer almost *insofar* as Russian sophiology has
influenced them:

> With both authors, the virginal motherhood of Mary presents the last
> and highest flowering of Sophia striving upward within the world pro-
> cess, just as Christ presents the definitive Incarnation of the Logos,
> increasingly made concrete by the same process. Both, accordingly, do
> not form two hypostatic unions, which as such would have to depict
> the suprasexual masculinity-femininity of God, but precisely that nup-
> tial "toward each other," which Saint Paul (Eph 5) and the entire tradi-
> tion describe in countless Christian commentaries on the Canticle of
> Canticles.[12]

Perhaps a more surprising example of Balthasar's friendliness to
thought which might be considered esoteric is his (measured, but
largely positive) appreciation of Valentin Tomberg, himself a much
clearer Catholic proponent of sophiology,[13] in Balthasar's forward to
the 1980 French version of Tomberg's unsettling *Meditations on the
Tarot*.[14] Balthasar is generally not shy about the possible contributions
of the esoteric, noting even in the first volume of the theological aesthetics that "so truly a 'church of the people' as the Catholic Church
does not abolish genuine esotericism."[15] Balthasar is certainly not
uncritical of Tomberg in the 1980 forward, noting instances where he
swerves too greatly away from the middle path, though he writes that

---

11. Ibid., 290. Also c.f. von Balthasar, *GL III*, 19.

12. Hans Urs von Balthasar, *Test Everything: Hold Fast to What is Good* (San Francisco: Ignatius Press, 1989), 46. See Louis Bouyer, *The Seat of Wisdom: An Essay on the
Place of the Virgin Mary in Christian Theology*, trans. A.V. Littledale (New York: Pan-
theon Books, 1962). Also see Davide Zordan, "De la Sagesse in théologie: Essai de con-
frontation entre Serge Boulgakov et Louis Bouyer," *Irénikon* 79: 2–3 (2006), 265–86, and
Keith Lemna, "Louis Bouyer's Sophiology: A Balthasarian Retrieval," *The Heythrop Journal* 52:4 (June 2011), 628–42.

13. See Michael Martin, *The Submerged Reality: Sophia and the Turn to a Poetic
Metaphysics* (Kettering, OH: Angelico Press, 2015), 189–202.

14. For an excellent treatment of Balthasar's forward to the 1980 edition, see Kevin
Mongrain, "Rule-Governed Christian Gnosis: Hans Urs von Balthasar on Valentin Tomberg's *Meditations on the Tarot*," *Modern Theology* 25:2 (April 2009), 285–314.

15. Balthasar, *GL I*, 34.

from these "excursions" into uncultivated territory he brings back an "almost enormous abundance of authentic and fruitful insights."[16] One particular point of commendation rather than damnation that Balthasar offers in this forward is the ludic, dialogical spirit with which Tomberg engages a gamut of thinkers both traditional and esoteric, including elements from

> the Sephirot (from the Cabbala), or a thought from Jacob Boehme or Rudolf Steiner, from Jung or Péladan, from Papus or Maître Philippe, or whoever it may be, let us not miss this finely humorous air with which he gathers every sort of flower from the side of the road to tie in his rich bouquet of imagination. Often he refers to the great philosophers and theologians, such as Thomas Aquinas, Bonaventure, Leibniz, Kant, Kierkegaard, Nietzsche, Bergson, Solovieff, Teilhard de Chardin; or to dramatists and poets, such as Shakespeare, Goethe, De Coster, Cervantes, Baudelaire, and many others. He easily plays with all registers of world literature.[17]

This commendation alone is enough to suggest that Balthasar is not terribly squeamish about playfully adopting certain aspects of a wide panoply of thinkers without offering them *carte blanche.*

Interestingly, in his excellent treatment of Balthasar's foreword to *MT*, Kevin Mongrain argues convincingly that Tomberg actually comes quite near the Russian sophiologists upon whom Balthasar himself already relies, especially Solovyov and Bulgakov.[18] It is notable here as well that Balthasar's exoneration of Tomberg, though marked by more pointed hesitancy, parallels that of Solovyov in that Balthasar believes both figures are ultimately regulated by Christocentric commitments which perform a kind of purifying operation upon the "dangerous" discourses

---

16. Hans Urs von Balthasar, Forward to Valentin Tomberg, *Méditations sure les 22 arcanes majeurs du Tarot* (Paris: Aubier Montaigne, 1980), 14; Mongrain 289–90; 308 n. 21.

17. See Balthasar, Foreword to Tomberg, 10–11; Mongrain, "Rule-Governed Christian Gnosis," 307 n. 20.

18. Mongrain expounds upon this connection in the following way: "First, Tomberg's general religious sensibility was very congenial to Russian Orthodoxy, so much so that he first tried to join the Russian church after becoming Christian. Second, he was obviously a reader and admirer of Vladimir Solovyov (see *MT*, 2002, 503, 519, 608); Soloviev is for him the ideal representative of Christian gnosis (608). Third, he seems to have assimilated Soloviev's theological interest in the cosmic-human 'Sophia': Tomberg frequently refers to the feminine creaturely principle of Sophia, and in many places he identifies it with the Virgin Mary (*MT* 2002, 39, 274, 279, 283, 548, 549, 574, 582, 633). Fourth ... his own basic theological perspective is extremely similar to the theology of Sergei Bulgakov, which is perhaps due to their common source in Soloviev" (309 n. 53).

of hermeticism, Gnosticism, idealism, and so on.[19] Furthermore, as Mongrain notes, Tomberg's concept of "Christian Hermeticism"— which is reflective, visionary, biblical, prayerful, ecclesial, and anchored in Christ—is not far from the "true" or "Christian" *gnosis*[20] which Balthasar advocates in the context of a sapiential reading of the Scriptures, a reading to which we shall now turn.

৯৯

By my lights, the sapiential mode in which Balthasar approaches the Scriptures as a whole actually is itself the hermeneutical key for consideration of the general sophianicity of his thinking, especially as he directly connects the Old Testament Wisdom literature to what he calls "true *gnosis*," traceable through the New Testament and emerging again recognizably in the Alexandrian theology of Origen and Clement. Balthasar sees the New Testament culmination of the contemplative tradition of the Wisdom literature in the Pauline and especially the Johannine literature, where *pistis* and *gnosis* are coincident, where a contemplative seeing of the hidden is possible and faith is prioritized.[21] The Johannine principle that knowledge of the Son in fact constitutes a knowledge of the Father (John 14:7) is operative insofar as the invisible is communicated in the sphere of the visible, though there is always a silent, cryptic remainder that is non-reducible to sense experience. These strands in Scripture from the Writings, the Gospels, and the Epistles are connected underground by the tangled common roots of "Biblical '*gnosis*' which is steeped in the same diffuse atmosphere of late antiquity as are Philo, the early Gnostic mystery texts, hermetic literature, and the beginnings of what would eventually produce Alexandrian Christianity."[22] For Balthasar, this sapiential *gnosis* is what capacitates

19. Compare, for instance, Balthasar's statement in the forward to *Meditations on the Tarot* that "if the author was able to enter into all the varieties of occult science with such sovereignty, it is because for him they are only secondary realities, which are only able to be truly known when they can be referred to the absolute mystery of divine love manifested in Christ" (11–12 and quoted in Mongrain, "Rule-Governed Christian Gnosis," 291–92) to his (probably a bit hyperbolic) claim about Solovyov's sources. Of Kabbala, Boehme, Swedenborg, Pordage, von Baader, and others, Balthasar writes of Solovyov that "in reading all these and many others he fully appropriates them for himself, the muddy stream runs through him as if through a purifying agent, and is distilled in crystal clear, disinfected waters" (*GL III*, 292).

20. Mongrain, "Rule-Governed Christian Gnosis," 296.

21. Balthasar, *GL I*, 137.

22. Ibid., 45.

the believer's theoretic vision to see the spirit in the letter, or, to make a different use of the artistic metaphor with which we began, to see by intuition the face underneath the face, which is to say, the glorious invisible that suffuses and illuminates the world—and, Balthasar says, even in the mundane forms of nature and art "we do in fact see it."[23]

Significantly, what both Tomberg's "Christian Hermeticism" and Balthasar's "true *gnosis*" forbear is a reduction of the mysterious reality of God's presence to purely rationalistic or formulaic theorems, systems, or discursive statements: thus, a reading of both the Bible and the world will include supernaturally amplified possibilities of contemplative perception, requiring a move from the academic discourse of a spectator to the praise of a participant. To see the world sophianically is to perceive it not as a mechanistic object of experimentation or a medium upon which power can be exercised, but with an awareness of the bright and hidden flame of divine presence that permeates the natural world and the human beings within it. The wisdom literature especially—born of a culture arguably prior to the hegemony of "argumentative prose," where song and story and hymn govern—is particularly in a poetic or aesthetic mode.[24] This brand of perception and response, therefore, requires non-discursive, contemplative modes of speech and of silence: it calls for rhapsody and confession, praise, and poetry, and prayer.

Indeed, according to Balthasar, contemplative prayer is the very condition of the possibility for Biblical *gnosis* not to devolve into logo-centric power plays, when readers and interpreters forget that within the form of the word or *littera* there is the unbounded, ineffable God. This forgetting leads to the absolutizing of word as "a human *logos* in philosophical logic or philology,"[25] but the Bible with its parade of images and genres is itself a sign of contradiction against logo-centric or rationalist reduction. Balthasar says that readers who would "see" God must attend to more than the word-character of the Scriptures, especially those byways which complicate the hegemony of word: "childlikeness (which . . . 'always sees the face of God,' Mt 18.10), simplicity (to which alone God's indivisible simplicity is revealed, Mt 11:25), peace ('that transcends all concepts,' Phil 4:7 . . . prayer (that yearns in the Spirit 'with unutterable groanings' for the glory of God, Rom 8:26), joy (which already now is 'unutterable' and 'glorified,' as it looks to the definitive gift

---

23. Ibid., 444. There are strong strands of Goethe here as well.
24. Ibid., 42.
25. Balthasar, *GL VII*, 266.

of God, 1 Pet 1:8; *c.f.* 1 Thess 2:20)," and so on.[26] Relatedly, a sapiential reading of the Bible and the world does not forget that "the Bible continually passes over into poetic diction, and comes to its close, in the last book, entirely in images ... there will *never* be a theology that gives a fully valid translation into abstract concepts of the dimensions of poetry and image in Scripture."[27] Insofar as Balthasar's "true *gnosis*" requires ecclesial grounding such that faith and knowledge are coincident, it does not sunder theology from spirituality. Balthasar's theology endeavors to bridge the gap, opening possibilities of the prayerful, the poetic, and the beautiful, such that the practice of theology exceeds merely discursive or dogmatic boundaries. Though these boundaries must, of course, be drawn, they must be drawn somewhat timorously with the understanding that within them there is always "the unbounded, the presence in the concept of what is beyond concept."[28] He calls for theologians to be "individuals who devote their lives to the glory of theology, that fierce fire burning in the dark night of adoration and obedience, whose abysses it illuminates."[29] This claim is resonant with Balthasar's well-known insistence that theology be done in a posture of wonder and prayer; it must be a *kniende Theologie*, a "kneeling theology."[30]

১৯৯১

When Balthasar interprets the Wisdom books (Book of Wisdom, Ben Sirach, Job, Song of Solomon, Psalms, Proverbs, Ecclesiastes), he understands the subject of these texts broadly as a kind of self-referential mirror in which the "Holy Spirit of Scripture reflect[s] on himself,"[31] which includes Sophia's reflection upon herself. The self-contemplation of Sophia herself is always in the register or mode of what Balthasar calls "glorious praise (*Rühmung*)," a self-reflection that by its rays illuminates past acts in salvation history, the beauty of the natural world, and human beings as well. [32] This association with mirrors in Balthasar's analysis is not insignificant, especially given Jacob Boehme's metaphor of Sophia as a "mirror of the divinity," which is repeated in

---

26. Ibid., 267.

27. Ibid., 267–68; italics added.

28. Hans Urs von Balthasar, "The Place of Theology," *Explorations in Theology, Volume I: The Word Made Flesh* (San Francisco: Ignatius Press, 1989), 155.

29. Ibid., 160.

30. See, for instance, "Theology and Sanctity," *Explorations I*, 181–210.

31. Balthasar, *GL I*, 43.

32. Ibid.

the Russians.[33] Moreover, the doubling that is suggested by a metaphoric appeal to the looking glass is also relevant considering further developments in sophiological thought, especially in Bulgakov, which posit both a "heavenly" and a "creaturely" Sophia, though Balthasar is loath to accept this premise.[34] In Balthasar's exegesis of the Wisdom literature:

> She is the purest "emanation"... of the "glory (*doxa*) of the Almighty": thus *she both is and is not the glory of God*: she is glory in the mode of not remaining alone by herself; she is the "reflection... of the eternal light," "spotless mirror of the working... of God," "image... of his sovereign goodness" (7:26); *thus always God in the act of going forth from himself, which is never an act of alienation from himself...*. [God is] the one who remains in himself, "without stepping outside himself," and yet at the same time can be his own emanation, reflection and image in the world.[35]

Balthasar does not speak to later sophiological developments in the context of this Old Testament exegesis. His reading of Sophia here is nevertheless instructive for his later embrace of Bulgakov's sophiologically-inflected notion of trinitarian distance/hiatus and the *Urkenosis*, which posits that the divine *ousia*—for Bulgakov nothing else but "Sophia"—is in fact the act of self-divestiture itself, the separation of "God from God" in the Father's consubstantial generation of the Son and subsequently in the creation of the world, the Incarnation, and the Cross.[36] This kenotic activity of the eternal relations of self-gift in the

33. See Jakob Böhme, *The Way to Christ*, trans. Peter Erb (New York: Paulist Press, 1978) and Judith Deutsch Kornblatt, "Who is Solovyov and What is Sophia," in Vladimir Soloviev, *Divine Sophia: The Wisdom Writings of Vladimir Solovyov*, ed. Judith Deutsch Kornblatt, trans. Boris Jakim, Judith Deutsch Kornblatt, and Laury Magnus (Ithaca, NY: Cornell University Press, 2009), especially 72–73.

34. Balthasar sees in Bulgakov's notion of divine and creaturely Sophia a threat to Christology which flirts with Gnosticism insofar as the created/uncreated reality of Sophia is the "'condition of possibility' for the union of the two natures in Christ, and thus, so to speak, a suprachristological scheme for Christology" (Balthasar, *Mysterium Paschale*, 46 n.69).

35. Hans Urs von Balthasar, *The Glory of the Lord: A Theological Aesthetics, Volume VI: Theology: The Old Covenant*, trans. Brian McNeil, C.R.V., and Erasmo Leiva-Merikakis; ed. John Riches (San Francisco: Ignatius Press, 1991), 360–62; italics added.

36. For affirmations of Bulgakov on this point, see Balthasar, *Mysterium Paschale*, 35; *GL VII*, 213–14; Hans Urs von Balthasar, *Theo-Drama: Theological Dramatic Theory, Volume IV: The Action*, trans. Graham Harrison (San Francisco: Ignatius Press, 1994), 323. I treat Balthasar's borrowing from Bulgakov at much greater length in "Ur-Kenosis and Paschal Trinitarianism: The Slain Lamb of the Apocalypse," in Martin, *Hans Urs von Balthasar and the Critical Appropriation of Russian Religious Thought*, 185–94.

Trinity is, for both Bulgakov and Balthasar, the reason that the world bears within it a sophianic brilliance of divine presence.[37] Again, for Bulgakov—at least in his clearest moments—Sophia and *ousia* are consonant rather than competing realities.

✍

Balthasar foregrounds Ben Sirach and the Book of Wisdom as primary examples of a cosmic broadening of the Old Testament into a more contemplative realm able to attend to the presence of divine Sophia in the world.[38] In Ben Sirach, true wisdom is accorded to the person who is able to perceive the shimmering, mysterious presence of divine glory in the world; this person is the "perfect *contemplator*."[39] The contemplator will not only recognize but will hunt single-mindedly after "Lady Wisdom" (Ben Sirach 24:9–20), a figure who, in striking arboreal imagery, pushes roots deep into the soil of the earth, and raises her aromatic branches of cedar or cypress or palm into the air—Wisdom who, Balthasar notes, is simultaneously virgin, mother, and bride (Ben Sirach 15:2). Indeed, throughout these texts, the figure of Sophia is enormously multivalent. As in Solovyov and Bulgakov, "Sophia" is a category-defying term referring not simply to the Logos;[40] Balthasar notes this multivalent character of the referents, though certainly not as a demerit. Rather, Balthasar reads Wisdom's refusal to be characterized exactly as a cipher for the impossibility of wrangling mystery into a human system.[41] What is required of the *contemplator* before this unclassifiable mystery is a posture of wonder (*thaumazein*), a concept taken up not only by Plato and Aristotle, but also by Heidegger, and this wonder is "directed to the marvels and beauties of the world," though through these immanent realities it can witness the transcendent Creator as their source.[42]

Wisdom in these texts is nothing less than a disclosure of "God's presence and providence" for human beings,[43] and yet the glory that is perceived in Sophia is *only* as in a mirror, a glass darkly; it is an attenuated

37. See Hans Urs von Balthasar, "The World is from the Trinity," *Theo-Drama: Theological Dramatic Theory, Volume V: The Last Act*, trans. Graham Harrison (San Francisco: Ignatius Press, 1998), 61–109. Cf. Hans Urs von Balthasar, "The Unknown Lying beyond the Word," *Explorations in Theology, Volume III: Creator Spirit*, trans. Brian McNeil, C.R.V. (San Francisco: Ignatius Press, 1993), 105–16.

38. Balthasar, *GL VI*, 345.

39. Ibid., 348.

40. Ibid., 360–61.

41. Ibid., 360.

42. Ibid., 351.

43. Ibid., 357.

reflection of divine presence and not God *himself*. [44] Attunement to the sophianic indicates the capacity to perceive and then to praise this hidden divine presence shining always and everywhere in the world, but in Balthasar's assessment the "glory" that is sung in the Old Testament sapiential books is insufficient due to its mildness and ubiquity, remaining, in his language, "ethereal and bloodless."[45] Though Balthasar does not make the interpretive mistake of subsuming Sophia to a property of the Son or Logos alone,[46] he is clear that the diffuse wisdom or divine presence in the world does not have the sharpness or specificity that will come with Christ.

ℱ∂

There is a similar trajectory of thought in Balthasar's aesthetic account of splendor, or luminesce, a light which pervades form, but which ultimately must be interpreted Christologically, which, however, is not to say non-sophiologically. If we concede that the sophianic has to do with a contemplative or poetic perception of the world, that it understands knowledge in terms of participation and intuition; that it is dialogical, Trinitarian, relational, luminous, and attentive to the divine presence in creation, in nature, in art and history, and so on, then Balthasar's concept of splendor—borrowed from Aquinas, medieval Neoplatonism, and the thought of Goethe—is certainly relevant. According to Balthasar's theological aesthetics, splendor is that unifying, luminous, visible-invisible depth of reality "which shines forth from the figure, making it into a worthy, a love-worthy thing."[47] It appears through the form, not apart from it or externally to it, and the form cannot be discarded or surpassed.[48] Furthermore, splendor exceeds the simply visual reception of proportion, color, symmetry, harmony, and so on: to perceive even worldly beauty is a great mystery. This depth-dimension of

44. Ibid., 358–59.

45. Ibid., 346.

46. Balthasar acknowledges that interpretations (whether patristic or modern) which correlate Sophia strictly to either Word or to Spirit alone are not actually adequate to the biblical record, which tends to "blur the boundaries between spirit, word, and wisdom" (*TL II*, 161). Even references to Wisdom/Sophia in the New Testament are not sufficiently understood if the assumption is made that Sophia is only a property of the second person of the Trinity. Rather, on Balthasar's reading there, Sophia is "an attribute of the divine essence" that is trinitarian, and not just Christological (*TL II*, 160. See the entire section, "The Position of the Logos in God," *TL II*, 151–70.) Also cf. Balthasar, *GL I*, 36.

47. Balthasar, *GL I*, 20.

48. Ibid., 119; cf. 151.

splendor that shines through and enlivens the form requires eyes to see it; that is, eyes capacitated and nurtured by contemplative Wisdom/ Sophia which is attentive to the glory shining all around it, in order, as in the Alexandrian theology of Clement and Origen, to see the spirit in the letter, the invisible through the visible, the face beyond the face.

For Balthasar, the notion of splendor definitely has a Christological mooring and Incarnational warrant; references specifically to splendor or radiance are correlative to Christ, who is the perfect singularity of infinite in the finite, the chiasmus at the very center of the world. Appealing to the Christmas Preface of the Roman Rite (*Quia per incarnati Verbi mysterium nova mentis nostrae oculis lux tuae claritatis infulsit: ut dum visibiliter Deum cognoscimus, per hunc in invisibilium amorem rapiamur*),[49] Balthasar situates this notion of splendor with an always Incarnational point of departure: the brightness that allows spiritual vision of the invisible is ultimately through the mystery of the Incarnate Word. Though this illuminative radiance or splendor (ἀπαύγασμα) originates "in the notion of the *logos* or *Sophia*,"[50] any tendency toward pantheism or impersonalism is corrected because the radiant expression of the divine is not lessened by the flesh of Christ but rather finds its apotheosis in the humanity of Jesus, particularly in his Resurrection, where "the glory of Christ unites splendor and radiance with solid reality."[51] According to Balthasar, the modern person—who no longer has eyes to see—must be confronted not only with the luminosity of Wisdom/Sophia, as in Ben Sirach or the Book of Wisdom, but precisely by the phenomenon of Christ, and thus, as Balthasar puts it, "experience the unclassifiable, total otherness of Christ as the outshining of God's sublimity and glory," which is to say, "to learn to see again"[52] with sapiential eyes.

What is crucial here is that for Balthasar the permeating radiance of the divine presence of Sophia in the created order—again, never quite reducible to the Logos—actually sharpens to a point neither upon Word or Wisdom but specifically upon a Face: that is, upon the face of the Son of Man, not Magritte's surrealist *Son of Man* with which we began these reflections, but the Son of Man of the Gospels and the Christ Jesus of Paul:

49. Ibid., 119–20.
50. Ibid., 435.
51. Ibid., 124.
52. Hans Urs von Balthasar, *Theo-Logic: Theological Logical Theory, Volume I: The Truth of the World*, trans. Adrian J. Walker (San Francisco: Ignatius Press, 2000), 20.

The centering in the New Testament of all δόξα in creation and salvation history upon the inmost focus can be seen at 1 Cor 4:6: "It is the same God who said, 'Let light shine out of darkness,' who has shone in our hearts, to give us the knowledge of the glory of God upon the *face* of Christ." Here at the end, there stands no longer "word," no longer "image," but "face": a face that is absolutely certainly a human face (as indeed before this, a ray of God's glory lay upon Moses' face; 2 Cor 3:13, 15), but the face of the Kyrios (3:18), that is substantially his as the pre-existent (2 Cor 8:9) Son.[53]

In Balthasar's reading of Paul, it is specifically the luminous face of the crucified Christ that must come "in the place of Sophia or of the Logos."[54] Balthasar makes it abundantly clear in his New Testament exegesis that the importation of the sophiological, whether in the *relectures* of the biblical Wisdom tradition or in appropriations from the surrounding culture like Plato and Philo, can find its fulfillment nowhere else than in the genuinely enfleshed and wounded face of the true Son of Man.[55]

⁊੭

This chapter has recommended the profitability of distinguishing between ascribing an explicit sophiology to Balthasar, which he does not seem to have in any uncomplicated sense, and a more pervasive "sophianicity" that can arguably be said to suffuse the entire complex edifice of Balthasar's thought, particularly in his conception of "Christian *gnosis*"; it is more than defensible to say that his thought is sophiologically aspirated or sophianic, suggesting something more pre-conceptual and indeterminate, having to do with a poetic, contemplative, and thoroughly sapiential posture not only as a reader of the Bible but also as reader of the world. There are other equally valuable possible entry points into the discussion of Balthasar's relation to the sophiological to which we could not attend, including an analysis of the overall Marian stamp of his thought, an examination of the way his pneumatology borrows from Bulgakov's *The Comforter*, or the markedly gendered or feminine character which emerges not only in his theological anthropology but also in his trinitarianism,[56] topics which all deserve further consideration in this context.

53. Balthasar, *GL VII*, 264. C.f. *GL I*, 437.
54. Balthasar, *GL VII*, 299.
55. Ibid., 280–84.
56. I have argued elsewhere, for instance, that when Balthasar borrows the symbol of *Urkenosis* from Bulgakov, he actually retains some of the deeply gendered structures of

If we might be indulged to revisit the image with which this chapter began, namely Magritte's painting *The Son of Man*, recall that the apple-face is actually coincident with the hidden, invisible, absent face intimated therein: for Magritte the surrealist, there are not actually two distinct faces there. So if Bulgakov is right in his claim that "Sophia" is a way of re-naming the divine essence as the act of self-evacuating love, then the sophianic is not esoteric at all but mainline, not at the fringes but at the very center of the Christian theological tradition and experience. This point is crucial. For Balthasar as with Bulgakov, and to the extent that Balthasar's thought is sophianic, it ought not be thought of as an exotic or external supplement to the tradition accessible only to elite initiates. It is simple, and simply another way of naming the reality of the triune God as substantially self-gift in creation, Incarnation, and Cross such that the apprehension of Sophia *is* the apprehension of God, not—analogous to the form-splendor dynamic in his aesthetics—something "extra" or "behind" God. Sophiology can thus never be more than redundant of what is already in the tradition. It summons only that which has always already existed, that which illuminates everything, the light—invisible in its very ubiquity—by which the "Christian gnostic" *contemplator* apprehends the hidden depths of reality, not in virtue of her own singular or private light, but only in light of that invisibility that is nothing other than what truly is.

Bulgakov's sophiology. That is, Balthasar seems to import the notion of Sophia as feminine, receptive, answering, ontologically secondary, and dual to some of his gendered constructions of the feminine, especially in trinitarian discourse. See Jennifer Newsome Martin, "The 'Whence' and the 'Whither' of Balthasar's Gendered Theology: Rehabilitating Kenosis for Feminist Theology," *Modern Theology* 31:2 (April 2015), 211–34.

Nature and Divine Wisdom:
How (Not) to Speak of Sophia[1]

Bruce V. Foltz

I. Why We Need a Lexicon of Divine Wisdom in Nature

A. The Sophiology of Dostoevsky

It is one of the most powerful scenes in the novel. The novice monk, quietly dreading the loss of his beloved spiritual father, is nonetheless excited to think that he himself will be among the few to hear his last words. Elder Zosima, the very "light of love" for his young disciple Alyosha, is dying.

The name for Alyosha (or Alexei), the gentle "hero" of *The Brothers Karamazov*, was derived from that of Dostoevsky's infant son and his character drawn from the author's young friend, Vladimir Solovyov, the great founder of Russian sophiology. After the child Alexei's death in 1878, the novelist traveled to the remote Monastery of Optina Pustyn accompanied by Solovyov in the hope of finding solace and healing for his intractable grief. According to his widow, after long discussions with Elder Ambrose, himself a model for Zosima in the novel, Dostoevsky found the peace he sought in this lovely monastery. Optina Pustyn or Optina-in-the-Wilderness—nestled on a hillside slope at the lower edge of a thick, largely coniferous forest, overlooking the Zhizdra River Valley and the fertile fields beyond—is an extraordinary place that to this day radiates the luxuriant beauty and simple goodness of creation, quietly testifying to why it was chosen as the place where great words were spoken concerning the holy goodness and sparkling beauty of nature. Thus,

---

1. This essay has greatly benefitted from readings by Hieromonk Alexios (Trader) of Karrakalou Monastery, Fr. Hans Jacobse of St. Peter Orthodox Church, and Prof. David Bradshaw of the University of Kentucky. Of course, any remaining weaknesses are attributable solely to the author.

to the select group of "his most faithful friends" sharing with him his last hours, the Elder delivers a remarkable series of recollections and reflections, lovingly recorded and preserved by the novice, Alyosha.

Perhaps it is not surprising, then, that these final thoughts and exhortations of Elder Zosima forming the spiritual heart of *The Brothers Karamazov* feature a theme that had hardly been central in Dostoevsky's previous novels: the understanding of nature as a locus for encountering God, nature as deeply expressive of God's love and wisdom. And this is all the more significant in view of the author's intention for this novel to serve as his final testament, the sum of his life-wisdom given to the world. In Zosima's reflections and recollections, we hear narrated a series of lives into which the divine radiance of creation has entered and shone brightly—lives for which, following acts of repentance and renewal, creation revealed itself differently, revealed its paradisiacal depths, showed that it had been Eden all along—and these narratives stand in stark contrast to the soliloquies of Ivan, for whom God is no more than a hypothesis and an abstraction, and who stands as the last in a series of unhappy, disappointed, Westernized intellectuals in Dostoevsky's fiction, from the Underground Man to Raskolnikov. These are figures whose hearts have been corrupted by their thoughts and by their attachment to their thoughts, and for whom created nature is an object of contempt (the battered and bitter Underground Man, for whom it is a realm of dumb necessity) or revulsion (Raskolnikov, who from within the Hell of his own making experiences nature as scorching and sulfuric, i.e., as itself infernal). These are nihilistic figures who have undergone neither the *katharsis* (purification of the heart) nor the subsequent *metanoia* (change of heart) that would allow them to experience God in nature and in others—men whose hearts are clouded with dark thoughts, not knowing that it is the pure in heart who shall see God— men who, not finding God in creation, conclude that they themselves are the creators of value. Cerebral, disembodied figures (shades, perhaps) believing only in the reign of the Man-God, humanity elevating itself to the status of world-creator.

In his last years, Dostoevsky saw this as the great decision forcing itself upon us today: the choice between the reign of the God-Man (Christ Himself, uniting God and humanity, drawing together heaven and earth) and the regime of the Man-God (humanity usurping the place of the Creator, elevating itself to the position of divinity). And if the first option is to be embraced, Dostoevsky seems to say, a sense of creation infused with divinity will play a critical role—a transfiguration of both environmental nature and human nature that is, even more radically, a revealing of their inner truth, of the depths in which they are rooted—of that first face they can turn to us, if we have a face to turn towards it. An experience of what certain Russian philosophers called "Sophia" or the divine wisdom in nature.

For if God is merely transcendent to the world, without at the same time being present within the world, then is He not (for us) merely an abstraction, one thought contending with others for legitimacy and preeminence? Dostoevsky understood that clever arguments against religious faith, such as those presented by Ivan Karamazov, cannot be overcome with other, even cleverer, arguments to the contrary, and that in the modern court of discursive thought—lacking the religious experience that could once be presupposed—the arguments for unbelief are invincible, capable of being overcome not by counter-arguments, but only by life itself: first the life of Elder Zosima, and then by the life of his disciple Alexei, whose warm and very real love for actual, living children depicted in the last pages finally triumphs over his brother Ivan's theoretical, abstract compassion for conjectural children and their hypothetical suffering. Dostoevsky, then, in this last statement of his thought shows that in this incipient age of the Man-God, it is today in the lives of holy people and in the beauty of nature that we can best encounter the living God, the God who will not be contained by His own transcendence.[2] And it is this numinous draw of creation, perhaps most evident to us in nature—this pull or persuasion or current within the visible that beckons into the invisible—this engaging and evocative interfacing between Creator and creation—that Dostoevsky's young colleague Solovyov, along with two generations of Russian thinkers, designated by the word "Sophia."

B. The Divine Wisdom in Nature

Zosima's discourses poetically depict a deep beauty and an enchanting mystery in created nature—a dimension of creation that can be apprehended only to the extent that the heart is purified. "Blessed are the pure in heart, for they shall see God," states Christ's counsel for being blessed or divinely happy, *makarios*. "The apprehension of the nature of things changes according to the inner disposition of the soul," states Nikitas Stithatos in the *Philokalia*.[3] "Each blade of grass, each little bug,

---

2. In Florensky's classic discussion, Sophia is first discussed not in nature, but in the lives of the saints and monastic elders, in "the beauty of spiritual life"; see Pavel Florensky, *The Pillar and Ground of the Truth*, tr. Boris Jakim (Princeton, NJ: Princeton University Press, 1997), 233f. Hereafter, *PGT*.

3. PGT 200, *The Philokalia*, Vol. 4, St. Nikodemos of the Holy Mountain and St. Makarios of Corinth; tr. G.E.H. Palmer, Philip Sherrard, and Kallistos Ware (London: Faber and Faber, 1979), 92; trans. altered.

ant, golden bee," exhorts Elder Zosima, witnesses "to the divine mystery, [because] they ceaselessly enact it."[4] And the narrative illustrates how purity of heart is required to see this divine wisdom at work in the world:

• For the cynical intellectual Ivan, nothing more is possible than a wistful glimpse of the spring-green leaves each year, although he confesses that it is this alone that allows him to keep on living.

• For the high-minded but passionate and unruly Dmitri, the inner beauty of nature is more accessible. "Let me be cursed, let me be base and vile," exclaims Dmitri, "but let me also kiss the hem of that garment in which my God is clothed."[5] And this garment is nothing other than Edenic nature—however it is to be found—with its shining sun, its clear sky, its green leaves, however clouded the perception.

• But for the third brother, Alyosha, whose embrace of suffering has brought about a certain purification of the soul, the experience of the night sky seems as if he were "touching other worlds": "The silence of the earth seemed to merge with the silence of the heavens, the mystery of the earth touched the mystery of the stars" as he ecstatically, rapturously falls to the ground and kisses the very earth itself.[6] Weeping and repentant, Alyosha encounters God within the element of the Divine Wisdom. But he doesn't name it. Rather, he is wordlessly caught up into its sublime silence. And we could call this Sophia.

Should we? According to St. Clement of Alexandria, Heraclitus had said: "That which is wise (*to sophon*) is one, and it both allows and does not allow itself to be called by the name of Zeus" (Fragment 32). And a central thesis of the present essay might be formulated as a gloss on this ancient fragment: *The Divine Wisdom, which is one with God, both allows and does not allow itself to be called Sophia.* For as soon as we name what is encountered by Alyosha; or by Zosima's young brother Markel, who apologized to the birds for ignoring their joyfulness; or by Zosima and an itinerant barge-hauler sitting quietly at the edge of a great, peaceful river on a starry summer's night—when we objectify this as something or someone, do we not render it a thing among things, or an individual among individuals, one more item in the ontic inventory—positing yet another obstruction between ourselves and God? Do

---

4. Fyodor Dostoevsky, *The Brothers Karamazov*, tr. Richard Pevear and Larissa Volikhonsky (New York: Vintage, 1991), 295. Hereafter, *BK*.

5. *BK*, 107.

6. Ibid., 362.

we not obscure the overwhelming and ineffable character of what is experienced, which is not one perception among others, but an eventful seeing, a privileged encounter, an initiatory unveiling that has been granted, and whose evanescence will not allow it to linger for long or be fixed in place—i.e., not something substantive, as Western metaphysics would hold, but rather something transitive—more an unfolding than an entity? But setting aside these reservations for later discussion, I shall for now speak of Sophia, and of our great need for an understanding of what it names—along with an experience of that to which it points. For surely the name "Sophia" is no more problematic than "nature" or "environment" as a name for what needs to be understood.

Indeed, the concept of "nature" is a central part of the problem, so heavily is it burdened with metaphysical baggage. Since the Latin Middle Ages, nature has been contrasted to, and opposed by, the supernatural. Nature here is non-porous, metaphysically discrete from the supernatural, substantially incommensurate with it. And with the Protestant Reformation, nature becomes radically opposed to grace as well. To this, metaphysics has added the opposition of nature and freedom, with the "spiritual" realm of freedom somehow standing ghostlike outside the realm of natural necessity. Add to this the longstanding equation of nature with substance, and the presupposition that true substance (*protē ousia*) is what can stand on its own, without need of anything else, and we have a monstrous distortion of creation: nature as something bereft of divinity and grace, a realm of blind necessity that, standing self-sufficiently by itself, has no need of, or inner connection to, anything transcendent, leaving qualities such as goodness and beauty merely subjective labels that we attach to things like little children putting stickers (values) on the household furniture (facts). Creation here becomes a harsh prison cell, a realm of impenetrable surfaces without depth, a frozen land in which visibility itself, rather than serving as an aperture to the invisible, becomes a weave of axiological barbed wire, blocking ingress and egress—in short, nature so understood and experienced becomes a cruel and escape-proof *gulag* into which it would today be considered unspeakably inhumane to place living human beings. And it is from precisely this kind of metaphysical imprisonment that "sophiology," the study of Sophia, would offer to free us.

Discussing sophiology in the work of Sergei Bulgakov, Fr. Andrew Louth provides us summary approaches to what is meant by Sophia, at least within the Russian succession from Solovyov to Florensky to Bulgakov. And it is with this body of work—surely the starting point for anything like a viable appropriation of this concept today—that this essay will concern itself. "The gulf between the uncreated God and Creation," writes Louth, "does not put Creation in opposition to God; rather Wisdom constitutes a kind of *metaxu*, 'between,' between God and humans/Creation, for Wisdom is that through which God created the universe, and it is equally through wisdom that the human quest for God finds fulfillment."[7] But, supplementing this concept of a bridge or link, a *tertium quid* between heaven and earth, Louth continues with a very different image: "Wisdom, one might say, is the face that God turns towards his Creation, and the face that Creation, in humankind, turns toward God."[8] The author draws here upon the ancient experience of the divine *prosōpon*, so prominent in the Old Testament, evoking the "face" or "presence" or "countenance" of God without which life has no meaning, is unendurable darkness. (And we may note in passing how radically different are the Psalmist's experiences of God within the gift of that Holy Countenance without which life is desperate and pointless and the modern experience—typified by Nietzsche—of a "supernatural" God as intrusive and meddling in the realm of an otherwise independent realm of "nature"—unneeded and unwanted in a self-sufficient world inhabited by confident, self-possessed hominids, haughty in their imagined independence.)[9] But apart from the important question of whether the sophianic element is more like a bridge or a facing, the same appraisal follows in either case: "Creation is not abandoned by God," Louth affirms: "Creation is graced, it is holy; in creation God may be encountered."[10] And in this holiness of creation, we find a promise of release from our metaphysical imprisonment in "nature," something we may hope sophiology can address. Moreover, we can arrive at this same nexus from several other directions as well:

1. The insight into a hidden depth of creation allows us to affirm that beneath the ontological ice, behind the hard edges, lies something very different: a loving presence, the welcoming embrace of a long-familiar face. Created nature is not made of cast iron, but is permeable, like the air, like the soil. As the Russian theologian Vladimir Lossky puts it: "The Eastern tradition knows nothing of 'pure nature' to which grace is added as a supernatural gift. For it, there is no natural or 'normal' state,

---

7. Andrew Louth, *Modern Orthodox Thinkers: From the Philokalia to the Present* (Downer's Grove, IL: InterVarsity Press Academic, 2015), 58.

8. Ibid.

9. On the modern, supernatural God of Western metaphysics as intrusive, see Michael Allen Gillespie, *Nihilism before Nietzsche* (Chicago: University of Chicago Press, 1996).

10. Louth, *Modern Orthodox Thinkers*, 58.

since grace is implied in the act of creation itself."[11] Nature is everywhere shot through with grace, permeated by what is misleadingly called "super-nature," inherently interwoven with freedom. As two centuries of nature poets have understood—figures from Hölderlin to Hopkins, from Traherne and Wordsworth to Emerson, Thoreau, and Muir—nature is still a place where we can meet God, just as surely as it was long ago in the Sinai Peninsula, in the Judean Desert, at the Sea of Galilee, in the Egyptian Thebaid.

It is doubtful whether there is any religion that has not in some way based itself upon experience. And if we are to experience God, to engage with God, then there must be some manner of divine immanence through which that encounter could take place. But in a world where only the nature of modern science is taken seriously, in a deistic world in which God is forever "off somewhere" leaving nature to function on its own, there are no apertures for the divine countenance to appear— no bushes so "charged with the grandeur of God" that they might burst into mystic flame before our eyes. Religious experience intrinsically demands something like Sophia, an infusion of the divine, of the invisible and heavenly, into the visible and earthly.

2. Moreover, the earthly as such cannot just be jettisoned into the briny waters of scientific objectification. Philosophical naturalism is the belief that what is, or better "what can be," is nothing other than the object of natural science. But if the naturalistic thesis is true, then goodness, beauty, and holiness are not genuinely attributable to nature, which has become nothing but an aggregate of nodal points for indifferent, scientific laws. What we call "facts" would be utterly lacking in what we, equally misleadingly, have come to call "values." We may think here of William Carlos Williams's poem in which bombs falling through space are compared to falling snowflakes, and of how the poem affirms the abysmal difference between them. The poem, "The Snow Begins," opens thus:

> A rain of bombs, well placed,
> is no less lovely
> but this comes gently over all...

The poet-physician Williams, educated as a medical scientist, knows that the laws of mechanics and aerodynamics are fundamentally inadequate to grasp the deepest differences between snowflakes and bombs. For without goodness, without a beauty that is more than merely

---

11. Vladimir Lossky, *The Mystical Theology of the Eastern Church* (Crestwood, NY: St. Vladimir's Seminary Press, 1976), 101.

"lovely," without the ultimate criterion of holiness, is not the distinction, upon which the poem hinges, itself opaque?[12] With the third line, "but this...," Williams snaps us out of the cultural trance, awakens us from "single vision" and Newton's Dream, restores to us a heart of flesh rather than a heart of stone. And the final stanza makes the point even more powerfully: the snow, "white as death," nevertheless dignifies what it covers "as no violence ever can/gently and silently in the night."[13] Williams's poem could rightfully be called sophianic, awakening us from the barrenness of naturalism and retrieving the realm of divinely created nature from its scientific facsimile.

3. Yet today, when ubiquitous video recordings show us in terrible detail the suffering arising from deadly tsunamis and devastating hurricanes, when nearly everyone knows someone stricken by cancer, in which the living body's very cells turn against it, we suffer profoundly from the lack of a natural theodicy. Even those whose Christian faith is robust enough to embrace the traditional view of nature as fallen—allowing them to insist that God did not create cancer nor does He send tsunamis—seem left with the equally counterintuitive view of nature as abandoned to corruption and devoid of grace, when it is plain to every soul that has not turned its back on poetry altogether that nature still, despite its being "bleared" and "smeared," nevertheless retains its original goodness and beauty and holiness, can still allow God's grandeur to "flame out." The concept of Sophia, understood as the "original creation" that still underlies the blight of sin and fallenness—i.e., the understanding of Sophia that I believe we find in Dostoevsky and Florensky—allows us to affirm the seemingly contradictory claims that nature is indeed fallen and corrupted, while still remaining *kalos*, both good and beautiful, as primordially proclaimed on each day of creation in the Greek Septuagint.

C. Nature and Human Nature: Creation as Normative

Every student of ethics knows about the modern claim of a naturalistic fallacy—so named by G.E. Moore in 1903, but based upon work by Hume two centuries earlier—rejecting the belief that one can derive "ought" from "is," that the way things *are* can be prescriptive for the way things *ought to be*. But neither Athens nor Jerusalem considered this to be fallacious at all. Throughout the Old Testament, and especially in the

12. For "the holy" as the highest order of axiology, see Max Scheler, *Formalism in Ethics and Non-Formal Ethics of Values: A New Attempt toward the Foundation of an Ethical Personalism* (Evanston, IL: Northwestern University Press, 1973), 93f.

13. William Carlos Williams, *The Collected Poems of William Carlos Williams: Volume II, 1939–1962*, ed. Christopher MacGowan, (New York: New Directions, 2001), 426.

Wisdom Books, nature is held up as exemplary and edifying. Nor is it accidental that Jesus, in his Sermon on the Mount, asks us to emulate the birds of the sky and the flowers of the field. And nature was prescriptive for the ancient Greeks as well, as is perhaps most evident in the Stoic commitment to living in accord with *physis* or nature, which they in turn identified with the deity. Until recently in the West, this view was associated with natural law theory, which claims that ethical norms can be based upon our observations of the natural order, a view that, while rooted in Plato, Aristotle, and the Stoics, is often associated with Thomas Aquinas. Unhappily, the belief in natural law is a decidedly minority view in philosophical ethics, jurisprudence, and even popular opinion. Why is this the case?

The first reason, I believe, derives from the fact that we have so much information about natural history. Yes, living species care for their young—except for those cases in which they get devoured by their parents. Yes, individual beings do strive to preserve themselves in being, except when they are rhizomatic and possess no individual being to begin with. And so on. Skeptical science teachers delight in pointing out countless examples in which cruelty and indifference to all human valuations prevail in nature. Indeed, students are typically presented with a view of Darwinism in which violence and cunning prevail over cooperation, while young males justify promiscuity through invoking the sociobiology they have been taught in class, in which male sexuality is presented as the indiscriminate drive to inseminate a maximum number of females.

The second objection to natural law theory is perhaps more subtle, but even more decisive. In positing a realm of pure nature, upon which reason alone can found moral precepts, its adherents are promulgating something of a fiction. For as has been argued already, there is no realm of this sort. Or, rather, pure nature would be nothing other than the nature of natural science, stripped beforehand of all "values," and hence not only worthless, but downright pernicious as a model for human behavior.[14] For only when we apprehend nature as divinely instituted, i.e., see it as creation, are we able to learn from it, to sense the divine wisdom interwoven throughout it. That is, only by means of *askēsis* (understood not primarily as fasting and vigils, but purification of the heart) can nature be seen deeply and the divine wisdom reigning within it be revealed. And this is precisely the view we find in Dostoevsky,

14. For a horrifying look at a set of moral values based purely on empirical, scientific nature, see the diabolical masterpiece of the Marquis de Sade, *Juliette*. Indeed, Horkheimer and Adorno see this monstrous work as the ultimate, and most consistent,

where characters fail to see any meaning in nature until their hearts are cleansed, until their souls begin to be set in order, until they learn how to love. And this insight, developed powerfully by Fr. Pavel Florensky in his *Pillar and Ground of the Truth*, is one of which we stand desperately in need today, in a dark age where traditional norms of human relationships are routinely mocked and discarded. An understanding of Sophia, then, or of some related set of ideas, is of the highest importance for us today, especially as we strive to learn how to live more harmoniously with what we call "nature," of whose ways, despite its claims, science alone cannot give us a sound understanding.

D. Nature as Original Creation

As a child during the last decades of the 19th century, Florensky experienced Batumi as a magical place, where nature seemed everywhere enchanted. It was the charmed setting where he first began to experience nature as brimming over with the mystery of divine wisdom. But now, a century and a quarter later, it is a major seaside resort for the Caucasus Republics and beyond to Turkey and Iran, as well as the primary port for oil piped in from the Caspian Sea. So I hardly expected that the enchantment would have lingered on. Nonetheless, here I stood upon the hotel balcony, looking out onto panoramas not just of the Black Sea with its tales of Jason and Medea, but also opening toward the lush mountains rising up from the city itself, cloud-covered like lofty Olympus and holy Athos. Yet these were not stately sentinels of sacred space but nascent and primal, simmering and roiling clouds, dynamic and animate, drawing in and out in acts of meteorological exhibitionism and metaphysical virtuosity. Clouds so massive and dense they looked tangible, yet so protean in their shape-shifting that they would have leapt out of the grip of any loutish giant seeking to clutch them. And in fact these cloud-ravished heights did look like places where mythical beings might still be stalking about. These clouds—so succulent that in their shadow, tea plantations are able to flourish here in the foothills of the Caucasus—seemed just as earthly as heavenly—brooding and reclusive, perhaps like those that must have just arisen on that second day of creation, when the Creator lifted up the expanse of land, and waters were first separated from other waters.

---

elaboration of the Enlightenment view of nature and its implications for human conduct, while Sade himself saw it as based squarely upon the materialistic understanding of nature in the French Encyclopedist Baron d'Holbach, especially his *Système de la Nature*. Max Horkheimer and Theodor W. Adorno, "*Juliette* or Enlightenment and Morality," in *Dialectic of Enlightenment: Philosophical Fragments*, tr. Edmund Jephcott (Stanford CA: Stanford University Press, 2002), 63–93.

Eager to get up into those cloud-hidden mountains, I spent an after-noon exploring a vast arboretum and forest preserve—dating to the nineteenth century, and precariously clinging to a mountainside that sloped down steeply to the sea itself—where the prodigious, profligately verdant character of this land was fully evident, teeming with flora and fauna in a manner that evoked those protocols of early explorers in the New World that abounded with words like "paradise" and "Eden." Nature here—now fog-shrouded, now sunlit, in just the kind of place the young Florensky must have wandered rapt in wonder—was capti-vating not only in its abundance and variety and dramatic visage, but in the sense that here nature seems to be just now emerging from the hand of God, as in the first beginning, or flying up like a white dove released to find Mount Ararat in that second beginning, when the world was once more purified and made new, sparkling and glistening, and all good things seemed possible.

Thinking back to his childhood years in Batumi, when he was "still nestled close to the life of nature," Florensky recalls that what he loved most "was air, wind, clouds"; "my brothers were cliffs, my spiritual kin-dred minerals, specially crystals. I loved birds, and most of all growing things and the sea . . . with all the power of my being, *I was in love with nature*."[15] However, it was not what philosophers would call empirical or positive nature that he loved, but something more, something deeper, more elemental: "I grew accustomed to seeing the roots of things. That habit of vision later grew though all my thought and defined its basic character—the will to move along verticals and a cer-tain indifference to horizontals."[16] In these reflections, we find intercon-nected thoughts that lie at the center of Florensky's philosophy. By means of *askēsis*, of repentance, of purification of the heart, we are able to break through the self-encrusted ego and, in an ecstatic act of loving and knowing, make contact with the very depths of creation, revealing those depths as only love can do. And this is precisely Florensky's funda-mental concept of Sophia. Sophia is not "merely all creation." Rather, "Sophia is the Great Root by which creation goes into the intra-Trinitar-ian life [of divine love] and through which it receives Life Eternal from the One Source of Life. *Sophia is the original nature of creation*."[17] But

---

15. Pavel Florensky, "On the Efimovs' Puppet Theatre," in Pavel Florensky, *Beyond Vision: Essays on the Perception of Art*, ed. Nicolette Misler, (London: Reaktion Books, 2002), 134; Pavel Florensky, *For My Children*, trans. in Avril Pyman, *Pavel Florensky: A Quiet Genius* (New York: Continuum, 2010), 5. Italics added.

16. Florensky, *For My Children*, 7.

17. *PGT* 237. Italics added.

the original nature of creation is its paradisiacal essence, nature as it issues from the hand of the Creator. As Florensky wrote in 1919, Sophia is "that spiritual aspect of being, one might call it a paradisiacal aspect, according to which there is as yet no knowledge of good and evil [but rather] there is only movement around God, a free playing in the presence of God . . . like the sea playing in the sun."[18] Or again: "Sophia is essential Beauty in all of creation," and therefore "purity of heart . . . is the necessary condition for seeing Sophia-Wisdom."[19] And with these passages, we also return to the great theme of Elder Zosima: repentant souls learning how to love, and thereby finding that they are now in paradise, finding that all is transfigured as its original nature is revealed. "Love all of God's creation," exhorts Elder Zosima, "both the whole of it, and every grain of sand. Love every leaf, every ray of God's light. Love animals, love plants, love each thing. If you love each thing, you will perceive the mystery of God in things."[20] This mystery, this depth in things, and in others, is for both Dostoevsky and Florensky "paradise," "God's glory" surrounding us, if only we are able to see it.[21]

Florensky uses many images, or more properly "symbols" as he would put it—links bringing together (*syn*) into one (*holon*) what Kant had bifurcated into the phenomenal and the noumenal—to convey what he means by "Sophia." In a single sentence, he refers to Sophia as:

- the Heavenly Jerusalem
- the Kingdom of God as the Ideal Person of Creation
- the Guardian Angel of Creation
- the world-creating thoughts of God
- the true pole and Incorruptible Aspect of creaturely being[22]

And many others follow. But I want to argue that they are all ways of speaking about this inner depth of creation, this beauty and mystery of creation that, like certain characters in Dostoevsky's novels, Florensky encountered in his experience of nature and of other people. And if we take such concepts as statements of Christian doctrine, or attempts to build a systematic theology, rather than poetic articulations of noetic experience, not only will they fall into impossible contradiction with one another, but we will misunderstand Florensky's entire project in *The Pillar and Ground of the Truth*, a book whose first sentence insists that "living religious experience [is] the sole legitimate way to gain

18. Florensky, "Celestial Signs," in *Beyond Vision*, 122.
19. Ibid., 254.
20. *BK*, 319.
21. Ibid., 289.
22. *PGT*, 241.

knowledge of dogmas," and adds that "only by relying on immediate experience can one survey the spiritual treasures of the Church and come to see their value."[23]

II. Why the Concept of Sophia is Problematic

The modern inaugurator of sophiological reflection, Vladimir Solovyov, also based his concept of Sophia on powerful, unforgettable experiences. But unlike Florensky's nature mysticism and Bulgakov's parallel and oft-cited experience of the Caucasus Mountains at sunset, Solovyov's experiences are, from the Orthodox point of view, highly suspect. For what he describes are not mystical experiences or noetic insights, but rather visionary interactions with a certain being named Sophia, visions (three of them) in which Sophia, who seems very much like a goddess, reveals to Solovyov as her follower a set of teachings. But in the tradition of Orthodox spiritual guidance, the consistent teaching is that such visions are most likely harbingers of *prelest* or spiritual delusion, and one must not seek them out, but rather assume until proven otherwise that their source is not divine at all, but rather demonic. Monks who report that Christ or the Mother of God have appeared to them in a vision are routinely advised to subject these visions to critical questioning and accept them only if they withstand scrutiny.

Nor are the occasions of these three visions at all auspicious. The first occurs when, during Divine Liturgy, the adolescent Solovyov is daydreaming about a girl with whom he is infatuated. The second vision takes place (during a period when Solovyov was practicing automatic writing and the "channeling of spirits") in the Reading Room of the British Museum, where he was doing research into Gnosticism, Hermeticism, and Occultism. And the third unfolds in the Sahara Desert near the Pyramids of Giza, themselves connected to the worship of Osiris, Egyptian god of death. Indeed, given Solovyov's lifelong interest in Gnosticism, theosophy, and the occult, one wonders whether this was a vision of the Sophia named in the Old Testament Wisdom Books, or rather a vision of Isis or Persephone, both identified with the Gnostic Sophia.[24] (The first major articulation of Blavatsky's theosophy was entitled *Isis Unveiled*.) Nor can these visions be dismissed as merely allegorical. As Avril Pyman relates, the generation of Russian intellectuals

23. *PGT*, 5.

24. The great Church historian Georges Florovsky, who knew him personally, argued that Solovyov's Sophia was that of "Valentinus and Cabbala," and complained that he had "pushed Russian society on the path of fascination with Gnosticism and theosophy." Paul L. Gavrilyuk, *Georges Florovsky and the Russian Religious Renaissance*

succeeding Solovyov in the quest for Sophia, many of whom knew him personally, all agreed upon one thing: these were real visions, representing genuine contact, with an actual supernatural entity named Sophia.[25] Thus, an element of goddess worship enters the tradition of sophianic inquiry from the very beginning and it is doubtful whether it is ever truly overcome.

But there are philosophical and theological problems here as well. For to the extent that Sophia is hypostasized, either as an individual person (a goddess), or as the world soul, or as a Fourth Hypostasis alongside the Three Persons of the Trinity (a proposal with its own, special problems), another reality is placed between God and the world. And the traditional name for this practice is idolatry. If there is a higher order of reality (x) that is closer to us than God Himself, does it not follow that we should worship (x) rather than God? Or, perhaps, worship both (x) and God? Indeed, this is the logic of the golden calf at the foot of Mt. Sinai, where God seems too distant, too inaccessible and indeed somewhat dubious, and the people demand a deity that is closer, more approachable, more reliable. This is the problem of any *metaxu*—Plato's term for a connecting link *between* the visible and the invisible, and upon which Bulgakov draws in his exposition of Sophia—i.e., of anything standing between God and Creation. For rather than connecting God and Creation, it tends instead, like a solar eclipse, to block the very source of Light itself. John Milbank, in his defense of Sophia, sees this problem clearly: "Between God and Creation then, there is no between. To suppose so would be idolatry."[26] Yet, within the framework of Western theology and its rejection of the Eastern understanding of divine energies, there seems to him no other way to bring God and Creation together. To resolve this dilemma, Milbank resorts to a formula that seems as arbitrary as it is incomprehensible: "Sophia names a *metaxu* which does not lie between two poles but rather remains simultaneously at both poles at once. As such it does not subsist before the two poles,

---

(Oxford: Oxford University Press, 2014), 102f. As later studies have shown, however, Russian society in the late nineteenth century was already quite fascinated with esotericism of this kind and hardly needed pushing from Solovyov. See, for example, Bernice Glatzer Rosenthal, ed., *The Occult in Russian and Soviet Culture* (Ithaca, NY: Cornell University Press, 1997).

25. Avril Pyman, *A History of Russian Symbolism* (Cambridge: Cambridge University Press, 1994), 228f.

26. John Milbank, "Sophiology and Theurgy: The New Theological Horizon," in Adrian Pabst and Christoph Schneider, eds., *Encounter Between Eastern Orthodoxy and Radical Orthodoxy: Transfiguring the World Through the Word* (Surrey, UK: Ashgate, 2009), 64.

but it co-arises with them such that they can only exist according to a mediated communication which remains purely occult, a matter of utterly inscrutable affinity."[27]

Moreover, a "between" of any sort does violence to our experience of God in nature and our discourse about it. If I look upon a beautiful landscape and say that it displays the divine wisdom, I do not mean that the beauty manifests some intermediate layer between God and world called "divine wisdom," which I must subsequently relate back to God. I simply mean that it is God Himself in His wisdom that I am experiencing. Likewise, if like Zosima's brother I say that the divine mystery addresses me through the singing of the birds, I don't mean that some hypostatic being called Mystery is singing and speaking—a being who would in fact merit my worship, were this the case. Rather, I mean that it is God Himself in His mystery that I am encountering.

Metaphysically, this too much resembles the concept of emanation in Neo-Platonism and Gnosticism, from which sources it is in fact partially imported. From the One a metaphysical layer of Nous emanates, and from the Nous emanates the Soul (and above all, the World Soul), and from the Soul the Visible World that we inhabit. To a given emanation, only the next-highest emanation is directly connected, relegating access to the One to initiate philosophers who can contemplatively climb the metaphysical ladder, leaving the Visible World behind, and doubtless rendering us (as Plotinus was said to be) ashamed of our own bodies.

Finally, both Florensky and Bulgakov maintain that Sophia reveals the very content of the divine essence. But this will not do. First, as Lossky points out, Wisdom is only one divine name among many that we know (such as Love, Being, Power, Justice, and Life) and no doubt innumerable others that we can neither experience nor know, no one of which can contain the divine fullness.[28] But second, any claim to comprehend the divine essence entails problems that are especially egregious for Orthodox theology, whose strong commitment to apophaticism insists that the divine essence is profoundly unknowable, forever mysterious, even to the highest ranks of the angelic orders. For a knowable God, a God whom we can know as He knows Himself, is a God who is commensurate with human knowledge, a God of our own size commensurate with our own concepts, i.e., an idol.

Do we really want, it might well be asked, to exhaust, or even compromise, the mystery of God, should that somehow be possible? Would we even want to exhaust the mystery of a human person we love, strip-

---

27. Ibid., 50.
28. Lossky, *Mystical Theology of the Eastern Church*, 80.

ping them of the possibility of surprising us, of leaving us in wonder, of continuing to inhabit a mystery that forever preserves them from being reduced to our own knowledge of them? Is it not of the very essence of a person not to be entirely known, even by that person himself? But if the very content of the divine essence has been delivered into Sophia, this would be precisely the result. As we came to understand God within the Wisdom layer that hovers above this finite world, we would become increasingly melancholy as we gradually exhausted the mystery of the divine essence. Must we not say that the mystery of God is utterly inexhaustible, and that we can no more progress toward a complete knowledge of the divine essence than we can make any progress in enumerating an infinite series, i.e., in counting up to infinity?

III. How (Not) to Speak of Sophia

But if God cannot be known in His essence (*ousia*), this does not mean that He cannot be known.

1. In Eastern Christianity, it has always been affirmed that God is everywhere present and knowable in His energies (*energeiai*), His activity or operation or work (*ergon*) in the world. For a person, any person, is present to varying degrees within his activity. A singer is present in her singing, as is the songwriter. I hear a woman singing on the radio, and I say "that's Baez." I recognize her. Or I can just as truthfully say, "that's Dylan." For if Baez sings Dylan, both are present in the singing—both are personally present. I glimpse a painting in an antique store and breathlessly whisper, "that's Van Gogh! I would recognize him anywhere." It is Dylan himself that I hear. And Baez herself. And Van Gogh himself that I see. Not representations of these human creators, but the persons themselves whom I recognize.[29] How much more, then, would

---

29. My example here is drawn from the contemporary Greek philosopher, Christos Yannaras, who points to the remarkable fact that in the work of art we can actually encounter the very person of the creator who has invested himself in the work. See Christos Yannaras, *Person and Eros*, tr. Norman Russell (Brookline, MA: Holy Cross Orthodox Press, 2007), 167–72. But already in the fourth century, we can find a similar claim in St. Gregory of Nyssa, who points to "human works of art where, in a way, the mind can perceive the maker of the product that is before it," St Gregory of Nyssa, *The Beatitudes*, in *St. Gregory of Nyssa: The Lord's Prayer and The Beatitudes*, tr. Hilda Graef, Ancient Christian Writers Vol. 18 (New York: Newman Press, 1954), 146. But it must be emphasized that this analogy is limited: the presence of God in His energies infinitely exceeds that of the human artist in his created work.

the Almighty Creator be present Himself within the continuous activity of His creation? As St. Gregory of Nyssa put it, God "is invisible by nature, but becomes visible in His energies."[30] If we have eyes to see, i.e., if our hearts are purified, we can discover God in all things, even through the crust of sin and corruption and fallenness. "The spiritual world of the invisible is not some infinitely far off kingdom," Florensky insists; "instead, it everywhere surrounds us as an ocean." "But we, from the habit of immature spiritual sight," he continues, "fail even to assume it exists, and therefore we only sense unclearly in our hearts the spiritual currents of what is really happening around us."[31]

2. As the Prologue to St. John's Gospel proclaims, God creates the world through the Logos, through his Eternal Word. Correspondingly, as maintained at least since St. Maximus the Confessor, at the deepest ground of each being there lies a unique *logos*, something that God has to say, something noetically intelligible and utterly unrepeatable. Each thing, "every little leaf," has an inexhaustible meaning, is an expression of the Word of God underlying all things. And in loving them, as Zosima prescribes, we are loving the Word expressed within them. Florensky explicitly draws upon this teaching in his exposition of Sophia, citing St. Clement of Alexandria, in whom we can already find the teaching of divine *logoi* articulated: "Before our creation we therefore existed in the thought of God, we who later turned out to be intelligent creatures of the Divine Word. Thanks to Him, we are very ancient in our origin, because 'in the beginning was the Word.'"[32]

3. That which is instituted by God's Word was originally in Greek named *ktisis* or creation. And still today what we call "nature" can be better understood as creation—that which God brings into being though his Word, the discourse of God that generates our world. The linguistic element is fundamental here. For the Greek *ktisis* signifies what is brought into being through its being spoken, something like the "performative" as understood in analytic philosophy, where the words "with this ring I thee wed" do not denote an already existing state of affairs, but rather bring that state of affairs (marriage) into being. In contrast to *ktisis* is *demiourgeia*, which is predicated of something made or produced, as a craftsman makes a finished product. And it is *ktisis* that is consistently

---

30. St. Gregory of Nyssa, 147.

31. Pavel Florensky, *Iconostasis*, tr. Donald Sheehan and Olga Andrejev (Crestwood, NY: St. Vladimir's Seminary Press, 1996), 64.

32. St. Clement of Alexandria, cited in *PGT*, 239.

used, in both the Septuagint Old Testament and the Greek New Testament, to denote creation as what is instituted by the Word of God. Creation, then, is less like a finished product and more like a proclamation being issued, something far more personal and far more evocative of the speaker—something that is indeed inhabited by the speaker.

4. The divine wisdom, then, could be understood as that within which the speaking of God coheres—the syntax of creation, its ordering (*taxis*) into something like verse and meter, stanza, chapter, and book—as well as the element of divine beauty or glory (*doxa*) that surrounds it, vouchsafing its origin.[33] Apprehending original creation would then be understood as something like the revealing and restoration of a text corrupted by moth or mold, or having been roughly translated from one language into another until its original beauty and order have become obscure. And I believe that most of what Florensky argues with regard to Sophia as original creation is quite compatible with this ancient notion of the divine wisdom ordering, and radiating from, creation as *ktisis*. Indeed, his final restatement at the end of the "Sophia" chapter employs precisely this language, while suggesting (as does Dostoevsky in *Karamozov*) that this revealing has an eschatological significance: "Sophia, the *true Creation* or *Creation in the Truth*, is a preliminary hint at the transfigured, spiritualized world as the manifestation, imperceptible for others, of the heavenly in the earthly."[34] But if this is the case, why risk the dangers of introducing the concept of Sophia, novel or marginal to both Eastern and Western traditions, with its questionable history and problematic implications?

5. Finally, what is said is always to one degree or another an image or *eikon* of the speaker, expressing the speaker without necessarily resembling him. The Byzantine or Russian icon is made (or "written," as it is said) to promote a kind of double seeing, a seeing in which we see through one thing (the image) in order to see another (the original). This double seeing was what the ancient Greeks called *eikasia*, or imagination, and it differed from *phantasia*, the production of *phantasmata*, the mere products of fancy or fantasy.[35] Like the shadow or mirror

33. "That everything is 'fitting' [*kata taxin*] is precisely what constitutes the beauty of creation, as well as its good and its truth." Florensky, *PGT*, 132.

34. *PGT*, 283, italics added.

35. The most important source in ancient philosophy for this understanding of *eikasia* is the "divided line" exegesis in Plato's Republic, where the "double-seeing" of an original through the image is used as a model for each step, proceeding up the divided line

image—which we must "see through" if we are to see it truly, i.e., see that it is "cast" by something else, and thereby see the original through it—the *eikon* in the proper sense is less a representation (*Vorstellung* in German) than a presentation (*Darstellung*) in which the original itself is brought forth, just as a performance of Hamlet is not a representation of the play, but a presentation of the play itself. Thus, creation can be seen as itself iconic, as God's first presentation of His Word, i.e., of Himself.[36] Creation can in this case be seen as presenting to us the very face or countenance or presence (*prosōpon*) of God, as is the case throughout the poetry of the Psalms.

But if God is present in creation as His own energies or activities; as the *logos* of each entity that makes it what it is, as something that God has to say; as the created order itself, in its coherence and wisdom and beauty; and as the original that is always present in the image, it would hardly seem necessary to resort to Sophia in order to mediate between God and world. As I have argued, this is not simply a matter of philosophical parsimony, but of avoiding serious theological and philosophical problems. Andrew Louth, in defense of Russian sophiology, has acknowledged that everything that is said through the concept of Sophia might well be said in more traditional ways. But how, he asks, would we then be able "to understand the coherence and mutual entailments" of the correlative concepts and "assertions"? But is a single concept, such as Sophia, in fact the best manner to accomplish this? Fr. Louth in fact proposes (without endorsing) an appealing answer to his own question in the suggestion that the "liturgical inspiration" that we find in Bulgakov's philosophical theology can bind together these concepts.[37] Perhaps. And no doubt the traditional Name of Divine Wisdom (without the Sophia encumbrances) needs to be much better developed,

---

to the highest step of the forms or *eidē* themselves. And even the latter are ultimately images of what in Plato is variously called the Good, the One, or the Same, and which Church Fathers understood as Plato's intuition of God. My reading of Plato has, in turn, been influenced by several works of former teachers and mentors: see Jacob Klein, *A Commentary on Plato's Meno* (Chapel Hill, NC: University of North Carolina Press, 1965), especially pages 112–15; Evan Brann, *The Music of the Republic: Essays on Socrates' Conversations and Plato's Writings* (Philadelphia: Paul Dry, 2011), especially 172–75, 18–94, 338–43; and John Sallis, *Being and Logos: Reading the Platonic Dialogues* (Bloomington, IN: Indiana University Press, 1996), especially 418–22.

36. For my understanding of creation as iconic, see Bruce V. Foltz, "The Iconic Earth: Nature Godly and Beautiful," Chapter Six of *The Noetics of Nature: Environmental Philosophy and the Holy Beauty of the Visible* (New York: Fordham University Press, 2014), 113–57.

37. Louth, *Modern Orthodox Thinkers*, 57.

something Florensky tried to do in his later research on space, time, mathematics, and natural science. For as St. Dionysius readily acknowledges in his *Divine Names*, Wisdom (or Sophia) is indeed a Name of God, allowing us to know God kataphatically, through His energies.

Perhaps the most successful applications of sophianic thinking are Bulgakov's *Philosophy of Economy* and Florensky's *Iconostasis*. In the former, Bulgakov very powerfully contrasts a sophianic economy (which reveals the divine goodness and beauty inherent in creation) to a diabolical economy (which does the opposite, obscuring and debasing and disfiguring original creation).[38] But would not a broader philosophical and theological articulation of creation as *ktisis* serve the same purpose, and in fact lead more productively to further modes of "coherence and mutual entailment" beyond those enumerated by Bulgakov? And in *Iconostasis*, his last published work, Florensky shows through art history how Western modes of thought and perception have served to sever heaven and earth, while the concept of the icon plays the role of linking them, without recourse to a between-element or any reference to Sophia at all. For the connection between image (*eikon*) and original is primal and ontological—the very being of an image is to be referential, to be ontologically transitive—without requiring any kind of a *metaxu* or "between" as a mediator. Moreover, the writings of both authors abound with rich, phenomenological accounts of the beauty of creation, and of the divine wisdom displayed in the astounding interconnectedness of every aspect of creation. I believe that there is much work to be done in assimilating these texts, which stand with the work of Scheler, Heidegger, and Merleau-Ponty as presenting the finest phenomenological research of the last century. A phenomenological, descriptive catalogue of the many modes of divine wisdom manifested in the world—a contemporary correlate to the bounteous expositions of divine wisdom woven throughout the Psalms and other Wisdom Books of scripture—would do much toward reclaiming the experienced world (the *Lebenswelt* of phenomenology) that we can rightfully claim as our truly human inheritance—encounter as *ktisis* or creation, rather than as a scientific object or a technological resource.

Surely the problems that Sophia seeks to remedy are urgent. Like Russia at the turn of the 20th century—its Church weakened by the Old Believer Schism and the Westernizing impositions and confiscations of

---

38. On Sophia in this Bulgakov text, see Bruce V. Foltz, "The Resurrection of Nature: Environmental Metaphysics in Sergei Bulgakov's *Philosophy of Economy*," Chapter Five of *Noetics of Nature*.

the Romanov Czars—the West today is caught between powerful but inchoate spiritual yearnings and religious institutions that seem incapable of meeting them. This situation constitutes perhaps the strongest reason for endorsing a bold claim made by John Milbank: "At the dawn of the 21st century, it increasingly appears that the most significant theology of the two preceding centuries has been that of the Russian sophiological tradition."[39] But it remains unclear whether the concept of Sophia is what will best address these urgent issues, especially given its controversial status in both orthodox Christian and Orthodox Christian circles. Perhaps the problems of sophiology that I have outlined, along with others that could easily be added, can all be surmounted. But in the meantime, I believe that the concepts of divine energies, of divine *logoi* in creation, of the ancient notion of creation as *ktisis*, of the Divine Wisdom in nature, and of iconic creation—all more traditional, better integrated into existing doctrine, and, I believe, inherently richer concepts—are more promising options to be further articulated and more fully developed.

39. Milbank, "Sophiology and Theurgy," 45.

The Catholic Imagination

A Sophiology Between Scatology and Eschatology

Artur Sebastian Rosman

...A pure thing, against the sad affairs of earth.
Pure, forbidden the use of certain words:
Toilet, telephone, ticket, ass, money...
Czeslaw Milosz, *A Treatise on Poetry*

THE IRISH PHILOSOPHER Richard Kearney differentiates the literary imagination of James Joyce as one where "the scatological and the eschatological rub shoulders."[1] In turn, James Joyce, in *Finnegans Wake*, imagined that a "truly catholic assemblage" would be one where H.C.E. reigns, that is, "Here Comes Everybody."[2] How are we to imagine such a boundless Catholicism, capable of embracing the wisdom (*sophia*) of God's world like Bernini's colonnades in St. Peter's Square? The concept of the imagination is fundamental to revitalizing such a properly Catholic way of hospitably engaging the world beyond superficial "liberal" and "conservative" labels that only serve the *status quo*. The imagination should not be confused with mere fancy; rather, an imagination has its own specific parameters that issue in an intellectual, physical, and material comportment to God, the world, and one's fellow man. I will provisionally venture the thesis that the concept of the imagination—more specifically the nature of the Catholic imagination—should be one of the foundations for anchoring the emerging discipline of Catho-

---

1. Richard Kearney, *Anatheism: Returning to God after God* (New York: Columbia University Press, 2010), 108.
2. James Joyce, *Finnegans Wake* (New York: Penguin, 1999), 32.

lic Studies in a rigorous manner.[3] Answers to the following basic questions will help us orient ourselves: What is an imagination? What are its implications? What is so unique about a Catholic imagination?

The symbolist poet Oskar Milosz[4] provides a preliminary answer to the first question in his *Epistle to Storge*. Here he speaks of a basic human need for placement within the cosmos: "It could be said of the compulsion to situate all things (including the space and time in which we situate them) that it is the first of our life's mental manifestations. Certainly there is no thought and emotion which does not derive from this essential activity of being."[5] The dynamic and intimate tie between the human mind, emotions, and the world—close in its thrust to what phenomenology understands by intentionality—is what we will understand as an imagination. The imagination's compulsion to situate all things does not come in one variety. Every intellectual-spiritual-material formation marks its members in its own unique ways.

One useful way of conceptualizing how an imagination works was outlined in David Tracy's now classic *The Analogical Imagination*. There he describes how an imagination arranges the relationship between three fundamental concepts: God, man, and the world.[6] Tracy characterizes the Catholic assemblage of things as "analogical," because it stresses the close interplay, the analogies, between God, man, and the world. This issues in a stress upon the immanence of the divine within (frequently painful and suffering-filled) human affairs and the cosmos. That is the eschatological in the scatological, if you will. Czeslaw Milosz describes thrust of the analogical imagination in a more poetic idiom:

> All humanity, past and present, is, in truth, a Church persisting outside ordinary space and time, a Church opposed to the necessity built into the universe. Catholicism is the most anthropocentric of religions and, in some sense, through its own excess of divine humanity, it resists the exact sciences which annihilate the individual. Thus, paradoxically, it is less susceptible than other religions to the disintegrative influence of science and technology. In Catholicism, even Heaven and Earth, the Descent and the Ascension of God are not like relations between

---

3. See James Fisher and Margaret McGuinness, eds., *The Catholic Studies Reader* (New York: Fordham University Press, 2011).

4. He was both uncle and the greatest spiritual inspiration of Nobelist poet Czeslaw Milosz.

5. Oskar Milosz, *The Noble Traveller: The Life and Writings of O.V. de Milosz*, ed. and trans. Czeslaw Milosz (West Stockbridge, MA: Lindisfarne, 1985), 234.

6. See David Tracy, *The Analogical Imagination: Christian Theology and the Culture of Pluralism* (New York: Crossroad, 1998), 405–45.

worlds but like those between human forms [and their suffering, tragic dimension].[7]

Yet, the eminence of science and technology, even in our late modern world, is undeniable. It is undeniable even when Bultmann's project of demythologizing the scriptures in the wake of mid-century scientific progress seems hopelessly out of date: "The world-view of the Scripture is mythological and is therefore unacceptable to modern man whose thinking has been shaped by science and is therefore no longer mythological."[8] In a late modern context, with a global ecological disaster looming, we are much more inclined, like Pope Francis in *Laudato Si'*, to demythologize science and its frequently less than salutary intentions and effects.

Czeslaw Milosz is also an invaluable guide here.[9] Here is how he describes the corrosive effects on the Catholic imagination of divorcing mind from matter, spirit from the body:

> Instead of leaving to theologians their worries, I have constantly meditated on religion [in my poetry]. Why? Simply because someone had to do this. . . . I lived in a time when a huge change in the contents of the human imagination was occurring. In my lifetime Heaven and Hell disappeared, the belief in life after death was considerably weakened [and so on]. . . . After two thousand years in which a huge edifice of creeds and dogmas has been erected, from Origen and Saint Augustine to Thomas Aquinas and Cardinal Newman, when every work of the human mind and of human hands was created within a system of reference, the age of homelessness has dawned. How could I not think of this?[10]

As Michael Martin points out in his *The Submerged Reality*, this state of affairs goes back much further than the Scientific Revolution. It is the end-result of a post-nominalist sundering of nature from grace.[11] It is impossible to avoid thinking about this, because that great divorce structures our possible ways of imagining and inhabiting the world. In some

---

7. Czeslaw Milosz, *Visions from San Francisco Bay*, trans. Richard Lourie (New York: Farrar Straus Giroux, 1982), 82–83.

8. Rudolf Bultmann, *Jesus Christ and Mythology* (New York: Scribner, 1958), 37.

9. I would argue Czeslaw Milosz was one of the most important undiscovered theological geniuses of the 20th century, much as Coleridge still remains mostly an unplumbed genius of 19th-century theology.

10. Czeslaw Milosz, *Roadside Dog*, trans. Robert Hass and Czeslaw Milosz (New York: Farrar, Straus and Giroux, 1998), 105.

11. Michael Martin, *The Submerged Reality: Sophiology and the Turn to a Poetic Metaphysics* (Kettering, OH: Angelico Press, 2015), 13–16.

ways, the Protestant imagination—followed by the scientific, literary-critical, neoliberal and other modern imaginations—institutionalized these tendencies through a dialectical emphasis of God's transcendence over and against man and the world.

What does it mean to speak of the dialectical emphasis of the Protestant imagination? Tracy's tripartite schema is useful here as well. The dialectical imagination places God over, above, and against humanity and the world. God's transcendence of creation is accentuated so as to almost form a complete break. The metaphors the Calvinist theologian Karl Barth uses in *The Epistle to the Romans* are a paradigmatic 20th-century example of what we mean when we speak of a Protestant dialectical imagination:

> The effulgence, or, rather, the crater made at the percussion point of an exploding shell, the void by which the point on the line of intersection makes itself known in the concrete world of history, is not—even though it be named the Life of Jesus—that other world which touches our world in Him. In so far as our world is touched in Jesus by the other world, it ceases to be capable of direct observation as history, time, or thing.[12]

Here not even the ascents or descents of the God-man form relations between this world and the other world, which only touches us with a void rather than a human presence. In Oskar Milosz's (and later Czeslaw's) terms this imagination of reality makes God homeless in the world. To be fair to Barth, later in his career he does say, in *The Humanity of God*, that the position he occupied in *The Epistle to the Romans* could not be and "was not the last word."[13] One must note that not all forms of Protestantism gravitate toward his earlier extremely dialectical position; some, like high Anglo-Catholicism, are not infrequently more analogical than most mainstream forms of Roman Catholicism. But it is also true that, if we go back to Czeslaw Milosz's analysis of the break-down of the Catholic edifice, a drift away from an analogical imagination toward a dialectical imagination is the source of the contemporary crisis of the Catholic imagination and its theologies.

The concept of the "imagination" requires further explication in order to take it out of its commonplace association with the realm of the "imaginary," "fanciful," and "wishful thinking" and the "pious pie-in-the-sky." The concept of the imagination needs more flesh to serve a

---

12. Karl Barth, *The Epistle to the Romans* (Oxford: Oxford University Press, 1968), 29.

13. Karl Barth, *The Humanity of God* (Knoxville, TN: Westminster John Knox, 1996), 39; however, the whole title essay is worthy of attention, 37–68.

truly incarnational Catholic imagination. The more refined definition for the concept of the "imagination" is as follows: *an imagination is a liturgically inculcated worldview that structures a way of life*. The concept of "liturgy," as it should be understood here, denotes a set of normative beliefs and practices that are inculcated through repetitive *praxis*, within a community.[14] These in turn create concrete forms of life, in the Catholic instance ones that should ideally stress the immanent presence of the transcendent God within creation. William T. Cavanaugh brings out this emphasis, its relevance to everyday life, in comparison to other familiar ways of imagining the world:

> Today the most significant misunderstanding of the Christian liturgy is that it is sacred. Let me clarify. The problem is that "sacred" has been opposed to "secular," and the two are presumed to describe two separate—but occasionally related—orbits. The problem is not simply that this separation leaves the church's liturgy begging for relevance to the "real world." The problem is rather that the supposedly "secular" world invents its own liturgies, with pretensions every bit as "sacred" as those of the Christian liturgy, and these liturgies can come to rival the church's liturgy for our bodies and our minds. . . . I want to explore in particular some of the liturgies of the American nation-state. I will suggest first that such liturgies are not properly called "secular," and second, that the Christian liturgy is not properly cordoned off into the realm of the "sacred."[15]

With such a definition it is easy to see how the imagination is neither insulated nor opposed to doctrine and religious practice into a safe immaterial realm of the mind. Those two dimensions of ecclesial existence (doctrine and practice) are integrated into our understanding of what the imagination is, which includes the body and the mind together. The imagination—whether Catholic or the competing American nationalist-patriotic imagination—always includes doctrine and practice, because there is always a dynamic interplay between beliefs, practices, and creativity. They play off of each other.

Now we can add an analogical twist to Czeslaw Milosz's analysis of the dialectical drift of the Catholic imagination. This can only be done by filling out some of the historical background behind nominalism,

---

14. The understanding of the imagination as a liturgically shaped worldview owes its inspiration to the work of religious scholars James K. A. Smith, William T. Cavanaugh, and the historian of philosophy Pierre Hadot. See Pierre Hadot, *Philosophy as a Way of Life: Spiritual Exercises from Socrates to Foucault* (Oxford: Wiley-Blackwell, 1995).

15. William T. Cavanaugh, *Migrations of the Holy* (Grand Rapids, MI: Eerdmans, 2011), 115.

the Reformation, and the Scientific Revolution. It is important to remember that the dialectical imagination was a legitimate, even necessary, response to ecclesial abuses of the fourteenth, fifteenth, and sixteenth centuries. The flagrant abuses of those centuries make those standing behind contemporary Catholic scandals look like choirboys. Most genealogical accounts of modernity overlook, forget, or paper over these historical facts. There was a real pressing need to sunder the ties between the corrupt worldliness of the Church and God. Nominalists such as Ockham were at the forefront of the Conciliarist Movement, which offered one potential solution, if in retrospect inadequate, to the political-ecclesiastical crises of the time. Even though Conciliarism did not win the day, the Reformation's institutionalization of the nominalist-dialectical imagination won in the long term and has shaped thought and deed since. Therefore, as Milosz notes, a collision with it is inevitable. It is the default worldview that any analogical-Catholic imagination cannot help but humbly face, because it has already internalized it to such an extent that any mindful believer is aware of their "edifice of creeds and dogmas" crumbling under the universal acid of nominalism. A new home needs to be erected not only for man, but also for God. Homelessness is unacceptable, because the compulsion to situate ourselves is irrepressible. However, making God too much at home in the world is an ever present danger for Catholic theology. The Late Middle Ages should serve as an abject object lesson.

Hans Urs von Balthasar, a Catholic theologian Karl Barth credits for helping his later work bend back toward the humanity of God, is one of the better guides for re-imagining a non-idolatrous analogical relation between God, man, and the world in our late modern context. In the introduction to his anthology of Origen's writings, *Spirit and Fire*, von Balthasar characterizes the incarnation kenotically, as "a wave of the sea which, rushing up on the flat beach, runs out, even thinner and more transparent, and does not return to its source but sinks into the sand and disappears."[16] Milosz puts this theological insight in a poetic idiom, using the Great Chain of Being analogy, in the final poem, "The Sun," from the cycle "The World: A Naive Poem":

> All colors come from the sun. And it does not have
> Any particular color, for it contains them all.
> And the whole Earth is like a poem
> While the sun above represents the artist.

---

16. *Origen: Spirit and Fire: A Thematic Anthology of His Writings* (Washington, DC: Catholic University of America Press, 2001), 18.

Whoever wants to paint the variegated world
Let him never look straight up at the sun
Or he will lose the memory of things he has seen.
Only burning tears will stay in his eyes.

Let him kneel down, lower his face to the grass,
And look at the light reflected by the ground.
There he will find everything we have lost:
The stars and the roses, the dusks and the dawns.[17]

This florilegium of natural analogies, of the divinity fully yet discretely present in creation, was unfortunately betrayed by the Swiss theologian and the Polish poet in their blind disdain for Darwinism in general, and Teilhard de Chardin in particular.[18]

In *The Phenomenon of Life* Jewish philosopher Hans Jonas seems to agree with the negative attitudes of the two Christian thinkers. Christianity, as he presents it, is inherently opposed to evolution because of what he deems its natural alliance with the very post-nominalist Cartesian thinking that has proven to be so ruinous for modern Catholic theology:

> Thus evolutionism undid Descartes' work more effectively than any metaphysical critique managed to do. In the hue and cry over the indignity done to man's metaphysical status in the doctrine of his animal descent, it was overlooked that by the same token some dignity had been restored to the realm of life as a whole. If man was the relative of animals, then animals were the relatives of man, and in degrees bearers of that inwardness of which man, the most advanced of their kin, is conscious in himself. Thus after the contradiction brought about by Christian transcendentalism and Cartesian dualism, the province of "soul," with feeling, striving, suffering, enjoyment, extended again, by the principle of continuous gradation, from man over the kingdom of life.[19]

Yet, Jonas sees evolution as an ally for religion in general, because it contains the seed of a possible retrieval of the religious metaphor of the Great Chain of Being. The Chain was a fundamental ingredient of the analogical imagination from at least the Church Fathers until the late Middle Ages—it gave us the cathedrals, the *Summas*, and the dazzling artworks. How is it possible to reconcile Jonas's positive appraisal of

17. Czeslaw Milosz, *Selected and Last Poems: 1931–2004*, trans. Anthony Milosz et al. (New York: Ecco, 2011), 32.

18. See especially Hans Urs Von Balthasar, *The Moment of Witness* (San Francisco: Ignatius, 1994) and Czeslaw Milosz, *The Land of Ulro* (New York: Farrar, Straus, and Giroux, 2000).

19. Hans Jonas, *The Phenomenon of Life: Toward a Philosophical Biology* (Evanston, IL: Northwestern University Press, 2001), 57.

evolution with the actual history of theology? First of all, by fastening onto Descartes he correctly identifies an early modern, vaguely Christian trend of thinking that separated nature and grace, mind and matter. However, this cannot be extended to the rest of the tradition that came before, nor to all of the tradition that came after it. For example, both John Henry Newman and Charles Kingsley (the Anglican whose attacks provoked *Apologia Pro Vita Sua*) praised *On the Origin of the Species by Natural Selection* when it first appeared. They did not see evolution as in any way competing with revelation, even if they had some quibbles with a few of Darwin's interpretations.[20] The Church never formally condemned evolution, because it had no reason to do so. However, there are plenty of reasons to embrace it, because, as Jonas correctly acknowledges, it is one possible avenue toward re-linking nature and grace.

More recently, the work of Oliver Davies concentrates upon how the encroachment of neuroscience upon the human mind is something that should be welcomed by theology rather than feared. The following passage is preceded by an account similar to the one from *The Phenomenon of Life* above. Davies rehearses the disincarnating tendencies of the Cartesian chasm between mind and matter. He then proceeds to argue that the non-dualism inherent to neurobiology makes it especially friendly to an incarnational faith such as Catholicism:

> But the effects of the scientific self-understanding which is emerging today are quite different. Here it is presupposed that we are materiality "all the way down." Neuroscience, genetics, and evolutionary biology show that mind and matter in us form a thoroughgoing continuity, each presupposing the other and each having causal effects upon the other within a continuum of human life as "intelligent embodiment" in a material world. Quantum physics does so even more radically. Consequently, there is no point at which the mind can be "outside" matter. We are free within materiality and not beyond it. Science is teaching us that we are both pure subjectivity and complex materiality at the same time. And in fact, there are no grounds for reducing one to the other (despite the best attempts of some).[21]

---

20. I cannot track back these statements to the published works of these Christian thinkers; however, their statements on the matter are readily available through internet archives. It appears they did not think their opinions on these matters controversial enough to publish major works defending them. They were simply in line with the mainline opinions of the orthodox theologians of their day.

21. Oliver Davies, *Theology of Transformation: Faith, Freedom, and the Christian Act* (Cambridge: Cambridge University Press, 2014), 14.

In the words of the Gospel of John, the word became flesh and dwelt among us. The wave of the sea non-competitively flows and waters the shore and sinks deep into the sand without disappearing. This is an old analogical insight that Herbert McCabe captures in a Thomistic idiom when he says that "The activity of God . . . is not an alternative to my free activity. It is its source."[22]

However, if God cannot be imagined as immanent and participating in creation then we are back at the quandary Louis Dupré identified as the principal problem of Hans Urs von Balthasar's theology:

> As a result of the nominalist separation between language and the nature of the real as well as of the humanist creative excess of language over nature, nature lost much of the symbolic power it had possessed before. The change not only affected the nature of religious symbolization, it also undermined the "beautiful" quality the objective forms of religion had enjoyed in the past.[23]

This is also the principal problem of the contemporary Catholic imagination. One aspect of the solution consists in wisely appropriating the most recent scientific discoveries as one way of regaining the symbolic power of nature. Only when theology and its liturgies can take the cosmos into their warm embrace can the Catholic imagination become more itself.

When Catholic theology accomplishes its analogical task, then we are able to say that H.C.E. not only means "Here Comes Everybody," but also "Here Comes Everything." As Gregory Wolfe summarizes the uniqueness of the God-man at the center of Christianity, "But what other kind is there? If God cannot become present in blood, guts, shit, piss, semen, saliva—He vanishes into the ether."[24] Therefore the task of theology in reinvigorating the Catholic imagination is both high and low. It needs to set itself the high goal of bringing the cosmic liturgy back into its discourse and practice. It is low, because it needs to reintegrate even the basest elements of natural reality. In other words, it can only become truly sophiological if it can make the scatological and eschatological rub shoulders. Then it will make itself more believable.

The reader has probably noticed by now that this essay devoted more space to Czeslaw Milosz's poetry and prose than to learned theologians. There is a reason for this. The Catholic imagination has always given

22. Herbert McCabe, *Faith within Reason* (NY: Bloomsbury Academic, 2007), 77.

23. Louis Dupré, *Religious Mystery and Rational Reflection* (Grand Rapids, MI: Eerdmans, 1998), 69.

24. Gregory Wolfe, "Editorial Statement: Picturing the Passion," *IMAGE Journal* 41 (2003): 6.

pride of place to creative writers and other types of artists in helping to articulate its complex multi-level view of the world. The trend goes back a long, long time:

> The inevitable consequence after Jesus had left this earth was for his followers to imitate his uses of imagination in the various ways that came naturally to them out of their own imagination in the various ways that came naturally to them out of their own imaginative lives. The story about the householder, the closed door, and the need for bread is but one way of imagining God's relationship to his people. Later Catholic artists using words, spoken or written, persisted in Jesus' imaginative search for viable images of God; so did painters, sculptors, musicians, and so on. Their work constituted a natural continuation—what I called earlier an "organic" continuation—of what Jesus had been doing.... Jesus, who never said anything about the arts, was the first Catholic artist, and Catholic art grew from how Jesus imagined and how he talked.[25]

Therefore, Catholics should look to writers as much as theologians in their attempts to revive the analogical core of their faith. Artists have been explicating the mystery of the Incarnation from the beginning. They worked in tandem with theologians until late in the modern period. The break between art and theology is very recent and there is nothing permanent about it. However, there is something unnatural about it.

It is high time to overcome such artificial divisions and reclaim the powerful imaginative insights of writers and other artists for rebuilding the Catholic edifice. The proof is in how much Czeslaw Milosz contributed to the present analysis—much more than most contemporary theologians, whether liberal or conservative, could contribute. The good news is that there is no shortage of living contemporary writers (not only dead ones from the 1950s) who can accompany us and the theologians on this journey: Artur Grabowski, Annie Dillard, Mary Karr, Heather King, Charles D'Ambrosio, Paul Mariani, Dana Gioia, Adam Zagajewski, Les Murray, Fanny Howe, Ron Hansen, and Tobias Wolff. The table of contents to the present volume is a kind of communion of such high-caliber artist-theologians, both living and dead, who bridge heaven and earth.

---

25. John Pfordresher, *Jesus and the Emergence of a Catholic Imagination* (Mahwah, NY: Paulist Press, 2008), 18.

The Poetic of Sophia

Michael Martin

IN HIS SEMINAL ESSAY "The Work of Art in the Age of Mechanical Reproduction" (1936), Walter Benjamin considers the changes—both subtle and abrupt—that accompanied the technological age and its colonization of the representative arts. He observes that such reproductive technologies not only widely disseminate works of art (or, rather, facsimiles of works of art), a gesture of democratization bringing artworks to the masses (the proletariat), but also turn works of art into objects of distraction at the expense of their role as objects of concentration and contemplation, a cultural development that, he believed, can lead to Fascism.[1] His intuition is keen, and one can only wonder what Benjamin would say were he to witness the eschatological aesthetic ramifications brought on by the democratizing reproductive technology we know as the internet.

Tellingly, Benjamin has almost nothing to say about poetry.

It is my position that poetry, the utterance of the poetic, is impervious to technological colonization. This is not to say that the technological has not impacted the craft of writing. Clearly, it has. Benjamin points to this aberration as arising out of Mallarme and Dada (to which I would add Gertrude Stein); and, indeed, this "aesthetic" carries on today in the profligate graduate MFA programs that have turned the writing of verses into a kind of careerism, negating poetry's and the poet's true vocation: the affirmative response to a summons, a calling analogous to the priesthood. The academy has been colonized by the technological. This technologization, this standardization of production, manifests in academia in the fetishization (read: idolatry) of what is called "professionalism" aligned according to the bureaucratic dictates of "best practices." Whatever those are. At the very least the technological colonization is dehumanizing; at worst it is something far more sin-

---

1. Walter Benjamin, *Illuminations: Essays and Reflections*, ed. Hannah Arendt and trans. Harry Zohn (New York: Schocken Books, 1968), 241.

ister. As Nicolas Berdyaev argued in 1935, "The world threatens to become an organized and technicized chaos in which only the most terrible forms of idolatry and demon-worship can live."[2] That day is here.

Yet, I still hold that poetry—authentic poetry—is impervious to this colonization. The poem—unlike the film, the photograph, the digital or lithographed image, the sound recording—does not exist in its medium of presentation. It exists beyond its medium, whether paper and ink or pixel. Its medium is not its medium, but only its point of appearance: as light only appears in its showing of the things of this world. Furthermore, the poem only truly comes alive through acts of contemplation. (There is much of what Michel Henry calls "Life" or "coming into the world" in this.)[3] One does not simply read a poem; one enters it. And, in a mysteriously reciprocal gesture, the poem enters into the reader, evidence of the "installation of a new ontological dimension."[4]

This opening certainly is potential in all art forms; but only in poetry is the medium ancillary to such a diminished degree. The forms of some poems—in George Herbert and e.e. cummings, for example—of course, are integral to their utterance: but they are not equal to it, and the poems, in any case, are not compromised by the mode of presentation. Poetry, though not as tied into the media of presentation as other art forms, still requires language, which, in the case of written poetry, generally means typography. The physicality of drama, painting, music, sculpture, and so forth are essential for the presence of their utterance to be experienced—a digital experience of these art forms, like the photographs of someone's vacation, are diminishment, compromise, *signum*. The poem is not compromised by the presentation of the medium. Its being exists elsewhere.

My considerations here, however, should not be construed as aesthetics, though I am concerned with the arrival of the Beautiful. Aesthetics is, ultimately, rationalization, Aristotelian, a categorical wrestling with the uncategorical. It is concerned with appearances and not with the appearing as such. The Beautiful, on the other hand, is what appears. Its appearing, furthermore, is experienced as personal, as an encounter. An encounter, it must be admitted, with being. With a being.

---

2. Nicolas Berdyaev, *The Fate of Man in the Modern World*, trans. Donald A. Lowrie (1935; reprt., Ann Arbor, MI: The University of Michigan Press, 1961), 127.

3. Michel Henry, *I Am the Truth: Toward a Philosophy of Christianity*, trans. Susan Emanuel, Cultural Memory in the Present (Stanford: Stanford University Press, 2003).

4. Michel Henry, interviewed by Jean-Marie Brohm and Magali Uhl, "Art et phénoménologie de la vie (entretien, Montpellier, 1996)" in *Auto-donation: Entretiens et Conferences* by Michael Henry (Paris: Editions Beauchesne, 2004), 197–222, at 197.

The arrival of the Beautiful is facilitated by—indeed, is unimaginable apart from—a contemplative presence to phenomena. Reverie, the playful abiding in an imaginal realm between the noumenal and physical worlds, provides an opening to this presence. Reverie, in the disappearance of time that seems to take place within its dimensions, allows us to be present to the things of this world and additionally, as Gaston Bachelard has observed, "puts us in the state of a soul being born."[5] For Percy Bysshe Shelley reverie was essential to the poetic act and rendered the soul more porous to the cosmos:

> There are some persons who in this respect are always children. Those who are subject to the state called reverie, feel as if their nature were dissolved into the surrounding universe, or as if the surrounding universe were absorbed into their being. They are conscious of no distinction. And these are states which precede, or accompany, or follow an unusually intense and vivid apprehension of life.[6]

Poetry, the poetic, indeed, any art "as the letting happen of the advent of the truth,"[7] can allow such an opening, but not without the proper disposition of soul, the appropriate pentecostal openness. And written poetry, perhaps more than any other art form, is especially conducive to entering such a state. For poetry cannot be experienced passively, as is often the case with music or drama, sculpture or painting. To read attentively, the only way poetry can be read, is to have a text enter the soul: it is a pure act, an act of absolute vulnerability. Literary theory, or at least the greater number of voices that have occupied this rhetorical space for most of the past forty years, can thus be seen to be a kind of anti-theory, anti-Θεωρία, absolutely alien, as it is, from contemplation (Θεωρία). It has poisoned the relationship of reader and text and tries to deliver poetry to the prisons of premeditation.

My appeal, then, is to what I have called (inspired by William Desmond) an *agapeic criticism*. In agapeic criticism we approach the text in an attitude of respect and reverence, avoiding the temptation to colonize it with premediated assumptions. Taking this approach, we participate with the text in a spirit of charity. Through the risk inherent to this participation, we expose ourselves to possibility. On the one hand stands the possibility of contamination—pornographic or other works that render

---

5. Gaston Bachelard, *The Poetics of Reverie: Childhood, Language, and the Cosmos*, trans. David Russell (1969; reprt., Boston: Beacon Press, 1971), 15.

6. Percy Bysshe Shelley, *Shelley's Poetry and Prose*, ed. Neil Fraistat and Donald H. Reiman, Norton Critical Editions (New York: W.W. Norton and Company, 1977), 477.

7. Martin Heidegger, "The Origin of the Work of Art" in *Poetry, Language, Thought*, trans. Albert Hofstadter (New York: Harper & Row Publishers, 1971), 72.

sin beautiful or appealing in some way certainly possess the ability to poison the soul. As Jacques Maritain has articulated so eloquently, "In making out of your sin beauty, you send it like an angel among your brothers. It kills them without a sound."[8] Such an opening is not an opening to life, but, rather, to death. On the other hand, participation can become an act, as Dionysius says, "by which it irrepressibly imparts being, life, wisdom and other gifts of *its* all creative goodness."[9] Some will call my appropriation of Dionysius here something of an ontological leap. It is not. My claim is that the life accessed through an agapeic engagement has as its source Dionysius's subject. *For what else is a revelation of the True, the Good, and the Beautiful?* This brings to the subject of Sophia.

> Sophia, as described in scripture, is identical with the life embedded in creation:

> He that shall find me, shall find life, and shall have salvation from the Lord.
> But he that shall sin against me shall hurt his own soul. All that hate me love death. (Proverbs 8:35–36)

> For Wisdom is more active than all active things: and reacheth everywhere by reason of her purity.
> For she is a vapour of the power of God, and a certain pure emanation of the glory of the almighty God: and therefore no defiled thing cometh into her.
> For she is the brightness of eternal light, and the unspotted mirror of God's majesty, and the image of his goodness.
> And being but one, she can do all things: and remaining in herself the same, she reneweth all things, and through nations conveyeth herself into holy souls, she maketh the friends of God and prophets. (Wisdom 7:23–26)

God's Wisdom, then, is *zoē* rather than *bios*, the light of the first day rather than that of the fourth.

Coinciding with these cosmological dimensions of Sophia are the sophiological dimensions implicit to the creative act itself, not only in that of God, but also in that of the human person who thereby becomes a truly sophianic subject. The creative act is essentially a transfigurative

---

8. Jacques Maritain, *Art and Poetry*, trans. Elva de P. Matthews (New York: Philosophical Library, 1943), 51.

9. From *The Divine Names* 644A. Taken from Pseudo-Dionysius, *The Complete Works*, trans. Colm Luibheid and Paul Rorem (New York: Paulist Press, 1987), 62. My emphasis.

act, whereby the human person participates in what Proverbs describes as Sophia's playfulness: "I was with him forming all things: and was delighted every day, playing before him at all times; Playing in the world: and my delights were to be with the children of men" (8:30–31). As Pavel Florensky writes, "Sophia, the true Creation or creation in the Truth, is a preliminary hint at the transfigured, spiritualized world as the manifestation, imperceptible for others, of the heavenly in the earthly."[10] This transfiguration is precisely what William Blake intuited when he wrote of "Wisdom in the Human Imagination / Which is the Divine Body of the Lord Jesus. blessed for ever."[11] It likewise underscores Nicolas Berdyaev's thesis in *The Meaning of the Creative Act* that through human creativity "man can discover limitless aid immanent within himself, by the creative act, all the power of God and the world, the true world, freed from the illusory world."[12] This is what Henry Vaughan and Thomas Traherne were consciously trying to effect. And William Wordsworth, without really trusting in it. Every imaginal act, however, is not redemptive; nor is every creative act identical with that which Berdyaev has in mind. And every piece of writing called a "poem" does not automatically qualify as poetry.

Poetry grounded in an exploration of being, then, would naturally tend to be more likely to disclose being—would it not?—in a way through which the sophianic nature not only of the poem but of the creative act itself might become actualized. This happens, for instance, in religious poetry that has the encounter with God—the source of all being—as object or addressee, a phenomenon traceable in the Metaphysical poets, for example, in the Sufi poet Rumi, and more recently in David Jones, Czeslaw Milosz, and Franz Wright. Such poems are essentially forms of *adoration*. Adoration, as Jean-Luc Nancy claims, "opens to the infinite, without which there would be no *relation* in the full sense that this word alone, perhaps, can take on, but only rapport, liaison, connection."[13] *Adoration*, that is, *awakens relation*. In this way, I would

---

10. Pavel Florensky, *The Pillar and Ground of the Truth: An Essay in Orthodox Theodicy in Twelve Letters*, trans. Boris Jakim (Princeton: Princeton University Press, 1997), 283.

11. William Blake, *Milton: a Poem in 2 Books*, 3.3, in *The Complete Poetry and Prose of William Blake*, ed. David V. Erdman with commentary by Harold Bloom, revised edition (Berkeley and Los Angeles: University of California Press, 1982).

12. Nicolas Berdyaev, *The Meaning of the Creative Act*, trans. Donald A. Lowrie (New York: Collier Books, 1962), 14.

13. Jean-Luc Nancy, *Adoration: The Deconstruction of Christianity II*, trans. John McKeane, Perspectives in Continental Philosophy (New York: Fordham University Press, 2013), 73.

add, poems that are not necessarily concerned with God directly can also disclose being through their own particular acts of adoration, say, in nature poetry or in love poetry. In this way, the poetic clearly has a relationship to prayer. The sophianic poetic act, then, functions as an awakening: the reader's intentionality awakens the adoration in the poem, which reciprocally awakens devotion in the reader. This adoration blossoms forth into acts of communion: of the reader with the poetic genius; of the reader and the poet with divinity. The reader's presence to the poem meets the poet's presence, informed by the presence beyond presences. The entire movement is thoroughly sacramental.

Some poetry, furthermore, is more explicitly sophiological, not only in its adorative aspects, but also in the ways it takes up some of the themes of sophiology proper (whether deliberately or not on the part of the poet is not important), which allows access to alternate dimensions and unfoldings of the poetic event. The apprehension of this event is characterized by a transfigurative attentiveness to Things, an awareness of what Hans Urs von Balthasar calls the "splendor" that shines *through* (and not from) them. There are several streams of this kind of poetry.

In one expression of this phenomenon, the writer, rather than adopting prose, couches his own religious experiences of a Sophia figure in poetic utterances, choosing a language of intimacy and reverie instead of one of empiricism, defenses, and proofs. Another is distinctly Marian in its theological aesthetic, attentive to the incarnational and sacramental role of the Virgin Mary in uniting divinity to the flesh and to the world, a reciprocating gesture both sacrificial and salvific. Still another turns its concern to that which shines through nature, through art, through human relationship, and through liturgy, revealing the Wisdom of God latent in the things of this world. And much sophiological poetry traverses all of these domains simultaneously.

First of all, the sophiological poetry explicitly concerned with Sophia as divine person begins with Russian Orthodox philosopher, literary critic, and poet Vladimir Solovyov. Solovyov had at least three religious experiences regarding Sophia (whom he only ever referred to as "My Eternal Friend"). The first occurred during Divine Liturgy on the Feast of the Ascension, May 1862, when the philosopher was nine years old.[14]

---

14. The story of Solovyov's visions of his Eternal Friend is oft repeated. See the account of his nephew, Fr. Sergey M. Solovyov's, *Vladimir Solovyov: His Life and Creative Evolution*, trans. Aleksey Gibson (Fairfax, VA: Eastern Christian Publications, 2000), 35–6 and 129–36; Paul M. Allen, *Vladimir Soloviev: Russian Mystic* (Blauvelt, NY: Steiner Books, 1978), 23–8 and 109–19.

He met Sophia again while researching her at the British Library. There she told him, "Meet me in the desert!" He immediately booked passage to Cairo, where she appeared to him once more—after he had been jumped and robbed by Bedouins. Solovyov recounts the experiences in his poem "Three Meetings."

The poem is narrative in form, long and with many digressions in which the poet pokes fun at himself (he was known for his puckish sense of humor and his outrageous laugh). He first touches on his religious experience as a nine-year-old:

> The sanctuary was open… But where were priest and deacon?
> Where was the crowd of praying people? Suddenly,
> The stream of passions dried up without a trace.
> Azure was all around; azure was in my soul.
>
> Suffused with a golden azure, and your hand
> Holding a flower that came from other lands,
> You stood there smiling a smile of radiance.
> You nodded to me, and vanished in the mist. (lines 25–32)[15]

Later in the poem, he describes his experience as a young scholar at the British Museum:

> But once—it was in autumn—I said to her:
> "O blossoming of divinity! I feel
> Your presence here. But why have you not revealed
> Yourself to my eyes since I was a child?"
>
> Hardly had I thought these words
> When all around was filled with golden azure
> And before me she was shining again—
> But only her face, it was her face alone.
>
> That instant was one of happiness much prolonged.
> My soul again became blind to things of earth.
> And if I spoke, any "sober" ear
> Would consider my speech incoherent and stupid. (lines 69–80)

And in the Egyptian desert, following his unfortunate encounter with the Bedouins, his third encounter arrives:

---

15. All translations of Solovyov's poetry here are from Boris Jakim and Laury Magnus and taken from Jakim's edited *The Religious Poetry of Vladimir Solovyov* (Kettering, OH: Semantron Press, 2014). The poems are also reproduced in this volume.

Long I lay there in a frightened slumber, till
At last, I heard a gentle whisper: "Sleep, my poor friend."
Then I fell into a deep sleep; and when I waked
The fragrance of roses wafted from earth and heaven.

And in the purple of the heavenly glow
You gazed with eyes full of an azure fire.
And your gaze was like the first shining
Of universal and creative day.

What is, what was, and what will be were here
Embraced within that one fixed gaze... The seas
And rivers all turned blue beneath me, as did
The distant forest and the snow-capped mountain heights.

I saw it all, and all of it was one,
One image there of beauty feminine...
The immeasurable was confined within that image.
Before me, in me, you alone were there. (lines 145–64)

Unlike almost all other sophiological poetry, Solovyov's is absent a relationship with the natural world. Things of nature—flowers, seas, mountains—though mentioned, have no actuality in this poetry. They are simply ciphers for another reality. His poetic landscape is utterly and absolutely a realm between heaven and earth, at the horizon of Sophia's appearing. He simply has no interest in anything else.

Solovyov's follower, the poet Alexander Blok, is a little more incarnated than his master, a little more attentive to the natural world—though not by much. Sophia, for Blok, still inhabits the *metaxu* between the ideal and the real, and, as with Solovyov, the idiom of dream seems to best fit Blok's rhetorical needs:

I seek strange and new things on the pages
Of old and familiar books;
I dream of white vanished birds
And sense the isolated instant.
Agitated rudely by the commotion of life
And dismayed by whispers and shouts,
I am anchored securely by my white dream
To the shore of the recent past.
White You are, imperturbable in the depths,
Stern and wrathful in life,
Mysteriously anxious and mysteriously loved,
Maiden, Dawn, Burning Bush.
The cheeks of golden-haired maidens fade,

> Dawns are not as eternal as dreams.
> Thorns crown the humble and wise
> With the white fire of the Burning Bush.[16]

Blok's Sophia is clearly divine, and, as "the white fire of the Burning Bush," certainly facilitates God's appearing (as the Virgin does for Christ). But her presence in the material world is tenuous, not a quality of its being, not a catalyst for the appearance of *zoē* in Things.

Beginning at least with the mystical speculation of Jacob Boehme, the sophianic role of the Virgin Mary has been an important aspect of sophiological metaphysics, and this has been reflected, perhaps most clearly of all, in poetry. Though as not every sophiological poem is Marian, neither is every Marian poem sophiological. To be sophiological, the poem should reveal the implicate order (to appropriate David Bohm's term) of Mary in her simultaneously cosmological, teleological, and incarnational offices as they are married to the disclosure of Truth, Beauty, and Goodness. A number of important poems engage this metaphysical space.

Perhaps the first poem to deliberately enter this theological aesthetic is Henry Vaughan's poem "The Knot." The poem was first published in the second part of Vaughan's *Silex Scintillans* (1655), issued five years after the work's first installment and apparently after Vaughan had encountered the writing of Boehme, which first began to appear in English translation in the late 1640s.[17] The poem illustrates the reciprocity between the heavenly and earthly realms effected by the Virgin Mary's affirmative participation in the Incarnation:

The Knot

> Bright Queen of Heaven! Gods Virgin Spouse!
>   The glad worlds blessed maid!
> Whose beauty tyed life to thy house,
>   And brought us saving ayd.
>
> Thou art the true Loves-knot; by thee
>   God is made our Allie,

---

16. Poem 111 of *Verses about the Beautiful Lady*. Taken from Alexander Blok, *Poems of Sophia*, trans. and ed. Boris Jakim (Kettering, OH: Semantron Press, 2014). Also featured in this volume.

17. I discuss Boehme's influence on both Henry and Thomas Vaughan in the chapter entitled "The Rosicrucian Mysticism of Henry and Thomas Vaughan" in my *Literature and the Encounter with God in Post-Reformation England* (Farnham, UK: Ashgate Publishing, 2014), especially pages 143–46.

And mans inferior Essence he
  With his did dignifie.

For Coalescent by that Band
  We are his body grown,
Nourished with favors from his hand
  Whom for our head we own.

And such a Knot, what arm dares loose,
  What life, what death can sever?
Which us in him, and him in us
  United keeps for ever.

Like Vaughan, Thomas Traherne perceives this quality behind the qualities of Things and names its author:

O what a world art Thou! A world within!
  All things appear
  All objects are
Alive in Thee! Supersubstantial, rare,
Above themselves, and nigh of kin
  To those pure things we find
  In His great mind
Who made the world! ("My Spirit," lines 110–17)

Traherne is acutely aware of the presence behind appearing, of the Life that informs life.

The end of Goethe's *Faust, Part II* and Novalis's exquisite *Hymnen an die Nacht* (*Hymns to the Night*) likewise espouse a sophiology more heavenly than earthly, though both are supremely concerned with Sophia-Mary's role as rescuer of souls as well as her ontological dimension as a quality of the cosmos. As Novalis writes,

Praise the world queen, the higher messenger of a holy word, a nurse of blessed love—she sends me you—tender, loved—Night's lovely sun,— now I wake—for I'm yours and mine—you called the Night to life for me,—humanized me—tear my body with spirit fire, so I can mix with you more inwardly, airily, and then the wedding night will last forever.[18]

What Vaughan and Traherne, Goethe and Novalis do not do in these poems—but what Vaughan does in many others (and Goethe certainly does in his scientific work)—is show the relationship between this binding of the natural and the supernatural in the language of Things, of the

---

18. Included in this volume.

world of growth, of the world of *bios* imbued by the world of *zoē*. This is the world explored in its Marian connotations in some of Gerard Manley Hopkins's poetry and in some important mid-20th-century Catholic poets.

Hopkins provided Catholic poets with a sophiological poetic idiom even though he could not have been aware of what subsequent generations came to know as sophiology. Hopkins's attention to "the dearest freshness deep down things" ("God's Grandeur," line 10) certainly speaks to such a sophiological sensibility, but nowhere is his sophiology as explicit as in his poem "The Blessed Virgin compared to the Air we Breathe." Its sophiology is apparent from the poem's first lines:

> Wild air, world-mothering air,
> Nestling me everywhere,
> That each eyelash or hair
> Girdles; goes home betwixt
> The fleeciest, frailest-flixed
> Snowflake; that's fairly mixed
> With, riddles, and is rife
> In every least thing's life. (lines 1–8)

The Virgin is, indeed, "rife/In every least thing's life," as Boehme would doubtlessly concur. As in Boehme, in Hopkins the Virgin is the catalyst, the vessel through which grace pours into the world, a divine principle of the world:

> Let all God's glory through,
> God's glory which would go
> Through her and from her flow
> Off, and no way but so. (lines 30–33)

This is all so because "her hand leaves his light/Sifted to suit our sight" (112–13). The Virgin makes grace perceivable, and, quite literally, makes Christ experienceable through the senses. Hopkins's theological aesthetic here is also articulated by Pierre Teilhard de Chardin in his imaginative work (I am inclined to call it a prose poem) "*L'Eternel féminin*" ("The Eternal Feminine") as well as in Thomas Merton's prose poem "Hagia Sophia."

Teilhard, who has received, I think, an undue amount of scorn from Catholic quarters (the Eastern Orthodox, ironically, seem to have a deeper appreciation for the much-maligned Jesuit), speaks a language highly conducive to sophiological insight. A scientist as well as a mystic, his genius proves particularly apt for describing the sophiological nature of Things and the sophiological office of the Virgin Mary:

Lying between God and the earth, as a zone of mutual attraction, I draw them both together in a passionate union.

—until the meeting takes place in me, in which the generation and plenitude of Christ are consummated throughout the centuries.

I am the Church, the bride of Christ.

I am Mary the Virgin, mother of all human kind.[19]

It is unclear whether or not Teilhard was familiar with Boehme or Russian sophiology, though it is certainly possible that he was. Merton, on the other hand, was well-read in Russian sophiology, the influence of which is palpable in "Hagia Sophia."

Merton presciently and beautifully arranges the poem according to the times of prayer in monastic life (Lauds, Prime, Tierce, and so on). In the Compline section, Merton writes of the Virgin in sophianic terms, of Sophia in Marian terms:

Now the Blessed Virgin Mary is the one created being who enacts and shows forth in her life all that is hidden in Sophia. Because of this she can be said to be a personal manifestation of Sophia, Who in God is *Ousia* rather than Person.

Natura in Mary becomes pure Mother. In her, *Natura* is as she was from the origin from her divine birth. In Mary *Natura* is all wise and is manifested as an all-prudent, all-loving, all-pure person: not a Creator, and not a Redeemer, but perfect Creature, perfectly Redeemed, the fruit of all God's great power, the perfect expression of wisdom in mercy.

It is she, it is Mary, Sophia, who in sadness and joy, with the full awareness of what she is doing, sets upon the Second Person, the Logos, a crown which is His Human Nature. Thus her consent opens the door of created nature, of time, of history, to the Word of God.

God enters into His creation. Through her wise answer, through her obedient understanding, through the sweet yielding consent of Sophia, God enters without publicity into the city of rapacious men.

She crowns Him not with what is glorious, but with what is greater than glory: the one thing greater than glory is weakness, nothingness, poverty.

She sends the infinitely Rich and Powerful One forth as poor and helpless, in His mission of inexpressible mercy, to die for us on the Cross.

The shadows fall. The stars appear. The birds begin to sleep. Night embraces the silent half of the earth.

19. Included in this volume.

A vagrant, a destitute wanderer with dusty feet, finds his way down a new road. A homeless God, lost in the night, without papers, without identification, without even a number, a frail expendable exile lies down in desolation under the sweet stars of the world and entrusts Himself to sleep.[20]

Merton describes here the *metaxu* of Sophia, the inhabiting of a realm between realms, the bestowal of *zoē* in the kingdom of *bios*, the immanent appearing of transcendent grace.

A poet too little read these days, William Everson (Brother Antoninus) also touches on a sophiological aesthetics in his poem "A Canticle to the Great Mother of God," and in the *metaxu* of his dream-language explores the ontological mystery of the Virgin Mary joined to the Virgin Sophia. In doing so, he alludes to the great Eastern Orthodox church, Hagia Sophia, and the poem takes on the virtue of a prayer:

> Hidden within the furlongs of those deeps, your fiery virtue impregnates the sky, irradiant with wisdom.
> You are Byzantium, domed awesomeness, the golden-ruddy richness of rare climes, great
> masterwork of God.
> Kneeling within thy moskey naves, seized in the luminous indult of those dusks,
> We hold the modal increase, subsumed in chant, ransomed of the balsam and the myrrh.
> Keeping an inmost essence, an invitational letting that never wholly spends, but solemnly recedes,
> You pause, you hover, virtue indemnable, at last made still, a synthesis unprobed.
> Checked there, we tremble on the brink, we dream the venue of those everlapsing deeps.

Everson, like Merton, attends to Sophia-Mary's role at the *metaxu* of nature and supernature and describes how the Church, likewise, participates in this holy effecting. That is, as Solovyov may have been the first to say, *Sophia is also an ontological dimension of the Church.*

Another 20th-century poet with pronounced sophiological intuitions is David Jones, whose poem "The Tutelar of the Place" is a tour-de-force of sophianic power. But unlike the poems here noted by Merton and Everson, the Welshman Jones takes Sophia's latency in the natural world as assumed and, instead, focuses upon that which obscures our perceptions of the sophianic shining: modernity and the Cartesian apotheosis

---

20. Included in this volume.

of the technological. For Jones, each particular locale possesses its particular quality, what Hopkins celebrated as "thisness" and Duns Scotus called *haecceitas*, and Jones, like them, affirms that it participates in a transcendent source:

> Tell us of the myriad names answers to but one name: From this tump she answers Jac o' the Tump only if he call Great-Jill-of-the-tump-that-bare-me, not if he cry by some new fangle moder of far gentes over the flud, fer-goddess name from anaphora of far folk wont woo her; she's a rare one for locality.[21]

Folk customs, in Jones's poetic idiom, though absolutely particular to place, are nevertheless manifestations of eternal truth, authentic eruptions of joy in its beauty:

> Though she inclines with attention from far fair-height outside all boundaries, beyond the known and kindly nomenclatures, where all names are one name, where all stones of demarcation dance and interchange, troia[22] the skipping mountains, nod recognitions. As when on known-site ritual frolics keep bucolic interval at eves and divisions when they mark the inflexions of the year and conjugate with trope and turn the seasons' syntax, with beating feet, with wands and pentagons to spell out the Trisagion.

In his communitarian ethos, Jones stands in the poetic lineage of Robert Herrick, who also rejected the poisonous fruit of modernity and division and their combined destruction of the integral union of religion and the wheel of the year.

Like Heidegger, Steiner, Huxley, and so many others who have raised concerns about the human, cultural, and spiritual costs of our infatuation with technology, Jones argues that we have made this technology into an idol, a Moloch-like demon he calls the Ram, and that this god demands the instrumentalization and subsequent sacrifice of human persons:

> Remember the mound-kin, the kith of the *tarren*[23] gone from this mountain because of the exorbitance of the Ram... remember them in the rectangular tenements, in the houses of the engines that fabricate the ingenuities of the Ram...
> Mother of Flowers save them then where no flower blows.
> > Though they shall not come again because of the requirements of the Ram with respect to the world plan,

---

21. Included in this volume.
22. "meander."
23. "knoll."

remember them where the dead forms multiply, where no stamen leans, where the carried pollen falls to the adamant surfaces, where is no crevice.[24]

Jones's incrimination here, I would argue, is a condemnation of the *anti-sophiology* that rules modernity, a modernity that can no longer recognize what a human person is, what gender is, what marriage is, or what is real. This is truly a modernity in which "dead forms multiply." And it is characterized by the fetishization of sterility.

As a final example of this kind of sophianic poem, I offer Franz Wright's beautiful "Rosary," a short, simple poem that quietly summarizes the sophiological qualities of the Virgin:

Rosary

Mother of space,
inner

virgin
with no one face—

See them flying to see you
be near you,

when you
are everywhere.

It requires no commentary.

It is curious, I think, that these 20th- and 21st-century Catholic poets write in a sophianic idiom so much more *incarnated* than even the Russians (even though Russian sophiology, particularly that of Bulgakov, is acutely aware of Sophia's shining through the natural world). There is in Catholicism something much more attentive to the sensual world, something seen perhaps only in Henry Vaughan (who is in many ways the most sophiological poet of all) among non-Catholics. Even Wendell Berry, known for his religious sensitivities and attentiveness to the natural world, is more a sabbatarian poet than a sophianic one. Protestantism's emphasis on God's transcendence at the expense of his immanence could have something to do with this. Similarly, these very different poetic ontologies may be tinged by one side's historical emphasis on preaching and the Word and the other's emphasis on the sensual and sacramental dimensions of the beholding, touching, and tasting implicit in participation in the Eucharist. The Orthodox poets partake of both of

---

24. Included in this volume.

these sensibilities, of course, though the emphasis with them is on otherworldliness and *theosis* as the center of their theological aesthetic witness.

A great many poems, however, disclose a sophianic sensibility without committing to a particularly religious or ontological position. Some, such as Wordsworth's "Ode: Intimations of Immortality from Recollections of Early Childhood," Hölderlin's "*Da ich ein Knabe war...*" ("When I was a boy..."), and even Dylan Thomas's "Fern Hill," lament the loss of what Owen Barfield would call the "original participation"[25] characteristic of childhood, the innate human affirmation of presence shining through Things. I do wonder how much the Enlightenment and the philosophy of Immanuel Kant may have poisoned even these Romantics (and, yes, I am calling Dylan Thomas a Romantic). All three simultaneously evoke wonder and loss, holding to the bittersweet residue of splendor before finally bending, however begrudgingly and lamentably, to modernity's totalizing demand that we regard the material world as the only and final master, even though we sing in our chains like the sea buried in thoughts that do often lie too deep for tears.

Other poems distanced from religious orthodoxy do not seem to be characterized by the same existential fatalism. Percy Bysshe Shelley in his freer, less politically actuated moments certainly evinces something of this (for example, in "Ode to the West Wind"), and certainly Keats expresses a similar confidence in the revelation of beauty. More recently, Robert Kelly, in his reminiscences of childhood reverie in the poem "The Heavenly Country," recognizes something shining through not only the landscape but also through literature—Tolkien and A. A. Milne no less than Blake and Wordsworth. The assurance, for Kelly, resides in the revelation of a nameless "It" seeking disclosure: "That it is a matter of It willing to reveal to Us I have never doubted."[26] The only difference is that I give It a name.

When I was a young graduate student, I found myself somewhat embarrassed by my devotion to Guillaume Apollinaire and his assertion that "*que seuls le renouvellent ceux qui sont fondés en poésie*"[27]—"only those remake the world who are rooted in poetry." Such a commitment did not seem becoming of a scholar in a postmodern milieu. When I confessed this to my professor, a gentle and learned Jesuit, all he could say

---

25. See Barfield's *Saving the Appearances: A Study in Idolatry*, 2nd edition (Middletown, CT: Wesleyan University Press, 1988), 42.

26. Included in this volume.

27. "Poeme lu au Mariage d'Andre Salmon," line 10.

was "Why not, Michael?" It took me most of twenty years to realize how right he was and that my initial intuition was, indeed, a realization of truth. Poetry as that which discloses the shining behind the universe, that itself participates in the shining, is what truly remakes the universe: for it participates, in however limited a way, in the source of that power. Thus, among other realms of human endeavor, the written word, scripture, the fine and performing arts, architecture, and liturgy all have the potential to participate in the poetic shining. Unfortunately, we live in times—like all times—in which those who think they can change the meanings of words can likewise change the universe. They are trapped in a prison of nominalism they mistake for freedom. And they are wrong. But as long as there is a shining, there will be the possibility of remaking the universe, *"parce que fondés en poésie nous avons des droits sur les paroles qui forment et défont l'Univers"*[28]—"because rooted in poetry, we have rights to make and unmake the universe." The name of this shining is Sophia.

28. Line 37.

Notes on Contributors

DAVID CRAIG has published fifteen collections of poetry, most recently *Whose Saints We Are* (Kaufmann, 2013), *St. Francis Poems* (Wipf & Stock, 2013), *Trouble in the Diocese* (Wipf & Stock, 2014), and *Pilgrim's Gait* (Wipf & Stock, 2015). He has also published two works of fiction, including *The Cheese Stands Alone* (CMJ Press, 1997). He teaches creative writing as a Professor at Franciscan University of Steubenville, where he edits both a poetry chapbook series and the Jacopone da Todi Poetry Prize.

BRUCE V. FOLTZ is Professor of Philosophy at Eckerd College in St Petersburg, Florida, and he has also taught at the University of Dallas and St John's College in Santa Fe, New Mexico. He is the author of two books, *Inhabiting the Earth* (Humanities Press, 1995) and *The Noetics of Nature* (Fordham University Press, 2014), and co-editor of two more: *Rethinking Nature* (Indiana University Press, 2004) and *Toward an Ecology of Transfiguration* (Fordham University Press, 2014). He has published numerous articles on Heidegger, Russian and Byzantine philosophy, mysticism, and the philosophy of the natural environment, while contributing more than thirty articles to five academic encyclopedias. Foltz is founder or co-founder of three professional societies, and his writings have been translated into Arabic, Greek, Portuguese, Romanian, and Russian.

GREGORY Y. GLAZOV is a professor of Old Testament Studies at Seton Hall University. He is the author of *The 'Bridling of the Tongue' and the 'Opening of the Mouth' in Biblical Prophecy* (Sheffield Academic Press, 2001), *The Scriptural Sources and Wisdom of the Lord's Prayer,* and *The Hail Mary, the Glory Be and the Sign of the Cross: A Scriptural Approach* (both forthcoming from Angelico Press, 2016). His translation, introduction and commentary on the work of the Russian religious philosopher Vladimir Solovyov, *The Burning Bush: Vladimir Solovyov's Writings on Judaism,* will be published by Notre Dame University Press in 2016.

JENNIFER NEWSOME MARTIN is Assistant Professor in the Program of Liberal Studies with a concurrent appointment in the department of theology at the University of Notre Dame. Martin's research engages the religious character of modern philosophical thought, particularly in the German Idealist and Romantic traditions, as well as pre- and early Soviet-era Russian religious philosophy. Her first book, *Hans Urs von Balthasar and the Critical Appropriation of Russian Religious Thought* (University of Notre Dame Press, 2015) analyzes the submerged presence of modern speculative Russian religious thinkers on the aesthetic, historical, and eschatological dimensions of the theology of Swiss Catholic theologian Hans Urs von Balthasar. Other work has appeared in *Modern Theology, Spiritus, Horizons*, and *Christianity and Literature.*

MICHAEL MARTIN, the editor of this volume, is Assistant Professor of Philosophy and English at Marygrove College. He is the author of *The Submerged Reality: Sophiology and the Turn to a Poetic Metaphysics* (Angelico, 2015) and *Literature and the Encounter with God in Post-Reformation England* (Ashgate, 2014) as well as a volume of poetry, *Meditations in Times of Wonder* (Angelico, 2014).

DANIEL JOSEPH POLIKOFF has published five books of poetry, translation, and criticism, including *In the Image of Orpheus: Rilke—A Soul History* (Chiron Publications, 2011) and a bilingual translation of Rilke's *Sonnets to Orpheus* (Angelico Press, 2015). A new creative non-fiction work, *Rue Rilke*, will appear from Chiron Publications in early 2016.

AARON RICHES teaches theology at the Seminario Mayor San Cecilio in Granada, Spain. He is a joint faculty member of the Instituto de Filosofía "Edith Stein" and the Instituto de Teología "Lumen Gentium," and is the author of *Ecce Homo: On the Divine Unity of Christ* (Eerdmans, 2016).

BRENT DEAN ROBBINS is Chair of the Department of Humanities & Human Sciences and Associate Professor of Psychology at Point Park University. He is Editor-in-Chief of the interdisciplinary journal *Janus Head*, and co-edited the volume *Drugging Our Children: How Profiteers are Pushing Antipsychotics on Our Youngest, and What We Can Do to Stop It* (Praeger, 2012).

ARTUR SEBASTIAN ROSMAN earned his PhD in Comparative Literature from the University of Washington with a dissertation entitled *The Catholic Imagination of Czeslaw Milosz.* He is an independent scholar who works as a freelance editor, translator from the Polish, and as a blogger (*Cosmos the in Lost*).

ROBERT SLESINSKI is a priest of the Byzantine Catholic Church. Fr. Slesinski is an independent researcher best known for his interest in Russian religious philosophy and related theological topics. He holds a doctorate from the Gregorian University, Rome. His monograph, *Pavel Florensky: A Metaphysics of Love* (St. Vladimir's Seminary Press, 1984), is the only book on this esteemed Russian Orthodox philosopher-theologian in English. A forthcoming book of his is entitled *The Theology of Sergius Bulgakov*. His articles in his philosophical-theological area of interest have appeared on the pages of various professional journals and collections both in America and abroad (Australia, Canada, and Europe).

LOURDES TORRES is an Associate Professor of Modern Languages at Marygrove College. Her areas of specialization include second language acquisition, Hispanic and Francophone popular culture, translation studies, Hispanic films and detective fiction in Latin America.

ARTHUR VERSLUIS is Chair of the Department of Religious Studies and Professor in the College of Arts & Letters at Michigan State University. Among his books are *Magic and Mysticism: An Introduction to Western Esotericism* (Rowman Littlefield, 2007), *The New Inquisitions: Heretic-hunting and the Intellectual Origins of Modern Totalitarianism* (Oxford UP, 2006), *Restoring Paradise: Esoteric Transmission through Literature and Art* (SUNY: 2004), *The Esoteric Origins of the American Renaissance* (Oxford UP, 2001), *Wisdom's Book: The Sophia Anthology* (Paragon House, 2000), *Wisdom's Children: A Christian Esoteric Tradition* (SUNY, 1999), *Theosophia: Hidden Dimensions of Christianity* (Lindisfarne, 1994) and *American Transcendentalism and Asian Religions* (Oxford UP, 1993). Versluis is the founding editor of *Esoterica*, co-editor of *JSR: Journal for the Study of Radicalism*, and the founding president of the Association for the Study of Esotericism.

Index of Poetry & Poets

General Index

CPSIA information can be obtained at www.ICGtesting.com
Printed in the USA
BVOW08*0327270816

460275BV00001B/4/P